The Willowbrook Wars

The Willowbrook Wars

Bringing the Mentally Disabled into the Community

David J. Rothman & Sheila M. Rothman

With a new afterword by the authors

Routledge
Taylor & Francis Group
LONDON AND NEW YORK

Originally published in 1984 by Harper & Row, Publishers, Inc.

First published 2005 by Transaction Publishers

2 Park Square, Milton Park, Abingdon, Oxfordshire OX14 4RN
711 Third Avenue, New York, NY 10017

Routledge is an imprint of the Taylor & Francis Group, an informa business

First issued in hardback 2017

Library of Congress Catalog Number: 2005041133

Library of Congress Cataloging-in-Publication Data

Rothman, David J.
The Willowbrook wars: bringing the mentally disabled into the community / David J. Rothman and Shelia M. Rothman; with a new afterword by the authors.
p. cm.
Previously published by Harper & Row in 1984 without subtitle.
ISBN 978-0-202-30757-2 (alk. paper)
1. New York Civil Liberties Union—Trials, litigation, etc. 2. Mental Health Law Project—Trials, litigation, etc. 3. Staten Island Developmental Center—Trials, litigation, etc. 4. Children with mental disabilities—Legal status, laws, etc.—New Yark (State) I. Rothman, Sheila M. II. Title.

KF228.N48R67 2005
344.7303'23—dc22
2005041133

ISBN 13: 978-0-202-30757-2 (pbk)
ISBN 13: 978-1-138-53949-5 (hbk)

To

Rose and Harry Miller

and

Edgar Leifer

for teaching us about caring

Contents

PART III
ALL TOGETHER NOW

PART IV
COMING APART

THE WILLOWBROOK WARS

The names of all Willowbrook residents and their parents have been changed except for those that became part of the official or public record, by speaking or appearing in public sessions, by being part of court transcripts or court documents, by appearing on television, by giving press interviews, and the like. We have also changed the names of all state employees except high-ranking officials and the names and details concerning the group homes in Chapter 10.

Going into the Field

On the Origins of the Project (David)

In May 1975, a few weeks after the three-year-long Willowbrook court case ended, Bruce Ennis, the lead attorney for the 5,400 retarded residents, sent me a copy of the consent judgment. Noting that he was proud of the agreement won from the State of New York, he thought I would be interested in its provisions. I knew a few things about the litigation, having served on the board of directors of both the New York Civil Liberties Union and the Mental Health Law Project, the public-interest law groups that had brought the suit. But I had followed the developments only casually. Although I had written extensively about prisons, mental hospitals, and reformatories, I paid almost no attention to institutions for the retarded. Even to someone ready to examine the underside of American history, the retarded seemed a group apart and, like many others, I placed them more in the category of incurably ill than of inmates of asylums. Far more methodically than the criminal or the mentally ill, the retarded were out of sight and out of mind.

Reading the twenty-nine-page judgment, I skimmed the many sections devoted to establishing standards of care for the institution. They seemed to me one more traditional and probably futile effort to reform the asylum; given a 150-year record of failure, another attempt to upgrade institutions did not interest me. But then I came to the final few pages, which pledged New York State to phase down Willowbrook. By 1981, it was to reduce the population of the 5,400-bed facility to no more than 250 people (all drawn from Staten Island), and to place everyone else in the community, in the language of the document, in the "least restrictive alternative" possible.

Here I became intrigued. Ever conscious of the ability of correctional and caretaker institutions to withstand exposés, to persist even when their record of performance was dismal, I wondered whether public-interest lawyers using the federal courts would exert a novel impact. Would a consent decree actually force the state to close down Willowbrook and return its residents to the community?

The potential for failure in this single largest venture in deinstitutionalization was overwhelming, and I was hard pressed even to think of useful models for such a program to follow. The release of mental patients in New York served only as a negative reference. To move inmates from hospital wards to sidewalk benches and single room occupancy hotels on Manhattan's Upper West Side, or to vacant hotels in the once fashionable resort section of Long Beach, or to dreary nursing homes all over the city, could not be considered progress. Moreover, the state, in disregard of the decree, might pour more money into institutions and neglect community placement altogether. Alabama was pursuing this very course after its institution for the retarded, Partlow, came under federal court supervision in 1972. The lawyers in that case, *Wyatt* v. *Stickney*, had assumed that establishing a constitutional "right to treatment" for inmates would force a closing of the facilities; treatment costs would be so beyond the state's ability to finance that it would have to release patients. I had been dubious about the strategy, and in the spring of 1975 my skepticism seemed warranted. Would the outcome at Willowbrook be any different? Would this suit manage to reverse a well-rooted tradition of reform without change?

I passed the decree along to Sheila, who was then doing research on American attitudes toward dependency and beginning her study of social reform in women's history (which would result in *Woman's Proper Place*). At the same time, I wrote Ennis congratulating him on his victory and asking whether he was arranging for a follow-up study: "In essence, you have started a marvelous experiment in deinstitutionalization and I am curious whether or not there will be a major effort to trace the results."

Ennis responded that no plans existed. The Willowbrook Review Panel, a court-appointed monitoring body, would oversee the implementation of the decree but would not be investigating either the process or the results of change. "I would like to see such a study," he remarked. "It is an extraordinary opportunity for a substantial bit of social research. . . . If you have any leads . . . please pursue them." That I might take a hand in organizing such a project, let alone codirect it, had been far from my mind. But the prospect, once raised, proved irresistible.

I was not without ambivalence. Trained as a historian, I was uneasy about leaving the archives to deal with "live" sources. I pictured myself midway through an investigation when participants decided to cut off access to their meetings and files. Nevertheless, more deeply involved in policy questions than most historians, I was ready to risk moving from the comforts of the archives to the unknowns in the field.

The route that led me to the Willowbrook project actually began in 1971 with the publication of *The Discovery of the Asylum.* I knew little about contemporary prisons or mental hospitals when I researched the nineteenth-century origins of these institutions, and not until I read galleys did I begin to think about the policy implications of my analysis. Then, immediately after the book's appearance, Aryeh Neier, head of the American Civil Liberties Union, asked me to address a Chicago conference (sponsored by the Playboy Foundation) that would be designing litigation strategies on behalf of prisoners' rights. I wondered what a historian who had never lectured to a nonacademic audience could contribute to such a meeting, but Neier persuaded me that the participants would find the analysis interesting.

It was a two-day meeting—I was to speak on the second day—and everything that I heard in the opening sessions made me anxious. The group was composed of lawyers and "consumers"—that is, ex-inmates —and the consumers had a very low tolerance for abstract discourse. On the first day, more than one attorney was greeted with shouts of "Cut the shit" and "Fuck off," leaving me to wonder what epithets would be left for a historian. Even dinner that night at Hugh Hefner's house (where I spent several hours telling him about the history of prisons) did little to calm me. But the talk the next day went surprisingly well. Ex-inmates did want to know about the origins of prisons and were ready to consider the fact that incarceration was not invented for the peculiar oppression of blacks. In the 1870s, the Irish had filled the cells; in the 1910s, the Italians and Slavs; the blacks were the latest in a long line of minorities. And the attorneys were astonished at how many prison practices of the 1830s still survived, an insight which they said would help them plot strategy against the dead hand of the past. At the same time, I started learning about a new breed of lawyer-reformers, and before very long, prisoners' rights and mental patients' rights were causes I wanted both to analyze and to influence.

Not long after the Chicago experience, I joined the boards of NYCLU and MHLP and began serving on a newly established Committee for the Study of Incarceration. These activities brought me directly into the debates on the proper aims of and tactics for social action. Was a right-to-treatment doctrine more mischievous than effective in closing institutions? Was it possible to design and implement alternatives to criminal incarceration? In effect, I found myself comfortable in dividing my time between historical research and policy debates, or, to borrow Robert Merton's terminology, between adding to our store of "certified knowledge" and thinking about "social technology."

The more I learned about public-interest law, the more I became fascinated with this latest chapter in the history of American reform. I appreciated just how unprecedented the involvement of attorneys and judges was. In the Progressive era, indeed from 1900 right through the 1950s, the prototypical reformers came from the helping professions (psychiatry, psychology, and social work), and they shared an enviable confidence in their ability to rehabilitate the deviant and the disabled. This optimism gave their movement its two chief characteristics. The reformers almost always brought their data and theories before the legislatures (not the courts) and won authority to exercise discretion in meeting what they defined as their clients' needs, no matter what their clients' formal rights might be. The paradigmatic Progressive reform was the juvenile court. A paternalistic-minded judge, assisted by the psychologist from the child guidance clinic, would act in the best interest of the delinquent. His ability to do good seemingly obviated the need for trial by jury and Fifth Amendment protections.

The post-Progressive reformers seemed to differ on almost every count. Attorneys now dominated the ranks, determined to uphold clients' rights before the courts. The change, I believed, had its origins in the civil rights movement of the 1950s. Over the next two decades, the prospect of reform through litigation invigorated movements on behalf of women's rights, children's rights, and, eventually, the rights of the retarded. Nothing less than a revolution in style and goals had occurred, and it was tempting to use the Willowbrook case to examine the results.

The temptation was all the greater because the change was generating a fierce and bitter debate on the proper role of the judiciary. A number of critics insisted that the entire enterprise was wrongheaded and ultimately self-defeating. A judge who would order a state to expend its funds to reorganize a prison or mental hospital was usurping a legislative function. Only elected officials should decide whether resources properly went to these institutions or to schools or to police. More, they claimed that courts could never be efficient or effective in attempts at amelioration. Not only were judges incompetent to oversee wardens or medical superintendents, but their interventions were bound to bring the judiciary itself into disrepute. However important it might be to upgrade a substandard institution, it was not worth undercutting the legitimacy of the courts.

These charges inspired rebuttals. Since courts were obliged to protect citizens against government abuse, why should a line be drawn at prison or hospital gates? True, judges might have to adopt novel tactics, but they were still fulfilling a traditional assignment. In a society dominated by bureaucracies, the aggrieved party would not be a person but a class (the 5,400 Willowbrook residents), and the wrong done, not a single act but a pattern of abuse (years of confinement without therapy or education). The wrongdoer would be a department (like Mental Hygiene), and the remedy would have to be prospective (such as closing down the institution and returning its residents to the community). All the while, however, the courts would be doing what they had always done, making certain that the spirit of constitutional protections pervaded societal practices.

As I reviewed these arguments (most of them written by law school professors and published in law journals), I was struck by how little was said about what really happened when lawyers and judges turned reformers. The debate was conducted almost exclusively by legal theorists, whose occasional assertions about reality were not well grounded. As important as it might be to analyze the principles of judicial intervention, it was no less critical to examine the results.

As I looked further, I discovered that some social scientists were interested in analyzing the impact of judicial intervention, but their research focused on two issues: the influence on school officials of desegregation decisions and the effect on police of decisions extending the rights of criminal suspects. Surprisingly, practically no work had been done on that group of cases which had become so prominent on court calendars, cases involving the reform of institutions. Indeed, the more

I read, the larger the gaps appeared. What attention had gone to the judiciary was riveted on the Supreme Court, not the federal district courts; and despite an awareness that contemporary government is run by bureacracies, the impact of court decisions on administrative bodies had been ignored. Morever, practically no one had attempted to explore the significance of judicial decisions for those that the court was trying to benefit, the consumers of a decree, if you will.

Thus, to follow the outcome of the Willowbrook case promised to be an exceptional opportunity for examining not only the phenomenon of deinstitutionalization but the dynamics of reform through litigation. The attorneys for the class had fashioned a twenty-nine-page consent judgment with several hundred stipulations; the state had signed and the court was committed to oversee its implementation. Would the parties live up to the agreement? Would the judge prove capable of enforcing the decree, gathering the requisite information and disciplining recalcitrants? Would the lawyers for the class prove as interested in satisfying clients' needs as they had been in winning clients' rights? Would the governor and his executive departments accept outside intervention, and for how long?

I recognized that the research would constitute a case study, and I had lived in New York too long to fantasize that it was typical of anything. But the city and the state provided a research stage on which every major actor in deinstitutionalization was likely to appear. Other jurisdictions might have one or another player, but New York had them all: a network of child welfare providers, unionized civil servants, nursing home operators, and public-interest litigators. The very crowd made tracking the performance all the more interesting.

I was acutely aware of the narrow time frames under which this research would operate. It would follow only the first act, the moment of creation, the time when innovators would be most enthusiastic and committed to their enterprise. Barring later returns to the field, the end of the story—the thirty-year legacy that the decree would leave—would be missing. But the trade-off seemed worth making. As a historian, I had always been the captive of survivals, of documents that happened to remain from past social experiments. Now I had the opportunity to generate my own data and intimately observe the process of change. In return for condensing the time frame, I gained the advantages of an inside look, and for once it might be illuminating to see events from this angle of vision.

However important all these considerations, the one that tipped the balance and brought me into the project was Sheila's enthusiasm. It was contagious. From the moment she read the decree, she wanted us jointly to follow the Willowbrook story, to become the biographers of the consent judgment.

On the Origins of the Project (Sheila)

The consent judgment struck me as an extraordinary document, although I came to it from a very different perspective than David. By temperament, I have little patience for discovering the reading of a constitutional clause that would convince a federal judge to intervene when the evidence of an institution's inhumanity should spark some sort of ameliorative action. By training, I was a social worker who recognized that a lengthy confinement in a custodial institution was almost always psychologically destructive. But at the same time, the policies of New York State that promoted massive discharges from mental hospitals with no provision for therapeutic services amounted to neglect. The consent judgment appeared to address this deficiency. It might actually create an extensive network of services for the one-time residents of back wards.

The document also addressed a dilemma that I had not been able to resolve more than a decade earlier. In 1963, in my second year at Simmons School of Social Work, I was assigned to a unit for "distrubed children," located in a sterile brick building on the grounds of the overgrown Metropolitan State Hospital in Waltham, Massachusetts. The residents exhibited every manner of bizarre behavior. Some set fires, others smeared feces, still others abused themselves or those near them, and yet others lived in their own world, beyond anyone's reach. The parents delivered these children to the unit with a mixture of relief and despair, knowing their children might never leave the facility. Even a dedicated staff could do little to help the residents or alter their fate. At the age of sixteen, most of them moved over to the adult unit, destined to live out their lives on one of its wards.

Working in this last-resort setting was not a plum assignment—not for the staff, and not for a student social worker either. Why had I been placed there? I was a high-risk student, which in 1963 meant that I was married and therefore likely to use the school's resources and then drop out to have a baby. (Another student at the unit was a recent refugee from Hungary who had spent several years in a concentration camp and was now learning English.) Occasionally, a staff member from one of the more prestigious mental health institutions (one that treated the acute rather than give custody to the hopeless) would come to the unit and lecture on new research findings. Shortly after I arrived, a social worker from the Massachusetts Mental Health Center described new policy directions for preventing institutionalization. State hospitals, she explained, neither rehabilitated their residents nor returned them to the community. I can still recall the details of her argument. If the patient left the dining room table for a month, the family stopped setting his place; a few months later, even the idea of his return seemed intrusive. She concluded that the community programs or day hospitals that gave clients the opportunity to go home at night might be able to keep them at the table and prevent their permanent confinement.

I decided to pursue some of the implications of her presentation for my master's essay. The children's unit had a long waiting list; for every child admitted, one was refused, and I wondered how those rejected fared several years later. I discovered that almost all of them were still living at home, and not because they were any less handicapped than those in the institution. The admit/reject decision had been based not on symptoms or type of illness, but on the number of beds available and the parents' political influence. To be sure, the situation was hardly ideal, and if the parents had had more money they might well have sent their children to a private hospital. Only a few of them were receiving social services or psychiatric assistance, and their families were constantly negotiating with authorities not to expel them from programs because of their unpredictable behavior. Nevertheless, the children were hanging on in the classroom, on the job, and at the dining room table, not sitting comatose on a state-hospital bench. Perhaps a variety of therapeutic programs in the community could prevent an initial commitment and promote responsible deinstitutionalization.

After graduation, I joined a newly established community mental health center to serve the residents of Boston's South Shore towns. Its largest program was a child guidance clinic that treated children exhibiting temper tantrums, stuttering, and phobias in order to prevent serious adult illness. The center also administered an aftercare clinic for patients discharged from state hospitals, on the theory that institutional stays could be shortened by making therapeutic assistance available outside. Hence I spent many hours counseling parents and coordinating care for children and ex–mental patients among physicians, school principals, welfare workers, and social workers.

The South Shore center was no less eager to assist retarded children. Knowing that many of them were excluded from public schools, it planned to open its own clinic-nursery. Some of the parents of prospective students were my clients, and their descriptions of life at home and the paucity of services introduced me to the field. (Social work curriculums generally ignored the retarded; Simmons was content to have the director of the Fernald State School come periodically to lecture on the differences between morons, imbeciles, and idiots.) Given the absence of community programs, I could only listen patiently as the mothers unburdened themselves.

During my tenure at South Shore, I learned a good deal about organizing community services and, along with other staff members, I was optimistic about alternatives to institutional care. Then in June 1964, David received his Ph.D. from Harvard and accepted a teaching position at Columbia, and we moved to New York. It was before the era of commuter marriages and I was inexperienced enough to believe that professional transitions were easily made. Centers like South Shore had to be found in a city like New York. I soon learned how wrong I was. No publicly funded community mental health facility existed in New York City that approximated the work of the South Shore. For want of alternatives, I took a post as a social worker with the inpatient psychiatric division of Mount Sinai Hospital.

By hospital policy, patients were allowed to remain at Mount Sinai no more than ninety days. During this time the psychiatrists attempted to stabilize them by establishing drug regimens to alleviate symptoms. They also did diagnostic workups, to learn the origins of and prognosis for the illness. Toward the end of the ninety days, the staff held a conference, presented results, and planned for discharge, and I, as the social worker, was responsible for carrying it out.

The task was near impossible because so few options existed. Many families were reluctant to take patients back home, even if the initial symptoms had abated, for fear that they could not cope with the demands of care. Hence I would search about for programs in the community, only to learn that despite the number and variety of private agencies, practically none of them were willing to accept patients recently discharged from a psychiatric facility. Nor were public agencies any more responsive. Social workers, however experienced or persistent, could not penetrate the welfare bureaucracy to turn paper entitlements into tangible ones. Provisions did exist for bringing homemakers to the mentally disabled, but city welfare workers, unwilling to spend three days on the necessary paperwork, had various strategies for avoiding requests from hospital social workers. (Much later in this project I would meet Sister Barbara Eirich, the only person I ever knew who managed to get homemakers for her clients.)

My frustration with the unresponsiveness of the system mounted. At first, I quietly carried out Sinai's standing policy. As the ninety-day period came to a close, I would tell parents about the necessity to transfer their daughter to, say, Creedmoor State Hospital, because no other options were available. But as this scene repeated itself, I became increasingly convinced that I was involved in a charade: Was this a hospital or a way station to an institution? I soon became uneasy with myself, with my assignment, and with Sinai. In mid-1965, I left the position and, as it turned out, the practice of social work.

At just this time, David was beginning to explore the origins of nineteenth-century asylums, and after an extensive but disappointing search for a psychiatric clinic on the South Shore model and a considered decision not to enter private practice, I decided to join him. Perhaps if I came to understand more about earlier policies around institutions, I would also understand more about my own experience and even locate the levers for change in the system. I started first with orphan asylums and soon discovered that day nurseries in the nineteenth century and foster care and widows' pensions in the twentieth century were designed as alternatives to institutionalization. Their proponents were frequently women who made these innovations part of a larger reform agenda that redefined domestic responsibility and family integrity.

The women reformers engaged me and I was soon exploring how a distinct perception of woman's proper place invigorated its supporters and set the direction for social policy toward women, children, and the family. More, as I examined the fate of the programs, I discovered that the solutions devised by one generation of women were altered and at times discarded by another. One generation of women led crusades to enact anticontraceptive legislation, believing that sexual abstinence assured female purity and ideal motherhood; the next led an equally passionate campaign to repeal these laws, maintaining, along with Margaret Sanger, that contraception, by encouraging romantic and sexual marriages, would promote family life. Then a third generation insisted that only abortion on demand and reproductive freedom guaranteed woman's personhood. In a similar spirit, one generation of women advocated protective legislation to enhance the health and welfare of women and children. Their successors fought to eliminate gender discrimination to secure equal opportunity.

As I turned from women's history to the consent decree, I was keenly aware of another cycle in reform. An earlier generation had wanted to protect the retarded in asylums; a new generation wanted to guarantee their rights in the community. I had no doubt that this latest reform would be as controversial as the women's movement, for it, too, was trying to alter fundamental definitions of a proper place. Only a handful of states, all much smaller than New York, had begun to reduce the size of their custodial institutions, and that by releasing the mildly or moderately retarded residents. Community placement for severely and profoundly retarded persons was unprecedented and no one knew how it would alter ideas and practices.

The experience of other social service programs provided little guidance. Child welfare reformers had substituted foster care and adoption for orphan asylums, but these solutions might not be suitable for multiply handicapped Willowbrook residents. A few jurisdictions had experimented with halfway houses for ex-offenders, but these were by definition temporary arrangements and the Willowbrook class required permanent care. Perhaps most important, there were few indications that a responsible group of voluntary agencies would agree to care for so disabled a population. The Willowbrook residents might end up in proprietary nursing homes—institutions smaller than Willowbrook, but institutions nevertheless. Or they might enter facilities run by for-profit operators, a version of day care's Kentucky Fried Children.

Since the experiment was new, an almost endless list of potential barriers came to mind. Yet New York had agreed to phase down Willowbrook, and a federal judge, a Willowbrook Review Panel, and a group of energetic attorneys were prepared to make it keep its promise. I sensed also that resistance to change was weakening. If women could become persons, perhaps the retarded could become citizens.

I sold the project to David by proposing a division of labor. I would analyze the implications of the decree's provisions for delivery of services, while he examined the politics of deinstitutionalization. Or in more autobiographical terms, I wanted to see if this attempt to bring the South Shore to New York would succeed.

PART I

MAKING THE CASE

Welcome to Willowbrook

Early in the afternoon of January 6, 1972, Michael Wilkins drove from Willowbrook to a nearby diner to keep an appointment with an old activist friend. They had worked together in the 1960s at a New York City clinic set up by the Young Lords, a Puerto Rican gang turned eleemosynary, to treat children who had contracted lead poisoning by eating paint chips from crumbling tenement walls. Wilkins had provided the clients with medical care, his friend had provided them with legal advice. The purpose of the meeting, however, was not to reminisce. The day before, Wilkins had been fired from his position as staff doctor at Willowbrook and he was outraged.

For almost a year now he had been providing a modicum of care for the very retarded children and adults confined to this massive state institution on Staten Island. The overcrowding was desperate—beds jammed one next to the other in the wards and along hallways—and the filth ubiquitous, so that virulent intestinal diseases like shigella spread through the population. Staffing was minimal, one attendant to fifty or sixty inmates, and injuries common, with residents abusing themselves or assaulting others. Working under these conditions, Wilkins had not been able to raise the level of medical care. Forced to provide emergency services, he had little time left to give the specialized treatment that such handicapped people required. The only encouraging development was that over the past several months, he and a fellow physician, William Bronston, had been able to raise the level of political protest.

Soon after arriving at Willowbrook, Wilkins and Bronston had tried to persuade the director, Dr. Jack Hammond, and the medical staff to demand larger appropriations and more staff from the state's Department of Mental Hygiene. But aside from winning over a handful of social workers, like Elizabeth Lee, their efforts brought them only professional and social ostracism. They were no more successful in making a white collar–blue collar alliance and mobilizing support from the nurses and attendants. As a last resort, they turned to the parents of the Willowbrook residents, a group with a well-deserved reputation for being guilt-ridden and passive. Yet, to their astonishment, they inspired a cadre of supporters, mounted several protest marches, and attracted attention from the local *Staten Island Advance.* Then, just as they were planning a large rally to usher in the new year, the administration panicked. It tried to ban their meeting with the parents, and failing, summarily fired Wilkins and Lee, who, unlike Bronston, were too new to Willowbrook to enjoy civil service tenure.

The dismissal caught them off guard. They were at once insulted (no one likes being fired, even from Willowbrook), angry, and uncertain of what to do. Lee went to see one of the director's assistants in an attempt to get the dismissal reversed, but he would not hear her out. She and Wilkins then called a few parent supporters, which brought them expressions of sympathy but little else. With Bronston out of town, the two of them mulled things over and Wilkins came up with an idea. His friend from the Young Lords clinic had since left the practice of law to become a fledgling news reporter for ABC television. Maybe Geraldo Rivera would be interested in doing a story about a doctor and a social worker who were fired for organizing parents to protest inhumane conditions.

Wilkins telephoned his friend Rivera and briefly recounted the details. Sensing a story, Rivera asked him to call back at the studio the next day, and when Wilkins did, Rivera checked whether a film crew was available. Learning that all were booked, he asked Wilkins if the story could wait a couple of days; Wilkins thought so, adding that since he had the keys to several buildings, Rivera had to bring a crew to film the "conditions." "What conditions?" asked Rivera. "In my building," responded Wilkins, "there are sixty retarded kids, with only one attendant to take care of them. Most are naked and they lie in their own shit." The image of naked kids lying in their own shit got Rivera a film crew and they immediately drove to the diner on Staten Island to meet with Wilkins and Lee.

At the diner, Wilkins explained that Willowbrook was laid out like a college campus, some forty low-slung buildings spread over several hundred acres. They would enter through a main gate, where a guard was on duty, but they were not to stop—hardly anyone ever did. Once inside, they were to drive about half a mile to reach his building. Easily said and easily done. No one interfered or asked any questions. They pulled up on the grass right outside Building 6, and with cameras rolling, Wilkins unlocked first an outer door and then a heavy metal inner door. Rivera entered, and breathing in foul air, hearing wailing noises, and seeing distorted forms, momentarily lost his bearings. As a floodlight pierced the darkened space, he exclaimed, "My God, they're children." To which Wilkins responded, "Welcome to Willowbrook."

They shot quickly. The hand-held camera rapidly panned the room; figures were framed in direct light, then lost in a shadowy blur. The images had a jumpy and elusive quality. This spindly and twisted limb was a leg; that grossly swollen organ was a head. The blotches smeared across the wall were feces; the white fabric covering the figure in the corner was a straitjacket. That crouching child, back to the camera, was naked and so was the one next to him. Both of them were on the floor; there was no furniture in the room save for a wooden bench and chair. The camera focused for a few seconds on an oddly smiling person, the only one fully clothed. That had to be the single attendant.

Even as he stood there, Rivera thought of the Nazi concentration camps. One could see similar scenes in the newsreels of American soldiers freeing the inmates of Dachau: the bulging, vacant eyes in emaciated faces, the giant heads and wasted bodies. Was Willowbrook America's concentration camp? Did we have such horrors too?

In less than ten minutes, the filming was over and the crew left, postponing interviews with the director and his staff. Rivera rushed to prepare the films for broadcast before anyone could protest the raid and block the story. Within a few hours his clips and text were ready. At six o'clock, Willowbrook went on the air.

The scene that Raymond and Ethel Silvers saw on the screen that evening was a familiar one, but they had never described it to anyone, family or friends. Every Sunday morning they left their home in Brooklyn to visit their daughter, Paula, at the facility, a visit that they dreaded but would not skip. They never knew in what condition they would find her. Sometimes they arrived to learn that she was sick; other times they saw welts or bites all over her body. No staff member ever called to inform them about an incident and Paula, profoundly retarded, was unable to explain what had happened.

Paula was born severely brain-damaged. Although the attending physician said there was no chance she would develop normally, the Silverses spent the first year and a quarter of her life going from one hospital to another. At fifteen months, Paula was evaluated at the Columbia Presbyterian Neurological Institute and its physicians recommended institutionalization; she was certain to become an emotional drain on her parents and exert a psychologically damaging influence on her siblings. The Silverses were in debt from the cost of consultations, and even Raymond's moonlighting to supplement his clerk's salary did not allow them to place her in a private facility. Hearing about the Willowbrook State School and reasoning that since it was close by they could visit her often, they decided to place Paula there.

Vicki and Murray Schneps, after an even more elaborate search, also sent their child to Willowbrook. Lara, their firstborn, had been a difficult delivery; Vicki had been in labor for almost a day when her physician finally performed a cesarean section. A few hours later, Lara turned blue and received oxygen. "She was placed in the intensive care unit," Vicki Schneps recalled, "and I visited her there. 'She's fine, just fine,' said the doctor as they discharged us. . . . Four months passed. Lara was slow, but children don't do much at four months of age. Suddenly she began having strange jerking motions and fluttering of her eyelids. My pediatrician said, 'You are a nervous mother. Just relax and forget it.' "

At her next checkup, Lara had a seizure in the pediatrician's office and he immediately sent her to Long Island Jewish Medical Center for neurological examination. "Lara's first hospitalization was followed by many more," Vicki Schneps continued. "From one expert to another. The outside world seemed to no longer exist. Murray's career came to a standstill. . . . I couldn't speak to anyone without breaking down in a flood of tears." The medical consensus was that Lara needed daily physical and occupational therapy. One physician recommended a private nursery in Westchester, but one visit convinced the Schnepses that "the place was no better than a cemetery above ground. No one touched the babies except to diaper and feed them." The director at a second nursery, which had no opening, told them to wait a few months. "Children are always dying. A bed will become available soon."

Meanwhile, the Schnepses learned about a new infant therapy unit at the Willowbrook State School. A staff member explained that were Lara to become a resident, she would receive six hours of physical and occupational therapy daily. "They had hopes for our Lara and once again we did too," Vicki Schneps explained. Still, placing her there was the "saddest day of my life."

Frances Jensen kept her profoundly retarded son, Martin, at home until he was five. By then, he had become so hyperactive and destructive that the "doctor begged me to place him. He said that I would have a breakdown if I didn't." She visited several upstate institutions, found them "horrible," and finally selected Willowbrook because at least "I could visit regularly and keep an eye on him."

All of these parents' initial encounters with the institution were positive. Grateful that their burdens had been lifted, they sought and found confirmation that the choice was right. Frances Jensen thought "the grounds are beautiful . . . like a college campus. The hospital roof reminded me of a cathedral in a small town. . . . It was like being in the country." After Lara had been at Willowbrook a short time, Murray Schneps wrote the director that he had "fulfilled all we had hoped for in the way of care, kindness, and consideration for our darling child." The Silverses were no less pleased. Within a few months at the school, Paula had learned to walk, which she had not been able to do at home.

Soon enough, however, they were disillusioned. Walking turned out to be the only thing that Paula learned at Willowbrook, and the ordeal of her parents' Sunday visits began. They would pack a bag of freshly laundered clothes, include soap and a towel, and set out for Willowbrook. Once there, they would sit around for an hour in a barren waiting room until Paula arrived. They were never allowed to see her ward. (Frances Jensen visited twice weekly, and pressed the staff to let her go on the ward. Later she admitted, "I was sorry I went. I didn't sleep for nights afterward. . . . Inside, everything was different. You could cut the smell with a knife.") When Paula finally came, they took her to a nearby washroom, scrubbed her from head to toe, and dressed her in clean clothing. In the washroom they learned about life on the wards. Her bruises told them all they needed to know about supervision and care.

One hot summer day, Paula arrived wearing a turtleneck. The Silverses frantically undressed her and found large bite marks covering her entire body. Raymond Silvers spent the next four days trying to discover what had happened. Getting no satisfaction from the doctor in charge of the ward or from the staff, he made an appointment with Jack Hammond, Willowbrook's director. As he paced outside the office, a supervisor happened to come by and asked what was wrong. He told her about the marks and she explained matter-of-factly that one of the other residents, Maggie, had been biting all the children on Paula's ward.

Silvers returned to Paula's building and confronted the doctor, who confirmed the story but offered no solution. Neither ashamed nor contrite, he turned on Silvers. Did he want him to sedate Maggie for days on end so that she would not bite the other children? How would Silvers feel if Maggie were his child? Silvers had no ready answer, although later he wondered why sedating Maggie was the only solution. Wasn't Willowbrook supposed to be a school? Couldn't they teach Maggie not to bite? And still later he realized that he had been lucky. The doctor might have told him that if he was dissatisfied he should take Paula home. Then what would he have done?

When Paula turned twelve, she left the children's unit and entered Building 76. Whatever misgivings the Silverses once had about her care now paled to insignificance. In 76, the waiting room itself stank of urine and they could only imagine the stench on the ward; Paula arrived bruised so often that they stopped asking questions. Now that she was older, the Silverses would take her to lunch at a Brooklyn restaurant. It was difficult to manage her, but at least they were doing something together as a family. Yet even this little amenity caused pain. No sooner was lunch over than Paula, sensing it was time to return, would begin to sob. As they drove back over the Verrazano Bridge to Staten Island, the sobs turned to moans and grew louder and louder. The Silverses, their eyes brimming with tears, would return Paula to the attendant and make their way home. What else were they to do? There was no money for a private facility, and they could not care for her themselves. It was Willowbrook or nothing.

Although the most disabled residents suffered the greatest neglect, even the less handicapped did not escape unharmed. Kenneth Becker was one of Willowbrook's first residents. His parents requested that he be transferred there from Letchworth, a state institution in Westchester County, so that they could visit more often. Kenneth was not as retarded as Lara or Paula, but he was blind and, like them, the frequent victim of abuse. At one visit, his parents learned that he had been struck by another resident and suffered a concussion; although the incident had occurred five days earlier, he was still wearing bloodstained clothing. Two weeks later, they discovered that the stitches for his head wound had not been removed. The Beckers sometimes found Kenneth hungry, and he was verbal enough to explain that his ward had not been served dinner the night before, or breakfast that morning.

The Beckers brought Kenneth home as frequently as possible (but not so frequently as to lose him his place at Willowbrook). They also tipped the ward staff on each visit. The Beckers thought the tipping was useless, but almost all the regulars did it; perhaps the dollars slipped to an attendant would bring their child a little better care.

In 1974, under different circumstances, another parent, Mr. Ben Rosepka, related his son's experiences at Willowbrook.

Q. Mr. Rosepka, can you briefly describe for the court how your son's physical condition has appeared to you over the past fifteen years?

A. Very bad. Very bad. Stevie was slashed. He had bruises on his back. He was struck like with a knife.

Q. When you visit him now, does he have any marks?

A. Yes. Stevie lost an eye four years ago. When I came to visit him on a Sunday, they brought him out from his ward. I saw Stevie with a swollen face with one eye closed. He was blue around his eye. I asked the supervisor, "What happened to Stevie?" She said, "Well, he must have had a fight with some kids and they hit him in his eye." I asked, "Was Stevie seen by a doctor?" She said, "Well, that is part of his sickness, that is why he keeps his eye closed." I let it go for a week later. I wrote a letter to Dr. Hammond about it. Dr. Hammond replied that Stevie was going to be seen by a doctor. Two weeks later I received a letter that Stevie has been taken to Building 2. That is the hospital. When I came back the following Sunday, I see Stevie's eye is no good in the hospital. I talked to Dr. Greenwood. He said, "Well, it's too late. We operated on his eye. I am sorry to tell you Stevie lost his eye."

Q. Did the doctor tell you anything else?

A. He did not tell me nothing else. I went back to the building. I asked for the supervisor and she said, "Well, it is one of the things that happens here at Willowbrook."

Occasionally, a parent would complain to the press. In May 1955, shortly after the institution opened, the parents of a five-year-old resident publicly charged the staff with brutality, claiming that during a recent visit they had discovered bruises and welts covering her body.

Willowbrook's then director, Dr. Harold Berman, flatly denied the charge; the girl had only a single one-inch sore. Besides, he countered, it was the first time the parents had ever visited, despite the fact that the girl had been on the critical list twice. No one ought to believe their accusations of abuse since they were guilty of neglect.

The particular miseries that each parent experienced did not generate group protest. The hell that each of them inhabited was a private hell, isolating one from the other, perhaps because of shame (at having a retarded child), or guilt (at having institutionalized the child). Left to themselves, they did little except curse their fate—"Why did God do this to me?"—or wait for the phone call announcing that the child had died of whatever it was, and spare us the details or the cause.

Willowbrook did have an official parent organization, the Benevolent Society, but its functions amounted to little more than occasional social events. It sponsored a few parties, complete with circus clowns, and arranged outings to a nearby park. It also sponsored an annual luncheon, where the director or a prominent official from the Department of Mental Hygiene would speak. Proceeds from the luncheon would go to paying for a few more parties and outings.

All the while, Benevolent remained steadfastly apolitical. Although it had one thousand dues-paying members, only twenty or thirty regulars came to its monthly meetings at the institution. Or more accurately, it was altogether political, the way a company union is. Willowbrook's director dominated the organization. Some parents gave him the deference due a doctor in charge of a critical case; others worried that to cross him might result in their child's getting a heavy dose of "ward therapy," a transfer to the worst units. Still others hoped that if they stood by the director, he might stand by their child. It was one of those fictions that parents who could do little else lived by.

What fictions did those responsible for Willowbrook live by? How could a Department of Mental Hygiene headed by prestigious psychiatrists, and a governor, for most of these years Nelson Rockefeller, ready to spend billions for university and office construction, allow such conditions to persist? How did Willowbrook get that way and how could it have been permitted to remain that way?

Some people are born under unlucky stars and maybe some institutions are too. From its inception in the 1930s down through the 1960s, Willowbrook was a subject of controversy and a scene of misery. It was almost stillborn. The New York legislature authorized its construction as a school for the retarded in 1938, but by the time the buildings were ready the country was at war and the federal government, in need of hospital beds, took it over as Halloran General Hospital. After the war, the Veterans Administration assumed control and New York officials had to go through long and acrimonious negotiations to recapture it. From 1947 to 1951, as veterans slowly left the wards, the new residents moved in. In April 1951, Willowbrook finally became a state institution serving the retarded.

It did not serve them well. Within four years, 3,600 residents were living in a facility with an official capacity of 2,950, and official capacity calculations are notably generous. By 1963, 6,000 residents were crammed into a space set for 4,275. The overcrowding went along with acute understaffing and an almost complete absence of educational and recreational activities. The predictable result was neglect and abuse. In 1964, a New York legislative committee, headed by State Senator William Conklin, toured Willowbrook and discovered for itself the "vile stench" in its buildings and the "crude way of life" forced upon its residents. These findings remained confidential, but other incidents attracted publicity. In the first half of 1965, a succession of violent deaths occurred which sparked a flurry of press reports and even a short-lived grand jury investigation. In February, a forty-two-year-old resident was scalded to death in a shower, the result of antiquated plumbing and the inexperience of his eighteen-year-old attendant. In May, the same fate befell a ten-year-old boy. Then, in June, a twelve-year-old strangled himself when the device restraining him came loose and twisted around his neck. In July, a twenty-six-year-old died when a fellow resident struck him in the throat.

In the fall of 1965, Willowbrook briefly captured national notoriety. Robert Kennedy, then U.S. senator from New York, made an unannounced visit. ("I answered a knock on the door," confessed Hammond, "and there was the senator.") Shocked by what he saw, Kennedy gave a graphic account to Conklin's committee and asked that its report become public. He told the press that Willowbrook's wards were "less comfortable and cheerful than the cages in which we put animals in a zoo. . . . [Willowbrook] was a reproach to us all. . . . We cannot tolerate a new snakepit."

The best beginning point for understanding the state's response to these exposés, its public strategies and private defenses, is a profile of

Willowbrook's residents, an account of their disabilities, age, and color. For it turns out that in a system that served the disadvantaged, Willowbrook served the most disadvantaged.

Classifications in retardation, as measurements go, are notably crude. The conventional scale is five points, ranging from profound (who before the 1960s were labeled idiots) to severe and moderate (the imbeciles), and on to the mild and the borderline (morons). But fitting a retarded person into one of these categories is not easy. The standard IQ tests cannot differentiate meaningfully among those at the lower end of the scale; physical handicaps, such as blindness and deafness, make the scoring all the more arbitrary. Nor is it clear just what these tests actually measure. The score may reflect environmental deprivation (the effect of being institutionalized) as much as genetic handicap. To complicate matters further, the tests at Willowbrook not only were administered infrequently but carried biases of their own. The directors instructed the staff to keep the scores low so as not to jeopardize any resident's eligibility for federal benefits. Not that in reality they had much to worry about, but nonetheless, staff would shave ten or fifteen points off a score. Hence the classifications and the tests are of little value in an absolute sense. They do, however, help to place Willowbrook in the context of the state system—that is, to establish its place at the bottom.

As of 1951, Willowbrook held a greater percentage of the profoundly retarded than any other state facility (one-quarter compared to 16 percent), and had fewer mild and borderline cases (18 percent compared to 36 percent). This difference grew more pronounced over the next decades. By 1969, three-fourths of Willowbrook's residents were profoundly or severely retarded, about 25 percent above the state institutional average. To use the language of mental health, Willowbrook's population was almost exclusively chronic patients, the fixtures of the back wards.

This negative selection was altogether unintended. Willowbrook had been built in order to relieve overcrowding at other state institutions, like Letchworth and Wassaic. But no sooner did it open than the older facilities took the occasion, as incarcerative institutions always do, to transfer their worst cases, their most difficult behavior problems and most severely retarded residents. A new institution is sure to become a dumping ground, receiving discards as in a draw poker game.

Moreover, Willowbrook admitted residents at the moment when

medical advances were keeping highly handicapped infants alive. The advent of antibiotics and the refinement of surgical techniques capable of correcting congenital neurological and intestinal defects brought to the institution many infants who in an earlier era would quickly have died. Indeed, as Willowbrook admitted more of these infants, only parents of those similarly afflicted would turn to the facility. Holding the most disabled residents, it attracted the most disabled residents.

Willowbrook had one other distinctive feature. Since it was a New York City institution, it held the greatest number of the state's black and Puerto Rican retarded. In all of the state's institutions, 84 percent of the residents were white and only 14 percent were minorities; in Willowbrook, two-thirds were white, one-third minorities. To be sure, the distribution of whites and blacks among the various levels of retardation was not significantly different. (In 1969, 37 percent of the whites at Willowbrook were profoundly retarded, as were 39 percent of the blacks.) But no New York institution held more profoundly retarded residents or more black profoundly retarded residents than Willowbrook. It was not intentional, but compared with other state facilities, Willowbrook's back wards were notably black back wards.

To the leaders of the Department of Mental Hygiene, to doctors Paul Hoch in the early 1960s, Alan Miller in the late 1960s, and Lawrence Kolb in the 1970s, Willowbrook's residents belonged under the same diagnostic label: They were the chronic cases, the incurables. All three men, products of the same medical and psychiatric training, were prepared to make the same triage decision. Confronted with what they perceived to be limited resources, they believed that available funds had to go first to the hopeful—to the curable mentally ill—and last to the senile, the chronic schizophrenic, the brain-damaged alcoholic, and the severe and profoundly retarded. They were, if you will, the grievously wounded who had to wait their turn until the seriously wounded had been thoroughly treated.

A readiness to think in triage terms (New York, after all, is not a battlefield and just how limited its resources were is arguable) was testimony not only to the strength of this tradition among physicians but to the particular biases of psychiatrists. There is no mistaking a deep-seated prejudice against the retarded. To highly verbal and intellectual professionals, retardation is the ultimate impairment. Equally important, psychiatrists had been taught that the failure of their discipline, more particularly the failure of the mental hospital, to deliver on its promise to cure patients was mostly due to the inability to separate the acute from the chronic, the treatable from the nontreatable. This was the precise message that Adolf Meyer, the Swiss-born psychiatrist and founder of the mental hygiene movement, had spread and that Hoch, Miller, and Kolb had learned. For psychiatry to achieve its proper rank in medicine, it had to maintain a rigid distinction between rehabilitation and custody. If it was to become a science, it had to stop confusing housekeeping chores with research, teaching, and therapy. Put in this context, Willowbrook was the price that had to be paid for advancement elsewhere. Squander resources on its incurables, and psychiatry in general and the treatable patients in particular would never progress.

Such a judgment, publicly offered, would have sounded far too callous, especially if it appeared at a time of scandal, and so the Department of Mental Hygiene, and the governor as well, promulgated a different sort of fiction, the five-year plan, the master design for reforming the system of care. The most notable example appeared in 1965, a seven-volume Comprehensive Mental Health and Mental Retardation Program. The result of two years of deliberation under the chairmanship of Alan Miller, with the assistance of an advisory board dominated by psychiatrists, the Comprehensive Program was based solidly on the triage principle—although its promise to accomplish everything for everybody disguised that. The program established two tracks in the Adolf Meyer tradition, and consigned the chronic mentally ill and the severely and profoundly retarded to the second and subsidiary track.

The 1965 plan made its priority the establishment of a network of community services for the treatable mentally ill and the borderline and mildly retarded. One hundred and fifty Community Mental Health Clinics and an equal number of Community Mental Retardation Clinics were to provide their respective clients with diagnostic and counseling services, outpatient treatment, and training in living and vocational skills. At the same time, the state committed itself to constructing a series of group homes and halfway houses to provide those likely to overcome their illness or handicap with an alternative to life in an institution. Since this part of the program was very much in accord with the 1963 Kennedy administration Community Mental Health Act, it had the distinct advantage of being able to attract federal funding.

The Comprehensive Program left the chronic, the back ward mental patient, and the severely and profoundly retarded in the institutions. "Even when specialized services are realized on an adequate scale, there will remain a real need for 24-hour residential care and training in state schools." To be sure, it promised to reduce the population of every state school and mental hospital to one thousand, and if that still seems large, remember that at the time some facilities held fifteen thousand. The program would also increase the number of staff and improve the rehabilitative services. But its thrust was unmistakable: first-rate treatment for the curable, second-rate confinement for the untreatable.

With great fanfare, Governor Rockefeller and the Department of Mental Hygiene unveiled the five-year plan. Praising it as "the most comprehensive and extensive in the nation," Rockefeller pledged to provide the financial support and the financial incentives to build community clinics and community residences, and to modernize existing facilities. Here, apparently, was the state's answer to Willowbrook and its scandals. The best of the retarded, along with the best of the mentally ill, would receive highly therapeutic services. The worst of them would be living in much-improved institutions.

What happened to the 1965 Comprehensive Program? Did it siphon off those whom the psychiatrists considered the most salvageable? Did it allot sufficient resources to give the unsalvageable conditions of minimal decency? The answer is an unqualified no. Over the next seven years, the state spent millions of dollars in mental hygiene, but when all was done, the major difference was that construction companies had new contracts and state bondholders, new investments.

Translating the five-year plan into a budget, Rockefeller called for the construction of four new one-thousand-bed state hospitals (at $90 million); thirteen new two-hundred-bed psychiatric institutions for children (at $58 million); and seven new state schools for the retarded (at $138 million). He also promised to upgrade existing facilities (at $222 million) and construct community mental health facilities (at $100 million). Thus Rockefeller actually reversed the priorities in the Comprehensive Program: $500 million of the $600 million were earmarked for institutions.

The disparity in funding between community clinics and institutions was even greater in mental retardation than in mental health. Practically all of the dollars went to constructing seven new state schools. One might argue that the extraordinary amount of overcrowding justified such an investment and that since four of the seven new facilities were designated for New York City (one for each borough excluding Staten Island, which already had Willowbrook), the four thousand additional beds would at least relieve the emergency at Willowbrook. But by 1972, Willowbrook's population was not significantly lower and the quality of life at the facility was as dismal as ever. What happened to the programs and the dollars? Why was the five-year plan at once oriented toward institutions and so unsuccessful?

The answer must begin with a recognition of the Department of Mental Hygiene's penchant for changing its mind after investing significant funds in an initial plan. First, DMH hired architects to design four new institutions for New York City, then it decided instead to purchase and renovate existing structures in two of the boroughs; but by the time it made this decision, architects' fees for the now discarded projects amounted to $1 million. Next, DMH decided to reduce the size of the new institutions from one thousand beds to 744 for Brooklyn and 384 for the Bronx. It defended this change by insisting that smaller was better, but the determining consideration was escalating costs, which had never been calculated accurately in the first place. Even with a 40 percent drop in capacity, the construction costs for all projects exceeded the original estimates by almost 20 percent (rising from $138 million to $162 million).

The newly created state Facilities Development Corporation, in charge of construction, was no more efficient. Not one of the institutions opened anywhere near schedule. Five of the state schools were supposed to be fully operating before 1972; none were. Rather than list here all that went wrong, suffice it to say that the conclusion of a 1973 state legislative committee was eminently justified: "After many years and the expenditure of many millions of dollars . . . New York State institutions still suffer from severe overcrowding."

The state did no better in creating alternatives to the institutions—in setting up the Community Mental Retardation Clinics or organizing community residences. Not that the need for such a program was in dispute. In 1969, DMH's own Office of Program Planning conducted a rather sophisticated survey of institutional residents to see how many of them were confined "by default," that is, because no services were available to them elsewhere. The investigation, in fact, made very conservative judgments on what types of retarded persons could function within the community. Following conventional wisdom, it assumed that all the severely and profoundly retarded should remain confined, along with the retarded who were nonambulatory or suffering from additional disabilities, such as epilepsy or blindness or psychological disturbances. But even by these criteria, the Office of Program Planning concluded that fully 7,000 of the 26,000 residents were institutionalized by default.

The reason these people remained confined, the report explained, was lack of support services in the community. They did require some help with housekeeping, shopping, cleaning, and cooking, the help that a modestly trained staff in a group home could easily provide. The report failed to analyze why this seemingly small investment was not being undertaken, but it made clear that very little of the community promise of the 1965 program was being realized.

Still nothing happened. The planning survey had no impact on departmental practices or the number of group homes. What was it that prevented change? Were there no persons or groups so affected by the wretchedness of the institutions or so offended by the numbers of residents confined by default that they would take up the cause?

Willowbrook's director for much of this period, Jack Hammond, was not about to confront the bureaucracy. He was prepared to accept the overcrowding at Willowbrook as the price to be paid for relieving parents of the burden of caring for their retarded children. The thankful letters he received from them convinced him that he was right; he had saved their marriages and protected the well-being of their other children. Willowbrook was "the only alternative to disruption and decompensation of the rest of the family." In priestly fashion, he took on their burdens and delivered absolution.

The few crumbs left over from the Rockefeller banquet gave him solace too. In 1961, when the governor was erecting a new university system for New York, he allotted $1 million to construct a new unit at Willowbrook. The sum was not generous, but for years Hammond had been hoping to establish an infant therapy center, and by expending the money prudently, he now would be able to build it. Since few staff ever took the children outdoors, he decided that the new center should be an interior hub connecting the four dormitories of the youngest residents. True, it would have no windows, but this design cost the least, and anyway, some experts believed that windows distracted the children.

The infant therapy center was completed in 1965, the same year that the series of violent deaths and Kennedy's visit publicized Willowbrook's miseries. When the press confronted Hammond about the abuses, he responded with descriptions of his new center and news of a federal grant for $100,000 to provide "intensive training" to thirty-five children. But how could he justify intensive training for thirty-five residents when the others were so neglected? "Can you imagine," Hammond answered, "what the costs would be for six thousand?" New York State would never spend $17 million to train all of Willowbrook's severely and profoundly retarded residents. Thus he took his satisfaction in reducing the plight of a handful of them. Kennedy arrived for a day, made a whirlwind tour, and then returned to the glitter of Washington; Hammond remained year after year. If the presence of ten good men could redeem the evil that was Sodom and Gomorrah, then the presence of an infant therapy center could redeem the misery that was Willowbrook.

His peers in institutions around the country made these same accommodations—which is why, throughout the 1960s, Willowbrook always passed professional accreditation examinations. Take, for example, the 1967 report on Willowbrook by a professional evaluation team of the American Association on Mental Deficiency. The team was fully aware of the facility's inadequacies, from overcrowding and lack of staff to the absence of programs and the shortages of clothing. Yet it responded not as a scrupulous auditor but as a sympathetic fellow administrator. The team appeared to believe that its job was to strengthen the hand of the director, to indicate failings in a way that would maximize his leverage against the central bureaucracy. Its approach, however, was more self-serving than effective, making its surveys misleading in substantive terms and impotent in political terms.

The equivocations in the introductory Statement of Strengths and Weaknesses of the AAMD survey make the point. The superintendent is "very dynamic and courageous"; Willowbrook is "on the move." Yet "the institution is plagued by overcrowding and understaffing." Still, there is a promised budget increase. The superintendent "has motivated many of the staff and has received outstanding support from the staff." However, "the turnover rate is very high and only the flagrant offenders are discharged." There is also "some concern about the quality of the people who are employed." Nevertheless, "there is every indication that Willowbrook State School is headed in the right direction." But "it still must be pointed out that . . . they have not attained all of their goals due to the inadequacies of overcrowding, understaffing, and complexities of the physical plant."

This combination of contradictions and sugar coating pervades the report. "The nursing staff is quite impressive. The institution has 59 nurses, but 113 vacancies remain." Consider the other possible formulations: Why are there twice as many places open as there are staff on hand? How can fifty-nine nurses possibly care for six thousand residents as handicapped as those at Willowbrook? Should the place be closed down as a health hazard? "The superintendent has introduced an ambitious plan for remotivation of attendant personnel. This is working very slowly, but effectively. . . . He has taken some positive steps in an attempt to do something about the excessive absenteeism." Possible variants: What is going on at Willowbrook that staff must be *re*motivated, that absenteeism is excessive, that remedial plans are working very slowly? "The clothing situation at the institution is considered to be inadequate. The allotment for clothing is insufficient." Or: Clients are frequently naked or in rags and tags. "The physical plant is quite inadequate. . . . Another need is to consider the use of more screens throughout the institution." Or: The toilets don't flush, the odors are incredible, the flies abound. In overall summary, "Willowbrook is an institution which is headed in the right direction. . . . Although the staff should be commended for their efforts, the level of care, treatment, and training must continue to improve before the standard of care is acceptable." The final potential variant: The standard of care is now unacceptable.

If such a report did little to undercut or embarrass the directors, it also did little to prod the state to action. The AAMD survey set off murmurs of understanding and consolation (variations on the theme "You fellows sure have a tough job to do down there"), but not much more. The directors did play the card, timidly, in Albany, but it was not trump. No viable threat stood behind it.

If those inside the system would not do battle for Willowbrook's residents, those outside were even less inclined. Powerful constituencies had a stake in capturing resources for highways, universities, and the Albany executive office mall, but practically no one had a stake in getting appropriations to the mentally disabled. One seeming exception confirms the rule. A powerful constituency of building contractors did favor constructing institutions, but they had no concern with what eventually happened inside them. No sooner were their bills paid than the rest was, quite literally, none of their business. Nor were other financial interests adversely affected if the operations were disastrous. In the marketplace, failure is generally followed by bankruptcy, at least if the company is less a giant than Lockheed or Chrysler. But let Willowbrook founder and no one lost, save its residents. Those who had, in a manner of speaking, invested in Willowbrook—that is, the bondholders of the state construction bonds—were thoroughly protected from the consequences of a dismal performance. In a variety of ways, New York State made certain that they were effectively insulated from the quality of the enterprise they had underwritten.

The agency responsible for financing as well as building the institutions was the state's Facilities Development Corporation. Chartered in 1963, it had two major sources of income: one, a first call on reimbursements for patient care (whether emanating from private or from public sources), and second, the moneys raised by the sale of bonds through the State Housing Finance Agency. The two incomes were interlocking, so that FDC used patient care reimbursements to pay off the bond debt. From an investor's viewpoint, the arrangement was highly secure, especially after 1966, when federal funds, through Medicaid, made up the bulk of reimbursements in the health care system. (In 1964, revenues from patients on which FDC had prior claims amounted to some $34 million, all paid by patients themselves; by 1972, FDC received $211 million, with $136 million coming from Medicaid.) Before turning over any of this money to the Department of Mental Hygiene to cover its operating costs, FDC made deposits in two separate reserve funds, one equal to the costs of funding the bond debt in this calendar year, and one equal to the costs of funding the debt in the next calendar year. Thus, before DMH received a dollar from patient reimbursements, the annual bond debt was twice secured.

Despite their soundness, these bonds returned a higher rate of interest than other state issues because they were not "general obligation" bonds (that is, secured with the "full faith and credit" of the state and sold by competitive bid), but "moral obligation" bonds (secured by particular state revenues and sold by negotiation). What this actually meant was that investors had a bond secured by Medicaid funds and covered by an annual income eleven times the annual debt level, and this bond returned better than average interest. To be sure, the investment was not one hundred percent safe. Should the federal government establish stiffer standards for institutions receiving funds and withdraw support from facilities not meeting those standards, problems could arise. But prior to 1972, such a prospect appeared very remote, which meant that bondholders had little to fear from scandals in state schools. (After 1972, as we shall see, the prospect of federal intervention became more real, but then the state adopted a different policy.) In sum, constituencies existed to support bond issues and to construct institutions, but not to secure appropriations that would run decent institutions, let alone appropriations that would run something other than institutions.

The grim consequences of this alignment became all too apparent in 1971 after the legislature slashed Governor Rockefeller's proposed budget, especially funds for social services. The scores being settled remain obscure (Rockefeller had no dearth of enemies in his own party), but the results of the cuts do not. DMH's budget dropped $35 million, and the governor's office imposed a hiring freeze. Since attrition at the state institutions was always high and every departure now became a permanent vacancy, the facilities lost five thousand staff members within a year. The results were nowhere more devastating than at Willowbrook. Its attrition was not only higher than that at most institutions, but at the moment of the freeze, it already had some 280 staff openings, which it now could not fill. By mid-1971, Willowbrook had lost 633 of its staff (22 percent), which together with its vacancies left it with 912 fewer employees. The shortage affected not only the direct care of residents but laundry and kitchen services and the purchase of medical and adaptive equipment as well. "It is obvious," one DMH official reported to Albany, "that the situation at Willowbrook State School has reached a highly critical point. . . . The care of patients has been seriously deteriorating." As for staff: "This is resulting in continuing of the high rate of absenteeism, lowering of morale, restlessness, irritation, increasing subordination, and what is potentially an explosive situation among the employees of the institution."

Still, few repercussions were felt outside Willowbrook. The *New York Times* ran an editorial on "Betraying the Helpless," declaring that the mentally disabled, those "passive" and "depressed" people who have "little or no competence to deal with ordinary problems of life," and who do not constitute a "pressure bloc of voters," deserved better. A handful of Willowbrook parents sent telegrams to the governor—which only served to document the sad truth that when resources are scarce, claimants are more likely to squabble among themselves than to unite against a common enemy. Thus one parent insisted: "We cannot afford the luxuries of out-patient day centers for those retarded who are fortunate enough to live at home . . . at the expense of funds needed to provide basic care for the mentally retarded in our residential institutions." The DMH commissioner, Alan Miller, did request more funds from the legislature, but at the same time demonstrated that bureaucrats can adjust to practically any situation. "The year 1971," his annual report began, "hardly the best of times but surely not the worst . . . Such setbacks are, perhaps, endemic to those who are engaged in the very special business of providing care and treatment needed for persons suffering from mental disorders. . . . In spite of criticism . . . there remains at Mental Hygiene an aura of optimism and a determination that we can and will control disorders."

Finally, Perry Duryea, speaker of the Assembly and the man most responsible for the budget cuts, composed a form letter to answer his critics. "Dear Constituent," it read. "The reductions in the Mental Hygiene Budget voted by the Legislature were aimed at administrative and collateral services, not at direct patient care." Which was, of course, nonsense, since the cuts were so large that the direct care staff had to be laid off.

In this atmosphere of crisis, William Bronston found an opportunity for change. If not for the protest movements of the 1960s, someone with his credentials was not likely to have come to Willowbrook. Born to wealth—his father was the movie mogul Samuel Bronston *(El Cid, The Fall of the Roman Empire)*—Bronston had been free to indulge his intellectual curiosity. After graduating from UCLA in 1961, he went to the University of Southern California School of Medicine and then served an internship in pediatrics. Interested in learning about the treatment of the mentally disabled, he toured Sweden to examine its innovative programs and then enrolled at the Hampstead Child Therapy Clinic in London. He returned to the States to begin a residency in psychiatry at the Menninger School and the Topeka State Hospital, which ended after he helped to lead the direct care staff at the hospital in a sit-in for higher wages and better working conditions.

In 1968, Bronston moved to New York, joining one of Manhattan's first neighborhood mental health clinics (organized by the Columbia Presbyterian psychiatry department) and working as part of a survey team on malnutrition in children. Bronston found the clinic a token effort and the diagnostic team too limited in resources and impact. In 1970, as he was turning thirty, he decided to become a staff physician at Willowbrook. He moved into a large Victorian house on Staten Island and together with a few friends, including Michael Wilkins, organized a commune. His goals were now clear: to reform Willowbrook and to get the United States out of Vietnam.

Even Bronston "was not prepared for the turmoil and shock of what the days and years unfolded" at Willowbrook. In Sweden, he had observed facilities that treated retarded people with dignity and trained them to their capacities. The USC Medical School professor he admired most, Dr. Richard Koch, ran a child development clinic at the Children's Hospital of Los Angeles, and Bronston had learned from him how skillful interventions could correct disabilities and enable parents to keep children at home. Although he assumed Willowbrook would be below such standards, he was stunned to discover how far below.

The first months on the wards were dizzying. Bronston found himself in charge of two hundred severely disabled children who had "every possible sort of medical, social, and education need." To assist him there were three nurses and a constantly changing staff of untrained attendants. Not surprisingly, he discovered "a general disregard of modern medical practice." "None of the children's records were intelligible to me. Medical diagnoses were inaccurate. Workups, the laboratory and physical evaluations that I thought were customary, were absent."

As soon as he recognized that these extraordinary conditions permeated the facility, he began to make weekly visits to Dr. Hammond. However radical his ultimate aims, his initial tactics were notably conservative. He informed Hammond of the deficiencies, described their devastating effects on the residents, and volunteered his considerable energy to effect reform. "I thought," he later confessed, "a solution was as close at hand as cooperation and good, basic medical practice."

The meetings between the two physicians, as Bronston recalls them, went poorly. Bronston spoke of the ideal: Willowbrook could become a rehabilitative setting. Hammond spoke of the real: The institution was a low priority for DMH and most of the residents would never receive help. As Bronston outlined the problems and remedies, he found Hammond growing defensive or ignoring him, and he was soon convinced that Hammond was unresponsive and uncaring. One failure, however, did not end Bronston's crusade. He became even more determined to learn how a situation he found so unyielding could be altered.

When conditions at Willowbrook deteriorated after the 1971 budget cuts, Bronston appealed to the forty other doctors on the staff to protest to the legislature and DMH. With the help of Michael Wilkins, who had now joined him at Willowbrook, he tried to galvanize the medical group to "take a stand on professional and moral grounds against this situation." Their united opposition, he insisted, would inspire all physicians employed by DMH to denounce the freeze. To open the campaign, Bronston and Wilkins sought joint election as the Willowbrook delegate to the annual state medical convention. Seeking a mandate from their colleagues to oppose "the forces that were responsible for the savage budget cuts and the 'job freeze,' " they distributed a "comprehensive" platform statement, a document that was in every way a product of the 1960s. The key to reforming Willowbrook was to alter the lines of authority within the institution. Power had to shift to the people, that is, to the health care "workers" (a term self-consciously chosen to include ward staff) and the residents' parents; together they would create "mass programs emphasizing productivity of residents," which was a way of saying that the retarded would receive rehabilitation. Bronston and Wilkins envisioned an alliance between Willowbrook and other cadres of the powerless—the ethnic minorities, the economically disadvantaged, and the victims of racism and sexism. The remote institution, the passive professionals within it, and the sleepy Staten Island community around it would become part of a nationwide movement for human rights.

For Bronston, Willowbrook exemplified all that was corrupt in the health care system, in the medical profession, indeed in American society. The institution, he asserted, was a "symbol of public abuse against powerless citizens," and he was determined, in one breath, to be "part of the movement to bring Willowbrook and the institutional system in America to account."

A decade later these phrases sound fanciful, but in 1970 such rhetoric had an appeal and even a basis in reality that is easily forgotten. A similar vision had prompted white middle-class students to travel south and help black sharecroppers register to vote and gain a share of political power. The vision had also activated white middle-class women to found the National Organization for Women and convince suburban housewives that they were an oppressed minority who needed power both in the family and in the workplace. Bronston and Wilkins looked to bring their Willowbrook colleagues into this coalition. Just as whites had become "brothers" with blacks, and middle-class women had become "sisters" with lower-class women, so the physicians would become "health care workers" with the untrained attendants. As things now stood, the physicians were "utterly isolated by their immense privileges from the rank and file working community"; but other groups had enlarged their sense of identity and so could doctors. It was not absurd to imagine that a proposal to "upgrade *all* employees' status, wages, working conditions and service skills" could win support at Willowbrook, or that such an alliance would transform the institution into a hospital for "neurologically impaired children."

Finally, the Bronston-Wilkins platform linked the suffering at Willowbrook directly to the adventure in Vietnam. The ultimate cause of the budget cuts and job freeze was the economic cost of the war. It was "the single greatest deterrent to realizing the desperately needed health and educational services in our community and by our country." Thus the last plank urged the Willowbrook doctors, for their own self-interest and for the sake of humanity, to "call for the immediate withdrawal of all U.S. troops from Southeast Asia."

To no one's surprise, save their own, the Bronston-Wilkins candidacy failed miserably. No sooner did they distribute their document to the meeting of Willowbrook physicians than, as Bronston recollects, the opposing candidate "jumped to his feet and literally screamed . . . every . . . epithet he could squeeze out." No one on the staff spoke up to challenge the accusations, let alone to support their candidacy. The opposition received every vote.

Bronston always believed that he and Wilkins could have won over the doctors, but the process "would have required more time than we could afford." That he could persist in this notion reflects a naïveté common to the radicals of the decade. They all shared a deep sense of moral rectitude and were convinced of their ability to garner allies. Just as student radicals believed that blue-collar workers and blacks would unite to topple a capitalist-imperialist system, so Bronston believed that his fellow professionals, who knew Willowbrook intimately, would rebel against the system. Born to privilege, he was comfortable confronting authority, whether that of an institutional director or that of a White House administration. He seemed unable to understand that those in more precarious positions, his Willowbrook colleagues, for example, found such confrontations impossible. Any number of the other physicians, for example, were foreign-born, refugees from Hitler's Germany or from third world countries, who took the job at Willowbrook because few other positions were available. To tilt with authority when they fully expected to remain at the facility until retirement was inconceivable. They were seeking asylum, not looking to lead a revolution. Thus, from the day they announced their platform, Bronston and Wilkins felt like outcasts.

When Bronston's attempt to persuade administration and medical staff to reform all of Willowbrook failed, he adopted a new tactic: Together with the untrained ward staff, he would reform one building. He would do good on a small scale and implement a program that would serve as a model for others. Bronston's focus became Building 76, where he served as physician in charge of over a hundred relatively high-functioning residents. He would educate its attendants, organize therapeutic programs, and demonstrate the residents' potential for rehabilitation. But once again he was disappointed.

Although Bronston was the chief medical officer for Building 76, he believed himself peripheral to the chain of command. He came to treat illnesses, to handle medical emergencies, and to prescribe drugs (usually tranquilizers like Thorazine), but the person in charge of the daily operation was the nursing supervisor. She was the one permanent fixture on a ward where staff turned over every six months and some attendants arrived four hours into an eight-hour shift. She assigned them their tasks—changing diapers, linen, and clothing (when these items were available), and feeding the residents (if they had time). She tried to be tough, for the jobs were menial and the attendants poorly paid (less than $5,000 a year), and the residents were a constant source of trouble (dirtying their diapers, choking on food, banging their heads against the wall). It was a thankless assignment, with as much left to do at the end of the shift as at the beginning.

Bronston was convinced that the organization of the ward around custodial chores exploited the unskilled blacks who were forced to take these dead-end jobs. "These workers were flung into the stench-filled barren wards without the slightest idea of what to do except hold on." But were attendants given responsibilities for teaching and caring for a small number of patients, the ward would become a therapeutic milieu, and the lives of the workers as well as the residents would be transformed.

Bronston tried to link his program to a form that Willowbrook physicians routinely filled out. In order to obtain Medicaid reimbursements, they twice yearly had to record the "estimate" of each resident's IQ. They were not to test the residents or even assess their potentials accurately, for the point of the exercise was to establish eligibility for federal support; any number would do, provided it was below 65. The physicians were also to list appropriate programs for the client—not in the expectation that they would be followed, but as additional justification for federal reimbursement. (The staff was cautioned not to include any program, however appropriate, that was obviously beyond the ability of Willowbrook to deliver.) The paperwork produced a steady and considerable flow of funds to the institution, some $3 million annually.

Finding the procedure scandalous, Bronston completed his set of forms correctly. Never one for subterfuge when protest was in order, he told Hammond that he "would not limit recommendations because of the absence of services and programs at Willowbrook." To Bronston's surprise, entering the precise programs that residents required led him to make a number of specific recommendations which, when brought together, constituted a reform agenda for his building, and by extension, for all of Willowbrook. As was his style, he rushed to tell others about the innovative design that flowed from doing paperwork honestly.

The plan actually replicated the Swedish system that Bronston had visited. In completing the forms, for example, he had noted that one client needed training in everyday life skills (combing hair, brushing teeth, setting a table), and recommended a daily schedule that taught these skills. From that to envisioning Building 76 not as large dormitories and dayrooms but as small apartments in which the residents lived with parent surrogates was only a short step—made all the shorter because this model followed the Scandinavians' concept of normalization. The institution should resemble an ordinary home as closely as possible, on the theory that the retarded would learn to behave more like the rest of us in such a setting. Bronston produced a fifteen-page draft of his idea and gave it to his immediate superior to read and pass on to Dr. Hammond.

The nursing supervisor also read his draft, and Bronston was certain that she took it as an attack on her own authority. She would not allow such a decentralization, for she could not control a staff divided up into household units and enabled to make their own decisions; and what would happen when the so-called surrogate parents failed to show up to work on Monday morning? Word began to circulate in the building that Bronston intended to fire some of the attendants and change the work shift of others. Soon he was noticing sullen expressions on attendants' faces and a growing unwillingness to talk to him.

After two months with no response, Bronston made an appointment to see Hammond. Their meeting should have served Bronston as a lesson in institutional facts of life. He recalls Hammond accusing him of provoking the staff, breeding dissension, and circumventing established lines of authority. Bronston responded alternately with moral indignation and professional analysis. How could one talk of lines of authority with a reality like Willowbrook's? And what about the import of the theory of normalization? The two men talked past each other. Hammond could not fire Bronston, who had civil service tenure, but he could do the next best thing: transfer Bronston, like a recalcitrant inmate, to the back wards.

The scene of Bronston's exile, Buildings 22 and 23, was the final home of 470 adult women whom the staff found most difficult to control. Many of these residents had taken a journey through Willowbrook not unlike Bronston's own. Admitted as infants, they began in the "baby complex"; in the course of time, they were moved to other buildings according to their behavior. The mild-mannered went to one unit, the more troublesome to another, the most troublesome to still another. It was a classification system that resembled a prison (minimum, medium, maximum security), not a school or hospital.

The residents of Buildings 22 and 23 rarely left the wards. There was not sufficient staff to supervise a walk outdoors or to run programs for them. Isolated in a barren environment, some stopped talking, others stopped hearing, still others stopped seeing. Many lost weight or became incontinent. With nothing to occupy their time, they spent their days and nights abusing themselves or other residents. The label "hopeless" became self-fulfilling.

The few parents who came to Buildings 22 and 23 knew little about disabilities and did not contest the notion that an effort to train their children was a waste of time. Occasionally, someone like Mrs. Lena Steuernagel, who was both a longtime employee of Willowbrook and the mother of a resident, tried to intervene. Her daughter from an earlier marriage, Patricia Parisi, entered Willowbrook in 1960, at the age of seven. As she grew older, she became increasingly hyperactive, and the physicians responded by prescribing larger doses of tranquilizers. She was labeled a troublemaker, and one day, after ripping an attendant's uniform, she received her final punishment, transfer to Building 22, to a ward with sixty other "highly disturbed, violent, and aggressive women."

With each visit, Mrs. Steuernagel became increasingly alarmed at the sight of Patricia's injuries and bruises. She repeatedly requested transfers to a less dangerous ward, but was always refused. The last rejection was almost too much for her to bear. Trying to provide some amusement for Patricia, Mrs. Steuernagel had brought her some crayons and a deck of playing cards. The director cited Patricia's misuse of these items as the main reason for not making the transfer. Patricia, he told her, "is prone to marking the walls with crayons," and her use of playing cards led to "difficulties with other children."

Bronston tried to reverse his sentence to Buildings 22 and 23, but his grievance petition was rejected. With nothing left to lose, he took on an impossible assignment: to politicize the parents of these residents. He was the first physician to suggest to them that their children's gross defects were not some curse of a malevolent deity but rather the predictable outcome of neglect. To publicize this message, Bronston began to hold meetings with the parents when they visited, and even arranged to bring in guest speakers to describe model programs. If only parents could be made to understand that many (though not all) of the children's problems reflected on Willowbrook, not on the children, then they might agitate for change.

At first, the parents sat and listened passively. They could not imagine a future Willowbrook divided into small bedroom apartments when now toilets did not flush and beds were inches apart. It was no less inconceivable that their children might someday work at a table when now they rocked back and forth in response to some unknown stimulus. Nevertheless, Bronston's message slowly penetrated. Maybe it was because these parents were denied even the few strands with which other parents wove nets of illusion. Or maybe it was because they became frantic about the effects of the recent budget cuts. A ward of sixty deeply disabled and disturbed residents that had been understaffed when four attendants were on duty now had to make do with two. Even those who thought themselves hardened to Willowbrook's worst conditions found the results devastating. Under Bronston's prodding, the parents began to consider organized protest, and some started to attend the Benevolent Society meetings to urge a joint campaign.

They soon found allies. A few social workers, like Ira Fischer and Elizabeth Lee, were encouraging the parents of Building 6 to unite against the cuts. Tim Casey, another social worker in search of a reform strategy, contacted the American Civil Liberties Union to explore the possibility of a lawsuit. Mary Feldt and her husband, Robert, the head of the Staten Island Legal Aid Society, let it be known that they were always available for consultation. The group was small and diverse, and the relationships among its members were not always cordial. Elizabeth Lee, who had been raised in a Staten Island Catholic family and went to work in Willowbrook on the recommendation of a relative employed there, had little in common with Bronston and became uncomfortable when he quoted Chairman Mao. But they all took satisfaction when larger numbers of parents arrived at Benevolent meetings to discuss the budget cuts, and strategies for getting them rescinded.

In November 1971, for the first time since arriving at Willowbrook, Bronston went public. He invited Richard Koch, his California teacher, to speak at one of the parent gatherings and arranged for him to tour Willowbrook. He also asked Jane Kurtin, a reporter for the *Staten Island Advance,* to join them. Kurtin, like everyone else who crossed the divide, could not believe what she saw; her account ran on the front page of the *Advance* under the headline: INSIDE THE CAGES. She returned to do a number of follow-up stories, and an *Advance* editorial asked, with Rockefeller's extravagant expenditures on his Albany Mall in mind: "Which is more important—concrete or these our fellows?"

Still, not very much happened. Hammond tried to use the adverse publicity to obtain funds from the legislature. He conceded the accuracy of Kurtin's account, but claimed he could do nothing if legislators ignored the institution. Not one of them, he complained, had toured Willowbrook in the six years since Robert Kennedy's highly publicized visit. After the *Advance* articles, a few public officials arrived, held press conferences, and recommended that an investigatory committee conduct special hearings. But all of this was traditional, and ineffective.

Then, at the end of November, something untraditional occurred. About one hundred parents first marched around the administration building and then blocked traffic on Victory Boulevard. As demonstrations go, it was low-key; only two parents were arrested, and when Kurtin went to interview them, they asked that she not use their names. Nevertheless, they had come out. They carried placards (END THE JOB

FREEZE) and told reporters, paraphrasing Robert Kennedy, that "animals in the Staten Island Zoo have more space and get better care than the children at Willowbrook." Hammond's response that Willowbrook was no worse than other state institutions, and had actually been more overcrowded and understaffed eight years before, sounded lame.

The parents made their next battleground the Benevolent Society. The sessions took on the tone of campus demonstrations as parents stood up to read non-negotiable demands to be made of Hammond. They publicly recounted their own horror stories, which now had the effect of whipping up anger. As though by contagion, other groups with no record of political agitation began passing similar resolutions. The Federation of Parents Organizations for the New York State Mental Institutions (coordinating all the Benevolent Societies) demanded that a grand jury inquire whether Willowbrook officials should be indicted for criminal neglect.

By temperament and experience, Hammond was ill-suited for handling open aggression and direct confrontation. He was accustomed to flattering notes from grateful parents, not curses and clenched fists, and the uproar unnerved him. He also seemed worried about the growing insubordination of attendants who feared that they were about to be used as scapegoats. He warned DMH that the situation had become "explosive." Furious parents might take him hostage or a frustrated staff assault him.

Soon Hammond was making a bad situation worse. He issued a directive—aimed at Bronston, Wilkins, and the social workers—that prohibited meetings with parents in any Willowbrook building. Next, he made a crude attempt to intimidate the dissidents. He had two of his assistant directors interrogate a resident, Bernard Carabello, who had become friendly with Bronston and Wilkins. Carabello, a twenty-one-year-old who suffered from cerebral palsy, was one of the most verbal and well-functioning residents at Willowbrook. He had the run of the place and was something of a staff favorite. He had often visited Bronston and Wilkins at their commune, taken day trips with them, and even attended some recent Benevolent meetings, where he served as a living example of the injustices committed at Willowbrook. With the help of Tim Casey, he had also written a letter to the *Advance* criticizing the institution. According to Carabello, the two assistant directors threatened to "lock him up" if he went off the grounds with Bronston and Wilkins. They were also looking for scandal, for they asked a number of leading questions about a possible homosexual relationship between Carabello and Wilkins.

The scheme backfired. Carabello immediately told his friends about the interrogation, and they contacted Robert Feldt at the Legal Aid Society; Feldt, in turn, had Carabello dictate an affidavit describing the incident. Carabello also recounted the substance of the story to Kurtin, and when it appeared in the *Advance,* the assistant directors admitted to questioning Carabello, but insisted that it was merely a routine inquiry. Given the pervasive neglect at Willowbrook, the notion that two assistant directors had suddenly become so solicitous of one resident strained credulity. Moreover, they admitted to ordering Carabello to keep the interview confidential, not "to go blabbing it around," which undercut the claim that the inquiry was for Carabello's protection.

Such heavy-handedness encouraged parents to protest and staff to leak to the press. During the last weeks of December, pickets became a familiar sight at Willowbrook and the *Advance* ran one exposé after another. Aware that institutional administrators either keep the streets quiet or lose their jobs, Hammond warned the group around Bronston that heads would roll if any more letters appeared in the *Advance* or reporters toured surreptitiously. Nevertheless, as the new year opened, another letter from Tim Casey appeared in the *Advance,* and another large parent rally was in the making. Hammond then played his final card.

On Wednesday, January 5, a security guard delivered slips to Michael Wilkins and Elizabeth Lee informing them that as of 5:00 P.M. their employment at Willowbrook was terminated. On Thursday, January 6, Geraldo Rivera introduced his TV audience to Willowbrook.

2

The Litigator as Reformer

The first campaign in Willowbrook's wars was waged in the media. Within twenty-four hours of Rivera's telecast, ABC received seven hundred telephone calls expressing outrage at Willowbrook, and other networks hastily dispatched reporters to cover the story. The *New York Times* ran an editorial on this "tragedy" and "disgrace," declaring that "the State dishonors itself by its dehumanization of these helpless children." The *Village Voice* provided a poignant account of two young women who had been confined to the facility all their lives, not because they were retarded but because they were the victims of a crippling disease. No one, of course, could predict the long-term impact of the publicity, and whether the scandal would generate change. It was not the first time that Willowbrook—or other institutions, for that matter—had been exposed, and it would not be the first time that a spasm of indignation would give way to malevolent neglect.

It quickly became obvious that the film crews affected the behavior of the protesters. The microphone was like a magic wand—wave it and parents once timid and helpless became radical and aggressive. When a reporter asked one of them, Rosalie Amoroso, whether the institution was really so terrible, she replied that it was horrible and then lashed out: "Why don't you ask the administration . . . why the children are so scratched and why they're full of cuts and bruises and why they're burned? All these things the administration must be accountable for." Bring a TV camera into a peaceable meeting and participants become charged; bring it to Willowbrook and the protesters became agitated—which guaranteed that the camera would return.

Taking their cue from the civil rights movement, the Willowbrook parents quickly learned to stage events for the media. The same techniques that evoked the cruelty of a Birmingham sheriff demonstrated the callousness of a Willowbrook superintendent. So, on a Tuesday morning in January, the demonstrators announced a rally for eight o'clock, but then postponed it for several hours until Rivera could arrive; he first had to "raid" another building for fresh film clips and interview Bernard Carabello, the cerebral palsied resident who had been cross-examined by the assistant directors.

The rally itself was well attended and the crowd played skillfully to the camera. Gathering outside the entrance to the institution, the parents held up placards that read: WILLOWBROOK IS A SNAKE PIT—LET'S CLEAN IT UP and REMEMBER DACHAU, REMEMBER BELSEN, REMEMBER WILLOWBROOK. They then marched half a mile (shades of Birmingham) to the administration building. In the lead was Bernard Carabello, arms linked with those of his mother and another parent (shades of Martin Luther King). When they reached the building, three security men blocked the door (shades of Wallace); the parents pushed past them and went up to Hammond's office, and the encounter became the highlight of the evening news. Malachy McCourt, a popular radio talk show host who was the stepfather of a Willowbrook resident, presided. In a resonant Irish brogue, he asked Hammond "how long it has been since you laid your hands on a child to heal him instead of fiddling your papers up here in this centrally air-conditioned building with carpets and beautiful furniture? There's no shit [beep] here. There's no piss [beep] here. There's no disease." Hammond was silent; on the screen he looked pathetic and tired. The Willowbrook agitators, like those in the civil rights movement, rarely lost a confrontation on camera.

Appearances on TV talk shows followed. Bill Bronston, Bernard Carabello, and a few Willowbrook parents told Dick Cavett their story and ripped apart the feeble efforts of two representatives from DMH to defend its record. Bronston and the others also testified at hearings in Albany. "The Pandora's box of our state school system for the retarded has been opened," Bronston told the legislators. "Our citizens have had a true glimpse of the misery, loneliness, and stench that have existed within for so many years."

No matter how exhilarating and personally satisfying these occasions were, the protesters knew better than to trust to the state to improve conditions. Aware that another scandal would eventually replace Willowbrook on the evening news, they were at once impatient to map out a reform campaign and uncertain of how to go about it. To resolve the dilemma, they convened a "Policy and Action" conference for the first weekend in March at Mount Augustine Retreat House in Staten Island, inviting the most concerned Willowbrook parents, sympathetic professionals in retardation, and several civil liberties attorneys.

At the retreat, fifty participants divided themselves into three separate working groups—parents, professionals, lawyers. Each group would conduct its own deliberations, and then join the others in a plenary session to frame decisions. The parents' discussions were more emotional than tactical. One of them would relate the horrors that had befallen his child, another would tell her story, and the tension in the room soon became intolerable. Useful as the confessions were psychologically to individual parents, they were of little help politically to the group. So at the plenary session they offered a few proposals ever so modestly, presenting themselves as only "ordinary people." Their first plank called for bringing Willowbrook up to "humane living standards," which to parents of back ward children meant placing "greater emphasis . . . on the care of the severely and profoundly retarded." They also wanted a governing board established for each institution, with parents composing a majority of the members. ("The responsibility for the care of the handicapped person should be exercised jointly by the parents and the state.") But how past policies were to be reversed, how residents' lives were to be enhanced and their guardians empowered, were questions they were unable to address.

The sessions of the professionals were led by members of Syracuse University's Center on Human Policy, whose ranks included the most radical thinkers in the field. Although one could never have known it from Willowbrook's history, the 1960s was a decade of remarkable creativity in mental retardation. Through World War I, professional and popular opinion alike had focused on the need to curb "the menace of the feeble-minded," to ensure that the retarded did not corrupt the eugenic stock of native America, a corruption that already seemed well under way with the rise of immigration. To this end, custodial care in institutions and sterilization procedures won approval on the grounds that three generations of imbeciles were enough. Over the next thirty years, as eugenic nightmares subsided (and eventually were discredited by the Nazi experience), a medical-psychiatric model took hold. Now the retarded were "sick," in need of hospital "treatment" as "patients." The proposition seemed more humane, save for the chilling fact that the severely and profoundly retarded were considered beyond the skills of medicine, falling into the category of incurable. Hence the shift in terminology from "menace" to "patient" meant little in practice. The retarded were still warehoused in distant institutions.

In reaction against these punitive and despairing judgments, a new generation of experts originated a concept of "normalization." Owing more to sociology than to medicine, it took its departure from labeling theory. In its most imaginative formulation, by Wolf Wolfensberger (who was then teaching at Syracuse), it conceived of a label (delinquent, mentally ill, or retarded) as a stage direction that told the director (the public) how to think about the actor (consider him deviant) and how to respond (segregate him). Thus, to label someone retarded was to evoke a strategy for "managing" or "coping" with him that would inevitably set him apart as an object of either pity (hopelessly ill) or fear (uncontrollably mad) or disdain (subhuman). In turn, the person so labeled took his own self-definition from this negative or hostile attitude and, in self-fulfilling fashion, fit his behavior to it. A child placed in an institution for the retarded would make less progress than his counterpart in the community, both because his instructors would be less inclined to teach him and because he would be less inclined to learn.

To counter the deleterious influence of the label, Wolfensberger (and others, particularly in Scandinavia) advanced the idea of the retarded as "normal," that is, deserving conditions of everyday life that are as close as possible to the mainstream of society. By this principle, the retarded child, like every other child, should be living in a family-like setting, attending public school, and receiving medical care in a doctor's neighborhood office. Normalization also answers seemingly tough questions: Should a retarded man and woman be allowed to share a bedroom or get married? The theory says yes; they should enjoy sexual expression like the rest of us. Should retarded people be allowed to travel alone on public transportation and spend their own money? Again the theory says yes; they, too, deserve "the dignity of risk." Normalization, let it be clear, is not intended as a legal regulation or a medical panacea. It does not insist that a retarded person must *never* be placed in a special class or be supervised on public transportation. Rather, it provides new directions and new goals: Set the stage in accord with what is normal and help the retarded to become insofar as possible like everyone else.

In the United States, normalization theory has had another policy implication: Do not incarcerate the retarded. Proponents have read Erving Goffman's *Asylums* carefully and are persuaded that institutions, whether they hold one hundred or one thousand inmates, are, perforce, total institutions. By necessity these facilities impose abnormal routines on their inmates; the very scale of operations force residents into rigid schedules (up at six, dinner at four-thirty), into uniformity of dress (the gray shift), and into impersonal relationships (identification not by name but by number). And inevitably such a regimen makes it all the more difficult for an inmate to adapt to life outside the institution.

Does this anti-institutional perspective allow for exceptions? The question is highly controversial, for although most retardation experts subscribe to the principles of normalization, only one wing is consistently and uncompromisingly anti-institutional. A significant segment of professional opinion (especially in Scandinavia) believes that institutions cannot be completely abolished. The severely and profoundly retarded will have to remain confined, and for them normalization should mean making large institutions smaller and more homelike. Other specialists, however, insist that normalization theory never (and they mean never) allows for institutionalization, no matter how handicapped the person or well designed the facility. It was such a group that was present at the retreat and helped to define the goals for Willowbrook's residents.

The professionals opened their workshop with an excess of ambition, attempting to describe the ideal service delivery system. But they soon recognized that the task required more than a weekend's work, and narrowed the assignment to composing Emergency Guidelines for Relief at Willowbrook. They reported to the plenary session that the institution should be divided into smaller units under team leaders and every resident should have a medical and an educational program. But the heart of their recommendations looked beyond the facility to the community. New York should undertake a program to build group homes. Important as it was to reduce Willowbrook's overcrowding immediately, no one should be transferred to another institution. Rather, all the residents should enter ten-bed group homes and begin using community services, schools, and doctors. The goal ought to be "integration into society, not segregation and dehumanization."

However advanced the agenda, the professionals, like the parents, did not have a sure sense of how to implement their demands. They all recognized that an enormous gap separated their rhetoric from Albany's reality, but they were unable to formulate a strategy to bridge it. Where were they to get the power to compel DMH to establish group homes?

The third group at the retreat, the attorneys, had a ready response and a total confidence in its efficacy. The power would come through the federal courts, in a class action suit on behalf of the Willowbrook residents that would culminate in a judicial decree. The others present had little idea what a class action suit was or why a federal court would assume jurisdiction over an institution like Willowbrook. But the lawyers, particularly Bruce Ennis, had come fully prepared to explain these matters.

Ennis's route to the retreat was a roundabout one. Trained at the University of Chicago Law School, he came to New York in the 1960s, joined a large Wall Street firm, and litigated on behalf of corporations. One night, after watching a television debate in which Aryeh Neier, then the director of the New York Civil Liberties Union, got the best of William Buckley, whom Ennis admired for his wit, he called Neier and volunteered to do some litigation for NYCLU. (One of his first assignments was to bail Neier out of jail following an anti–Vietnam War demonstration. Neier was embarrassed by the incident, not because of a few hours in a lockup, but because he had carefully instructed NYCLU legal observers on how not to get arrested.) In the fall of 1970, Ennis became restless in his Wall Street practice and asked Neier whether NYCLU had an opening for a full-time attorney. Neier had no vacant general staff positions, but invited Ennis to apply to direct a new litigation project on behalf of mental patients' rights.

Ennis was not familiar with psychiatry or psychiatrists and no one in his family had ever been institutionalized. But he started reading, mostly books by Thomas Szasz on the "myth of mental illness," and finding the "abstract legal and social policy issues" fascinating, decided to apply. His ignorance was little barrier—no one in 1970 knew what mental health law was or what the rights of the mentally ill might be.

NYCLU's eagerness to litigate in mental health testifies to a revolution in the history of American reform that had occurred during the

1960s, a revolution that altered both the composition of the reformers' ranks and the strategies they pursued. The roots of this transformation lay in the civil rights movement. Until the campaign that culminated in the Supreme Court's *Brown* v. *Board of Education* decision in 1954, those who agitated on behalf of minorities, especially the poor and the mentally disabled, typically came from the helping professions and argued their cause before legislators. Whether it was Jane Addams advocating more generous support for needy widows with children or Harry Hopkins negotiating for larger relief appropriations for the unemployed, social workers with their allies conducted what were essentially lobbying campaigns. They would marshal their facts, offer testimony, join together with other constituent groups, and regularly get their bills approved. Later, historians would note the frequency with which reform fell short of its goals, but at the time, the strategy seemed effective and the innovations significant.

Progressives and New Dealers were wary of the judiciary, and with good reason. State and federal courts, elevating property rights over the general welfare, struck down Progressive legislation regulating workers' hours and wages and early New Deal legislation setting prices. Indeed, reformers distrusted not only courts but lawyers as well. Attorneys who focused on client's rights, who valued procedural protections more than open-ended therapeutic encounters, would disrupt the rehabilitative process by which social workers assisted the delinquent and the poor.

The first movement to break with this tradition was civil rights. No black determined to desegregate Southern schools could conceive of the legislature as anything but *the* enemy. Imagine mounting an integration effort in the 1930s in Jackson, Mississippi, or in the 1940s in Montgomery, Alabama. Those who would end segregation saw only one option, a move to the courts. Hence, in the 1930s, the National Association for the Advancement of Colored People began a twenty-five-year litigating effort that would culminate in *Brown,* and for the first time, lawyers, like Thurgood Marshall, determined the tactics. Take on graduate schools first; make initial inroads in desegregating law schools, where it would be easier to demonstrate that separate was unequal (compare libraries and faculty). Culminate with a plaintiff who is a girl and wants to enter a white public school when the colored school is miles away and in primitive condition.

The civil rights movement encouraged women, prisoners, and,

eventually, the disabled to define themselves as oppressed minorities and to search for constitutional, not political, grounds for winning their rights. It taught them to think of themselves not as poor unfortunates who should be the object of paternalism, but as competent individuals who had entitlements. This shift marks a major divide in twentieth-century social thought and social action. It moves us from Progressive protective legislation, which prohibited women from working in strenuous occupations, to agitation for equal rights; from involuntary commitment laws, which incarcerated the incompetent, to agitation for mental patients' rights.

Civil rights also engaged a generation of law students in a great crusade. Dozens of graduates of prestigious Eastern law schools, for example, traveled to Mississippi in the early 1960s to assist illiterate blacks in registering to vote; and although they spent only a short time there, the experience stimulated them to use their legal skills on behalf of the disadvantaged. (When Ennis was still a law student, he applied to the Mississippi project, and was keenly disappointed to learn that so many law school graduates were volunteering that students were ineligible.) Frequently, one encounter with social injustice led to another. Attorneys like Alvin Bronstein learned from their black clients about Southern jails and prisons where conditions of incarceration were barbaric. Arkansas had the "Tucker Telephone," which guards used to apply electric shocks to inmates' genitals. Texas had the "hole," solitary confinement for months on end in bare, airless, and dimly lit cement boxes. Certain that such conditions violated Eighth Amendment injunctions against cruel and unusual punishment, Bronstein, with Neier's encouragement and support, established the National Prison Project and began litigating on behalf of prisoners' rights.

He and fellow attorneys in the movement were notably successful in persuading federal judges to look behind "administrative expertise" to the practices themselves. Traditionally, when inmates complained (as they regularly did) about inadequate conditions or unfair procedures, judges had steadfastly maintained a hands-off posture. As late as 1951, one court of appeals judge, reviewing a prisoner's claim to a right to receive and send letters, insisted: "We think it is well settled that it is not the function of the courts to superintend the treatment or discipline of persons in penitentiaries." His colleague wrote a concurring opinion just to decry the waste of time involved in even considering such a suit: "I think that a judge of a court as busy as the one below should not be compelled to listen to such nonsense."

By the late 1960s, however, judges were no longer willing to keep "hands off" the prisons and trust to their administrators' supposed expertise. Not that they were eager to exercise oversight, but when the factual record of horrendous circumstances came into the lower courts in the days when Earl Warren presided over the Supreme Court, it made a powerful case for judicial intervention. Were judges really to look the other way after learning that Arkansas guards cranked up their Tucker Telephone? Or that inmates in Texas solitary cells were forced to live in their own excrement? Surely judges could rule that the Eighth Amendment prohibited such practices without themselves becoming entangled in the day-to-day running of a prison. But no sooner did the doctrine of abstention weaken than other abuses, only somewhat less severe, were on the court dockets. If the Constitution did not stop at the prison walls, was it appropriate to punish a prisoner without giving him a hearing? Was it fair to deprive him of reading material, or lawbooks, or the right to practice his religion as he saw fit? And what were judges to do when states persisted in violating their orders? Was it not necessary to appoint a master to make certain that the orders were enforced? One decision followed another, until it was apparent, in the words of one Tennessee federal judge in 1969, that, "As to the traditional preference for leaving matters of internal prison management to state officials, an analysis of recent cases indicated that . . . the federal judiciary . . . will not hesitate to intervene in appropriate cases."

No reform group worked harder to expand the roster of clients and causes who might benefit from expanded judicial oversight than the American Civil Liberties Union, which in the process transformed its own character. From its founding in the Progressive period through the 1950s, ACLU had focused its energies on protecting free speech, on ensuring that the First Amendment covered pacifists, Communists, Ku Klux Klan members, and, eventually, neo-Nazis in Skokie, Illinois. Although it certainly supported the early civil rights movement, it did not exercise leadership; desegregation was not a First Amendment issue. But in the aftermath of the civil rights movement, Aryeh Neier (who became its director in 1972), together with Ira Glasser (who succeeded Neier first at NYCLU and then at ACLU), took the organization beyond the First Amendment to litigate on behalf of women, prisoners, students, and children. With this enlarged purpose, an altogether predictable split occurred between ACLU traditionalists (who wished to maintain the centrality of free speech issues) and the Neier-Glasser camp (which wanted to do battle for other rights), and many of the new projects alienated an old-guard constituency. To sue a principal on behalf of a student's right to dress as he wished was to receive an angry call from the principal demanding to know why ACLU would sue one of its own members; to proceed with the suit was inevitably to offend New York schoolteachers and lose them and their friends as members and donors. But the rights strategy also won support, particularly from those eager to extend the civil rights model to other minorities. Since a significant number of them were foundation directors (like Leslie Dunbar at Field, McGeorge Bundy at Ford, and, later, John Coleman at Clark), Neier had the resources to hire Bruce Ennis to begin litigating on mental health.

From 1970 to 1972, Ennis helped to establish some of the first principles of mental health law, to bring the Constitution behind not only prison but asylum walls. Courts now ruled that a diagnosis of mental illness did not automatically render a defendant incapable of standing trial, and thus made it more difficult for prosecutors to use competency hearings as a way of avoiding criminal trial when their evidence for conviction was weak. Courts also determined that patients did not lose all their rights when entering a mental hospital, thus making it more difficult for psychiatrists to impose treatment regimens against a patient's wishes.

Perhaps most notable was the litigation that Ennis was helping to conduct on behalf of patients' right to treatment. The idea that a mental hospital was obliged under the Constitution to provide residents with therapy originated in a 1960 article by a Brooklyn physician and lawyer, Morton Birnbaum; searching for some legal remedy for substandard state institutions, he suggested that anyone involuntarily committed and denied treatment was unfairly deprived of his liberty, imprisoned as though guilty of a criminal act. It was Birnbaum's hope that the courts would find such a constitutional right and compel states to turn their warehouses into genuine hospitals.*

The argument was first tried out before the federal court in the District of Columbia, because one of its leading judges, David Bazelon,

*As we noted earlier, not every advocate of right to treatment shared Birnbaum's goals. Many lawyers, including Ennis, wanted to use the doctrine as a way of emptying mental hospitals; confident that the states would never be able to make the institutions therapeutic, they saw right to treatment as a tool for prying patients loose from horrendous settings.

wanted the judiciary active in cleaning up the snake pits. It received its important test in the case of Kenneth Donaldson, a patient at the Florida State Hospital.

Donaldson had entered the hospital in 1956 when his eighty-year-old parents petitioned the local county court to commit their forty-eight-year-old son because he was suffering from a "persecution complex." Two physicians (not psychiatrists) and a deputy sheriff concurred, and so did a judge (after a few minutes of questioning). For the next fifteen years, Donaldson remained confined, the victim of neglect—for the hospital provided no treatment—and of the animosity of two staff psychiatrists. He kept up a steady barrage of petitions to the courts for release, which the hospital psychiatrists successfully opposed. Then, by accident, his predicament came to the attention of Morton Birnbaum, who wanted to apply his theory on right to treatment to Donaldson's case. For five years no court would so much as grant him a hearing. Then, in 1971, to everyone's astonishment, the Supreme Court instructed the Florida district court to give Donaldson a hearing.

Knowing of Ennis's involvement in mental health law, Birnbaum invited him to serve as co-counsel, and together they argued that Donaldson's right to treatment had been violated by the Florida State Hospital and that he was entitled both to release and to $100,000 in damages. In an effort to moot the case, the state immediately released Donaldson (after fifteen years he was suddenly pronounced cured); but since the action for damages stood, the case continued. After Donaldson prevailed in several lower-court decisions, the suit reached the Supreme Court, which in 1975 also found in Donaldson's favor. Nondangerous patients could not simply be kept in custody against their will; something more had to be done for them. In the absence of danger to himself or others and in the absence of treatment (left undefined), a person cannot be committed against his will to a mental hospital. To Ennis, the ruling was a victory that established the first significant limits on the practice of involuntary commitment. Perhaps someday he might win a ruling that hospitals could not hold patients against their will under any circumstances.

Ennis received other requests for assistance from would-be plaintiffs and other attorneys. In the fall of 1970, George Dean, an Alabama lawyer, asked him for help in a case before federal judge Frank Johnson, known for his uncompromising orders in desegregation suits. The Alabama commissioner of mental health, Dr. Stonewall Stickney, had ordered the dismissal of some one hundred employees at Bryce, the state mental hospital, and a group of psychologists, social workers, and nurses retained Dean to argue that the dismissals violated their contracts and jeopardized the well-being of the patients. In a preliminary session, Johnson gave short shrift to the contractual claims—the state courts could adjudicate them—but he asked Dean (this before Donaldson was litigated) to brief him on whether the state could enforce involuntary hospitalization without providing suitable and adequate treatment. Dean, who had little familiarity with right-to-treatment principles, was referred to Ennis, who rushed off a packet of cases and articles.

Dean's brief to Johnson contended that "patients confined to any state-operated mental health facility are constitutionally entitled to adequate, competent treatment," and Johnson, intrigued, asked him to pursue the point in a full trial. Dean again contacted Ennis, and he, together with another public-interest lawyer, Charles Halpern, toured Bryce, and joined Dean as special amici (which gave the right to examine and cross-examine witnesses). The experience prompted Halpern and Ennis to create the Mental Health Law Project. Halpern headed up the Washington office and Ennis the New York office, as an adjunct to NYCLU.

As George Dean learned more about the dismal conditions at Bryce, he became increasingly concerned about patient care at Alabama's other facilities. He went to visit Partlow, the institution for the retarded, and discovered that however much a warehouse Bryce was, Partlow was worse, its floors and walls covered with urine and excrement. Dean petitioned Johnson to include Partlow in the complaint against the state, and in August 1971, Johnson agreed.

Through the fall of 1971 and into the winter of 1972, Dean, Halpern, and Ennis prepared and then conducted a two-day trial before Judge Johnson. Their aim in *Wyatt* v. *Stickney,* as the case was called, was to make the deficiencies of Bryce and Partlow declared a violation of a right to treatment. In the division of labor, Dean handled most of the local witnesses, and Halpern assembled a supporting coalition of the leading mental health and retardation organizations. The Department of Justice joined plaintiffs, invited in by Judge Johnson, who was accustomed to relying upon its resources in desegregation cases.

Ennis assisted generally but was freed of many of the burdens of preparing a case for trial. He therefore had time to learn about retardation and institutions for the retarded, and soon was wondering why he had only litigated for the mentally ill. Hardened to institutional sights and smells, he still gagged upon entering Partlow—even the standard practice of taking short breaths inside the building and gulping air outside did not work. As expert witnesses came to tour and prepare testimony, Ennis met many of the leading practitioners, including James Clements (who directed a highly regarded institution in Atlanta), Linda Glenn (who directed research and planning for an exemplary community placement program in Omaha), and Philip Roos (who headed the largest voluntary association for the retarded in the nation). The experts taught him the most critical lesson about the institutionalized retarded: The gross disabilities and bizarre behavior that the visitor saw, limbs twisted into brambles and residents banging their heads against the wall, were not the reason for incarceration but the result of incarceration.

Tours of Partlow reinforced Ennis's already deep distrust of custodial institutions. As a civil libertarian, he instinctively thought of inmates not in clinical categories but as citizens. A Rockefeller five-year mental hygiene plan might opt to place the mildly retarded in the community and leave the severely retarded in institutions; but Ennis saw little reason to make such a distinction and to parcel out constitutional entitlements by degree of retardation. Indeed, as he began to learn about normalization theory, he found it completely congruent with his own position. Both the professionals and the litigators wanted to avoid stigmatizing labels and to integrate the retarded into the community.

As Ennis was formulating these ideas, Wilkins and Lee were bringing the television camera to Willowbrook. Ennis was in Alabama finishing up the *Wyatt* trial when Rivera broadcast his story, and he immediately knew what his next case would be. Arriving in New York at the start of February, he began drafting a formal court complaint without even visiting Willowbrook. Its hell, he reckoned, could not be significantly different from Partlow's.

In preparing the class action, Ennis's first, and simplest, assignment was to enlist the cooperation of experts whose testimony in *Wyatt* had impressed him. "I will soon be filing a similar lawsuit," he wrote Clements, Glenn, and Roos among others, "seeking to establish a constitutional right to habilitation for the [Willowbrook] residents." He also met with parents of Willowbrook residents who might be willing to serve as named plaintiffs or testify in the case. In the course of this, he learned that Robert Feldt, from the Staten Island Legal Aid Society, was thinking of bringing his own case. (In fact, litigation was so much in the air that Edward Koch, then congressman from Manhattan's "silk stocking" district, had suggested to Aryeh Neier that ACLU sue New York over Willowbrook, and he volunteered to serve as one of the complainants.) Ennis worried about too many lawyers sitting around the plaintiffs' table, not only because of the possibility of contradictory strategies but because of clashes in personality as well. In Alabama he had spent considerable energy keeping peace among the attorneys, whose swollen egos kept bumping into each other, and he had no desire to repeat the experience in New York.

For Ennis, going to the Mount Augustine Retreat was an occasion not to decide strategy but to advance strategy. Once the parents and the professionals completed their presentations, he explained the legal principles that had been so successfully presented in *Wyatt.* He reported on Frank Johnson's receptivity to a right to treatment and how he had already issued a preliminary decree ordering the state to hire three hundred additional staff, correct fire hazards, improve the diet, and initiate an immunization program. Ennis outlined additional improvements that the attorneys wanted the court to impose and with which he was confident it would concur. A few weeks later, on April 13, 1972, his prediction proved right. Finding conditions at Alabama's institutions so "grossly substandard" as to violate residents' "right to habilitation," Johnson issued a twenty-one-page order which specified the "minimum standards for constitutional care." It included precise definitions of staff-client ratios (1:1 for the severely retarded), adequate living space (ten square feet per resident in the dining room, forty in the dayroom), and the correct building temperatures (no less than 68 degrees, no more than 83). Johnson also ruled that residents "have a right to the least restrictive conditions necessary to achieve the purposes of habilitation." Hence the state was to "make every attempt to move residents from (1) more to less structured living; (2) larger to smaller facilities; (3) larger to smaller living units; (4) group to individual residence; (5) segregated from the community to integrated into the community living; (6) dependent to independent living."

Ennis, then, was fully confident of winning a Willowbrook case in New York—and he had no difficulty arousing the enthusiasm of others at the retreat. The principal resolution of the plenary session was to avoid taking "direct legislative action . . . because of the impending federal class action law suits [on the] 'right to treatment.' " Given the federal court's readiness to "encompass so many areas of proposed improvement in the care of the handicapped," the conference decided "not to . . . endorse any action which, in the opinion of the legal group . . . might in any way jeopardize the outcome of the litigation." In short, the lawyers were now in command.

Behind this transfer of leadership was a widespread and well-warranted distrust of going to the New York legislature. Those at the retreat could see little sense in lobbying the body that had neglected Willowbrook for years and, through its recent budget cuts, precipitated the crisis. Moreover, litigation seemed to promise something for everybody. Many of the parents who had no desire other than to see Willowbrook improved were encouraged that Judge Johnson's first order was for more staff, and that most of his emergency remedies looked to improve institutional conditions. The professionals, on the other hand, sensed immediately and correctly that Ennis's civil liberties principles were at one with their notions of normalization and the ultimate aim of the suit was community placement. No one dampened the glow of Ennis's presentation by suggesting that a suit would take years, or that the legislature might someday have to be reckoned with, or that the parents' intention to upgrade institutions did not coincide with the professionals' intention to close them down. What mattered most now was that someone was ready and seemingly able to do something about Willowbrook.

Immediately after the retreat, Ennis and Feldt met to resolve questions of turf. Feldt, with an insider's knowledge of Willowbrook, was afraid that Ennis would be unable to convey to a judge its true misery. He was also concerned, not unwisely as it turned out, that Ennis, NYCLU, and MHLP would receive all the publicity, leaving Feldt and Legal Aid in the cold. For his part, Ennis worried that Feldt would drown the case in atrocity stories, obscuring the relevant constitutional principles. In the end, they compromised. Each would initially file his own suit and then, after a few months, they would ask the court to consolidate them. In this way, both organizations would take credit for the case and both attorneys would have standing to examine witnesses. The only remaining issue was the order in which the lawyers would file their suits, which of them technically would be first. They decided to flip a coin, and for those who take portents seriously, Ennis won.

The details resolved, Ennis had to identify his named plaintiffs and assemble a group that justified a motion for a class action suit. He needed a broad base, first to make certain that the state did not here, as it had so often in mental health, moot the case by releasing the client. Moreover, so many groups and subgroups made up Willowbrook's population (from different level of retardation to different level of physical disability) that the state might challenge the eligibility of a handful of parents to represent the interest of the entire class. Accordingly, Ennis chose eight individual parents, most of whom he had met at the retreat, and almost all of whom had been leaders in the protests. Murray Schneps was ready to join him, and so were Diana McCourt, Rosalie Amoroso, Ida Rios, and Jerry Isaacs. Ennis also enlisted the now radicalized Willowbrook Benevolent Society, whose leaders, Jerry Gavin and Tony Pinto, were eager to cooperate. But he was well aware that Benevolent was an organization with no fixed rules on membership or procedures. It was not inconceivable that a hundred people would show up at a meeting, capture the organization, and immediately dismiss Ennis or redefine the purpose of the lawsuit. He had enough to do in the courtroom without looking over his shoulder to monitor Benevolent's politics.

These considerations left him facing his most delicate decision: Should he bring into the case the New York State Association for Retarded Children (NYARC) as a named plaintiff? More precisely, should he try to cooperate with its director, Joseph Weingold, who had a reputation for being as politically well-connected as he was personally irascible?

NYARC was, and is, the state's single largest and most powerful parent organization in retardation. Its origins, although modest, reveal its ongoing aims. In the winter of 1948, two Bronx families whose children were mildly retarded tried to enroll them in public school. When they were refused admission and no other public or private classes were available, the parents created their own program. They advertised in the *New York Post,* seeking other parents of retarded children interested in organizing a day nursery, and within a month, two hundred people attended the association's first meeting. Within a year, the group was large enough to hire from among its parent members a professional executive director, Joseph Weingold.

Over the next two decades, NYARC grew in size to some thirty thousand members, with chapters all over the state, and its political influence grew too. Weingold, an indefatigable lobbyist, was able to win legislative appropriations for several community programs. What he could not do was loosen the hold that psychiatrists (and mental health concerns) had on the Department of Mental Hygiene. Weingold repeatedly urged a separate department for retardation, but when his bill finally passed the legislature, Rockefeller vetoed it.

Weingold did persuade the Benevolent Societies at three state institutions, including Willowbrook, to come under the ARC umbrella, but the alliance was always uneasy. ARC periodically protested institutional overcrowding, the lengthy wait for admissions, and substandard physical conditions. But its major purpose was to serve parents who kept their retarded children at home, to obtain for them more workshops and camp programs. The two groups squabbled over their rightful share of state appropriations. Benevolent Society members feared that dollars allotted to community programs meant reduced expenditures for institutions. ARC parents believed that because dollars were locked into institutional budgets, community services were stunted.

Weingold's own style exacerbated these differences. There is a story, perhaps apocryphal but widely circulated, that when Weingold met with the Willowbrook Benevolent Society in early 1972 and its members asked him to join the agitation, he retorted that those who institutionalized their children deserved what they got. At his most consistent, Weingold probably preferred a triage in services: institutions for the severely and profoundly retarded, community programs for mildly and moderately retarded.

This history had very particular implications for Ennis. To include the most important parent association among the plaintiffs would probably resolve any doubts about his legal standing to represent the Willowbrook class. Ennis also anticipated that the governor might try to negotiate a settlement before trial, in which instance Weingold's Albany connections would prove useful. And if Ennis excluded Weingold, he might find ARC using its political influence to sabotage the case.

Equally compelling reasons suggested not including ARC. Not only were the Benevolent parents suspicious of it, but so were many of Ennis's retardation experts. Although the New York chapter had been the moving force in organizing the national ARC, it had subsequently severed ties because of fundamental differences in perspective. A terminological distinction framed one issue: National changed its title from

Association for Retarded Children to Association for Retarded *Citizens.* The New York group kept the designation *Children.* And the difference between thinking about the retarded as citizens and thinking of them as children was at the heart of Ennis's case.

Yet Ennis did not want to give up on Weingold. Too much was to be gained if an agreement could be reached. To explore the possibility while protecting himself from later embarrassment, Ennis had recourse to a practice that is commonplace in the world of commercial law but unusual in the world of public-interest law. He drew up a three-page retainer agreement defining the aims of the litigation: ARC retained him to challenge "the adequacy and constitutionality of conditions at Willowbrook," and agreed to remain with the case "to its conclusion." Ennis hoped "to secure [institutional] standards of education, care, treatment, training and habilitation which are as good as, or better than, the [*Wyatt* v. *Stickney*] standards for Partlow." But more:

> The ultimate goal of the lawsuit is to make it necessary for the State of New York to provide community-based alternatives (including halfway houses, hostels, group homes, community education and training programs, etc.), so that Willowbrook (and similar institutions) can be promptly and completely phased out of existence.

The goal in absolute terms was to close institutions for the retarded.

To this end, the retainer explained that "it will be necessary to demonstrate (a) that the conditions at Willowbrook are barbaric . . . (b) that the administrative personnel in the Department of Mental Hygiene and at Willowbrook have long been aware of those conditions and are unable or unwilling to correct them." Ennis intended to ask the court to order that Willowbrook be run in a "humane and constitutional manner" until it was "phased out" with a community-based system, and to appoint a master, or a panel of experts, to oversee the effort. Finally, he promised to "regularly consult" with Weingold, although "counsel will exercise final authority with regard to litigation strategy."

Never one to leave a loophole open, Ennis demanded not only that Weingold, as ARC executive director, sign the document, but that the president of his board, Robert Hodgson, do so too. Lest anyone claim later that a salaried employee had no authority to commit ARC to a lawsuit, both of them had to sign. And they did. Not to join the suit would create public relations problems and, at worst, provoke the radical parents to try to take over this organization the way they had

Benevolent. So the alliance was made and, for the moment, Ennis had his named plaintiffs in place.

The Willowbrook retainer demonstrates a more formal arrangement between a public-interest lawyer and his client than those who think of such lawyers as runaway horses, litigating at will, normally concede. Nevertheless, it is true that Ennis, and not the clients or their guardians, set the terms of the suit. Further, Ennis treated the document as a private treaty, not circulating it to any of the other parties, not even the parents named as plaintiffs. This fact poses sharply one of the central controversies around reform efforts on behalf of the dependent. Who has the right to speak for disabled persons, especially when, as in the case of Willowbrook, the vast majority are unable to speak for themselves? If not the attorneys, then who? The parents—who, until the exposé, suffered from personal and political constraints that rendered them immobile or who had never gone out to visit Willowbrook or their children? The state—which had let the facility degenerate? The legislature—which made budget cuts with impunity? The professionals —who accredited the institution even at its most inhumane? One point is clear: Ennis did not wrest power from other claimants. Everyone, from parents to professionals, had a long record of failure; insofar as reforming Willowbrook was concerned, power was lying in the streets until Ennis picked it up. Who ought to speak for the retarded? In 1972, there was good reason to select someone with a clean record, someone who, with whatever presumptuousness, defined himself as acting in the public interest.

One last assignment remained: to draw up the formal complaint initiating the lawsuit in federal court. Ennis took his facts from the parent plaintiffs and his theories from *Wyatt.* The facts were depressingly easy to marshal:

Lara Schneps, aged four, profoundly retarded and severely disabled. She "is not engaged in any program"; she is on a ward that is "for substantial periods of time . . . left entirely unattended." She does not receive "minimally adequate medical care," and because of this, in July of 1970, she fell into a coma and almost died.

Nina Galin, aged ten, IQ of 19, "receives no schooling or training." Her room has no toys, she is given tranquilizers four times a day. On their frequent visits, her parents "almost always discover new physical problems and injuries."

Evelyn Cruz, aged thirteen, lives on a ward with one hundred other children "which is staffed by approximately four employees." When her parents visit, they find her "almost always . . . severely scratched." "Except for Dr. Bill Bronston, no employee at Willowbrook has ever told Evelyn's parents anything about her."

David Amoroso, aged twelve, has suffered frequent injuries and second degree burns. Drs. Michael Wilkins and Bill Bronston got him enrolled in a school program. But the teacher soon suspended him from class "because he had started to soil himself," and now he is only receiving an hour a day of instruction.

Lowell Isaacs, aged seven, is retarded, deaf, and mute. He was assigned to a hearing program but then removed "for being 'too active.' " Lowell's clothing is "deplorable," his ward has no toys. "He is forced to eat only mashed meals, even though he is able to consume solid food."

These widespread abuses, the complaint averred, violated residents' right to habilitation. Willowbrook "is not a therapeutic institution. It more closely resembles a prison"; and no one could be confined there unless the facility "provided an adequate habilitation program." Its residents were deprived of "the habilitation necessary to enable them to speak, read, communicate, in violation of the First Amendment; deprived of rights to privacy and dignity, in violation of the Fourth and Fourteenth; deprived of services given to others, in violation of the Fourteenth; and subjected to cruel and unusual punishment, in violation of the Eighth."

Given these denials of rights, the complaint asked the court to hold a hearing to determine standards of adequate habilitation and then to order appropriate relief. The court should also enjoin the defendants from expending funds on any institution for the retarded in the state until it was satisfied that adequate community facilities existed. Finally, the court should appoint a receiver or a master to oversee implemention. In effect, the court should declare the institution bankrupt and assume control.

Where chance predominates, myths flourish. The Willowbrook case was to be filed in the Federal Court of the Eastern District of New York, which sits at Cadman Plaza in downtown Brooklyn. Twelve judges serve on it, some by record and temperament close to civil libertarian positions, others less sympathetic. One myth has it that liberal judges work longer and harder, and thus are more likely to be in chambers on

Friday afternoon. The lawyer who files his papers late that day and asks for emergency relief may draw one of these judges. So on Friday afternoon, March 17, 1972, Ennis met with the Legal Aid lawyers at the courthouse to initiate the case. Their fantasy was that they would get Jack Weinstein, a former Columbia University law professor whose civil libertarian credentials were impeccable. But fantasies are not so easily realized. It was Orrin Judd who was working late that Friday, and in his courtroom *New York ARC* v. *Rockefeller* was not destined to become a simple replay of *Wyatt* v. *Stickney*.

3

A Keen Intellect and a Love of Man

It could have been an easy case, open and shut. Since Willowbrook was an obvious hellhole, the court would order the state immediately to correct the worst abuses and later to create a system for returning the residents to the community. In fact, for a brief moment, Ennis thought that the litigation would move quickly and smoothly. His first discussions with Alan Miller, head of the Department of Mental Hygiene (whom he had sued before on behalf of mental patients), were amicable, with Miller promising, as Ennis remembered it, to put up "as defenseless a defense as possible." After all, a court order would enable DMH to pry appropriations loose from the legislature and get Willowbrook off the front page. But nothing in the suit turned out to be simple. Between the filing of the complaint in March 1972 and Orrin Judd's decision on preliminary relief, more than a year elapsed. Another fourteen months went by before the trial on permanent relief was held (in December 1974), and still another four months were devoted to negotiating a settlement. All told, it took three years to go from first papers to the signing of the consent judgment.

The duration does not point to crowded court dockets and a backlog of cases, which make the wheels of justice turn as though it were always mud season in Vermont. Rather, the unwavering unyieldingness of the state and the extraordinary circumspection of the judge made this a suit in which nothing could be taken for granted—no fact about the conditions at Willowbrook, no premise about the appropriateness of judicial intervention.

An adversarial posture affected every aspect of the case. Louis Lefkowitz and the attorney general's office, not Alan Miller and DMH, set the courtroom strategy. They contested every motion from their opponents, both to increase plaintiffs' work load and to slow the progress of the suit. Often two sides to an institutional case will "stipulate" to certain of the facts; if the litigation, for example, is about prison conditions, they will agree on the number of inmates and the ratio of staff. Although the defendants might be conceding a high degree of overcrowding or neglect, they know that plaintiffs will eventually get the facts and opt to demonstrate good faith. (Your Honor, we do not disagree that conditions must be upgraded, but we are committed to all necessary improvements.) In Willowbrook, however, the attorney general's office refused to stipulate to almost anything, forcing the plaintiffs to verify every detail. Its aim was to delay matters as long as possible, on the theory that the more time passed, the better DMH would be able to demonstrate its competence. (Your Honor, Willowbrook *was* a nightmare, but we have reduced the population, hired more staff, reorganized the administration, and thus do not require court oversight.) From the attorney general's perspective, it was the only feasible strategy. Even were the state to fail in its ameliorative efforts, the defense would be no worse off. The Willowbrook residents, it is true, might be worse off, but the attorney general took his client to be the state and its agencies, not the institutionalized retarded.

Thus, when Ennis and his co-attorneys from Legal Aid, Robert Feldt and Anita Barrett, began going to Willowbrook to interview clients, investigate conditions, and tour with expert witnesses, the state moved to restrict their access. Brenda Soloff, the assistant attorney general handling the suit, protested to Ennis that he had no right to walk through three buildings and talk to attendants on duty on a late evening visit. "I must insist," Soloff wrote, "that this sort of action not be repeated. . . . Such an intrusion is disruptive and harassing particularly at such a late hour." Ennis countered that DMH policy required institutions to "establish the most liberal visitation policies . . . feasible," including at least three visiting hours every evening. Moreover, since attendants were not named defendants, he was entitled to interview them. ("The first amendment, after all, has not yet been repealed.") The judge resolved the dispute to Ennis's complete satisfaction, but the opening exchange indicated just how acrimonious and protracted the proceedings would be.

Ennis had originally estimated that the cost of bringing a motion for the preliminary relief (exclusive of attorneys' fees) would amount to some $12,500. Once the state's tactics became apparent, he had to revise it upward. "The attorney general told me," he informed Ira Glasser, NYCLU's executive director, in May 1972, "that the defendants no longer intend to negotiate anything. Accordingly, we now have an all-out fight on our hands, which will require even more money." He would have to depose more state officials and invite more expert witnesses to document conditions. The $5,000 he had received from the New York State Association for Retarded Children, which was to have covered almost half his costs, was now a pittance. The suit was likely to take a few years and cost at least a quarter of a million dollars.

And it might not bring a victory. Ennis could not predict the attitude of the presiding judge, Orrin Judd. By reputation, Judd was well trained and hardworking; when he was not in court he was either in the law library or in church—his custom was to work late on Friday, which is why Ennis's ploy to draw Judge Weinstein failed. A graduate of Harvard Law School and an editor of the *Harvard Law Review*, Judd had clerked in 1930–31 for the distinguished New York jurist Learned Hand; after a brief stint in private practice, he became New York State solicitor general under Governor Thomas Dewey, then a state judge and, in 1968, a federal judge. A devout Baptist, Judd was also active in interdenominational organizations. For several years he chaired New York State's Council of Churches and was honored by the United Church of Christ as Churchman of the Year.

Judd was known to be scrupulously fair, ready to uphold his reading of the law whatever the consequences. Over the course of the Willowbrook suit, he ruled on a number of prison cases, invariably demanding that institutional conditions be improved under penalty of discharging inmates or closing down the facilities. In one case, Judd ordered that defendants denied bail had to be brought to trial within seven and a half months or released from detention; in another, he decreed that if conditions in the Brooklyn and Queens jails were not improved "within a reasonable time," all pretrial detainees would have to be released. And in his most famous decision, delivered in July 1973, he ordered the United States to halt the bombing of Cambodia.

Then why was Ennis not enthusiastic about drawing an independent-minded, liberal-Republican, churchgoing judge? Surely anyone ready to halt military operations in Cambodia would be prepared to improve conditions at one inhumane institution on Staten Island? The answer was that for Judd, Cambodia was the easy case and Willowbrook the difficult one.

Cambodia was easy because, Judd believed, the suit posed a constitutional question that the federal courts ought to resolve. At issue was the right of the President, as commander in chief of the armed forces, to order bombing sorties into Cambodia. No one disputed the fact that as of August 15, 1973, congressional action required the termination of all military activity there. What remained uncertain was whether the sorties could continue right up to that date—in effect, from mid-April until August 15. The antiwar groups (represented by ACLU) insisted that all incursions into Cambodia halt immediately because Congress had never explicitly authorized the intervention. The Justice Department responded that Cambodia was part of the larger military effort in Southeast Asia which had received congressional approval, and hence the bombing could continue until the cutoff date. Judd could have ducked so controversial a case by ruling it nonjusticiable, that is, involving a political, not constitutional, dispute between the President and the Congress. More, by the time he heard arguments it was already June 1973; he would need at least a month to render his decision, and so the matter came down to a few weeks. Nevertheless, he plunged in, the moral imperative seeming obvious: "The court cannot say that the Cambodian and American lives which may be lost during the next three weeks are so unimportant that it should defer action in this case still further." And he had no doubt that "the question of the balance of constitutional authority to declare war, between the executive and legislative branches, is not a political question."

After reviewing the record, Judd found that "Congress did not acquiesce in the Presidential statement that the Indochina war was all of one piece," and since it had never authorized military action in Cambodia, he banned the bombing immediately. The court of appeals reversed him, siding with Irving Kaufman's view that judges who were "deficient in military knowledge . . . and sitting thousands of miles from the field of action" ought to stay out of such disputes. But for Judd the question did not require military training or proximity to the battlefield, but rather an understanding of the doctrine of separation of powers, and thus for him Cambodia was the easy case.

What made Willowbrook so difficult was Judd's doubts on first principles, on the very propriety of federal court involvement. For one, he was predisposed to respect a "rule of abstention." The principle, as Felix Frankfurter once explained, directed federal judges to "restrain their authority because of 'scrupulous regard for the right independence of state governments' and the smooth workings of the federal judiciary." Willowbrook was a state institution, operating under state laws, and state judges could be expected to have proper regard for the welfare of its residents. (In fact, a few Willowbrook parents had already sued the facility in a state court and the judge was responding favorably.) To be sure, the rule of restraint had not ranked high for the Warren Court. But Judd took his guidance from Learned Hand, who had so eloquently urged federal judges to give deference to the findings of state courts, indeed to respect decisions of elected officials. Acting in this tradition, Judd should have told Ennis to bring his case to the state court and to base his complaint on statutory, not constitutional, grounds; or to go lobby the legislature and persuade it to increase its expenditures for Willowbrook.

Judd had even more serious reservations about intervention because confinement in Willowbrook in law (if not in reality) seemed different from confinement in a prison or a mental hospital. Although most of Willowbrook's residents were admitted through a court order, they were, in fact, free to leave at any time. (To substantiate this point, the director wrote to the families immediately after the suit was filed, inviting them to take their children home—an invitation no one accepted.) Their legal status appeared to both remove the constitutional grounds for court intervention and exclude the remedies courts had been granting in prison and mental hospital cases. There judges could reason (as Judd himself did) that involuntary confinement (whether as punishment for a crime or as protection against harming oneself or others) had to meet certain constitutional standards. Eighth Amendment prohibitions against cruel and unusual punishment were obviously applicable when someone was incarcerated against his will. Moreover, a judge who found constitutional violations in a facility could order the state either to administer an institution in accord with constitutional standards or to close it down. Admittedly, this might appear an idle threat, but in constitutional terms it had the advantage of avoiding encroachment on the legislature's power of the purse. By telling the legislature to run a constitutionally acceptable prison or not run one at all, the court was not actually determining appropriations; the legislature was free, at least in theory, to abandon prison administration and save its money. All this might appear to be hair splitting, since states were not about to stop using prisons or mental hospitals. Nevertheless, to a great number of judges, and legislators as well, the fact that the court did not directly order legislatures to spend money was of genuine significance.

Such approaches, however, did not seem even remotely applicable to Willowbrook. How could one invoke the Eighth Amendment when all its residents were free to leave the institution? And plaintiffs were not asking the state to get out of the business of caring for the retarded but asking it to spend more on the retarded, which allowed the court no face-saving gesture in ordering a state expenditure. Moreover, the lack of coercion over residents seemed to make Willowbrook part of the state's social service network, a "benefit" available to those who wanted it. Every judicial precedent agreed that federal judges were not to allocate tax dollars among social programs, to decide how many dollars should go to the retarded as against, say, the aged. Judd was sensitive to the import of these points and frequently observed that "a federal court should not second-guess a State on the allocation of limited funds for social and welfare purposes," and that "a Federal judge really can't mandamus the Legislature as to what it should do."

Beyond these conceptual difficulties, Judd had a practical concern with the ability of a federal judge to oversee the implementation of a remedial order. Suppose he resolved the constitutional issues in favor of the plaintiffs and ordered improvements. How would he know if the orders were carried out? Would he have to move his courtroom to Willowbrook? In prison and mental hospital cases, the court could rely on inmate complaints. Most residents at Willowbrook, however, were too disabled to report at all, let alone to report accurately. Moreover, Judd was reluctant "to get into detailed housekeeping matters," afraid that he would suffocate in detail and be consumed by bickering. Recognizing that "maintenance is really never to the satisfaction of those who use it," he anticipated endless complaints about the number of towels and the number of attendants. "I can't have somebody over there at Willowbrook to see what's going on and I don't want to hear a lot of reports about one night when there were supposed to be fifteen [staff] people in the baby complex and there were only ten [and] that I have to hold hearings about it."

Fully aware of Judd's misgivings, Ennis constructed his case by heading to Willowbrook's wards, not the law library. First the facts, then the theory; first the realities, then the constitutional doctrine. This design followed Ennis's own predilections. His strength as an advocate was not so much in devising original constitutional theories to expand court jurisdiction as in conducting exhaustive and detailed discovery to undercut defense arguments and prod the court to action. More, he expected theory to bend to fit reality, the right starting point even for a constitutional argument being the facts of the case. Not that he considered federal judges in general, let alone Orrin Judd in particular, to be prepared to reach a result no matter what the Constitution or judicial precedent said. Rather, his sense was that within bounds, judges had a bias toward equity, toward accomplishing what they believed ought to be.

Beginning in March 1972 and continuing through the summer, Ennis, Feldt, and Barrett made regular trips out to Willowbrook, bringing along the experts in retardation who would serve as witnesses. No tour was without its surprises. His first time there, Ennis met several residents who could read and write fluently; why they were confined remained unanswered. Later that same day, he entered Ward A of Building 23: "The dayroom, which is not large to begin with, is informally divided by an imaginary line into four separate areas. The residents are each assigned to a separate area in the dayroom and are not permitted to cross the imaginary line into other areas. That restriction on their movement in the dayroom is considered necessary in order to enable the attendants to keep track of their charges. We saw residents yelled at whenever they tried to cross the imaginary line to play with other residents."

Soon enough, a pattern of deprivation became apparent. On every visit Ennis saw some residents nude on the wards and others, in violation of formal regulations, locked in solitary confinement. On every visit he found such high rates of staff absenteeism that a single attendant was in charge of fifty or a hundred residents. On every visit, too, he discovered showers that did not run and toilets that did not flush.

The experts that often accompanied him—physicians, psychologists, and administrators from other states—described still more neglect and abuse.

Mary Stewart Goodwin, pediatrician, former consultant to DMH, visits of March 30, 31, 1972:

> 10:00 P.M. Door of seclusion room opened by request; bare unlighted room, closed screened window, mattress and crumpled sheet and single

> thin blanket on floor, barefoot 17-year-old girl in dingy loose gown standing by the door—pale pasty appearance. Took my hand when offered—responded to questions with gestures and monosyllables. Has been in seclusion for *7* years; heavily tranquilized, teeth extracted long ago because "she bit someone"—no signs of aggressive behavior during our visit.

Robert Kugel, professor of pediatrics, dean, College of Medicine, University of Nebraska, visit of April 17, 1972:

> Building 2, Floor number four is . . . where hospitalized patients were located. The patients' names were written on their legs with indelible ink. I found this to be an extraordinary procedure.
>
> On many of the wards I was told that anywhere from 75 to 95 percent of the patients were on tranquilizers. This percent would be very high and would suggest that behavior is being controlled more through drugs than through programs, activity, or other therapy.

As the process of discovery continued, Ennis maneuvered the case through various pretrial procedures. First he had to win class action status and the right to represent the 5,400 clients at Willowbrook. The abuses, he argued, affected all residents alike and the remedies could not be achieved on an individual-by-individual basis. The state objected that Ennis wanted to shut down the institution, which "may not be appropriate or desired by all Willowbrook residents." Clutching at straws, it also contended that since the suit would require access to the names of Willowbrook residents and their guardians, "it could mean an invasion of privacy." Judd unhesitantly dismissed the privacy claims and granted class action status. "The interests of the individual plaintiffs and the character of the plaintiff organization are sufficient to assure that all members of the class will be adequately represented."

Then Ennis asked the court for "emergency relief . . . necessary to protect the lives, physical health, safety and well-being of the residents." This motion, he explained, did not look to permanent remedies that would "improve" residents' functioning (and thus involve arguments about a right to treatment); for now he was only seeking temporary measures to "maintain" residents' functioning and prevent their deterioration while preparing the case for permanent relief. The facts Ennis presented related mostly to overcrowding, understaffing, and the use of seclusion and restraint; and his remedy was for the court to order the state to hire more personnel, to conduct a medical screening of all residents, and to develop a foster home program. The state responded by asking Judd to respect its good-faith efforts: The governor had just made an emergency allocation of $5 million and DMH was already implementing many of the plaintiffs' requests.

When Frank Johnson had heard these same arguments in *Wyatt,* he held two days of hearings and then overnight granted plaintiffs' motion for preliminary relief. Judd, however, was more hesitant. Responding to Ennis's first plea in June 1972, he conceded that "conditions at Willowbrook are largely inhumane, and this situation has continued over a period of years. . . . The need to improve conditions at Willowbrook has been known to New York State officials from at least 1964." Nevertheless, "in spite of the urgency of the conditions, and the assertions that the defendants are moving too slowly," the court had to give "thoughtful study to the extent to which a federal court order is appropriate." So he urged the two sides to negotiate their differences. If the state was already doing most of what the plaintiffs wanted, surely they could agree on preliminary relief measures.

But the two sides could not agree to anything. No sooner did plaintiffs win their class action motion than a dispute of several months followed on who was to notify the parents and what the announcement should say. Eventually, Judd had to decide that the state would mail the notice, that the plaintiffs would pay the postage and duplication costs, and the letter would have to say more than that plaintiffs wanted to close down Willowbrook—a point the state wished to emphasize, in the hope that it would disturb many parents and lead them to hire their own attorneys, and thus create havoc for the plaintiffs. With this level of animosity, substantive negotiations on remedial measures went nowhere. The state kept insisting that it had a plan to meet all the residents' needs. Plaintiffs were certain that the plan was "really no plan at all."

The dispute unresolved, Ennis petitioned Judd for a hearing on preliminary relief, which Judd scheduled for mid-November. Then a criminal case came up on his docket, and to Ennis's chagrin, he postponed Willowbrook. "We do not know if the defendant in that case is in custody," protested Ennis. "We do know that our clients are in custody. . . . It is our position that Willowbrook is a prison, and in many respects is worse than a prison." But Judd would not change the calendar. The criminal case lasted nearly a month, and not until December 18, 1972, did the five-day hearing on preliminary relief finally open.

* * *

Ennis's presentation of the case had the quality of a well-crafted film. Start with a close-up, parents testifying about incidents of abuse to their children. Pan to a medium-range shot, the staff analyzing the problems endemic to Willowbrook. Then pull back for a wide-angle view, the experts putting Willowbrook in the context of human development—all demonstrating that unless remedial measures were introduced immediately, the residents would deteriorate physically and mentally.

Thus plaintiffs' case began with the mother of Patricia Parisi telling the court about the bruises that covered her daughter's body. The mother of Sheldon Rosenthal described burns on her son's back from radiators without protective covers. The sister-in-law of Ulga De Alzate, in Building 22, recounted the most grisly story of all:

Q. I direct your attention to April, 1972. Do you recall a specific injury which occurred to her at that time?

A. Well, yes. . . . We drove up to Willowbrook . . . and we found Ulga with her ear bitten off, part of the nose torn off this way [indicating] and her knees completely bruised, black and blue, scratches on her face and arms.

Testimony about the chambers of horrors came next from whistle blowers on the staff who were ready to risk their jobs (and even more certainly, the enmity of administration and co-workers) to expose the system. Inez Stevens, a nurse, first described the Kardex record system on the patients, with so few entries that continuity of treatment was impossible. Then she told of the haphazard maintenance in the buildings.

Q. Mrs. Stevens, let me ask you about the physical plant environment in buildings 20, 22, and 23. . . .

A. They are inadequate. The buildings are in a deplorable state. As far as plumbing goes, we are constantly having floods. The water backs up through the drains. The sinks don't work. The lights are always out . . . there are no night lights in the building. They never get replaced. The physical condition is really bad.

Q. Do you have any insect problems in 20, 22, or 23?

A. The insect problem is terrible. They have just taken over the building. . . . Cockroaches I mean as far as insects.

Q. Did you have any insect problem in Building 2 in the infirmary when you were working there?

A. Oh, yes, cockroaches just run all over the place. In fact, when I had a patient under oxygen, I had a cockroach in the oxygen tent with the patient.

The star witness from inside Willowbrook was Bill Bronston. At the March retreat he had greeted Ennis's plan for a lawsuit enthusiastically, and he remained at Willowbrook expressly to collect damaging evidence. His own testimony was imaginatively conceived; between September 8 and 10 he had photographed patients he treated (or at least those among them who demonstrated the effects of gross abuse and neglect). On the witness stand, Bronston discussed each photograph: Here was a shot of Patricia's laceration, which took nineteen sutures; there was a photograph of the gash across Peter's lip, which took six or seven. Elaine had a scalp cut an inch and a half deep, caused when another resident struck her on the head with a shoe. Mildred had two lacerations, each requiring two to three stitches: "These have been caused by keys," explained Bronston. "They are a very peculiar lesion. They are a puncture and Y-shaped cut, which is caused by the heavy door keys that open the main doors." Do residents carry keys? he was asked. "No," he answered, only the professionals, the administrators, and the attendants have them. Bronston's testimony continued with a disheartening repetitiveness—a photograph of an arm with a dozen sutures followed by one of a scalp with fresh sutures crisscrossing the lines of old ones.

The most persuasive expert testimony came from Dr. James Clements, head of the Georgia Retardation Center, where residents lived in small, apartment-like units, received decent food, and followed daily programs. At the least, the center was scandal-free. At its best, it resembled a real school. Ennis had first met Clements during the *Wyatt* trial. One of the lawyers had happened upon an early American Association on Mental Deficiency survey of Partlow, which, unlike most such surveys, was frankly critical of conditions. The attorneys contacted the author of the survey, Jim Clements, and were delighted to hear a Southern accent. Expecting him to be highly effective in Johnson's courtroom, they asked him to testify on Partlow. This was the first of dozens of court appearances that Clements would make over the next ten years, and invariably he was an exemplary witness, informed, cool, and methodical.

Clements gave Judd a moving account of his several days at Willowbrook. He described meeting a Catholic priest who was doing penance by working at the institution. The priest was pacing around an enclosed pen for the children at Building 16, "not verbalizing or making any attempt at verbal communication, and the youngsters there were so eager for human contact that there was a youngster holding onto each leg, being dragged around and around this endless circle within this pen." Clements could imagine the sins that brought the priest into the circle, but what could the children have done to belong in it too?

The heart of his testimony went to research findings on the damaging effects when "individuals are not being subjected to at least minimal safe-keeping custodial care. . . . Those children who were toilet trained will lose this skill. Children who were talking will likely stop talking. Children who are walking are likely to stop walking." He reviewed John Bowlby's and Sally Provence's findings on the damaging consequences of barren environments on infant development, how abandoned children placed in institutions had more acute psychological problems than those placed in family care. He also recounted Richard Davenport's work at the Yerkes Primate Center; newborn chimps who were taken from their mothers and placed in isolation (food tossed into their cages, no external stimuli presented) manifested "all sorts of behavioral difficulties . . . head-banging, twirling, aggressive behavior." For Clements, the analogy to Willowbrook was obvious and no one challenged him on it. With his testimony, plaintiffs rested their case.

There is a popularly held image of the public-interest lawyer as David against the state's Goliath. It may hold true insofar as dollars are concerned, but the Goliath in the first Willowbrook class action suit was remarkably unprepared and lackluster. Its lawyers had been able to delay the proceedings and increase Ennis's costs, but they were unable to mount a creditable defense, and not merely because they had been dealt a poor hand. For Brenda Soloff (who is now a state judge and enjoys a solid reputation), Willowbrook was one of several cases on a desk piled high with papers in an attorney general's office which was accustomed to handling appellate arguments, not conducting long and complicated trials. Soloff did not have the days open or the assistants available to travel to Willowbrook, find witnesses, and prepare testimony. For Ennis and his fellow attorneys, Willowbrook was *the* case, the cause to win. For Soloff, it was another responsibility, worse than most, an ordeal to survive. And almost every moment in the courtroom demonstrated the import of this difference.

The state's cross-examination of plaintiffs' witnesses appeared amateurish. Its questions to Bronston involved the length of time it took him to snap the pictures, as though his dereliction of duty was the real issue. Even Judd lost patience. Calculating that forty pictures at thirty seconds a picture amounted to twenty minutes, he told the attorney that the line of questioning was "not too significant." By the time cross was over, Judd was more impressed with Bronston, asking his opinion on the value of volunteers at Willowbrook and the likelihood that a larger staff would perform better. So, too, the state mainly questioned Clements about how much he could learn about Willowbrook in four days, which, to listen to him, was clearly a lot.

Witnesses for the defense often sounded like witnesses for the plaintiffs. The most that Dr. Frederic Grunberg, deputy commissioner in charge of mental retardation, was willing to say for the state was that in 1967, Willowbrook's "conditions were grimmer than they are now." But citing past dereliction did not enhance DMH's reputation. In fact, the bulk of Grunberg's testimony confirmed pervasive "dehumanization" (his term) and "extremely poor staff morale." Willowbrook was "completely out of scale with the [Staten Island] community that it's supposed to serve." Although he recounted several new programs to reduce overcrowding, he concluded: "If we are talking of taking care of very, very basic needs and preventing some very gross life-threatening situations, I would say that we may meet it. But on the other hand, if we do mention adequate custodial care, no, we are not meeting it."

To refute any notion that DMH was likely to improve its performance, Ennis, on cross-examination, took Grunberg through the record on community placements. Grunberg testified that some five hundred to seven hundred Willowbrook residents belonged in group homes, but that only one residence was open in Manhattan and none were under construction. When Ennis finished his questions, Judd asked one of his own:

The Court: Dr. Grunberg, do you think that a Court Order would help speed up the shift from planning to performance?
The Witness: No, Your Honor.
The Court: You don't?
The Witness: I don't think so.
The Court: It seems to take a long time from plan to results.

The only nasty exchanges occurred at the close of the hearing, when Ennis cross-examined Miodrag Ristich, the latest of Willowbrook's directors and the only witness who really tried to defend the institution. "At our worst," he testified, "we are meeting the basic levels of need, just barely. . . . I would include attention to physical need, feeding, clothing, keeping clean, attention to acute medical problems, protection from common physical dangers." He insisted that the incidents Bronston had reported were unavoidable: "There are some people who bang their heads much of the time, continually." Closer supervision might prevent a few accidents, "but there are other people who I have seen who once in a week or once in two weeks certainly for no apparent reason hit their head against the corner of a table, and one just knows that periodically these people come up for suturing. This type of injury is not really preventable." Ristich also contended that he had not seen "any deterioration over the six months that I have been in Willowbrook. I cannot truthfully say that anyone functions at a perceptible lower level than he did six months ago."

Ennis set out to demolish his testimony. He turned first to the "incident" reports filed at Willowbrook in cases of injury and the like, which were not only consistently high in number but increasing during Ristich's tenure.

Q. Incident reports have gone up an average of one hundred incidents per month. Is that correct?
A. That is correct.
Q. What kind of trend is that? Is that an upward trend or a downward trend?
A. It is an upward trend in reports.

When Ristich tried to slip away by claiming that the incident reports covered more than injuries, Ennis pursued:

Q. Let's see what kind of incidents are reported in these books. Let's take the last page, since it's the most recent. Will you read off the classification of the incident involved?
A. Injury, injury, injury, injury, patient assault, injury, patient assault.
Q. Let's try the preceding page. Would you read off the classifications of what those incident reports were about?
A. Patient assault, injury—do you want me to read every single one?
Q. They are all the same?
A. Yes, except for one patient fight, yes.

Ennis concluded his cross-examination with questions on Ristich's claim that Willowbrook was satisfying residents' "basic level of need."

Q. Dr. Ristich, we have heard testimony that many residents are requested to stand naked for long periods of time, waiting to be hosed down (as a shower) in a line. Does that process meet their basic human needs?

A. I have always said that their privacy leaves much to be desired, and this is one of the instances that—

Q. We have also heard testimony that residents drink water from toilet bowls. Does that meet their basic human needs?

A. I don't know how to answer that. There is a school of thought that people have entitlement to [not] being restrained. I don't know if that's your school of thought, but there are problems. How does one stop people from drinking water from toilets?

Q. How about more staff?

A. But even then, that means that the staff must go with the resident every time he goes to the bathroom, and that's an invasion of privacy.

Q. How about fountains on wards?

A. The experience shows it wouldn't last.

Q. Because the environment is so destructive?

A. Yes.

Q. In these respects, privacy and other matters, it's fair to say that Willowbrook does not meet the residents' basic level of needs?

A. As long as we keep a distinction between safekeeping and another basic level, which is custody with dignity—yes, I'd say it does not.

Whatever terminological games Ristich was playing, Ennis was content to let the images make the point.

The evidence at the hearings constituted a powerful indictment of the state, and yet to Ennis's dismay, Judd would periodically comment on how difficult he found this case. On one occasion, in excluding a minor piece of evidence, he exclaimed: "I am not going into [that]. I am deciding what to do with the children at Willowbrook. That's hard enough." Then, on the last afternoon, Judd made clear that he was uninterested in whatever injustices had already been committed at Willowbrook. "There is no point in my punishing the department for something they did in the past." Rather, "Your only question is whether there is a risk in the future that justifies my granting some kind of injunction." As if his unwillingness to see a predictive value to past performance were not discouraging enough, Judd asked the lawyers to include in their posttrial briefs arguments over the practicality of court-ordered remedies. "Assuming that I find I have jurisdiction to do anything, what can I feasibly do? There is no good of my granting an injunction if it's one that I can't enforce." On that note of caution, the trial closed.

The posttrial briefs complicated Judd's deliberations, for the state ably laid out the constitutional objections to court intervention. Reminding him that no "legal fetters confined the retarded to Willowbrook," the defense's brief carefully argued that a court had the right to abolish discriminatory practices *within* a social service system—to prohibit, for example, a relief regulation that gave higher stipends to whites than to blacks. It did not, however, have the right to compel a social system to increase the welfare stipend for all whites and blacks, even where it fell below subsistence levels. Whatever the judge's own sentiments, there was no constitutional right to adequate welfare payments, and allocation decisions were properly left to the legislature. So in the case of Willowbrook, plaintiffs might be dissatisfied with the limited budget devoted to the residents and the conditions that resulted from it. But then they should have the parents take their children home and make their protests to the legislature.

The state's brief was notably weaker in establishing its own ability to administer a humane system. Trying to cover its bets (as briefs always do), it argued that should the court find improvements necessary, DMH could manage the assignment without outside interference. Yet when it came to particulars, to implementing new programs, the state seemed ever so uncaring, as though the difficulty of change obviated the need for change.

Plaintiff Demand:	Willowbrook should hire 134 more nurses immediately.
Defense Response:	It is simply a fact of life that nurses are in short supply and nurses who will work with the retarded are in even shorter supply.
Demand:	Willowbrook should hire more physical therapists, even if it requires higher salaries.
Response:	The numbers of personnel available is limited and not attracted to clients who show relatively undramatic progress. Civil service requirements are rigid. No court order will change these facts.
Demand:	Repair all exposed heating units.

Response: Plaintiffs did not show that the problem is with exposed units rather the problem is that the covers conduct heat. No solution has yet been devised.

The plaintiffs' two-hundred-page brief relentlessly piled fact upon fact (demonstrating why "there is probably no more dangerous place to live in New York City than the back wards of Willowbrook") but it added little on the court's proper role. Ennis continued to rest most of his case on the argument that Willowbrook was a prison and Eighth Amendment standards applied. But what if Judd took seriously the fact that residents were not confined against their will? Ennis also cited Frank Johnson's ruling in *Wyatt* advancing a right to treatment. But the decision was new and if Judd found it too strained a reading of the Constitution, he would have grave difficulty in fashioning a remedy for Willowbrook.

It is a fortunate person who never confronts an irreconcilable conflict between two prized values, and by such a standard, Judd was not a fortunate person. One of his closest friends said of him: "He was blessed by God with two endowments which do not often appear in the same person, a keenness of intellect and a love of man." For most of his life, these two traits fit well together and Judd was genuinely a man of conscience and of mind. But then came Willowbrook—and he found himself forced to choose between a moral and a judicial position, to choose, quite literally, between his intellect and his love of man.

His intellect suggested several compelling reasons to keep judicial hands off Willowbrook. If its residents were there by choice, if Willowbrook was truly a social service, then the only basis for court intervention would be an overriding constitutional obligation to provide treatment—and Judd was very skeptical of such an obligation. He knew the history of the "right to treatment" well. After Morton Birnbaum originated the idea, it appeared in a 1966 decision, *Rouse* v. *Cameron,* involving the long-term commitment of a minor offender found criminally insane to St. Elizabeth's mental hospital. David Bazelon, the presiding judge of the district court, followed Birnbaum's quid pro quo argument: For the state to deprive someone of his liberty against his will, it was constitutionally obligated to provide treatment. But as Judd was careful to note, Bazelon had merely *suggested* the existence of such a right; he actually freed Rouse on statutory grounds. St. Elizabeth's was a federal hospital and Congress had legislated (in 1964) a right to treatment in federal hospitals. Thus the *Rouse* decision had no bearing to the case at hand. Willowbrook did not hold inmates against their will—thereby making any quid pro quo unnecessary—and New York had not legislated a right to treatment.

The second outstanding case in the annals of right to treatment was, of course, Frank Johnson's 1971 opinion in *Wyatt,* which Judd found unpersuasive. He was convinced that Johnson had read *Rouse* uncritically, going well beyond Bazelon's conclusions. Furthermore, Johnson's original findings had been directed against Bryce, the state mental hospital; when the case was broadened to include Partlow, the state's mental retardation institution, Johnson merely asserted that it was "clear beyond cavil" that the retarded also had "a constitutional right to receive individual habilitation." To Judd, the point was by no means clear beyond cavil. By what logic did the state have a constitutional duty to refit the retarded for life in society? It might choose to do so, or not choose to do so: "The allocation of state resources among conflicting needs is a matter for the state legislature." In short, Judd could find no theory in *Rouse* or in *Wyatt* that established constitutional rights for those at Willowbrook. Seemingly the plaintiffs should leave the court and head for Albany.

But the facts, the grim record, remained. Would Judd really turn the case away? Did judicial restraint mean this kind of restraint? The choice was agonizing, pitting the dreadful details that he had heard in the courtroom against a scrupulous reading of judicial precedent. In an effort to escape this conflict, Judd took an extraordinary step: With the final briefs in and the testimony reviewed, he decided to see Willowbrook for himself.

Why make this trip? With hundreds of pages of testimony and depositions, what was the point of going to Willowbrook? Yes, juries do on occasion visit the scene of the crime, but that is to understand better the testimony or the geography of the site, not to substitute their observations for those of the witnesses. But here the question was not geography, the location of Building 2 in relation to Building 22. It was a test. Were the experts for the plaintiffs right? Were the toilets broken? Did the wards stink? Were the residents naked? It was Judd second-guessing the testimony, which indicates the depth of his discomfort.

Just how equivocal Judd's visit was emerges from a later remark of Frank Johnson's. Johnson was not an unbiased source—he had to be aware of Judd's highly critical view of the *Wyatt* decision. But in a 1980 television interview, Bill Moyers asked Johnson, who was by then overseeing Alabama's corrections as well as its mental health and retardations systems, whether he ever toured an institution before writing an opinion. "Absolutely no," Johnson responded. "A judge shouldn't go visiting a place that he has under scrutiny in a lawsuit, and base his decision in whole or in part on what he's observed, unless he's going to submit himself to cross-examination." A judge had to rely on the court proceedings and papers. "He should do it on the basis of evidence that's presented during the adversary proceeding. And so, I've been criticized for not going to Bryce Hospital. I've been criticized for not visiting the penitentiaries. But that's not the approach, in my judgment."

Judd's position was less persuasive. Suppose he traveled out to Willowbrook and found it much better than testimony suggested. What was he to do with that finding? Act on it—without being certain whether the state had engineered a show for his announced visit? Or what if he found conditions worse than the testimony? Would the state have the opportunity to refute his impressions? Why, then, did he go? Probably because he was hoping against hope that Willowbrook was not as terrible as the witnesses had said. Perhaps their professional commitment to improving retardation services had colored their testimony, and wanting the best (which the state was surely not obliged to provide), they had exaggerated the worst. Judd did not doubt that Willowbrook was in need of improvement, but maybe its conditions did not shock the conscience.

Notes from the Field
Judge Orrin Judd Visits Willowbrook
February 12, 1973

The day's tour had been planned well in advance. The judge, not one for surprise visits, wanted to see only the buildings about which he had heard testimony. *The Court* [as Judd reported] *visited Willowbrook State School on February 12, 1973. Necessarily, what a layman could learn from such a visit was limited. The decision must be based primarily on the factual and expert testimony received in court.*

On arrival, Judd went to the deputy director's office in Building 1, to be joined there by two lawyers, one from each side. At 9:30 A.M., the tour of ten of the forty buildings began.

The group went first to Building 2, one of the largest of the Willowbrook structures, with something of the look of a college administration building. But despite the cupola with its flag and the grassy fields around, the fantasy of being on a campus lasted only for a moment. *The wards in almost every building are enclosed by metal doors which lock with a key, somewhat like the arrangements in a mental hospital.* And the visitors had to come to grips with what went on behind the doors.

In Building 2, the group climbed up to the third floor and entered Ward A. *There was a young boy standing up chewing the rail of his playpen.* Spastic children also lay about in cripple carts—wooden wheelbarrow-like devices—or in rows on mats on the floor. In Ward B, *there were many women sitting around half dressed.* Judd counted the number of residents, forty-three, and the number of attendants, four, and noted that no nurses were present anywhere. He and the others climbed to the fourth floor, and as they entered Ward B, a woman toppled out of her wheelchair. The judge asked the attendant to show him the residents' records; she explained that there was no time to maintain a system. *The Kardex records in Building 2 were still not up to date, and the medication instructions did not have clear terminal dates.* Remembering that one of the experts had testified about pervasive malnutrition, and that one resident of Building 2 was reputedly so undernourished that she had "pipe stem legs," Judd asked to see her. The attendant pointed to the woman who had just fallen out of her chair.

The group passed strewn garbage and litter to enter Building 20. *A typical residential unit is a two-story brick building, containing two wards per floor—one on each side of a central stairway. Entrance onto the wards is through a metal door which is locked and must be opened with a key. On the other side of the door is the dayroom, a large rectangular space. Most of the dayrooms are dimly lit and the furniture is limited to plastic chairs and an occasional table. Some dayrooms have TVs which are usually turned to a soap opera or a quiz show. Residents in the dayroom in Building 20 were mostly doing nothing; one was rocking continually and another was oddly contorted. Most of the ward attendants merely stood and watched the idle residents.* The supervisor informed Judd that although he was supposed to have responsibility for no more than 100 residents, staff shortages forced him to worry about 220.

In every ward that he entered, Judd went over to the bank of toilets and tried to flush them. Hours of testimony had been offered about the filth and the malfunctioning of the plumbing, but he learned for himself that on every row of toilets at least one did not operate and another was filled with stool. Finding no towels, he asked the supervisor where they were, and was told that they "were somewhere," only he did not know exactly where. Judd made his way down to the basement, saw four residents watching television, asked if they could go back up to the dormitory if they wished to, and was told that they could not. *The residents for the most part sleep in dormitories and are not confined to cells like prisoners, but even those who are ambulatory cannot move about freely.*

The visit continued at Building 22. Judd noted that the smells here and elsewhere were not as bad as he had expected. *The court did not observe the stench of urine which was described by the witnesses in court, but the combination of odors in many buildings made it a pleasure to be able to go outdoors.* He climbed a flight of stairs to enter Ward C, counted the chairs and counted the residents, and asked why there were fewer chairs than residents. The answer was that one resident, Carmen, destroyed chairs and beds too, and was strong enough to be able to pull nails out of the walls bare-handed. *The court was told of one young woman in Building 22 who broke twelve chairs in one day. Since the purpose of the visit was to observe and not to obtain additional testimony, the court did not pursue these matters.* On the way down, a woman resident coming upstairs drew even with Judd, suddenly spat on him, and shook him. When two of the group went to his aid, she struck one on the back of the neck and scratched the other across the face. *The court party should have waited until the staircase was clear. Nevertheless, the incident illustrates that, in dealing with residents who may fling their arms about aimlessly without any malevolence, considerable supervision is required to protect their fellow residents.*

After a brief stop for medical attention, the group went to Building 8, where the judge again inspected the toilets. *There was still generally at least one toilet which did not flush in each battery. There was no toilet paper. The court is convinced that delays in plumbing repairs are not merely an inconvenience but a detriment to teaching or maintaining personal hygiene.*

They moved to Building 16, the "Baby Complex," the pride of Willowbrook. *The dayrooms have chest-high partitions running the length of the room, creating two large pens on either side. The residents were confined in the pens: the large center area of the dayroom went unused. At the far end of the dayrooms another locked door leads to the dormitory area. In the dormitory about 50 beds are spread out in long rows, but little space between the beds. February 12 was a sort of holiday (the Stock Exchange was open, but banks and schools were closed) for people outside Willowbrook and for some of the professional staff. But there were no special celebrations or special activities. Except in Building 78, and in the "Baby Complex," there were no toys or apparatus observable in the dayrooms. Granted that many of the residents are destructive, it should be possible with a more generous budget and better supervision to keep at least a minimum supply of equipment to encourage some activity on the part of the residents.* Judd noticed a water fountain; experts had testified about some residents suffering from dehydration. *The water fountain in Building 16 was out of order. Granted that children might squirt water at each other if the fountain was operating, it still should be fixed. Adequate supervision might make a water fountain useful not only to quench thirst, but to provide training in life habits.*

The group proceeded to Building 6. When Judd asked why some forty residents in one of the wards were doing nothing, the attendant responded that they were enjoying a "relaxation period." Plaintiffs' attorney, Robert Feldt, commented that

6 was actually a "demonstration building" and therefore had a greater number of staff. Perhaps the judge would like to tour Building 7, which was not on the itinerary? Judd demurred, remarking that no trial testimony had been offered on 7.

It was late afternoon by the time the group entered Building 78, one of Willowbrook's best units. *One attendant in Building 78 was playing a record and leading the children in a sort of dance, but this was almost the only activity that was observed.* As Judd left the building, he proposed that they visit Building 7 after all.

Here the nightmare that was Willowbrook sprang to life. It was the snake pit, or worse. In Ward A, Judd saw fifty-three men without an attendant in sight, some of them nude, lying on the floor, others moving about aimlessly and rapidly. *A sign in B Ward of this building read: "Keep your clothes on." Two attendants covering 35 boys, however, could not be expected to be sure that they live up to the admonition on the walls.* The stench of urine and sweat was pervasive. *In Building 7, the court observed a boy whose right eye was swollen shut and whose forehead was covered with fresh blood from several open wounds. There was no immediate response from the nearest attendant to the team leader's inquiry as to how it had happened, and no entry had yet been made on the incident sheet for the building.* Judd stopped to talk with Miss Kao, a small and slight Korean woman who seemed especially frail against the backdrop of the larger and aggressive men in the ward. She complained of chronic shortages of clothing, sheets, and bedding, adding that the nudity Judd saw was commonplace on weekends and holidays because no clothing was available.

As Judd left Building 7, he commented that all this was "disreputable." And just about this time he began introducing himself to Willowbrook staff as "the judge who has to try to do something about these problems."

The tour completed, Judd returned to write his opinion, putting his mind at the service of his conscience. The reasoning was weak, the arguments unpersuasive, but he decided for the plaintiffs. Judd was not able to accept a right to treatment and instead devised his own theory, a right to protection from harm.

His starting point was with the established principle that "persons who live in state custodial institutions are owed certain constitutional duties." Reviewing the 1960s prisoners' rights cases, Judd found that "a tolerable living environment is now guaranteed by law." Prisoners had a right to protection against assault, to medical care, to the opportunity for exercise, to adequate heat, to "the necessary elements of basic hygiene." His list was intended to be not exhaustive but exemplary, to illustrate the content and scope of the protection from harm. And such a protection, he ruled, should be extended to Willowbrook as well. The essentials that had been established for prisons held for schools for the retarded.

But exactly how did Judd get from prisons to institutions for the retarded, which had been the major problem all along? How did he overcome the objections that no one was at Willowbrook against his or her will? The answer: "Since Willowbrook residents are for the most part confined behind locked gates . . . they must be entitled to at least the same living conditions as prisoners." Yet what did it mean to say that Willowbrook residents were "confined behind locked gates"? If Judd meant it literally, his visit told him he was wrong. There were no walls enclosing the several hundred acres and not a locked gate in sight. Although wards were frequently locked, Judd undoubtedly meant the observation to be taken metaphorically. The problem was that he himself had already undercut the point by noting that "none [of the residents] have been denied a right to release." In effect, Judd asserted the prison analogy, not demonstrated it. His opinion represented an unwillingness to allow federal judges to raise prisons to a standard of decency while remaining powerless to ameliorate institutions for the retarded.

Judd disposed of other objections to federal court intervention more quickly but not much more persuasively. He overcame his reluctance to have courts dictate the allocation of social resources by noting that Willowbrook was out of compliance with HEW's minimum standards for federal reimbursement. His decision would not represent unwarranted interference because: "For all practical purposes, the state must ultimately meet the requirements of the Department of Health, Education and Welfare or lose the substantial federal assistance. . . . The relief granted here is substantially less than what the HEW regulations will ultimately require." In other words, because the state might later decide to expend "substantially more" funds to obtain federal reimbursements, he was entitled to compel it to expend substantially less funds immediately.

Judd then granted preliminary relief, ordering the state to: (1) prohibit seclusion (thereby making violators subject to contempt of court); (2) hire and train more ward attendants, physicians, nurses, physical therapists, and recreational staff; (3) repair all inoperable toilets. To demonstrate how protection from harm differed from right to treatment, Judd specifically commented that he was not compelling the state to conduct a medical screening of each resident. Such a measure would have constituted treatment.

Judd closed with a line that clarified the moving force in the entire document. With Deputy Commissioner Frederic Grunberg about to leave DMH, Judd remarked: "It may be hoped that [his successor] will read the affidavits submitted in this case so that he may be aware of the inhumane and shocking conditions which have heretofore existed at Willowbrook." In Judd's decision, a love of man triumphed over keenness of intellect.

4

The Numbers Game

No one was pleased with Judd's opinion on preliminary relief and his strenuous effort to steer a course between judicial intervention and restraint. The Department of Mental Hygiene fitfully attempted to dispose of the Willowbrook scandal and resented any intrusions on its autonomy. Plaintiffs were deeply disappointed with Judd's rejection of a right to treatment, fearful that he meant to accomplish little more than make Willowbrook into a safer warehouse. In their mutual discontent, the two sides would eventually reach their own agreement, like two petty nations inclined to strike a bargain rather than allow a superpower to impose its will. But before the parties could fashion a consent decree, defendants spent several (futile) years trying to make the Willowbrook scandal disappear and plaintiffs learned about the frustrations inherent in trying to enforce a preliminary injunction and persuade a reluctant judge to close down a facility.

From the day Rivera's film clips aired right through the start of the second Willowbrook trial, the state attempted to demonstrate to the court and the press its ability to resolve the scandal. That it proved incapable of self-correction provides not only a lesson in bureaucratic ineptitude but, far more important, an exemplification of what would have happened to Willowbrook's 5,400 residents without sustained court involvement. Between 1972 and 1975, DMH played a numbers game whose rules were simple, really crude: Reduce the institutional census at Willowbrook by whatever means. Transfer its residents anywhere and everywhere, regardless of the quality or character of the alternate setting. Absent a lawsuit, with the state left to its own solutions, Willowbrook would have been another exercise in dumping, this time into other custodial and barren settings.

The person who as head of DMH had the task of resolving the crisis was Alan Miller. He had arrived at DMH as an associate commissioner in 1964, having chaired the community services planning division at the National Institute of Mental Health (NIMH). He helped to draft the 1965 Rockefeller five-year plan, and after the sudden death of Paul Hoch, Rockefeller appointed him commissioner. Unlike his predecessors he lacked a major academic reputation in psychiatry, but turned loose in the Albany jungle, he knew when to take on the protective camouflage of drabness and when to seek visibility as an energetic man on the move.

Miller's agenda was, first, to get Rockefeller and DMH out of their embarrassment as quickly as possible; second, to avert the fiscal disaster that the scandal might generate. At the start of 1972, HEW, in an effort to reduce overcrowding in state institutions, was tightening its Medicaid regulations. Under its new space-resident ratios, Willowbrook was to hold no more than 2,900 residents by 1977 or lose its federal funding. Miller was worried about not only the long-term deadline but also the possibility that the scandal might bring HEW auditors to New York, who finding Willowbrook so out of compliance, might recommend an immediate cutoff of funds. The state would then lose millions of dollars in income and, in the ultimate nightmare, jeopardize the security of the construction bonds that were the cornerstone of the Rockefeller administration.

His eye trained on Washington, Miller set out to make a highly visible display of New York's commitment to the retarded. He helped arrange for the appointment of an HEW task force (with an old friend from NIMH, Bertram Brown, heading it) that would "find ways of assisting New York to improve the situation at the Willowbrook State School as well as the other mental retardation programs within the State." Miller understood that HEW took good-faith efforts to be almost as important as actual performance—so if New York seized the initiative, the threat of a sudden Medicaid cutoff would be eliminated.

At the end of February 1972, the task force arrived for a two-day visit. It toured Willowbrook (predictably finding the level of care "substandard and inadequate") and met with city and state health, mental health, and social service officials as well as the leaders of the protests. The result, oddly enough, was that the task force came away convinced that DMH's problems were manageable. Despite the grossness of the scandal, it concluded that the core of the problem was not official incompetence or even a scarcity of funds, but rather a lack of communication among various departments. Ostensibly, the difficulties were not structural, reflecting an unwillingness to commit resources, but administrative, reflecting an absence of coordination.

The inadequacy of this explanation was amply demonstrated by the fate of the task force's recommendations. Since its "most disheartening" discovery was that no one had identified the special needs of each client, a prerequisite for arranging and coordinating services, it suggested that DMH compile an individualized treatment plan for all Willowbrook residents. Although such plans were already mandated by Medicaid regulations, and Willowbrook should have devised them long ago, NIMH now offered New York a planning grant of some $200,000 to establish a diagnostic unit; DMH was to hire a professional team of evaluators whose first responsibility would be to locate the Willowbrook residents with the highest "potential for community living." These residents would be released quickly, thereby reducing overcrowding; eventually, every resident would be screened and the census would drop to 2,900. Those remaining at the facility would be in a rehabilitative setting; those in the community would have the right amalgam of programs. The scandal would be over.

The strategy seemed not only professionally correct but simple to implement. The task force estimated that a ten-person team could evaluate three to four residents a day, completing four hundred cases by the end of six months; by the end of a year, 20 percent of the resident population would have been screened and Willowbrook would be on the right track. DMH proved it wrong. The state accepted the grant, hired an evaluation team, and established Project Exodus, but the name belied the reality. Very few people left in this exodus, and almost no one reached the promised land.

Between July 1, 1972, and June 30, 1973, the evaluation unit of the Exodus team completed 311 diagnostic studies, about a third of the task force estimate. Part of the problem was that the screening had to begin from scratch; many residents had never received physical or mental tests, and for those who had, the results were frequently outdated. More distressing, the team's recommendations about placement for residents could not be carried out because existing community services were more primitive than the task force believed. HEW had put the cart before the horse, funding an evaluation unit to write prescriptions for programs that did not exist. Thus the Exodus team determined that 184 of the 311 residents should enter foster care and that another 67 should be returned to their families or live in supervised group homes. In fact, only 11 of the 184 residents recommended for foster care entered a foster home, and only 8 of the 67 went into community residences. Indeed, of the 311 residents it evaluated, only 55 left Willowbrook—and 36 of them went to another state institution.*

All the while, DMH continued to make transfers from Willowbrook with scant attention to the work done, or remaining to be done, by the Exodus team. Over 1973 and 1974, some 1,500 inmates left the facility (although given the dismal recordkeeping, these figures must be treated with great skepticism). The majority (55 percent) went to another state facility for the retarded; the rest were dumped into a variety of makeshift settings. They were transferred to vacant wards in state mental hospitals (20 percent); or boarding homes (16 percent); or nursing homes (9 percent). Eight residents, less than 0.5 percent of the total transfers, moved into group homes.

Because the other mental retardation facilities in the state were already overcrowded, the transfers from Willowbrook went mostly to the recently opened borough developmental centers funded under Rockefeller's five-year plan. Their location made a mockery of the notion of community-based services. The Brooklyn Developmental Center, for example, was built at the southwestern tip of the borough, overlooking miles of marshland. It took well over an hour by public transportation to reach the facility from downtown Brooklyn, and once there, the visitor was greeted by the pungent smell of a nearby garbage dump. (Later, it was learned that the site was also an illegal toxic waste dump.) The Williamsburg Residential and Training Center was in an area of abandoned and burned-out buildings. The structure earlier served as a Jewish day school, but after its members moved away, the congregation sold the school to the state, which intended to convert it into a halfway house for the mildly retarded. The facility, however,

*However disappointing these figures, they suggest a degree of organization that distorts the record. The most salient feature of Project Exodus was a confusion so pervasive that for years afterward it would be impossible to know how many residents had actually left the institution and where they had gone.

remained unoccupied until 1973 (the Burns Detective Agency vainly trying to prevent vandalism), when DMH, with a minimum of renovations, moved in forty-five Willowbrook residents.

In the summer of 1972, someone in DMH had the brainstorm to transfer residents from Willowbrook to the empty wards in the state's mental hospitals. Since the mid-1960s, these institutions had been releasing patients indiscriminately to nursing homes and park benches, and to those charged to resolve the Willowbrook crisis, the space was a godsend. DMH intended to open five or six major mental retardation units in these hospitals, each to serve some three hundred of Willowbrook's most troublesome cases. In fact, it managed only to open four small units for a total of some three hundred residents.

Since speed of movement was the dominant consideration, the units were exceptionally grim and lacked sufficient staff. Glen Oaks, at Creedmoor State Hospital, sounds like a golf club; it actually constituted the twelfth through fifteenth floors of the medical-surgical building, a setting as remote and chilling as Willowbrook itself. Wingdale, on Harlem Valley's extensive grounds, was composed of two buildings, one of which would soon be closed for violating fire and safety codes. The Keener Unit had been constructed in the nineteenth century as part of the city's charity hospital on Ward's Island; later it became part of Manhattan State Psychiatric Hospital, and eventually it would serve as a shelter for homeless men. After the scandal it became the home of eighty Willowbrook residents, and not a very inviting one. Its walls had flaking plaster and peeling paint (which, given its age, had a high lead content). Visitors complained about the "cold looking and sparsely furnished day rooms and the lack of amenities."

Why did it accomplish only some 15 percent of the projected transfers to the mental hospitals? DMH had assumed that the buses would roll into Willowbrook, pick up their passengers, drive to the psychiatric centers, and drop them off. But nothing at Willowbrook ever worked (or would work) simply. First, DMH had to reckon with the fact that the hospital wards were generally inaccessible to multiply disabled and wheelchair-bound Willowbrook residents. Doors had to be widened, toilets changed, ramps installed, and all that took time. The selection of the clients to be moved was hindered by the blankness of records and charts. Then parental permission had to be secured, and to the state's surprise, that permission was often denied. The stigma of insanity may be more oppressive than the stigma of retardation, for a number of parents did not want their children going to a psychiatric facility—not because of geography or poor programming, but simply because their children did not belong in mad houses. The result was that the number of transfers remained small and the group that did eventually enter the psychiatric facilities was incredibly heterogeneous. Aggressive teenagers mixed with the senile, the very handicapped with the mildly disabled, the verbal with the nonverbal, giving the wards the atmosphere and appearance of a nineteenth-century almshouse.

A more traditional alternative to institutional care was foster care (or family care, as it was also known). The Exodus team estimated that a total of five hundred Willowbrook residents were sufficiently "high functioning," possessing "vocational potential," to be suitable candidates. Obviously, that many people could not be relocated in Staten Island, nor, it seemed, in New York City. The team, therefore, started to search for an economically depressed agricultural area where farmers might be ready to take in boarders for $200 a month, an area that was not near another institution which would have already exhausted the demand. In short order it identified the region around Broome County as having an "almost unlimited potential for family care placements." Its population of less than a quarter of a million people lived scattered over seven hundred square miles, with a per capita income 20 percent lower than the state average. The team justified transfers there with well-worn images of rural life. "Many of the family care homes selected will be small farms and the residents would be expected to perform some tasks in relation to the operation of the farm, e.g., milking cows, feeding poultry and livestock, harvesting fruits and vegetables." Bring foster care to Broome County and Willowbrook would shrink in size, the boarders would live more healthy and productive lives, and a depressed economy would receive over a million dollars annually.

Approvals for this dream-come-true project were rapidly forthcoming, and in the summer of 1973, the Willowbrook–Broome County exchange began. The plan was to bus twenty-five Willowbrook residents weekly to Broome County and discharge them to foster families that had already been selected—so that by December 1973, Willowbrook's population would decline by five hundred.

Once again, the expectations were fanciful. By April 1975, only a little over one hundred ex-Willowbrook residents were living in Broome County. Some of the slippage occurred at the institution. The case records might describe a client as mildly handicapped, but then he turned out to be ineligible because of major physical disabilities or a lack of elementary living skills. Even when suitable residents were identified, parents or guardians frequently objected to the transfer. More problems arose in Broome County. To some farm families, the idea of taking in a black boarder, never mind that he was retarded, was the obstacle. To others, the burden of care was too great and the likelihood of a significant return of labor too small; the resident was too young or too old, or had seizures, or was prone to run away. Thus at times the Willowbrook bus returned more residents from Broome County than it brought there.

That any caretakers would have welcomed the Willowbrook residents seemed unlikely, but such a group existed: the operators of proprietary, for-profit, nursing homes. To have expected DMH to resist doing business with them would have been expecting too much. No opportunity to reduce the size of Willowbrook was passed over.

In the fall of 1973, one DMH official arranged for a 320-bed proprietary nursing home located on the boardwalk in Atlantic City, to accept twenty-two Willowbrook residents. That only two of the clients were from New Jersey and that ten were under fifty years of age did not disturb DMH. The home not only had empty beds but was Medicaid approved, which meant that federal funds would cover much of the cost. The New Jersey facility, it is true, was cleaner, less crowded, and better staffed than Willowbrook. But by any other standard, it was unacceptable. The daily routine consisted of wandering about the halls or sitting before a television set. In fact, three years later the nursing home was the subject of an exposé, which produced a consent decree with monitors to inspect conditions.

DMH entered into even more elaborate negotiations with another proprietary nursing home operator, Solomon Scharf. Scharf was just about to open a new nursing home on Castle Hill Avenue in the Bronx when, recognizing the pressure that DMH was under, he inquired whether his facility could admit some seventy Willowbrook residents. He undoubtedly knew that higher reimbursement rates were available to take in the retarded; he also recognized that more residents would be leaving Willowbrook and he may well have wanted to build a reputation as a major provider of alternative care. Discussions went smoothly and on February 12, 1973, Castle Hill Manor received its operating certificate.

Life at Scharf's facility closely resembled life in most proprietary nursing homes of the 1960s and 1970s—it was monotonous and joyless. DMH staff reported on the vacuousness of the daily routine. "What struck the visitor as he entered the facility was the blatant inactivity with clients sitting in front of a big television, clients roaming aimlessly around the facility and clients arguing with each other and with the staff." They both complained to Scharf's manager, but to no avail, or almost no avail. One day the manager spotted a large mirror on sale, and remembering that a DMH staff member had urged him to purchase furnishings that would assist clients in learning good grooming habits, he bought it and proudly displayed it. The only problem was that the mirror was cracked.

DMH was so determined to play a numbers game that it was especially vulnerable to the schemes of others. A scandal within a scandal began when the nursing home mogul Bernard Bergman and several of his associates attempted to fill a vacant and unlicensed 240-bed facility on Staten Island with Willowbrook residents. Despite rounds of secret negotiations and interventions from well-placed officials in Albany, the deal fell through. Nevertheless, the publicity surrounding the incident started the chain of events that led to the Moreland Commission's investigation of nursing homes and the conviction of Bergman for Medicaid fraud. Nothing in these events reflected well on DMH officials. But for the Willowbrook suit, the residents would have been left to the tender mercies of the Bernard Bergmans.

What happened at Willowbrook itself between 1972–75? Could DMH upgrade the quality of care? In March 1972, Nelson Rockefeller appointed a committee to "thoroughly examine the conditions at Willowbrook and prepare recommendations on what needs to be done to improve the institution." Alton Marshall, the governor's close friend and the head of Rockefeller Center, was chairman; serving with him were several state commissioners, associate commissioners, and directors of private agencies (such as Robert Schonhorn of United Cerebral Palsy, Tom Coughlin, director of an upstate chapter of ARC, and Joseph Weingold of ARC). They spent a year developing proposals that were, in their opinion, "responsive, responsible, and achievable."

The committee was too sophisticated to believe that Willowbrook would automatically improve even should its population drop to 2,900. The facility would "still be too large by modern program concepts," incapable of meeting the individual needs of the residents and of preparing them for community life. So it offered a novel recommendation to cut through layers of bureaucratic inertia. "Willowbrook, as it stands today," declared the report, "should be dissolved. Its improved facilities and services should be used to support five independently administered units, each relating to one of the five Boroughs. This should be a temporary measure until the day when the current site will serve only the needs of Staten Island."

The committee wanted Willowbrook divided into five mini-institutions, each headed by a borough director. He would be responsible both for one-fifth of Willowbrook (the buildings in which clients from his borough lived) and for running his own borough developmental center (centers were already operating in Brooklyn, Queens, and Manhattan). The director was to give "top priority" to transferring residents from his unit at Willowbrook to his unit in the borough. And to provide an incentive, as clients moved so would staff; the more residents repatriated, the larger the borough feifdom. Thus Geographic Unitization (as the plan was called in bureaucratese) would transform Willowbrook into a small facility for some 250 Staten Island residents. Everyone else would be back home.

The simplicity of this solution bred an optimism that it might work. The committee issued its recommendations in February 1973. DMH pondered them for a year, and then in April 1974 established the Willowbrook Geographic Unitization Council (WGUC). Composed of six deputy directors, one appointed by each of the borough directors and one by the DMH regional office, WGUC had as its task the making of detailed plans to implement the committee's recommendations.

The original proposal had not addressed specifics, like which borough a Willowbrook resident should be assigned to—the borough he was born in (borough of origin) or the borough his family now lived in (borough of interest). WGUC, convinced that placement should be as near the family as possible, quite sensibly opted for the borough of interest. But then what should be done about those with no known families? WGUC proposed that these eight hundred residents go into the Staten Island pool. Willowbrook's director liked having more clients to care for if the day should arrive when the Willowbrook census neared 250. And the other borough directors agreed, looking to minimize their own responsibilities. But the DMH regional office objected. Its stated reason was that Staten Island did not have sufficient community services for this group. More telling, clients without families were most easily moved out of Willowbrook, for there was no one to protest a scheme like sending them off to Broome County.

So it went, with every practical decision arousing opposition. What should be done about decentralizing services at Willowbrook? Were there to be five laundry systems, five cleaning staffs, and five food preparation units? The borough directors wanted no decentralization at all, so as to avoid running the services themselves. But then the whole scheme broke down. Suppose the "Bronx buildings" at Willowbrook were filthy. The director would call central administration to inspect and clean them; however, if central administration was short on staff, it would inform the borough director that no help was available and the building would remain dirty—which was the present state of affairs.

As these disputes surfaced, the borough directors, in an unusual display of unity, wrote to the regional DMH commissioner to condemn the new plan as "unworkable." It would pose "very serious obstacles" to satisfying their own "heavy burden of responsibilities." They recommended that the commissioner keep the institution under a central director, give the borough directors the opportunity to develop their own community services, and then later transfer the Willowbrook residents. The directors also told (or warned) the regional office that they would instruct their deputies on WGUC to devise a "feasible plan within these guidelines."

Slowly but inevitably the enterprise wound down. In October 1974, WGUC backed away from unitization, reporting that "any large-scale attempt at complete borough unitization at this time is precipitous." At the same time, a newly appointed acting director at Willowbrook, James Forde, made his opposition clear. "There seems to be some feeling that this facility will be operated by some committee of people who are representative of some superior forces in far distant places and have been placed on these grounds to bring about salvation. I just can't believe that this is the answer to the problems that admittedly exist here."

Thus, in January 1975, the institution's administrative organization was essentially what it had been in January 1972. The bureaucracy seemed impervious to outside influences. Neither an exposé, a federal task force, a court preliminary injunction, nor a gubernatorial commission could generate a fundamental change in its organization or procedures.

One final story about one of the eight Willowbrook residents who went to a group home during these years makes evident why such successes were—and would have remained—rare. In December 1973, the Guild for Exceptional Children, a Brooklyn voluntary agency, asked a social worker at Willowbrook to select a resident who would "benefit from living in our community residence." The choice was made, and the social worker agreed to set a date for the young man to visit the home for a weekend as part of a "weaning-in process." Weeks passed and the social worker never called. The director inquired about the delay and was told that "Willowbrook could not provide the young man with transportation," despite the fact that the home was only a fifteen-minute drive away. The Guild agreed to provide the transportation, but again no one called to set a date. The director pursued the matter, and this time learned that Willowbrook had no clothes for the resident. An irate call to Dr. Ristich did bring a message that clothing had been located and he would be coming. Nevertheless, when he finally arrived, he was wearing "threadbare pants and a shirt."

Then, just when his joining the home seemed set, it turned out that the Willowbrook staff had never notified his family. His sisters arrived at Willowbrook to visit him (having first called to confirm the arrangements), only to discover he was at the hostel. Since they had never given permission for the transfer, they were understandably furious and arrived at the residence threatening to sue. An afternoon at the hostel changed their attitude. They liked what they saw, and the transfer went through.

Understandably, the Guild was not optimistic about taking a second resident. "We certainly hope," the director concluded, "that we can give another young man the home-like atmosphere and opportunity afforded by our hostel, without the insurmountable delay, confusion, and contradiction which I have described."

DMH's misadventures were small consolation to plaintiffs. Although the state's behavior came as no surprise to them, their clients were suffering and the court seemed unresponsive to their plight. When Judd's opinion came down in April 1973, Ennis, to gain some room for maneuver, submitted a new brief asking the judge to reserve "final judgment" on the merits of a right to treatment until "plaintiffs had an opportunity to introduce relevant evidence, expert testimony, and further legal argument." Citing the inadequate conditions at Willowbrook once again, he noted that "the existence or non-existence of a constitutional right to treatment or habilitation depends upon the factual context in which that right is claimed." Judd agreed to permit further argument, but given an obvious impatience with the doctrine, Ennis was not optimistic.

Ennis was not alone in his misgivings. The attorneys from the Civil Rights Division of the Department of Justice who had just won recognition of a right to treatment in Frank Johnson's court were now concerned about a split in the lower federal judiciary and the possibility of reversal when Alabama officials appealed *Wyatt.* Accordingly, Justice decided to enter the Willowbrook case, putting its resources and, yes, the resources of the Federal Bureau of Investigation on the side of the plaintiffs to "convince the judge . . . that mere custodial care will not protect the residents of Willowbrook from physical harm and will in fact result in a lack of any progress and deterioration. This would provide the factual basis on which Judge Judd could easily reconsider his . . . views on right to treatment."

Particularly during the 1970s, Justice and the FBI were not popularly perceived as champions of minorities in general or the disabled in particular. The images first to mind are of prosecutions of draft resisters and the machinations of agents provocateurs, yet during the Nixon administration those in the Civil Rights Division had both the autonomy and the commitment to pursue causes that to some citizens were highly controversial. The division, created in 1957, concentrated initially on winning voter registration rights for Southern blacks and ending discrimination in housing, education, and employment. These activities led division lawyers, like the public-interest lawyers, to defend prisoners' rights; it made no sense to promote integration if the result was that blacks and whites shared equally in the atrocities of an Arkansas or a Texas prison system. Thus, by 1974, Justice lawsuits looked to abolish the practice of arming prisoners as trusty guards (with abuses familiar to moviegoers from *Cool Hand Luke* and *Brubaker*) and to prohibit the worst abuses of solitary confinement.

Division attorneys then had to confront the fact that residents in state mental hospitals and facilities for the retarded were often living in environments at least as punitive. They immediately responded to Frank Johnson's invitation to join the *Wyatt* suit and were eager to assist with Willowbrook. On May 1, 1972, Michael Thrasher, the division attorney in *Wyatt,* submitted a forty-page "justification memorandum" to his superiors, but approval was not forthcoming. They were reluctant to see so much time and resources devoted to institutional litigation. But once Judd's opinion came down, the debate over entering resumed with new urgency. In the interim, Stanley Pottinger had come to Justice from HEW; having worked vigorously to compel universities to adopt affirmative action programs for women faculty, he was ready to improve the lot of other minorities. With him came Michael Lottman, a Harvard College graduate who in the 1960s had moved to Alabama to defend civil rights activists and now, with a law degree earned at night, wanted to litigate on behalf of the disabled. On May 10, 1973, Thrasher sent Pottinger a memorandum urging Justice to participate in the Willowbrook case. Emphasizing how disastrous Judd's opinion was, he wanted the division to enter not merely as a general amicus (with the right to submit briefs) but as a "litigating amicus," with rights to depose, examine, and cross-examine witnesses, because "so much of the establishment of a 'right to treatment' depends upon a proper factual basis." Pottinger agreed and so did Elliot Richardson, who was attorney general. On June 13, 1973, the department formally requested and received Judd's permission to join the suit as a litigating amicus.

Ennis had some initial misgivings about the collaboration, not wanting to lose control of the case and more than a little wary of working with people who were, after all, inside the Nixon administration. But the advantages far outweighed the risks. Justice would bear a large part of the litigation costs. Ennis was also finding New York officials so recalcitrant that he wanted the investigative resources of the FBI to keep the state honest and the judge informed.

Barely three weeks after Judd issued his preliminary relief order, Ennis was embroiled in a fierce dispute with DMH on its compliance with the order's three principal provisions: a 1:9 attendant-resident ratio, outdoor exercise for residents five times a week, and all toilets in repair. Convinced that DMH's estimates of the number of staff necessary to meet the requirement were short by three hundred positions, he asked for a meeting to resolve the differences, which DMH refused. A few weeks later, he toured Willowbrook, counted heads, and flushed toilets, and discovered pervasive noncompliance. "We are not playing a numbers game here," Ennis complained to Brenda Soloff. "Residents continue to be injured, to choke on their food, and to lie in urine-soaked cribs because there are not enough attendants to care for them." Again he proposed discussions on "the steps that should be taken to implement the Court's order," and again he was rebuffed.

Dismayed at the lack of progress and encouraged by Justice's presence, Ennis asked Judd in mid-June to hold the state in contempt. He described the inadequacies at Willowbrook ("Building 6: On A Ward we found . . . three attendants for 45 residents. We found four totally nude boys. There was one newly broken toilet. On B Ward we found . . . three attendants for 50 residents"). He also complained that the summer recreation staff "would not even be sufficient to take the residents out of the front door, walk them around the building, and take them back to the wards." It was his "honest belief that defendants still do not understand, and have not adequately responded to, the urgency of the situation. . . . No step short of a contempt proceeding will induce defendants to comply."

The state countered with an affidavit from Willowbrook's director Miodrag Ristich, explaining, with only a modicum of embarrassment, that staffing errors had occurred because DMH had rushed its calculations in order to meet budget deadlines; but Judd was not to worry, for the department was appointing a special task force to design a new compliance plan. Ristich also noted that an unexpectedly large number of attendants had recently resigned, preventing DMH from reaching its staffing goals. "Valuable time . . . has been lost due to circumstances beyond the defendant's control. . . . No finding of contempt is required to bring the message of this court's order home to the defendants."

With the contempt motion before the court, the attorneys from Justice offered the services of the FBI to monitor Willowbrook's staff ratios, to count the number of residents in outdoor recreation, and to investigate the number of toilets in disrepair. DMH protested that Willowbrook "does not require a police force to oversee compliance [and] it does not take the FBI to . . . flush toilets and count heads." But plaintiffs responded that the FBI was the ideal body to measure compliance and collect "accurate information of an objective character." Indeed, its agents were already monitoring conditions for Justice in mental hospitals, juvenile institutions, prisons, and jails, compiling "an exemplary record in these highly sensitive areas."

Mounting charges and countercharges made the need for accurate information obvious to Judd, and at the end of July, he approved the FBI monitoring and postponed action on plaintiffs' motion for contempt—whereupon Willowbrook received its most unusual visitors. On

August 8 and 9, two FBI agents arrived at the facility, collected maps of the grounds, and examined the client record system. Shortly thereafter, thirty-seven agents received their instructions:

1. Enter each ward of all resident buildings.
   a) Count the number of residents present.
   b) Count the number of attendants present.
   c) Inspect the toilet facilities for each ward to ascertain:
      1) the total number of toilets;
      2) the number of missing, leaking, or inoperative toilets (flush each toilet);
      3) the number of toilets without seats or with broken seats;
      4) whether all lights in the bathroom area are operative;
      5) whether there is water, feces, or urine on the floor of the toilet area.
2. Observe the ground around *all* resident buildings . . . to determine whether any group(s) of residents is (are) outdoors. For each group of residents outdoors, describe exactly what the residents are doing.
3. In carrying out the foregoing, please observe the following procedures:
   a) Perform the monitoring activities on a sunny day or at least on a day when rain does not appear likely. . . .

On August 21, the FBI agents inspected the facility and found substantial noncompliance. Staff did not meet the 1:9 ratio in twenty-five of eighty-two dayrooms; very few residents were outdoors, some 10 percent of the toilets were inoperative. DMH continued to object to "the blanketing [of] Willowbrook with FBI agents," insisting that Willowbrook's toilets "are probably in somewhat better repair than the toilets in public areas in most large buildings." Justice "could not have found a more intrusive, less necessary role to play."

Still Judd kept to his middle-of-the-road position, not citing the state for contempt, but not halting the FBI investigations either. After receiving the August report, he asked the agents to return in November, when they learned that twenty-six of seventy-one dayrooms did not have staff at the 1:9 ratio, that "a total of 23 residents (of over 4,000) . . . were outdoors, although the weather on November 14 was fair, clear and mild." The most encouraging finding was that less than 4 percent of the toilets were defective. Judd took all this to mean that DMH was making some progress. Indeed, he made a second visit to Willowbrook, toured five buildings, found that "all toilets seemed to be functioning properly," and that the wards had an average staff ratio of 1:12. The critical problem was supervision of the staff, and everyone agreed that more midlevel supervisors had to be hired. So once again Judd declined to hold the state in contempt and urged the plaintiffs to keep pressing their demands.

Thus the first year following the preliminary order left everybody uneasy. Ennis was disturbed by Judd's reluctance to take bold steps, either in interpreting constitutional doctrines or in disciplining the state. The state saw itself as victim, trying to take ameliorative action but harassed by such intruders as the FBI. Judd was probably the most troubled of all. Utterly reluctant to manage an institution, here he was dispatching FBI agents to flush toilets and worrying about how many residents were outside on a sunny day. On its face, it all seemed a bit mad. But if one traced each step from the initial scandal to the state's inability to obey the court order, the sequence became inevitable, if no less controversial. In the end, the court could not poke its nose under the tent without sooner or later, comfortably or uncomfortably, coming all the way in.

5

Uninformed Consent

In the spring of 1974, the plaintiffs' lawyers put aside skirmishes with DMH to organize the second Willowbrook trial, seeking permanent relief and a new system of care. The attorneys' ranks had grown. Chris Hansen, who, like Ennis, had graduated from the University of Chicago Law School, originally joined the Mental Health Law Project and NYCLU to litigate all the cases except Willowbrook, and was now devoting himself exclusively to Willowbrook. "The case was a sink," sucking up time, energy, and money, Ennis later remarked. Anita Barrett took over at Legal Aid; Michael Lottman and Diane Dorfman represented Justice. The team worked together with remarkable harmony, with Ennis as the first among equals.

It soon became apparent that the plaintiffs' intention to persuade the court of a constitutional right to treatment was unrealistic. Judd made clear in discussions in chambers that he was disinclined even to admit arguments on the doctrine. So plaintiffs imaginatively devised an alternative strategy: They would enlarge the concept of a right to protection from harm until it was the equivalent of a right to treatment.

Several experts in mental disabilities helped plaintiffs rework their argument. Sidney Lecker, director of a mental health clinic, suggested a concept of "mental starvation." Just as the body deteriorated without proper nourishment, so the mind deteriorated without proper stimulation; thus the only way to protect Willowbrook's residents from harm was to treat them, not merely keep them in custody. Lecker's formulation also allowed Ennis to draw an analogy between the question before the court and legal precedent. The federal courts had consistently ruled that children had a right to an education, though they had no right to the best education. Ennis argued that he was asking no more for the residents of the Willowbrook State School: They asserted no right to the best programs, but merely a right to adequate ones.

Earl Butterfield, a psychologist from the University of Kansas, helped refine the point. As Butterfield eventually explained on the witness stand, Willowbrook's environment was so "grossly inadequate" that its residents "had suffered intellectual harm, social harm, and emotional harm." Given a lack of interaction with staff, residents filled the void by rocking back and forth, abusing themselves, wriggling their fingers in front of their eyes, and other repetitive and purposeless motions. Judd's goal of "a clean, safe, custodial environment" would not protect the residents from harm; unless one intervened actively, they would deteriorate. So, too, "preserving the capacity for growth and development" (a phrase Judd used synonymously with protection from harm) was of little help to the mentally disabled. Human growth could not be preserved in a deep freeze; one could not keep a child, let alone a developmentally disabled child, in perpetual readiness for some future learning experience. "Time out, time lost prior to early adulthood, is just time lost. It comes off the other end of your attainments." Judd's do-less position also made little practical sense. There was no point to preserving a capacity for growth and development if the court was going to permit the retarded to remain in custodial institutions for the rest of their lives.

Plaintiffs' final effort to enlarge the concept of protection from harm relied on the anti-institutional principles of normalization. Custodial care even in a clean and well-lit warehouse was not neutral but damaging. It forced the retarded to live in an abnormal setting, to mix only with other retarded, rendering them unfit to return to society. The circle of argument was now closed: The only way to protect residents from harm was to care for them in the community.

As presented before Judge Judd in October 1974, plaintiffs' case had a textbook quality. In 1972, most of the witnesses had been parents or whistle blowers from the staff. This time, experts in retardation predominated. They, too, had horror stories to tell. Earl Butterfield testified that he had "never seen a facility in which the inadequacies were so widespread and rampant." Linda Glenn, who had toured Willowbrook for Ennis in 1972, reported that the facility was now "a little less crowded. There wasn't as much abrasive odor, but I couldn't say it is in any way better for the development of the people there." Dr. James Clements, a veteran of both *Wyatt* and the 1972 trial, testified that although the staff was larger, "there are more people who are doing less than I noticed before." And to leave Judd with at least one ghastly image, plaintiffs had Juanita Hutter, a registered nurse at the public health hospital to which Willowbrook sent its residents, testify about a cast on one patient's leg:

Q. What did the cast itself look like?
A. It was rotted and broken in several places. . . . There was an extremely foul odor from his cast, the odor of urine and feces.
Q. Did you notice anything unusual . . . before the cast was removed?
A. Yes, there were maggots crawling out from underneath it. . . . We picked them off the cast with forceps and put them in a covered jar.
Q. How many maggots did you find?
A. Before the cast was removed we picked off 35 or 40.
Q. When the cast was taken off?
A. There were numerous maggots in the wound itself. And there was a large black bug embedded in the wound.
Q. I refer to one photograph . . . Can you identify it?
A. It is a photograph of the container with the maggots in it.

Rather than dwell on such revolting incidents, plaintiffs had their experts testify to the potential of the retarded for growth. Earl Butterfield described the many programs that could teach the severely and profoundly retarded basic living skills, from toilet training to grooming and feeding, with "exceptionally dramatic" results. As soon as teachers stopped thinking about raising a score on the IQ test and taught behavior that would facilitate placement in a group home, then the learning capacity of the retarded was considerable. In the same spirit, James Clements suggested that a visitor to Willowbrook would find that "some of the residents are physically different than most of us. Some were dirty, many . . . behave in a bizarre manner." The visitor would be disgusted by much of what he saw, that is, disgusted "not with the people at Willowbrook but with the place. . . . Retarded persons . . . didn't have to look the way they did and did not have to act in the way they acted [at Willowbrook]. . . . They have more similarities to normal persons than differences." Judd had trouble grasping the point. "Aren't some of these people people who just naturally tear their clothes off?"

To which Clements replied, "Your Honor, I have not seen the mentally retarded person who was in an adequately stimulating environment who naturally tore clothes off. This I have not observed."

Plaintiffs next argued the relevance of normalization theory. Paul Dockeki, a clinical psychologist, explained that at Willowbrook "we have both a non-stimulating environment on the one hand and the ability for residents to learn from each other, but what would they be learning from each other but garbage behavior." His observations led logically to plaintiffs' remedy, placing residents in group homes and foster families. The experts' final and probably most important task was to persuade Judd of both the appropriateness and the feasibility of the goal. Accordingly, Linda Glenn brought along a series of "before" and "after" photographs of Nebraska's community placement experience. These pictures contrasted drab and idle inmates with community residents who were dressed in sport shirts and pants, sitting at workbenches, looking (almost) normal and smiling. Could this feat be accomplished with Willowbrook residents? "I was really amazed," insisted Glenn, "that about eighty percent of the children would be very, very easy to serve. They do not have medical problems. Most of them do not have behavioral problems that would [prevent] . . . their moving into a foster home or group home."

The results of such a program, Earl Butterfield testified, would be impressive. "From a large body of research data," he announced, "foster homes will promote more intellectual, social and emotional growth than institutions." And to personalize all of this, a foster mother to a retarded child testified that when her foster child first arrived, "he did not know how to eat. He ate with his face in the bowl. He did not know what a spoon was, he was not toilet trained and he walked with a gait. When he ate he covered his food as if I was trying to take it away. But then after a while I assured him that nobody was going to take his food. I taught him how to eat with a spoon and now he eats with a fork. He walks 100 percent better—he is just a different child."

Plaintiffs' closing point was that community care would be far cheaper than institutional care and all the requisite funds were already available to the Department of Mental Hygiene. Ennis led Max Schneier, the organizer of the first effective parent lobbying group in mental health, through all the complexities of the Facilities Development Corporation and its bonds; Schneier calculated that the cost of providing a single new institutional bed, if one included *all* interest charges that the state had to pay out to bondholders over the life of the bond, amounted to $100,000, at least three times that of a group-home bed. Judge Judd could close Willowbrook without costing the state money.

How much of this expert testimony was based on hard data and how much on ideological commitment? Did substantial empirical evidence support the postulates about normalization, the capabilities of the retarded, and the superiority of group homes and foster care to institutions? The question is crucial, for at least since *Brown* v. *Board of Education* the validity of the social science data used in the courtroom cannot be assumed. It is now clear that the studies which plaintiffs' attorneys used in *Brown* to establish the debilitating effects of segregation on black pupils were not reliable. Psychologists like Kenneth Clark were certainly well-intentioned in their eagerness to demonstrate that separate could not be equal, but their methods lacked rigor. Black pupils in segregated schools may have had a lower self-image than blacks in nonsegregated schools, but to confirm such a hypothesis would require carefully matched groups with precise criteria for measuring something as elusive as self-image, not merely a collection of anecdotes drawn from brief visits to assorted schools. Clark, and many others, were so determined to persuade the court to abolish segregation that they collected their evidence to advance that cause. Should the same be said of the experts in the Willowbrook case? Did they gather their facts to be rid of institutions?

The answer is ambiguous. Assertions that the great majority of the retarded had the capacity to learn living skills, that their "garbage behavior" could be reduced, were well founded. Placed in a stimulating environment, the mentally disabled did not tear off their clothes; in a barren setting, without role models, they did learn the worst from each other. Furthermore, no anti-institutional bias colored the experts' perception of Willowbrook's conditions; the state itself did not really dispute their testimony. But what of the larger issues? Could the claim that residents would make better progress in community programs than in institutions be proved?

Not really. Linda Glenn's before-and-after Nebraska photographs seem to be illustrations for a position, not data for a conclusion. By the same token, Earl Butterfield's testimony on the superiority of foster care to institutional care rested on thin data: The foster care success stories were about the high-functioning retarded, while the Willowbrook class was composed of the low-functioning retarded. Indeed, the state of research in 1974–75 (it is not very different ten years later) was such that the data comparing institutional with noninstitutional care was skimpy, at most suggesting that the retarded fared better in community programs.

Some of the gaps in the research had to do with the almost impossible task of designing and carrying out a controlled study that compared the same sorts of clients (be they mildly or profoundly impaired) in the same sorts of settings (be they substandard or excellent). To say that profoundly retarded residents in wretched institutions did not do as well as mildly retarded residents in outstanding group homes was not persuasive; why not try to upgrade the institutions to see whether that mattered? Or why not blame the extent of the disability? Indeed, how was one to know in 1974–75 if severely retarded residents could actually function in a group home? Too few disabled clients were in community residences to permit statistically reliable findings; for that matter, too few were in high-quality institutions to serve as a control population. Only by a leap of faith could community care be presented as more habilitative than institutional care.

To be sure, proponents were entitled to argue that the institutional record was so disappointing that one either took such a leap or remained mired in the mud. Moreover, a handful of studies carried out in England by John Tizard did point to significant differences between congregate institutions and group homes; the former were more rigid, regimented, and depersonalizing than the latter. And these differences appeared to affect residents' behavior. Children in the group homes "were significantly more advanced in feeding and dressing skills and in speech than were those in institution-oriented units." Research in this country by Edward Zigler, a psychologist at Yale University, agreed with Tizard's findings, although just which one of the many negative qualities of large institutions reduced the level of residents' functioning was unclear.

The courtroom, however, was not the place to analyze precisely what was and was not known. The experts did not lecture on the state of the discipline. They did not tell Judd that community care for the retarded was an experiment, that one could not be confident of its outcome, although given the history of institutions, the risks seemed worth taking. Instead they delivered unqualified opinions, as though deinstitutionalization were the only legitimate option. When social science entered the courtroom, the litigant might win but the discipline did not. Testifying and carrying out research, whether the case be desegregation or deinstitutionalization, are activities more antithetical than anyone who does both would like to admit.

In the adversarial setting of the courtroom, partisan assertions by one side are supposed to be rebutted by the other. But in the second Willowbrook trial, as in the first, the defense offered few challenges. The plaintiffs' witnesses did not face telling cross-examination and the state's own case was weakly constructed and ineffectively presented. In the spring of 1974, Brenda Soloff had left the attorney general's office and was replaced by George Mantzoros—who had very little time to prepare. But even under the best of circumstances, defending Willowbrook would be an unenviable task.

The lead witness for the defense, Dr. Herbert Grossman, director of an institution for the retarded in Illinois and a witness for the state in 1972, found Willowbrook upgraded. "There was no urine and fecal matter on the walls and floors. . . . There was indeed substantial improvement in living areas, in dining rooms. . . . The linen and clothing supply was improved. . . . In the serving of meals . . . we had food, both hot and cold items, being delivered in an attractive manner." But under Ennis's cross-examination, Grossman testified about overcrowding, shortages of clothing, lack of appropriate wheelchairs, and the general drabness of the place. Ennis finished by asking Grossman to update his 1972 comments that Willowbrook should be "bombed," and that "reforming Willowbrook would be like attaching an artificial limb to a cadaver":

Ennis: Willowbrook, in your opinion, was [in 1972] a major problem?
Grossman: I said that.
Ennis: And today it is a minor tragedy?
Grossman: It is moderate.
Ennis: A moderate tragedy?
Grossman: Yes.

The testimony of Stephen Zoltan, in charge of Willowbrook's laundry system, explained a new "total cleaning concept," with a color-coding system designed to ensure that the right clothing went back to the right buildings. But "total" turned out to be not quite accurate.

Q. An unnamed employee testified . . . the residents didn't have enough clothing and often got rags back from the laundry.
A. The linen service . . . consists of shipping clean clothes to a building. . . . There is no system set up for removing articles from the system that are no longer satisfactory to wear. If I receive nonsatisfactory pieces of clothing in the shipment . . . I have no way of removing it from the system and will return it to the building. . . . If unrepaired, torn clothing is in the system, I am sorry. But at this point the laundry is not in any way set up to eliminate it.
Q. Until this administrative problem is firmly in control there will be rags in the Willowbrook system?
A. I am afraid that is correct.

Of poorly collected quantitative data fed into high-powered computers, one often hears: Garbage in, garbage out. A variant held for the Willowbrook laundry: Rags in, rags out.

The state did no better in rebutting plaintiffs' unqualified endorsement of the virtues of community placement. One Willowbrook parent, Gerald Hammer, testified that his daughter was making substantial progress in Willowbrook and he wanted nothing to do with foster care because all foster care parents were interested only in money. On cross-examination, Michael Lottman first established that unknown to Hammer, his daughter was regularly receiving powerful tranquilizers, that she continued to behave aggressively (her school record noted that "she seems to enjoy abusing her peers and adults"), and that while at Willowbrook she had not only contracted shigella but had been subjected to an experiment in which she was fed live hepatitis virus (a project we will have more to say about later). Mr. Hammer also knew nothing about foster care, never having visited a home. All of this would be damning enough to Willowbrook, but that plaintiffs elicited it from defendants' witness made it almost pathetic.

Even as these exchanges were taking place, attention was shifting from the courtroom to the negotiating table. Plaintiffs' lawyers, representatives of DMH, and most important, members of the transition team of the new governor, Hugh Carey, were exploring the possibility of a consent decree.

Ever since May 1974, Ennis and Justice's Diane Dorfman had been fashioning a document that would serve as the basis either for an agreement between the parties or for Judd's order on permanent relief. Once

Carey defeated Malcolm Wilson, Rockefeller's hand-picked successor, in the November 1974 elections, it seemed appropriate to explore the new administration's reaction to the proposal. Carey had made a campaign pledge to clean up Willowbrook; he had even attended a meeting of parents of the retarded and hinted or promised (depending upon your source) that he would establish a separate department of mental retardation. The new administration might also wish to take credit for ending "three years of acrimony and legal confrontations" and for ushering in a "new era of cooperation" (to quote from the eventual press release). It was possible, too, that the outgoing administration might want to leave on a conciliatory note, signing a decree and leaving the headache of implementation to the Carey administration. Finally, by now Judge Judd had fairly well tipped his hand, which meant that both sides had ample reason to compromise. The state recognized that Judd was certain to insist on some degree of court oversight; plaintiffs understood that Judd was not likely to close down Willowbrook. Nevertheless, the parties needed five months to reach agreement, and for most of that time they seemed stalemated.

When plaintiffs composed the first drafts of the consent decree—setting new standards for Willowbrook and requiring that its residents return promptly to the community—they turned first to officially promulgated criteria for institutions, specifically to the Joint Commission for the Accreditation of Hospitals *Standards for Residential Facilities for the Mentally Retarded,* and the HEW *Guidelines for Facilities for the Mentally Retarded,* which itself drew heavily on the JCAH document. Relying upon these standards not only spared the attorneys from reinventing the wheel but gave their document professional legitimacy; they were asking not for radical solutions but merely for standards established by the regulatory authority. Inevitably, many of these stipulations were very precise—and critics who later sniped that God gave his commandments in ten lines but plaintiffs needed twenty-nine single-spaced pages ignored the fact that JCAH took 159 pages and HEW fifteen triple-columned pages to set out their guidelines. Thus JCAH declared that:

> Seclusion, defined as the placement of a resident alone, in a locked room, not under direct supervision and not as part of a systematic time-out program that meets all applicable standards, shall not be employed.

The federal regulations went further, omitting the exception for a time-out program:

> Seclusion, defined as the placement of a resident alone in a locked room, shall not be employed.

The proposed consent decree followed the federal variant, adding a Willowbrook touch of its own (which would not survive the negotiations):

> Seclusion shall be defined as placing a resident alone in a locked room, ward or area, which the resident cannot leave at will. All seclusion shall be eliminated. K.F. [a resident who had spent over five years in seclusion at Willowbrook] shall be taken out of seclusion immediately.

In this same fashion, the JCAH standards on nutrition declared:

> Denial of a nutritionally adequate diet shall not be used as a punishment [no bread-and-water diet allowed]. At least three meals shall be served daily, at regular times with not more than a 14-hour span between a substantial evening meal and breakfast on the following day. Residents' meal times shall be comparable to those normally obtaining in the community [no giving breakfast at 5:00 A.M. and dinner at 4:00 P.M.]. Residents shall be fed at a leisurely rate, and the time allowed for eating shall be such as to . . . encourage socialization [no assembly line methods here].

The proposed consent decree followed this language closely:

> Denial of a nutritionally adequate diet shall not be used as a punishment, or as part of a behavior modification program [changing the name will not change the prohibition]. The time for meals shall be modified to correspond to the standard community times for meals. . . . Eating should be leisurely. Residents shall ordinarily be allowed at least 30–45 minutes for each meal.

Plaintiffs, however, did more than edit the JCAH document. The proposed decree typically added specificity to more general exhortations. JCAH stated that meals should be leisurely; the decree would require meals of no less than thirty to forty-five minutes. JCAH provided that speech and hearing tests should be administered "as needed." Plaintiffs insisted that the evaluations be done semiannually (later compromised to annually). JCAH wanted "an array of those services that will enable each resident to develop to his maximum potential"; plaintiffs required that "every resident shall have a minimum of six hours of programming each day." JCAH declared that severely and profoundly retarded residents "shall be provided" with educational programs; the proposed decree stipulated that "there shall be no more than six residents in a class for severely and profoundly retarded residents, nine in a class for moderately retarded residents, and twelve in a class for mildly retarded residents. Generally classes shall be conducted for six hours per day."

In part, the decree's preciseness reflected the lawyers' unwillingness to give Willowbrook administrators the discretion to decide when evaluations were "necessary," for they might never see the need. In part, too, the lawyers assumed that specificity was necessary to determine whether the stipulations were fulfilled. Contracts do not read that builders are to do their best to finish "before winter," and promise to construct a "handsome building"; by the same token, the decree did not rely upon terms like "leisurely" or "as necessary." In a courtroom, one looks to ask whether a full six hours of programming had been provided —and hence the precision of the lawyers and the indignation of the administrators.

Although almost all the standards in the proposed consent decree pertained to institutions, one brief and vague section addressed deinstitutionalization. The difficulty was that guidelines for so massive an effort at community placement were in short supply. JCAH affirmed the goal, and the decree repeated its words verbatim: "The facility shall make every attempt to move residents from: More to less structured living; Larger to smaller facilities; Larger living units to smaller living units; Group to individual residences; Dependent to independent living; Segregated to integrated living." However, it said nothing about the appropriate means.

Nor were other models available. Contrary to popular belief, the Scandinavians had not (and still have not) established many alternatives to institutions. Their facilities are exceptionally clean, well furnished, and comfortable, but running first-rate institutions has not encouraged (or perhaps allowed) investment in community homes. Their few group homes serve mostly the mildly retarded and it is not unusual to find residents sitting and reading newspapers—which not only reduces the relevance of the experience to the placement of severely and profoundly retarded from Willowbrook but raises the question why literate people were institutionalized in the first place.

The primitive state of the art meant that plaintiffs had to improvise provisions about community placement, and the texts demonstrated the novelty of the undertaking. The initial draft not only disposed of the subject in a few short sentences; it even called upon the "existing community service office" at Willowbrook to devise alternatives—which in 1974 was obviously a weak suggestion. A later draft represented only a minor advance. It asked DMH to "prepare a plan for the phasing out of Willowbrook," the only time the document trusted DMH to devise its own remedies. In effect, the proposed decree was out of balance, with almost all provisions devoted to institutional improvement and only a few governing community placement. Those who read the document without knowledge of plaintiffs' commitments could easily have been led to believe that improving Willowbrook was more important than closing it down.

The same problems plagued plaintiffs' effort to design an oversight mechanism. To ask the court to appoint a master who would have a supercommissioner's status with full authority to issue orders seemed futile. If Frank Johnson had backed away from so drastic a remedy in Alabama, Judd would not be persuaded here. Besides, plaintiffs were not confident that a master was the best solution. Their ultimate purpose was to revamp the system of care so that the residents of all state institutions for the retarded returned to the community. To this end, DMH would have to be reformed from within—which was not something that a master specifically for Willowbrook could accomplish. Hence the proposed consent degree begged the question, referring to a "monitor" whose powers were unspecified or to a "human rights committee" whose relationship to the bureaucracy was undefined. Plaintiffs were least precise when confronting the most complicated issues in the case.

The draft's explicit reliance upon official standards and its vagueness on community placement and monitoring actually facilitated negotiations. State officials had few grounds for objecting to JCAH guidelines, and Ennis methodically pursued this advantage. In a lengthy pretrial deposition, he queried Commissioner Alan Miller about each of the proposed decree provisions, and got his endorsement for practically every one of them; at trial, Ennis cross-examined Associate Commissioner Robert Hayes and obtained his approval for the draft as well. Indeed, the puzzle was why the state did not agree to the consent judgment right away when DMH's leadership was on record supporting the settlement.

For a moment, it looked as if the outgoing Republican administration would sign the decree. Over the course of November and December (immediately after plaintiffs rested their case), negotiations went smoothly. But then at the start of December (when defendants were about to present their side), the defense attorneys informed Judd that Governor Wilson, over the opposition of his commissioners, would not conclude an agreement. Ennis then contacted Governor-elect Hugh Carey, who had been quoted in the press as preferring a consent decree to continuing litigation. Ennis asked Carey to "indicate by letter that you will in fact sign the proposed consent judgment shortly after you become Governor. I would then show that letter to Judge Judd as a basis for adjourning the Willowbrook litigation until after you become Governor." But Carey held back. "As a matter of policy," he responded, "I do not believe it is appropriate for me to bind myself in advance to execute a particular legal document after January 1, 1975." He was optimistic about an eventual settlement: "I believe we will be able to reach agreement on the Consent Judgment promptly after my inauguration, and certainly by January 15, 1975." But neither Ennis nor the judge considered this binding enough to adjourn the case. Hence, through December and January, the state presented its defense and Judd began preparing his decision.

Once installed in office, the Carey administration began negotiations. However wary the governor might be about ceding authority to a federal court, he was less happy about being tarred with a Rockefeller scandal; he also had a long and deep personal and political commitment to helping the handicapped. Hence, he asked Peter Goldmark, director of the budget, a former commissioner of social services in Massachusetts, a well-known advocate of community services, and one of his most trusted advisers, to see if an agreement could be reached.

Discussions began at the start of February and continued through April, just as Carey and Goldmark were frantically attempting to rescue New York City from bankruptcy. The fiscal crisis had to be first on Goldmark's daily agenda, and so it was generally late in the evening when he and his staff met with Ennis and his colleagues, and they often did not break off until the early hours of the morning. The schedule mattered little to plaintiffs, who were free to spend the day preparing points. But Goldmark was under constant pressure as he shuttled from one budget meeting to another.

Goldmark's first impression of the draft was totally negative. On February 13, he advised Carey to either negotiate an entirely new document or risk a court decision. He was convinced, first, that the decree was so overdetailed as to be impossible to administer. "Just documenting compliance," he complained, "would require a full-time staff unit at Willowbrook." He was also uneasy with the monitoring mechanism, now called a review panel, which seemed to him to have all the powers of a master and was likely to make the administration of Willowbrook "almost impossible." More, "the proposed decree would be too costly," amounting to some $20–$30 million a year for Willowbrook, and since DMH had to be prepared to make the program statewide, the price tag would reach $150–$160 million a year.

Worst of all, the decree was at war with itself, requiring an enormous investment in an institution that was about to be closed. "The proposed decree does not reflect a coherent, effective program for the retarded. While the decree calls for the 'phasing out' of Willowbrook, its actual provisions provide for an elaborate enrichment of present institutional staffing patterns." Goldmark recognized that convincing plaintiffs to negotiate a new decree "when they think they have won everything including the kitchen sink . . . will be extremely difficult." And if the governor informed them that he was ready to accept a court order, "we must be prepared to do it." To take a hard line, Goldmark warned Carey, was likely to be "attacked as a retreat from your previous disposition to seek a rapid settlement." Still, he concluded, "I believe that the present decree is unacceptable."

Perhaps at another time and place—with New York City in better financial shape or with a court decision not imminent or with a team of mental retardation experts already in place—drafting an alternative decree would have been feasible. But since Goldmark was devoting most of his time to keeping New York solvent and Lawrence Kolb, the newly installed commissioner for mental hygiene, was not involved with mental retardation, preparing another settlement was impossible. Instead, Ennis, Goldmark, and their staffs began a line-by-line review of the plaintiffs' proposals—which meant that while a particular provision might be amended or omitted, the essence of the decree was likely to remain intact.

The lore among those who followed the negotiations was that the only difference the talks made was that Ennis had the sixty-one-page draft decree retyped into a single-spaced, twenty-nine-page version so that it would appear as if Goldmark had reduced the number of stipulations. As in many such stories, an element of truth can be detected. The final document was retyped in just this way, and scrawled on one page of Ennis's notes taken during the negotiations is the phrase "single space if possible." But the sessions were not meaningless, and Goldmark made significant changes.

For one thing, he frequently managed to gain greater latitude and discretion for DMH. The draft read: "Residents over 13 ordinarily shall not be expected to live according to the timetable of a younger child." The final document changed "over 13" to "older residents." The draft stipulated that beds on the wards were to be four feet apart; the final version called for "spacious living and sleeping areas."

Goldmark also eliminated stipulations that were condescending or demeaning to the state. The injunction that "all broken windows shall be replaced within 8 hours and all strewn glass . . . shall be picked up immediately" was omitted, as were the provisions that "Residents shall not be forced to sit in chairs simply for staff convenience" and "All toilets shall have toilet seats." Occasionally, Goldmark was even able to reduce the weight of a demand. Ennis would have required six hours of programs daily; Goldmark reduced it to weekdays. Ennis, aware of how often mental hospitals exploited the labor of inmates, wanted the Willowbrook residents not only paid for whatever labor they performed but not charged the cost of room and board; Goldmark won deductions from wages for up to half a resident's earnings.

More important, the two sides negotiated a compromise on the structure of the monitoring body, one that plaintiffs were prepared to make because Judd was not likely to be more generous. The arrangement was for a seven-person review panel (two members chosen by the defendants, three by the plaintiffs, and the remaining two by the panel itself) that would both audit DMH's performance and recommend improvements in procedures. The panel would employ a professional staff (with all expenses borne by the state) and their investigations of clients and facilities would form the basis of six-month reports to the court on DMH's progress in meeting consent decree goals. At the same time, the panel (by majority vote) could recommend measures to fulfill the decree's stipulations. It would also resolve (again by majority vote) whatever differences arose between defendants and plaintiffs in interpreting the decree. (If either party disagreed with a panel finding, it could appeal to the court.) By design, then, the panel lacked the direct authority of a master to implement procedures. Instead it was to serve as a monitor of performance, an arbiter of disputes, and a provider of professional assistance.

Finally, the Ennis-Goldmark sessions resolved the issue of community placement, in large measure by asking the review panel to prepare "a detailed and comprehensive plan for . . . community facilities and programs." But some significant guidelines were adopted, including the maximum size permitted for a community residence. Ennis wanted to keep it to no more than ten residents; Goldmark preferred fifteen. The compromise was fifteen or fewer for the mildly retarded, ten or fewer for all others. The state also pledged to request from the legislature the necessary appropriations and agreed to operate group homes and foster care if the voluntary agencies were slow to develop them. After much discussion, the negotiators agreed to a timetable. DMH was to accomplish two hundred placements in the first year; within six years, Willowbrook was to be reduced to no more than 250 beds (the number coming from the state's estimation of the requirements of the Staten Island community). As Ennis remembers it, the years suggested ranged from plaintiffs' three to DMH's fifteen. It was Goldmark who came up with the six-year figure, his estimate of how long it would take him, were he head of DMH, to fulfill the mandate.

Goldmark's victories, however substantial, would not necessarily have blunted his earlier opposition to the document. There still remained twenty-nine single-spaced pages of stipulations which required Willowbrook to be at once emptied and improved, to the point of installing a costly air-conditioning system. And if the review panel was not a master, it certainly was an arm of the court with a very long reach. The changes in the proposed decree, in comparison to what remained, were minor—so why, then, did Goldmark advise Carey to sign the decree?

Some of the answer has to do with Goldmark's personal commitment to a program that he generally admired. Most of his discussions with Ennis were substantive, not tactical, with a genuine desire on both sides to promote the best interest of the Willowbrook class. Political considerations, it is true, were never far off, but the negotiations represented an honest effort to serve the retarded. Some of the answer, too, involves the pride, perhaps the excessive pride, of a new administration. To the Carey team, the disasters that had befallen DMH's efforts to upgrade Willowbrook represented the ineptitude of Rockefeller's officials. Thus the signing of the consent decree testified not only to a change in administration but to the timing of the change. The Carey group had not held power long enough to know the limits of its own competence. It recognized the misadventures of its predecessors (all too well, given the threat of New York City's going bankrupt), but it did not yet reckon with the possibility of its own impotence.

One last but by no means insignificant consideration led Goldmark to favor the decree. By his calculation, New York would be obliged to satisfy many of its stipulations in order to remain eligible for federal reimbursements after 1977. Goldmark commissioned his staff to compare HEW and consent decree provisions; since the decree borrowed liberally from the federal code, the differences, particularly for institutional conditions, did not seem great. All these considerations, then, pointed Goldmark in the same direction: sign the consent decree because it appeared to be politically wise, ideologically correct, and federally mandated.

Nevertheless, neither Goldmark nor Carey grasped the full magnitude of the assignment they were undertaking. They had little idea of how difficult implementation would be. The novelty of the assignment should have worried them, but they did not pause to consider that no state as complex as New York had actually closed down a retardation facility and returned 5,400 residents to the community.

What of those in the state with more experience, like the directors of institutions? Goldmark did not consult with them; apparently judging them to be a major part of the problem, he thought them ill-suited to advise on the solution. And his opinion was confirmed by the directors' response to the decree. They were offended by its detailed standards for services and care. Indeed, one of them distributed a twenty-five page attack on the decree for stipulating, among other things, that the class should have "adequate toilet paper, soap and towels," when "the profoundly and severely retarded, disturbed, do not know how to use toilet paper, soap or towels." To have followed the directors' advice would have stifled the prospect for change. To ignore them completely was to exaggerate the ease of change.

Most important, Goldmark, Carey, and the others failed to understand how unconditional the plaintiffs' commitment to deinstitutionalization was. Goldmark was all in favor of restructuring DMH and opening group homes, but he did not think that he was agreeing to a document that, as interpreted by the plaintiffs, intended to put every single member of the class into residences of fifteen beds or less. He believed he was starting a much-needed process of change, pointing state policy in the right direction, not signing an irrevocable contract. The press release with which Carey celebrated the signing of the decree reveals the extent of the misinterpretation: "This is a fundamental change. . . . There will be an environment in the institution which approximates that of a normal community setting. . . . Residents will be prepared for transition to the least restrictive environment—*in the community if possible—compatible with his or her development.*" Willowbrook's population was to drop to 250, but: "The reduction will be achieved *by transfers to developmental centers* in the metropolitan area and to more suitable living environments, *with an emphasis on placement in the community.*" (Italics added.)

For the plaintiffs, on the other hand, this was not to be a decree to return residents to the community "if possible." It was not a decree that presupposed that the severely retarded might end up in handsome, Scandinavian-like "normal" institutions which would be "compatible" with their development. Nor was it a decree that intended to substitute for Willowbrook confinement in borough developmental centers of three to five hundred residents. And they would never be content with only "an emphasis" on community placement. Goldmark and Carey were thinking in terms of balance, of a *shift* from institutional to community care, of new group homes coexisting with improved institutions. By contrast, the plaintiffs perceived a revolution. No more than 250 people would remain at Willowbrook; all the others were to enter the community. They even fantasized that the revolution would spread from Willowbrook to other state facilities so that the day would soon come when every retarded person, irrespective of handicap, would live in a normal, homelike setting. Goldmark thought he had agreed to take a new tack in an old race. Ennis thought he had won approval for a new boat in a new race. And in truth, neither of them had much idea what it meant to navigate in these waters.

On April 30, the parties gathered in Judge Judd's courtroom to obtain official approval. "The court," he declared, "has reviewed the proposed judgment and each of the steps, standards and procedures, and finds them neither impractical, improper nor beyond the scope of the complaint." Noting that they provided "greater relief than did the

[1973] preliminary injunction," he now discounted his earlier efforts to distinguish sharply between "right to treatment" and "protection from harm." "It appears that there is no bright line separating these standards."

As the proceedings came to a close, many of those involved believed that the case was over at last. The review panel would soon be selected and its members, together with DMH, would implement the decree. Ennis thought he was, more or less, finished with the suit. Judd retained jurisdiction over implementation, but considered that a formality: "The court hopes it will not have to consider requests for action by the Review Panel." They all imagined they had signed a treaty ending the war. In fact, they had only opened a new theater for a new campaign.

PART II

THE BIOGRAPHY OF A CONSENT DECREE

6

Ready, Fire, Aim

When the seven members of the Willowbrook Review Panel first met together in June 1975, neither they nor plaintiffs' lawyers nor Judge Orrin Judd had a coherent design for action. The assignment seemed straightforward, to oversee the implementation of the consent judgment, but how the panel was to fulfill it remained obscure. Born of a political compromise, standing somewhere between a master (with ample authority) and a consultant (with no authority at all), the panel had no precedents to follow. Ennis attended the opening meeting to review the provisions of the judgment, but offered few suggestions. More surprisingly, Orrin Judd did not, either then or later, communicate with the members to spell out his expectations. He kept a careful distance, perhaps because the panel had not been his idea or because he could not make his peace with such judicial intervention.

In the absence of binding instructions, the personalities and commitments of the members became decisive, and a solid majority of them were uncompromising critics of institutions. Neither the style nor the bias was accidental. The first task facing plaintiffs and defendants once the decree was signed was to select the panel, and Ennis, compensating for compromises made over formal powers, painstakingly searched for resolute advocates of deinstitutionalization. He put them not only into the three plaintiff slots, but by a combination of shrewd manipulation and DMH lassitude, into the joint slots as well. Linda Glenn, whose slide show on Nebraska's community programs had so impressed Judd, was one appointee; Michael Lottman, co-counsel from Justice during the trial and an expert in the law of the handicapped, was another. Murray Schneps, a leader of the parent protests in 1972 and a lawyer as well, was the third. One of the joint appointments went to James Clements, star witness in both Willowbrook trials, and the other to David Rosen, who had charge of Detroit's community programs and had supplied a powerful deposition on the feasibility of opening group homes for the retarded.

Thus all five had furthered the litigation, all were keen proponents of deinstitutionalization, and all, with the exception of Rosen, were fiercely uncompromising and deeply distrusted politics. Glenn had outraged her superiors in Nebraska by publicly accusing the governor of killing retarded children by not moving them out of substandard institutions more quickly. Lottman's practice of law constituted defending minority rights against majority prejudices, and Schneps thought the New York legislature in general and DMH in particular considered the retarded less than human. (When a *New York Times* editorial referred to Karen Quinlan as a "living vegetable" and criticized a judge for not allowing doctors to remove her from the respirator, Schneps wrote in protest: "Your newspaper has arrogantly set itself up . . . to determine standards for full humanity. . . . How dare you pompously and arrogantly sentence people to death who cannot function on some arbitrary level.") Clements was a twentieth-century Dorothea Dix, testifying, in courts all over the country, against the primitive conditions in state institutions. Together, these four gave the panel a majority that would energetically defend every last provision of the consent judgment.

Notes from the Field
Breakfast with Jim Clements (Sheila)
November 1975

When I first met Jim Clements, David and I were still debating whether to follow the Willowbrook case. David had returned from the October board of trustees meeting of the Mental Health Law Project in Washington and told me that the chairmanship of the new review panel had gone to Clements, a fellow trustee. Although Clements religiously attended the board meetings, he did not take an active part in the debates over litigative strategies and David did not know him well. Nevertheless, when he told Clements of our "possible interest" in following Willowbrook, Clements immediately suggested that the three of us have breakfast when he next came to New York.

Seven weeks later, on a gray November morning, as David and I walked the long crosstown blocks from the West Side subway to the Barbizon Plaza, we debated the problems of doing a contemporary history. What would happen if participants disliked what we, or they, were doing and cut off access to the Willowbrook files and meetings? The panel was also an arm of the court, and courts are often secretive about their activities. By the time we reached the hotel, we anticipated a brush-off or, at best, a lukewarm reception.

We could not have been more wrong. Clements, a tall and courtly man, was waiting in the lobby and greeted us with the reserved manner of a well-bred Southerner. We went to the dining room, settled ourselves in the overstuffed chairs, and began what turned out to be a four-hour talk. Clements spoke in carefully measured cadences with a distinct Southern accent. The tone of his voice did not vary much, but his dedication to returning the institutionalized retarded to the community was evident. He dominated the conversation, always watching our reactions to his statements. Partway through the breakfast, I realized that we were not asking for access to conduct research but that he was selling us on doing the project. This was a story he wanted told.

Clements recounted in detail his upbringing in a small Southern town (not far from Plains, Georgia), in a family that was progressive enough on racial issues to have trouble with the local Ku Klux Klan. He gave a few details on his education (Emory and Yale), but spent more time discussing segregation and his part in trying to end it. As the head of a Georgia institution for the retarded, he had been able to abolish the practice in his own facility. He reported fully on the *Wyatt* case, how he as a Southern physician had been willing to testify for bearded Northern lawyers and against Southern lawyers. On the witness stand he had described the inhumane conditions at Partlow, alienating Alabama professionals and officials. Such institutions, he told us, were "places where children were sent to die, except they didn't."

I thought the phrase summed up all I needed to know about the facility, but Clements went on to describe the twisted bodies of children lying in cribs, their limbs contorted, their faces lifeless. He explained the therapies that could straighten their arms and legs and move their minds. He seemed to be bearing witness that the retarded were the victims of our perverse practices and perceptions.

Our access was not an issue for Clements. To the contrary, he wanted to guide us into this territory. He had no doubt that the panel would permit us to attend its meetings and examine its files. He assured us that whatever the problems we would encounter in doing the research, panel cooperation would not be one of them.

We left Clements at noon, a little startled at the hour. We both understood that his reserved and distant manner masked a fierce determination to close down Willowbrook, one that would not bend to accommodate politics. Clements was a maverick, and just as he had once worked to integrate whites and blacks within his institution, he would now work to integrate the retarded into the larger society.

Willowbrook was his *Brown* v. *Board of Education* in another guise. More than ever before, we appreciated that analyzing the outcome of the consent judgment was an opportunity to learn not only about deinstitutionalization and the role of the courts, but about the impact of the civil rights movement on the rest of us.

DMH, unlike Ennis, gave short shrift to making its appointments to the panel, as if by disposing of the business quickly it could make the panel disappear. After a few unsuccessful efforts to recruit prestigious members (like Justine Polier, the prominent family court judge who had just retired), the state retreated to its own bureaucrats. William Bitner, an assistant commissioner with the Department of Education, received one post, James Forde, Willowbrook's newest acting director, the other. Although both men were competent civil servants, they had little of the crusader's zeal, at least when compared to Clements or Schneps.

More surprisingly, the state made little effort to challenge the plaintiffs' appointments or to block the selection of Clements and Rosen for the joint positions. It could have argued that the panel should begin as a neutral body, that it was inappropriate for five of its members to have assisted the plaintiffs' case. Instead DMH sloughed over the issue, made a minor protest against Lottman, which the judge disallowed, and accepted the rest of the slate passively.

The only one unhappy with the panel was Joseph Weingold, the head of New York State's ARC. Indeed, Weingold thought the entire judgment wrongheaded, with the panel only one of its many disastrous provisions. Ennis did not consult him initially about its composition, and when Weingold learned thirdhand that the slots were being filled, he tried to get someone from ARC on the body. His first choice was Helen Kaplan, the head of ARC's Nassau chapter, but Ennis refused to go along, doubtful of her commitment to place very retarded institutional residents in the community. Weingold complained to Judd that ARC was not represented on the panel and that six of its seven members, coming from outside New York, were ignorant of state conditions. Judd, however, dismissed his objection: "There is no evidence that any member lacks professional qualifications, experience or integrity." Moreover, "One of the impressions the court received from the trial is that other states have achieved more than New York had done at Willowbrook."

Buried beneath the self-serving quality of Weingold's complaint was an alternate, and not unimportant, definition of the proper membership for a review panel. The court, the lawyers, and even DMH assumed that professionals in retardation should predominate. The panel's tasks seemed purely technical—to help design and implement the most effective habilitative community residence system—and those with credentials in the field were best qualified for the assignment. Indeed, this perspective was standard. Judges had first used masters in commercial cases to settle the affairs of bankrupt corporations and assumed that financial expertise, not political skill, was required. But even as the function of masters changed, ideas about appropriate credentials did not. By the mid-1970s, courts were appointing masters to enforce orders to desegregate school systems or upgrade prisons, which often required more of them than technical skills. It might be crucial, for example, to cajole a legislature or pacify a community, but few people considered whether political know-how would be useful in implementing court decrees. Certainly Ennis did not. For him, the consent decree was a contract the state was obliged to honor; thus only the services of experts would be needed. Indeed, he was so confident that the judgment was outside politics, he had written a clause which provided merely that the governor was to "request" funds for implementation from the legislature.

Because politics seemed so very irrelevant, Ennis did not bother to pacify Weingold. In 1972, he had anticipated that Weingold's Albany connections might be useful in negotiating a settlement. In 1975, with the judgment in hand, he considered these connections unimportant. Nor did Ennis think it vital to recruit panel members well connected to New York political leaders or constituencies. He did not foresee the panel's traveling to Albany to brief a committee chairman or to Brooklyn to consult with the heads of private charities. The panel was not to bargain with the state to fit clients' rights to available remedies. Rather, it was to compel the state to expand remedies to satisfy the client's absolute rights.

The panel lived up to this expectation, and in so doing earned the opprobrium of almost everyone else involved in implementation, from DMH to the voluntary agencies. Few people had a good word to say about it, at least publicly. Yet, particularly in the first year and a half after the judgment, the panel ensured that events post-1975 would not recapitulate events post-1972.

Throughout its five-year life, the panel met monthly, usually for two all-day sessions, and its members spent additional time inspecting facilities and composing reports. The five staff assistants were no less active, particularly the executive director, Jennifer Howse. A Ph.D. in linguistics who joined Florida's Division of Retardation and organized its monitoring procedures, she mirrored the characteristics of the panel: expert skills and, in the panel's words, "the motivation needed to sustain the extra demands of this position including long hours and weekend work." The panel's annual expenditures amounted to some $350,-000, with each member receiving $200 a day for expenses and honorarium. Most of them billed less than $10,000 a year, which did not keep critics from charging that the assignment was a boondoggle.

So committed a group inevitably experienced internal friction. The most uncompromising member was Murray Schneps. Secure in his sense of self-righteousness for having been involved with Willowbrook protest longer than anyone else, he indulged in table-banging habits which drove Clements to despair. Even Michael Lottman, intellectually closest to Schneps, complained to Clements: "If he tells me one more time that he doesn't care what the panel decides, he's a plaintiff and he can do what he wants, I'm going to be tempted to kill him."

But Schneps had a sure sense of how far to go, and the panel itself, if unyielding, was not foolhardy. A bitter fight broke out in November 1975 on how the panel should phrase its first definition of purpose to the court. Schneps wanted to make the statement tough and combative: "The Willowbrook Panel is not a neutral body seeking to appease the parties by negotiating or accepting anything less than full compliance. . . . [It] is not a passive monitoring group, and will continue to be most active, diligent and aggressive in assuring compliance." He even threatened to submit a minority statement if the full body would not accept his language. Yet, when the others balked, he backed down, knowing that one dissent might yield to others and having no significant quarrel with the final version: "The Panel does not automatically act as either a sword or a shield to the Department of Mental Hygiene. Rather the Panel is obliged to evaluate each issue separately, and to offer strong encouragement to good faith efforts to achieve compliance, or to give heavy criticism when compliance efforts are inappropriate or nonexistent."

By the time this language was formulated, every panel member recognized that it was going to offer more heavy criticism than strong encouragement. In the first six months after the decree, almost all of

DMH's energies went into bureaucratic infighting, with nothing left over for fulfilling the judgment. What would have been the fate of the decree without a panel and without continuous court intervention? One example provides the full answer: the short, unhappy history of the Willowbrook Task Force.

Shortly after the signing of the judgment, the Division of the Budget under Peter Goldmark, with Governor Carey's approval, assigned DMH the task of fulfilling the decree and warned its commissioner, Lawrence Kolb, that the administration intended "to meet all the conditions of the decree within the dates specified. Delays which might be expected in ordinary business will be unacceptable to me." In response, Kolb established the Willowbrook Task Force under associate commissioner Samuel Ornstein, with responsibility "for coordinating and directing the transfer of residents to other institutions and community placement."

The task force, however, was born into a family of jealous siblings who fought desperately not to cede it authority. The directors of the institutions wanted to retain the power to make community placements; the regional DMH director did not want "a Task Force . . . confusing the situation with even more fragmentation." Together they subverted Ornstein's mandate, taking away the substance of power—operational authority, with him and his staff doing placements—and substituting the shadow of power—the right to "observe and assess progress." Within two months, DMH ruled that "there is no implicit or implied line of authority for the implementation of the Consent Judgment vested in the Task Force." All this maneuvering, of course, was standard procedure in DMH. The task force, like the earlier Willowbrook Geographic Unitization plan, fell victim to entrenched interests, and seemingly this would be the fate of any attempt to redraw lines of authority.

What little energy remained after such wrangling went into fantastic proposals for satisfying all the decree's provisions at one stroke, which came perilously close to searching for the lost ark. Harold Piepenbrink, another of those who moved through the revolving door that was the Willowbrook directorship, suggested that a private contractor build eighty-five four-bedroom houses on the grounds of Willowbrook; the state would lease them and move in seven hundred inmates. When the decree expired in 1981, the houses would be returned to the contractors, who would then be free to sell them to the public. What would happen to the seven hundred residents was not addressed, a reality lost in the chimera of closing Willowbrook with no capital expenses. The regional directors actually endorsed this proposal ("We would . . . be offering our residential population the very finest in living arrangements"). But others, including Ornstein, recognized that the judgment did not intend to make Willowbrook into a village for the retarded. Yet until that recognition spread through DMH, more memos changed hands than people left the institution.

The intervention of the review panel forced events to take a different turn. The panel knew enough about the machinations around the Willowbrook Task Force to recognize that DMH had "severe management problems." "Almost seven months after the entry of the [court] order," it informed Judge Judd, "it does not seem to us that the Department has appropriately assigned responsibility for implementation. . . . Indeed, Department officials have conceded to us that they 'have not gotten their act together.' " The panel also believed that DMH was acting in bad faith, treating every request for information as an intrusion and every investigation as an affront. The department refused to give the panel copies of client records, submitted its progress reports late, and insisted on supervising all staff communication with the panel. When the panel protested that gag measures violated the judgment, Commissioner Kolb retreated, but only after confirming the panel's mounting sense of a highly adversarial relationship.

So, too, the panel was distressed to learn that DMH interpreted the judgment to mean that six hours of programming were required only for Willowbrook residents under the age of twenty-one—and when it pointed out to Kolb the error (obvious in the document), it received a hairsplitting letter debating just what constituted "education." Again the panel prevailed, but DMH placed the adults in programs slowly and grudgingly. Perhaps most aggravating of all, panel members visiting Willowbrook discovered that the direct care staff did not meet required ratios and still did not know how to feed clients without raising the risk of choking them. Nudity was commonplace and residents were still tied to beds or locked in seclusion.

Then, to underscore the gravity of the situation, one Willowbrook resident, Luis Ramirez, disappeared from his ward sometime during the afternoon of Wednesday, December 24, 1975. The ward attendant noticed his absence early that evening and notified the building supervisor, who in turn telephoned the grounds supervisor, the security office, and the New York City police and sent a telegram to his parents. Yet nothing was done about the disappearance for the next three days. Only when Ramirez's parents arrived on Sunday and asked to visit their son did a thorough search begin. Monday morning, his half-clad body was found in a clump of woods fifteen hundred feet from the administration building; he had died, the coroner reported, of exposure. The latest acting director at Willowbrook, Dr. Stanley Slawinski, told reporters that "on the surface it appears that proper procedures were not followed completely after Luis Ramirez's disappearance." The subsequent investigation revealed that the security office had no record of the call and so its personnel did nothing about the disappearance. The ward journal contained an entry about his absence, but each succeeding shift assumed that the appropriate persons had been notified and no one bothered to ask about the progress of the search. So sometime over the four frigid winter days, Ramirez died.

To the panel, this "horrifying death" was less an unavoidable accident than the inevitable outcome of a "systematic managerial problem which continues to exist at Willowbrook." It immediately began an investigation of its own, asking Kolb for the relevant records and the right to attend the hearings at Willowbrook—which he refused. (Kolb, whose dislike of the panel was matched only by his resourcefulness in finding reasons to deny its requests, insisted that the panel would interfere with disciplinary proceedings.) The panel, by now almost reflexively, appealed to the court and DMH relented, but here was one more instance of a fundamental hostility. At the same time, the panel received a painful lesson in the price of failure. The Ramirez death reflected badly not only on DMH but also on the panel—and a number of critics, particularly from among the parents, told it so in shouts. The panel responded that it did not "administer the Department of Mental Hygiene, nor could it instantly change conditions which are as old as Willowbrook." But the accusations hurt and the answer, however fair, gave small comfort.

All the while, DMH made practically no progress in moving clients into the community. Over the first six months it managed to send out some thirty-five residents—and the effort was so haphazard that no one was certain of the exact number placed or the quality of the group homes. The judgment's provision that DMH accomplish two hundred placements by the end of the first year seemed altogether illusory.

For all the disappointments, the panel was having more of an effect than was immediately apparent. Its skirmishes with DMH were helping alert Budget to managerial incompetence in the agency. Budget's diagnosis, like the panel's, was that "the various elements of the Department, including the Task Force, the Regional Office and the Willowbrook staff, appear more concerned with posturing over rules and authority than with focusing on specific problems and roles. . . . Our present concern [is] that the Department is unlikely to comply with . . . critical aspects of the Judgment."

Under growing pressure from the panel and from Budget, Carey's advisers resolved to bring new leadership to DMH. At a September 1975 press conference, the governor pledged to recruit staff to meet his "personal commitment to more effective care . . . and to ensure conformance with the Willowbrook standards," and within a month he appointed Thomas Coughlin deputy commissioner. Although the panel would never quite see it this way (and Budget would later develop its own doubts), Coughlin's arrival was the first major victory in the campaign to get DMH moving.

Like many others in the field, Coughlin came to retardation not by choice but by necessity. He was a state trooper in northern New York when his daughter was born retarded. Reluctant to institutionalize her, he worked with the Watertown chapter of ARC to organize programs, and was soon so involved with its activities that he became the full-time director and won a reputation for innovative leadership. In fact, Ennis considered appointing him to the review panel, and the panel considered appointing him its executive director.

Carey first met Coughlin during a tour of state programs for the mentally retarded, and Coughlin offered the governor some useful suggestions about education laws for the handicapped. A few weeks later, Coughlin was invited to Albany to discuss his proposals with one of Carey's advisers, and when the meeting was over, Robert Morgado, the governor's chief assistant, told him to see the governor. The interview was short and to the point. Carey asked Coughlin what he thought about the consent judgment; Coughlin said it was difficult to satisfy and should be modified if at all possible. Carey then asked whether he would come to work on it as deputy commissioner, and Coughlin immediately agreed. Carey told Morgado to break the news to Kolb and then warned Coughlin that although many people over at DMH did not like him, he was just what they needed, a state trooper, a first sergeant. "Go to it," was the governor's closing line. "You've got my support."

Coughlin complied, skillfully maneuvering to grab the reins of power, worn and tattered as they were. A warm and genial man with a broad smile, he had an intuitive feel for politics and was ready to follow the maxim of many innovative administrators: Ready, Fire, Aim! He immediately recognized that his own ambitions were intertwined with the judgment, that fulfilling its provisions would bring him additional resources and authority. Although publicly he complained about the intransigence and pettiness of the panel, privately, in the corridors of executive buildings, he used its threats to pry more money loose. On the back of the panel, Coughlin rode to power. Mental Retardation eventually broke off from Mental Hygiene to become a separate department—the Office of Mental Retardation and Developmental Disabilities (OMRDD)—and he became its first commissioner.

Over the winter of 1975–76, every crisis in implementation became a stepping-stone in Coughlin's steady climb upward. When the panel returned to court in mid-November to have DMH declared in contempt, Coughlin took the occasion to announce in Kolb's presence: "We've had competing groups involved in handling the Willowbrook case. . . . It took forever to get a procedure out. But now that I've been made responsible . . . I'm the bag holder. And I think there will be some movement." As the intensity of the conflicts rose, so did Kolb's willingness to defer to Coughlin. (Since Coughlin had come into the department as Carey's man, he would cite, and if necessary exaggerate, his influence in the governor's office the few times Kolb tried to contain him.) At the end of November, DMH issued a directive announcing that "in view of the need for quicker and tighter communication . . . authority in all matters relating to mental retardation and the Willowbrook Consent Judgment [goes] to Mr. Thomas A. Coughlin." It was a crucial change, and the panel deserves the bulk of the credit. Its readiness to seek judicial intervention shook up the bureaucracy and altered department priorities. To Coughlin, the decree was not an encroachment on his territory but a means for advancing his interests. With his promotion, some identity of interests existed between the holders of power and the outside agitators.

Notes from the Field

A Session with Tom Coughlin (David)

December 1975

I scheduled my first meeting with Tom Coughlin after Ennis, Clements, and the full panel had promised Sheila and me full cooperation in following the implementation of the consent judgment. One hurdle remained, to my mind the most difficult.

DMH had a track record on Willowbrook that most administrators would be eager to bury, and bureaucracies, whether in Washington or Albany, were not known to be sympathetic to prying outsiders. I was altogether skeptical about Coughlin's willingness to let us into his meetings or his files.

When I telephoned him in Albany, he suggested that we get together when he was in New York at the review panel's office in the World Trade Center. I would have preferred more neutral territory, wondering whether my relationship to Ennis and Clements would put him off—but that was not to be the case. With Coughlin perched on the end of a worktable (for the panel offices were still unfurnished) and me meandering around the room, we got acquainted.

Coughlin was frankly curious to understand why a historian would want to take on such a project and asked all the right questions with candor and good humor. As I talked about the history of opening (and closing) institutions, he was attentive, surprised that places like Willowbrook and Attica actually had a history and were the focus of academic research. When the conversation shifted to the decree and recent Willowbrook developments, he gave me some clues about the Albany game, but what emerged most clearly was not the substance of his points, but his style. He exuded confidence, almost cockiness, and a clear sense of pleasure at being in the hot seat. He even joked about having this conversation in the heart of the enemy (panel) camp. Perhaps it was going from state trooper to deputy commissioner, perhaps it was a matter of an ebullient personality, but Coughlin was clearly having a good time.

When I asked about access to the relevant files and sessions, Coughlin explained that some other researchers from within the Albany bureaucracy had recently approached him with the same request, but he thought an outsider would do the job better and he was ready to facilitate the research. Once Coughlin signed on, the project got under way.

Why his willingness to cooperate? For one, because any historian would be more objective than someone from DMH or Budget. For another, Coughlin was confident that he would be successful; he intended to implement this incredible decree and do it in a way that might well warrant a book. Besides, how many state officials had their own historian? For sure, he must have come to the right place at the right time.

Several panel members did not see it this way. Clements and Schneps neither liked nor trusted Coughlin. Unlike Coughlin, they would not smooth over differences in an effort to make limited gains. They also took his criticisms of the panel personally, not prepared to see them as part of a strategy for increasing his leverage in Albany. Finally, they were convinced that Coughlin would work for the decree only up to the point of political expediency. Entitlements that they would consider non-negotiable he would be prepared to bargain away.

In fact, the panel's very rigidity expanded the roster of benefits that Coughlin was required to deliver to claim a victory. His implementation of the decree had to satisfy not only Albany administrators—who would be content with a rough measure of compliance—but the panel, to whom every paragraph was sacrosanct; otherwise the commissioner and the governor might have to take the witness stand in a contempt hearing. In effect, the panel's fierce defense of the decree added to the pressures on Coughlin. The less it budged, the more he had to do—at least up to the point where implementation provoked an even stronger backlash.

If the panel's first great accomplishment was to reorder personnel and priorities within DMH, its second was to have its interpretation of the essence of the consent judgment prevail, at least for a time. It fought a constant battle to ensure that compliance meant not merely reducing Willowbrook's population (the state's position) but placing the entire class in community residences. In a sense, the conflict was over whether DMH had to satisfy only HEW (and secure funding for a smaller and improved Willowbrook) or the plaintiffs as well (and translate into reality the precepts of least restrictive alternatives). Its tenacity was never more in evidence and probably never more important than in this conflict.

Review panel members were deeply distrustful of DMH's commitment to community placement. They feared that the department would attempt to resolve the Willowbrook crisis by transferring residents to other institutions, and soon enough their suspicions were confirmed. In August 1975, just as the panel was organizing itself, DMH announced its intention to transfer thirty-two Willowbrook residents to the Westchester Developmental Center. Clements sought assurances from Kolb that these thirty-two people would be moved to "true community placements" within five months. But Kolb would not agree, declaring that "it is not possible to make such a definite commitment at this time." At its October meeting, the panel passed its first formal court recommendation (binding unless the state objected): All class members had to be placed directly in a community setting, not transferred first to another facility and only later into the community.

Never having understood precisely what the decree meant either to the plaintiffs' lawyers or to their hand-picked representatives, Kolb was astonished by the one-step proposal. To him, the judgment's language of "least restrictive environment possible" meant the least restrictive environment *"presently* available." To keep a resident at Willowbrook until the most ideal setting imaginable came into existence would "irretrievably damage the child . . . sacrificing . . . immediate welfare to goals which while desirable are not now reached." Since the Westchester Developmental Center was far less crowded than Willowbrook, its staff would be better able to train residents who had for some twenty years lived in a five-thousand-bed facility for life in a group home. The panel's fanaticism on deinstitutionalization, he believed, made it impatient with gradual progress. Surely a two-step process, a transfer first to a smaller facility and then to the community, was in the clients' best interest.

Unsaid publicly but well understood privately, the two-step process was also in the state's best interest. Budget calculated that 1,258 residents would have to leave Willowbrook over the next eighteen months in order for the facility to meet HEW standards. Even if DMH managed to make its first-year quota of two hundred community placements, the shortfall would be close to one thousand residents. Willowbrook's population had to be permitted to enter other institutions or the state might lose several million dollars.

The panel had little understanding of the role of HEW, but even if it had understood, it would probably not have retreated. Its one-step recommendation, as it explained to Orrin Judd in January 1976, was "the cornerstone of the Consent Judgment, an absolute necessity without which implementation . . . will be rendered impossible." Since "the defendants' emphasis continues to be institutional both philosophically and financially . . . community placement . . . will thereby be delayed indefinitely." The definition of the least restrictive environment "possible" had to mean "required and appropriate for the client, not simply available." The judgment, after all, was entered into "for the benefits of the members of the Class and not for the convenience of the defendants."

To the panel's keen disappointment and the state's immense relief, Judd disagreed. As reluctant as ever to widen the scope of the court's intervention, he preferred to interpret the specific language of the decree rather than to insist upon one particular strategy for implementation. Observing that nothing in the judgment prohibited a two-step placement process, Judd saw no reason to restrict DMH's options. He candidly noted, too, that parents of residents about to be transferred (especially those selected to go to Westchester) had written and telephoned him to express indignation at their children spending one day longer than necessary at Willowbrook. Hence Judd ruled that the immediate benefits that class members would enjoy should not be delayed, so as "to put pressure on the defendants to speed the provision of community placement facilities." He and the panel would make certain that DMH did not renege on its promises or divert funds from community programs to institutional improvements.

The decision turned out to be the last that Judd issued on Willowbrook, for in June 1976, while attending a seminar in Aspen, Colorado (his briefcase stuffed with Willowbrook papers to review), he collapsed and died of a heart attack. His widow, it is said, blamed Willowbrook for his death, her way, perhaps, of acknowledging the tensions under which he labored. The obituaries and tributes, recognizing the importance of the case to Judd, all gave it a prominent place in their accounts.

A period of suspense followed. Again the plaintiffs had the fantasy that Judge Jack Weinstein would take over the case, and again they were disappointed. The assignment went to John R. Bartels, a seventy-eight-year-old senior judge appointed to the federal bench in 1959 by President Eisenhower, and a close friend of Judd's. At age sixty-seven, he chose not to retire but to sit on fewer cases a year. He had obviously requested the case, but why he wished to assume the burden remained unclear.

During the transition, Schneps, Clements, Glenn, and Lottman kept searching for ways to revive the issue of institutional transfers. The slow pace of community placement left them more convinced than ever that the state's reliance on transfers to developmental centers inhibited the creation of alternatives. It was not easy to reopen the question, but in August 1976, right after Judd's death, something of an opportunity arose. The state was about to begin operating the Bronx Developmental Center, a $26 million, prize-winning design, and it might just be possible to make this an occasion to review the one-step, two-step ruling.

The origins of the Bronx Developmental Center date back to 1965, when Governor Rockefeller embarked on his grandiose building program. The project, like so many others, started behind schedule and underwent numerous modifications. Originally, BDC was to house 1,500 retarded people, but in 1969, when construction costs jumped ahead of even Rockefeller's willingness to float bonds, the number was reduced to 750. As if to compensate for the drop in size, Rockefeller encouraged the Facilities Development Corporation to hire a first-rate architect, and the assignment went to Richard Meier.

Meier, one of the most original young architects in New York, was on the brink of a brilliant career, but by happenstance, he still did not have a major building to his credit. His reputation rested on the design of several private residences for the wealthy, usually summer houses on Long Island. These were highly formal and geometric structures, intellectual to the core, in which strong horizontal lines were broken by cylinders, squares, and rectangles. Meier had, in the opinion of one architectural critic, mastered "the art of the cube." His mastery, however, had been displayed only on a limited scale. Meier had won several national competitions and received handsome commissions, but a spell of bad luck kept the designs from being built. There is probably no other profession in which the chance of a commissioned work's not moving from blueprint to reality is as great as architecture. Imagine the frustration of a composer paid for his composition, winning awards for the score, but never able to get the piece performed, and one has a sense of Meier's feelings. He had done a superb model for a dormitory at Cornell, but then the student riots broke out, alumni donations dropped, and the plans were scuttled. He made an equally impressive design for the Olivetti Corporation, but then a downturn in profits eliminated the building plans. He had renovated the Westbeth apartments in lower Manhattan and completed a developmental center in Rochester (which was highly conventional, campus-like in approach, and did not enhance his reputation). Thus the commission for the Bronx Developmental Center finally gave Meier the opportunity to work on a substantial scale.

As commissions go, the BDC one had more than its fair share of headaches. First, Meier had to contend with the site itself. Located at the back end of the Bronx Psychiatric Hospital, it was surrounded by a parkway, factories, railroad tracks, and the gloomy buildings of the hospital itself; the only reason to use the site was that it was state-owned and hence would cost nothing to acquire and would not generate neighborhood protest. Second, Meier had to contend with DMH. Architects may complain about the exhausting experience of designing a private home in which the location of each electrical outlet is the subject of a three-day discussion. But working for DMH was far more frustrating.

One year into the project, it again changed its mind about the size of the facility, dropping it to 600 beds, and then a year later it reduced the number to 384, all the while insisting that Meier economize on materials. Meier also had to clear each design with numerous committees—he estimated that over the life of the project he took counsel with at least one hundred DMH representatives. He also had to comply with several hundred pages of plan specifications that the department produced.

Accommodating himself to his client's demands while trying to express his own architectural instincts, Meier self-consciously chose as his model a Le Corbusier monastery. By turning the facility inward, Meier would shut out the ugliness, as well as the noise and wind, of the surrounding environment. He could also give rein to an imaginative effort to shape an aesthetically pleasing environment. He divided the building in two, one part public and the other private, locating in the one the schoolrooms, exercise rooms, playrooms, and cafeteria, and in the other, apartments of four bedrooms each, not unlike those to be found in a nearby housing project. Meier added little touches that he thought served the retarded well. Going to Scandinavia to examine its institutions (which he had been told were the best-designed in the world) and noting that the retarded often spent a considerable part of their day sitting on the floor, he placed a number of windows in the living quarters at floor level. Finally, he wrapped the entire structure in a silver-toned aluminum skin—giving it a highly futuristic appearance. (The producers of *Simon,* a movie about crackpot scientific geniuses, used it as the set for their super think tank.) When Meier was done, the retarded had a world unto themselves, as handsomely crafted as he could make it.

Praise for the building came quickly from the profession. *Progressive Architecture* called it "a breath-taking silver machine for healing." John Hejduk, dean of the school of architecture at Cooper Union, found its "message" to be "that architecture can lift up the spirit and make life a little better." In the *New York Times,* Ada Louise Huxtable declared that "it is a landmark before its doors open . . . [to] those pathetic shards of humanity. . . . This building has a richness of composition and a finesse and originality of form that mark an important new phase of architectural design." The facility won four architectural prizes, including one from the President's Committee on the Employment of the Handicapped and another from the American Institute of Architects. In the spring of 1977, Meier was understandably proud of his achievements. He had brought the building in on time, stayed within the $26 million budget, put his ideas to work on a grand scale, secured his reputation, and provided the retarded with an exemplary facility.

None of this enthusiasm infected the review panel. To James Clements, the Bronx Developmental Center exemplified all that was outmoded in the care of retarded persons. It represented the wrong concept (institutionalization) in the wrong place (the distant grounds of a psychiatric hospital) at the wrong time. To confine retarded persons to a monastery, however pleasing the structure might be, was perverse. The goal was to integrate them into the community, not segregate them in a world of their own. The panel's executive director, Jennifer Howse, tried to explain this viewpoint to Ada Louise Huxtable, with little success. "The residents of Willowbrook," Howse noted, "are not 'pathetic shards of humanity.' They are human beings and citizens . . . entitled to all the rights and privileges such citizenship implies." And those rights included not being incarcerated in a setting which creates "its own environment. Handicapped people [should] live among others who are not handicapped." Perhaps it was expecting too much of DMH or of Richard Meier to have appreciated this principle in 1970, although by then numerous presidential commissions had endorsed community-based programs and popularized the principles of normalization. In all events, the panel was convinced that such a facility violated the basic precepts of the field.

The panel was not alone in its opposition. The consumer advisory board, appointed under the consent judgment to serve as guardians for the Willowbrook class members who had no known parents (and not incidentally, dominated by the leaders in the 1972 protests), toured the Bronx facility and issued a scathing critique of this "gigantic submarine." It complained bitterly about the segregation of the future residents and the lack of safety precautions; the building had too few elevators and too many open walkways and balconies with low guardrails. "Why do we," the CAB asked, "continue to treat people who happen to be mentally retarded as subhuman organisms to be stacked in huge, isolated structures, where they are overwhelmed by the physical environment? . . . The new Bronx facility is a masterfully and futuristic designed replication of every institution ever constructed to alienate, devalue, and destroy people who have differences." A number of architects concurred. David Sokoloff, chairman of a design committee for the National Association for Retarded Citizens, protested to the AIA that the building it had praised was considered by "recognized and accepted authorities [to] be socially and/or psychologically harmful to those who will use it."

The critique of the Bronx facility represented an attack not only on institutionalization but, in a way that was especially puzzling to Meier and his admirers, on "moral architecture," on the belief that a successfully engineered and pleasing environment would generate a therapy of its own. The idea was a very old one, dating back to the 1820s and 1830s, when reformers insisted that crime and insanity could be eliminated through the proper physical design of the penitentiary and the mental hospital. In its contemporary version, moral architecture presumed that life in the Bronx Developmental Center was bound to be more habilitative than life in an ordinary and grimy apartment, and anyone who disagreed lacked taste and sensibility. But to the panel and its supporters, life in an ordinary and even grimy Bronx apartment was better for their clients. Their goal was to eliminate the separateness of the retarded, to have them blend into the landscape, not jut out from it. In effect, the Meier camp, following a tradition of artistic excellence, was devoted to the exceptional; the panel camp, following the principles of normalization, was committed to the commonplace—and each side was convinced that the other had not the slightest appreciation of its position.

For all that, the panel seemed in no position to do much about the Bronx facility. Since Judd's opinion allowed institutional transfers, it had no way to keep the Willowbrook class out of Meier's monastery. Nevertheless, it tried. In August 1976, Murray Schneps wrote to Kolb expressing the panel's wish that the facility "never be utilized, even temporarily, as a residential institution for the mentally retarded." Kolb, of course, rejected his suggestion, contrasting his own dedication to "compassionate care of the more severely affected of the retarded" to the panel's "ideological stance." Next, the panel attempted to strike a bargain with Coughlin, but Coughlin would not agree to the proposal to limit the number of residents to 144, who would then be placed in the community after six months. Judd had given DMH much more latitude and he saw no reason to make concessions.

Since the state was unwilling to forgo use of the new facility, Clements, Schneps, Lottman, and Glenn voted to plunge ahead and formally recommended to the court that Willowbrook residents not be admitted there. Not only were their three colleagues opposed but so were Bruce Ennis and Chris Hansen (who was about to take over as head attorney). By their reasoning, the Judd opinion was determinative and it made no sense to go before a judge who was new to the case on an issue already resolved in favor of the state. Better to wait and cultivate a relationship with him than to start off with a sure loser. But the four were uncompromising. BDC was an institution, the decree called for community placement, and here was an occasion to educate Bartels to its principles. As was expected, OMRDD immediately rejected their recommendation, appealed to the court, and on May 10 and 12, 1977, Judge Bartels presided over his first Willowbrook trial. Should the state be prohibited from placing class members in its $26 million, award-winning facility?

On its face, the Bronx suit seems ripe for an award as the most outrageous case of the year. How could anyone doubt that the new facility was preferable to Willowbrook? But in the context of the panel's desire to promote community care, the issue becomes far more complex. In fact, the state had a difficult time presenting a consistent or persuasive defense. Its opening witness, Dr. Herbert Cohen, the director of the facility and a well-known advocate of community services, had opposed the plan of construction, and still remained ambivalent about its usefulness. Cohen did claim that the Bronx Developmental Center could serve as a "transitional" facility, providing short-term, intensive training in community living skills to the exceptionally disabled Willowbrook residents. However, under cross-examination by Murray Schneps, he conceded that no DMH directive limited the size of the facility or the length of residents' stay. Cohen was ready to "negotiate and discuss" policy with Albany, but he could make no promises about the outcome. Schneps used questions about the shortage of elevators and low balcony railings to elicit Cohen's own concerns for residents' safety. Finally, he posed a hypothetical:

Q. Attorneys have this magical power to give you authority . . . in 1970 to direct that the building not have been built. . . . Would you have taken that authority and prevented its opening?

A. With what I know now, possibly. . . . I think there is need for a small facility, for a place that people can get intensive rehabilitation. . . .

Q. Do you consider Bronx Developmental Center as it stands now not a large institution?
A. I consider it relatively large.

Cohen's equivocations buttressed the panel's position.

Tom Coughlin, next to testify, did no better by the state's case. He conceded that even if he would rather see his own child at the Bronx facility than at Willowbrook, most of all he would want her in a community residence. And when he was asked the hypothetical: "If the Bronx Developmental Center had not already been built, would you . . . build it now?" his answer was unambiguous: "I would not build it."

If the pains of working for the state and the debate over the building had not already dimmed Richard Meier's enthusiasm for the project, then the court contest and the offhand reception given his testimony surely did. Meier described the various stages that his design had moved through, from study models to working drawings, with each step reviewed at weekly meetings with DMH. He staunchly defended the safety of the structure—three-foot railings were adequate—and the wisdom of turning the building inward. But Judge Bartels was uninterested in the quality of the design. He only wanted to know whether the developmental center would accelerate or impede community placement, a matter on which Meier had nothing to say.

As usual, James Clements led off the case for the panel, and addressed this very point. He contended that transferring residents from Willowbrook to the Bronx facility and then to the community was certain to harm them. Clements also claimed, albeit without any substantiating data, that his own experience in moving residents from the Georgia Retardation Center to the community demonstrated greater success with a one-step than with a two-step process. Although the bulk of Clements's testimony repeated points made in earlier court appearances, Bartels had never heard him before; he hung on every word and regularly interrupted with his own questions.

Toward the close of the second and final day of the trial, Bartels turned the courtroom into an informal seminar, moderating a debate between Clements (still in the witness chair) and Cohen and Coughlin (sitting in the spectator section). The judge pressed the two state officials to explain why an intermediary placement in the Bronx facility was necessary, and when they described the value of preparing clients for community living, he wanted to know why such training was not already being given at Willowbrook. Cohen responded that he could not speak for Willowbrook, to which Bartels said, "That's what bothers me. I cannot understand that. You seem to just look at Willowbrook as just a place where nothing seems to happen." When Cohen explained what he hoped to accomplish in the Bronx, Bartels interrupted to ask why he was so confident that the Bronx experience would not recapitulate Willowbrook's. The judge also pressed Clements to justify his opposition to BDC; this sparked another round, which Bartels closed by expressing his own doubts that a resident at an "island" facility would be any more part of a community than at Willowbrook.

One final consideration undercut the state's case. The more Coughlin boasted of initial successes in community placement, the more Bartels wondered why the Bronx facility had to be used at all. If the state was finally mastering the art of placement, then why not forget about the Bronx facility? The state was caught in a no-win situation. It was not making all the placements the decree mandated, but it was promising to make too many placements to justify an intermediate facility. Damned if you do, damned if you don't—a prescription for frustration with courts, lawyers, and review panels.

Those who had followed Bartels's comments closely, and discounted his frequent protestations that he was merely trying to clarify the issues, were hardly surprised when his June opinion ruled in favor of the review panel. Observing that all the parties subscribed to the principles of normalization (which they took to mean that group homes were preferable to institutions), Bartels asked whether the Bronx facility would accelerate or frustrate community placement. He noted the "sharp disagreement among experts," but found that "on balance . . . the class members should not be transferred from Willowbrook to the Bronx Developmental Center." For one thing, the review panel as well as the Consumer Advisory Board were opposed; for another, community placement "offers the principal hope in the elimination of the indifference and negligence which have characterized the institutional care of the retarded and handicapped for many years." In sum, "The court is convinced that transfers . . . will create . . . delay in community placement, where the only real improvement in the handicapped and retarded can be expected."

The ruling had a substantial impact. It was no small matter to forbid the use of a $26 million facility. Equally important, Bartels's opinion rested on two axioms that would guide his future decisions: a deep distrust of institutions and a conviction that community living would be genuinely rehabilitative. This was not a bias that he brought to the case so much as a logical outcome of the testimony he heard. He presided at a moment when not only the review panel but the representatives of OMRDD unreservedly and persuasively extolled the benefits of community care, in part because they had to pledge support for the consent judgment, but also because they believed it. No one advanced the argument that normalization could be satisfied in smaller and homelike institutions (which was the authentic Scandinavian model), or argued that the empirical data demonstrating the rehabilitative effects of group homes were scant. The courtroom was not a forum in which the several possibilities open to public policy were presented and debated. Rather, the panel and Coughlin had more ideas in common than their acrimonious exchanges would suggest.

Bartels also worried less than Judd about judicial restraint. During the trial he did declare that "I don't want anybody to feel that the Federal Court . . . [is] invading the field of the executive branch. . . . I am perfectly cognizant of what does happen in the various social and economic fields . . . by decisions of federal courts . . . so I really don't want any of you to get any feeling that I am very anxious to come in here . . . and interfere with the Department of Mental Health. I'm not." Then he added the critical qualification: "But I do have an obligation . . . a legal and moral obligation . . . and I do feel strongly about the care and health and future of these children." Perhaps it was because the plight of Willowbrook's residents was so horrendous, or because Bartels intended the Willowbrook case to serve as a memorial to the humanitarian impulses of Orrin Judd—the best guess is that he requested the case to make certain that his friend's work did not go unrealized—or because a consent judgment did not raise for him problems about courts coercing legislatures. Whatever the reason, Bartels was entirely comfortable with protecting "those poor unfortunates at Willowbrook." He was ready to relax formal procedures to moderate a debate between witness and spectators, for "we are more or less in the position of an investigative body. . . . All of us are here trying to search for the truth and not necessarily as adverse parties." In this way we will advance "the welfare of these patients out at Willowbrook."

Finally, Bartels was ready to trust to the review panel's judgments and empower it to police the state. He appreciated the dedication of Coughlin, but at the same time reckoned that he needed help. As well-intentioned as the commissioner might be, he could be overridden by Budget if it seemed cheaper to enlarge a 144-bed facility to 380, or more convenient to transfer Willowbrook residents to other institutions. To implement the decree required an active, vigilant, and engaged judge, and Bartels was fully prepared to be all three.

From the panel's perspective, events could not have turned out better. It had acted on principle and won a resounding victory. It had a firm supporter in Bartels, increasing the likelihood that the panel's oversight and the court's authority would protect the class. Winning this case confirmed for the panel the wisdom of depending exclusively upon the court to secure state compliance. Judge Bartels was its best friend.

7

Who Cares?

Translating courtroom victories into new life chances for the Willowbrook class required that the state design and implement an entirely new system of care. Whatever the consent judgment envisioned, the reality was that New York City had only a handful of group homes and community programs, and only a handful of organizations interested in developing more. To survey the landscape of noninstitutional services was to discover how utterly barren it was.

In signing the decree, the state assumed the responsibility for constructing a network of community services for the Willowbrook class—which over the years 1976–79 it did with remarkable inventiveness. Once the court and the panel ruled out business as usual, a bureaucracy notable for its lethargy created a special unit to implement the decree—the Metropolitan Placement Unit (MPU)—and found a special person to head it—Barbara Blum.

Blum's record of accomplishment at MPU demonstrated, first, that diverse organizations with few interconnections or prior experience in retardation were prepared to cooperate, provided someone galvanized them. Among others, the Catholic Church (after Vatican II) and black ghetto organizations (after the war on poverty) proved to be willing to care for the handicapped. Moreover, as Blum identified and funded agencies to serve Willowbrook's residents, she built a coalition in favor of returning handicapped persons to the community. The involvement of these agencies had the unanticipated consequence of creating a constituency for deinstitutionalization *after the fact.* Before the decree, no one stood to gain from the release of the retarded. Following the decree, a network of providers had a stake in the movement.

In the fall of 1975, Sam Ornstein recommended creating a unit "whose sole function will be the development of community residences" for Willowbrook's residents. "It would not run institutions or programs [but] contain all the necessary personnel and authority to expedite the development of potential locations and programs." The proposal generated the same opposition that had undercut the Willowbrook Task Force. The institutional directors complained bitterly to Tom Coughlin that the unit would add another dead end to the bureaucratic maze. Despite these protests, or more likely because of them, Coughlin adopted Ornstein's plan. Circumventing the directors gave him a chance to succeed, and he, as well as the judge, would know whom to hold accountable in case of failure.

Empowering MPU had the effect of insulating the judgment from all the other parts of the state bureaucracy. Whatever MPU did for the class would be distinct from what the Department of Mental Hygiene did, or did not do, for the rest of the retarded. This arrangement freed MPU to innovate. Charged with only one assignment, it did not have to agonize over the allocation of scarce resources among competing groups, to balance the needs of the Willowbrook class against, say, the needs of those confined elsewhere. MPU had its own orders, its own budget, and a single standard against which its performance would be measured. But such a situation had disadvantages too. MPU's work might not have significant impact on the fate of other retarded persons, institutionalized or not. Thus the creation of MPU at once made it more likely that the judgment would be implemented and less likely that its influence would ripple outward. If deinstitutionalization was contagious, MPU was a perfect quarantine.

Finding someone to head the unit proved difficult. Coughlin asked Robert Schonhorn, executive director of United Cerebral Palsy of New York State, but Schonhorn was unwilling to work for DMH. With no other choices at hand and with the panel threatening contempt citations unless the number of placements increased, Coughlin asked Alvin Mesnikoff, a new DMH regional director, for advice. Mesnikoff strongly recommended Barbara Blum; although he barely knew her, he was impressed with her successes in opening group homes for New York's abandoned children. Without so much as an interview, Coughlin had

Mesnikoff offer her the job. If she performed well, so much to his credit. If she failed, she could be fed to the panel.

When Barbara Blum had first read the consent judgment in the spring of 1975, she found it a revolutionary document and wondered, as did many others, whether the state would satisfy its provisions. She was astonished six months later to be offered the MPU position, but accepted it immediately. Her current assignment as director of the New York City office of the State Board of Social Welfare (supervising the agencies caring for children and disabled adults) had become routine, and implementing the decree intrigued her. In uncharacteristic fashion, she jumped without looking, taking the post without meeting the panel, the judge, or even Coughlin. Within forty-eight hours she got her just deserts: a negotiating session with the panel about an elaborate placement plan that she had never read and attendance at a court hearing about the state's failure to make the two hundred placements promised in the judgment. It was a baptism by fire, except that during her two-year tenure the temperature never dropped.

A more cautious administrator, determined to climb the departmental ladder, would have refused the post. Not only was the task formidable, but MPU was by mandate a temporary division, created to solve a particular problem and then disappear. Its staff was either "borrowed" from the developmental centers (to the director's unhappiness) or "provisional," without civil service tenure. Coughlin actually boasted that "when all members of the [Willowbrook] class have been satisfactorily placed, the MPU will no longer have any function." Blum also sensed that she was being set up as a scapegoat, should implementation fail. "Normally when you enter a governmental position, it is very tedious getting on the payroll. You fill out forms and don't get checks for weeks after you begin to work." This time, "without ever having filled out a form for DMH, they somehow got me on the payroll," and did it so quickly that for a few weeks she was being paid at both her old job and her new one. The explanation was obvious to an insider: "There seemed to be a kind of precipitous desire to see that I was there for the court, to have evidence that I was being paid."

Nevertheless, Blum was confident of holding her own. Her tone was soft-spoken and her manner demure, but her appearance was misleading, almost intentionally so. "Men tend to assume that you're not very bright," Blum believed. "And if they think you're stupid, and you're smart, you have a real advantage in figuring out how to outwit them." Even less sexist men, she found, often succumbed to an impulse to defend a woman when the fighting got rough. "As a member of the protected sex, you're a little safer." Her most critical advantage, however, was that she treated this assignment not as a job but as a mission, and in a system where incompetence was rivaled only by cynicism, this proved no small advantage.

Blum, like Coughlin, learned about retardation by necessity, not by choice. A major in economics at Vassar College, she graduated in 1950 and, like most of her classmates, was soon married and raising children. Her second child, Jonathan, was born in 1953, and although his development at first was normal, by the age of three he demonstrated severe behavior problems. He was not speaking and his conduct was so erratic that no nursery school would accept him. Blum looked for help but could not find special programs in or around New York City. Unwilling to institutionalize him, she, with a group of similarly situated parents, organized a not-for-profit agency to run a nursery school.

While Blum was organizing the project, her husband, Robert, a lawyer (and an Olympic Games fencer), joined the staff of the newly elected congressman from their district, John Lindsay. The two men formed a close friendship and Lindsay was soon learning about the frustrations of finding programs for Johnny. When Lindsay successfully ran for mayor, both Blums worked overtime in his campaign, and one of his first official acts was to establish a Task Force on Mental Health and Mental Retardation and put Barbara Blum in charge. In this capacity, Blum interviewed parents and professionals all over the city, confirming what she already suspected, that there were few community services or funds for mentally disabled children.

Blum's task force recommended expanding programs by involving the voluntary agencies that served dependent (albeit normal) children—and this strategy became the hallmark of her efforts through her tenure at MPU. Heretofore, voluntary agencies presumed that serving the handicapped was too expensive and frustrating. Blum was convinced, however, that were sufficient resources committed, the agencies would respond favorably. Lindsay agreed, eager to tap newly available federal dollars and promote fledgling ghetto self-help organizations, such as the new antipoverty councils. It was an opportunity to do good and build up a political base outside the regular Democratic party clubs, which had little enthusiasm for the mayor.

Lindsay appointed Blum deputy commissioner for the city Department of Mental Hygiene and she ably implemented the task force recommendations. In 1966, the city had expended $1 million to purchase services for the mentally handicapped living in the community, with almost all the sums going to diagnostic clinics located in municipal hospitals. By 1971, when Blum left the post, the city was expending some $9 million, with substantial support going to voluntary agency community programs, including parent-run and minority-run agencies. The ninefold increase in spending and the involvement of new agencies was an impressive start, even if large gaps remained in serving the most severely handicapped.

In 1971, after a series of scandals erupted at city shelters for homeless and abandoned children, Lindsay asked Blum to head another task force. She found that the facilities had too many children and too few staff, and no alternatives were available. The child welfare agencies had been reluctant to supervise the difficult cases—black and Hispanic children with aggressive behavior—and Blum once again recommended larger appropriations to attract the voluntary sector. Following her lead, Lindsay established a Department of Special Services for Children and appointed her to head it.

At Special Services, Blum persuaded several foundations to provide start-up funds for group homes and assisted a number of imaginative social workers, like Sister Mary Paul (who would later join her at MPU), in getting projects under way. The sister wanted to organize a neighborhood crisis center to keep children at home and out of foster care, and Blum provided sound managerial advice and an introduction to a foundation for a first grant. In these ways, Blum managed to close down some shelters and reduce the population at others, not, to be sure, solving the problem but making a dent.

At MPU, Blum confidently pursued this same approach, persuading not-for-profit agencies to run foster care programs and open group homes. Why so automatic an appeal to the voluntary sector? Why not have the state organize and administer community programs? The answer rests not in a scrupulous appraisal of the relative merits of these alternatives, but in the 150-year history of social welfare.

In the early nineteenth century, in the Jacksonian period, states first constructed orphanages, reformatories, mental hospitals, and prisons for the deviant and dependent. They were confident that the asylums would be islands of order, their rigid routines and bell-ringing punctuality inculcating habits of discipline and obedience. Within twenty to thirty years, however, the institutions turned into islands of disorder, with rampant corruption and brutality. Reaction and reform were slow in coming, but in the opening decades of the twentieth century, the system changed. Repeated exposés of institutional abuses bred a disillusionment with incarceration, particularly for children. At the same time, a new generation of university-trained psychologists and social workers objected to asylum routines which were rigid and military-like; only a familial setting could produce well-adjusted children. These new perspectives inspired professionally run foster care and adoption programs, at least for those who were young and nonaggressive. Coincidentally, the burgeoning immigrant communities were also wary of public, essentially Protestant, charities, convinced (not unfairly) that relief was leavened with a heavy dose of proselytizing. Hence, as ethnic leaders captured political power in states like New York, Massachusetts, and Illinois, legislators made appropriations to Jewish and Catholic agencies to take care of their own children. (The attempt to use public moneys for parochial schools was another part of this effort, but generally more controversial and less successful.)

The net effect of these trends was to create a new division of responsibility in social welfare. Generally, the state provided for the hard-core cases in institutions, typically the older, aggressive, and handicapped children. The private agencies provided foster homes and adoption for the others. To be sure, some private agencies, particularly Catholic ones, also administered large facilities, thereby blurring these lines. But the guiding principle was that the state restricted itself to institutions and left the community to the voluntaries.

Blum's policies broke with this tradition in one notable way: it became her mission to get those usually defined as untreatable, whether they were shelter children or the severely and profoundly retarded, out of institutions. But in another way, Blum was faithful to the legacy in looking to private agencies, not the state, to develop programs in the community. She had adopted this strategy in the Lindsay administration and was now about to follow it again at MPU.

Despite the need to build a system from the ground up, Blum was optimistic. She assumed that the voluntaries would want to protect their turf and maintain a monopoly over services in the community. She also expected that the private charities, facing hard financial times, would be ready to enter a new field. Many of the sectarian agencies' clients had moved to the suburbs and so had many of their donors. An increasing percentage of agency budgets was already coming from public contracts—by 1975, almost 90 percent—which Blum believed would make them willing partners with MPU.

MPU could reimburse the agencies handsomely for their services. Coughlin's use of the consent judgment to pry dollars loose from Budget meant that Blum could take advantage of two new funding arrangements. Before the decree, the state spent only some $9,000 per client annually in the few group homes that it supported, half of the money coming from the client's own federal Social Security supplement and half from the state's matching funds. But $9,000 was not nearly enough for MPU to attract the voluntary agencies and satisfy the many requirements of the decree. Coughlin and Blum increased the allotment so that each Willowbrook class client who entered a group home commanded between $25,000 and $50,000 annually, depending on the severity of the disability. All the additional sums came from the state, not federal, treasury. The first source was "620 funds," under which the state assumed full costs of care for anyone who had been institutionalized five years or longer (in effect, the entire Willowbrook class). The other was Purchase of Service (POS) funds, which allowed MPU to make individual contracts with each voluntary agency. Coughlin did have to negotiate an agency budget with the powers in Albany, but MPU could overspend without much difficulty. It could write generous contracts with individual voluntary agencies, knowing that its POS commitments would all be honored in one way or another. In a pinch, Coughlin could transfer dollars from the institutional budget or he could request a supplementary appropriation, which he did regularly and successfully. All told, Blum would not (and did not) have trouble satisfying the financial requests of the agencies.

Indeed, Blum trusted the voluntary agencies. Unlike some critics, who insist that the major difference between for-profit and not-for-profit agencies is that the one takes its returns in dividends while the other takes it in salaries, she counted on a difference in ethos. Her experience in child welfare was that not-for-profits did not misuse public moneys; the hard bargains they drove went to service expansion, not self-enrichment. The one group she did not contract with to serve the Willowbrook class was the for-profit providers. Alert to the nursing home scandals but not able to write a regulation that banned for-profit agencies from setting up homes for the retarded, Blum discouraged staff from dealing with proprietary operators. (This discouragement was not standard practice. Minnesota, for example, regularly contracted with for-profit agencies to run group homes and somehow managed to administer a decent system.) Blum's position was easy for staff to accommodate because most of the operators owned large facilities, well beyond the ten-to-fifteen-bed limit imposed by the consent judgment. Thus, when one nursing home operator sent Blum floor plans for two of his empty buildings and informed her that both were "beautiful new constructions, fully furnished and equipped, including drapes and curtains," she wrote back that her program did not use "sites of this size."

At MPU, Blum devoted her energy to capturing resources to meet the decree's requirements, not to policing the voluntary agencies. If some of them inflated their administrative overhead by putting agency costs onto the Willowbrook budget rather than distributing them evenly across all their activities, she could live with that. The clients would be the ultimate beneficiaries.

Despite Blum's best efforts, many of the larger and more prestigious agencies were reluctant to cooperate. In the Lindsay days, they had been willing to take responsibility for some of the mildly handicapped and homeless children. But the Willowbrook assignment made totally different demands. They would have to serve the severely disabled, meet quotas and timetables, and undergo monitoring by the the court and the review panel. These considerations discouraged participation from the voluntary sector, thereby making Blum's job the most demanding of her career.

The bad news came quickly. One of the first groups Blum contacted was the Federation of Jewish Philanthropies, an umbrella organization for high-quality and wealthy child care agencies. Blum was hopeful that they would serve the Willowbrook class, or at least that fifteen percent of them who were Jewish. She was particularly eager to enlist the energies of one of the stars of the Federation, the Jewish Child Care Association (JCCA), which served almost one thousand children in a well-supervised network of foster homes, group residences, and child care institutions. JCCA had a budget of some $10 million (two-thirds of which came from public funds, the rest from its own endowment and Federation fund drives), and had a reputation for providing treatment, not custody. It also was one of the few agencies that ran a group home for emotionally disturbed children.

Blum was pleased when a JCCA vice-president promised to "explore vigorously and expeditiously a plan to be of maximum assistance," but then weeks passed without a word. Finally, months later, he reported that the agency had canvassed its foster parents, to learn that none of them were interested in caring for retarded children, even with additional stipends. In a token gesture, JCCA offered to open one home in a predominantly Jewish neighborhood, but it was much more enthusiastic about leasing an empty cottage at one of its institutions; since the agency considered institutions a last resort for normal children, it was hoping to get rid of surplus property via the Willowbrook class. Blum rejected the offer, not prepared (or allowed) to reinstitutionalize her charges.

Blum fared no better with other Jewish Federation agencies. Most of them were accustomed to providing short-term psychiatric treatment to emotionally disturbed children and had no wish to become "a life-time care agency" for retarded children. Troubled by the plight of Willowbrook's Jewish residents, the Federation did appoint a committee to explore why Jews, who were generally "in the forefront in providing services . . . [were] in this area . . . behind other faiths." (The answer came back that "the emphasis in Judaism on intellectual achievement tends to set off Jewish retardates more sharply from other Jews.") Still, the Federation moved very cautiously. A few agencies which were running sheltered workshops and providing counseling services began to include some clients from the Willowbrook class and one child care society opened a group home. But the commitment was too minimal to help Blum in meeting the decree's provisions.

The Federation of Protestant Welfare Agencies was no more cooperative. Representing non-Jewish and non-Catholic child welfare agencies, it had had difficulty arriving at a positive self-definition. In 1920, the New York City Commissioner of Welfare requested Protestant agencies to follow the Jewish and Catholic example and appoint an advisory committee; but the Protestants objected to a sectarian designation. Under pressure, they finally formed a federation, but then spent years debating what a Protestant agency was. As late as 1940, board members still did not understand what made their federation distinctive. "I don't know what it is," one of them remarked, "but it is different from Jewish and Catholic Federations."

In practice, Jews comfortably served Jews, Catholics served Catholics, but Protestant agencies, at least in the twentieth century, still wanted to serve everyone. Their approach was partly principled—who should represent the general welfare if not they? It was also strategic—in this immigrant-filled city, where would they find Protestant clients? So the agencies aimed to help all those who were homeless and dependent, which through World War II really meant some blacks, a few white Protestants, and children of no known religious denomination.

The situation changed drastically after 1945, when large numbers of Southern blacks moved to New York and swelled its welfare rolls. As late as 1947, the city Department of Welfare had 400 children, half white, half black, waiting for foster homes. By 1966, the department had to place 760 children, of whom 660 were black. The Protestant Federation responded to this crisis by expanding its foster care programs. It recruited black foster parents for black children, advertising in subway cars ("Take two—they're small") and sending mobile units through black neighborhoods urging residents "to open your hearts and homes to foster children." The campaigns proved successful and Protestant agencies grew into multimillion-dollar operations, with practically all their funds coming from the public treasury.

With some confidence, Blum brought her agenda to the Protestant Federation. Organizations that had proven capable of meeting the needs of so many black children without expanding institutional beds might do the same for the Willowbrook class. Besides, the agencies, perceiving a future reduction in the number of black clients (because of either declining migration to the city or rising rates of abortion), might well want to negotiate substantial contracts. But once again, Blum was disappointed. The Federation canvassed its members, but it was those with half-empty and expensive institutions who responded positively. Only a handful of agencies providing foster care were even willing to question the parents about taking in retarded children, and only three followed through.

The difficulties that overwhelmed one agency willing to cooperate with Blum explain why the others were not. Windham Child Care, one of the oldest agencies in the city, was expending \$3 million annually (90 percent from city contracts). Windham's directors, like Blum, initially believed that serving retarded children would not be especially demanding, but they soon discovered that foster parents who were already working with the agency would not accept the new assignment. When Windham mounted one of its usual campaigns to recruit parents, the response was minimal. In the end, the agency offered Blum one group home, which not coincidentally was too large for the three residents presently occupying it. Blum accepted it, but such ad hoc arrangements would never satisfy the consent judgment.

In retrospect, it appears Blum miscalculated the prospects of an alliance with major Jewish and Protestant agencies because she minimized the distinction between emotionally disturbed children and retarded children. With her own son, the differences were slight; no one knew where Johnny's emotional problems ended and his cognitive ones began. But these voluntary agencies drew rigid lines. In psychiatric terms (which were the most relevant for them), disturbed children were the acute, often curable cases, while retarded children were the chronic, hopeless ones. Moreover, the established agencies were closely tied to city, not state government. Staff moved freely between municipal and agency positions and the city did not monitor closely for compliance with its contracts. The agencies also had no urge to be associated with the bureaucracy that had perpetuated Willowbrook. Lastly, they had no assurance that the state would continue to fund group homes and foster care once the case was over. Hence, not even Blum's credentials could overcome agency reluctance to work with the retarded, the state, and the court.

Catholic Charities gave Blum her most favorable reception. Even before the decree, it had provided a wide range of community services, including several group homes. Its commitment reflected a recognition that any organization that counseled a mother with a defective fetus to forgo an abortion incurred a moral obligation to assist her and her handicapped newborn. More important, Vatican II charged the religious orders to undergo a renewal, to be more attentive to their social mission, and that gave a new relevance to working on behalf of retarded persons.

Vatican II's message to the clergy was to embrace "the Christ of a poor and hungry people." In this spirit, some clerics in Latin America took up the cause of landless peasants, while others in North America advanced the rights of blacks through the civil rights movement. Still others sought to serve the underprivileged by turning an empty parish house into a home for runaway youths. This commitment changed the lives of many priests. It revolutionized the lives of still more nuns. The authoritarian organization of the convent crumbled. The sisters not only put away the habit and donned street clothes but moved out of the convents and into apartments. They set their own schedules (breathing a sigh of relief at not having to rise at 5:00 A.M. and spend the first half hour getting into the habit) and selected their own assignments. In the 1950s, the mother superior had decided how sisters should be "serving God's will in holy obedience." In the 1970s, the sister herself sought to discern the Spirit's direction.

In a totally unpredictable way, Vatican II's injunctions dovetailed in the United States with changes in government policy toward the disadvantaged. The introduction of federal health insurance for the poor substituted an entitlement for a charity and insisted upon a professionalization of benevolence. Medicaid policies governing hospital reimbursements required that staff possess diplomas (dedication was not enough), and accordingly, Catholic hospitals had to send their sister nurses and sister social workers to graduate schools. Thus, just when Vatican II was urging members of the orders to pursue justice in the secular world, Medicaid was compelling them to be trained in the secular world, a combination that broke down the insularity of the convent.

For the sisters, the new freedom was at once liberating and traumatic. They were seemingly indistinguishable from other women, save that they had taken their vows. Forced to ponder what made them different, many of them could find no satisfactory answer and left the orders. Their flight was contagious, one departure prompting another. ("I felt I was on a sinking ship, and wanted to get out where I didn't have to struggle to find meaning for my life.") Between 1966 and 1976, the ranks of nuns in the United States declined from 180,000 to 131,000. In 1960, some 10,000 women had joined one of 287 orders; in 1970, only 6,800 joined.

What became of those who remained? How did they justify their continued commitment and renunciation of worldly goods and pleasures? A significant number deliberately chose assignments that lay people shunned, such as caring for the severely disabled.

Sister Barbara Eirich's career exemplified both the turmoil and the resolution of those who stayed in the life. An earnest and self-effacing woman, Sister Barbara rarely raised her voice or displayed emotion, at most evincing a weak smile or a pursing of her lips. But beneath the placid, almost aloof appearance was an unwavering dedication. She seemed driven by an inner voice to care for the least of her brethren.

Trained as a nurse, Sister Barbara joined the Order of the Sisters of St. Francis and cared for hospitalized crippled children. When the Salk polio vaccine reduced the hospital population, the archdiocese arranged to close the facility; simultaneously, her order experienced its renewal, and Sister Barbara went back to school to get a master's degree in social work. She then assisted Catholic community groups in raising funds for social action programs. In this capacity, she met Sister Lorraine Reilly, who was trying to organize programs for teenage girls who dropped out of school. With the assistance of Sister Barbara, Sister Lorraine incorporated GLIE (Group Live-In Experience) and began looking for resources to rent a home and hire neighborhood workers, which brought her to Barbara Blum, then at Special Services for Children. Blum thought GLIE a terrific idea—these adolescents often ended up in the shelters and detention centers she was trying to close —and she helped Sister Lorraine start GLIE.

The two sisters frequently discussed Sister Barbara's desire to provide a home for severely physically disabled children like those she had nursed at the St. Francis hospital. Even as that hospital closed, she had arranged for the children to move into their own apartments; although public welfare funds were available to pay for furnishings and homemakers, only someone as persistent as Sister Barbara could force the bureaucracy to translate paper entitlements into goods and services. Seeing these young adults living independently in the community and not as inmates in an institution validated her commitment.

In April 1976, Sister Lorraine attended a hastily called meeting in the Bronx, at which Barbara Blum, now head of MPU, asked voluntary agencies to provide group homes for the Willowbrook class. Sister Lorraine reported the details to Sister Barbara and the two of them drafted a proposal to have GLIE open two apartments in the South Bronx for twelve nonambulatory Willowbrook residents. Blum was delighted with it, especially because neither the clientele nor the neighborhood had been sought after by other agencies.

With a touch of the theatrical, Sister Barbara took her new charges from Willowbrook to their Bronx home by way of the fifty-sixth floor at Two World Trade Center. The sister and her assistants rolled the wheelchair-bound clients, each holding a plant on his or her lap, into the MPU offices. They had come, she told Blum, to meet the person who had made it possible for them to have a home. There was not a dry eye in the room, except for Jennifer Howse, the executive director of the panel. Not thinking it proper for a representative of the court to cry, she bit her lip to hold back the tears.

However helpful Catholic Charities and individual sisters might be, Blum understood that they alone could not resettle the Willowbrook class. Accordingly, she explored two different strategies: to have MPU itself recruit foster parents, and to attract a new cadre of voluntary agencies outside the major federations. Although the first turned out far less successful than the second, both broke new ground in serving the retarded in the community.

The foster care system had originally been designed to assist parents confronting sudden illness or economic hardship. Their child would *temporarily* go to a foster family (resembling the natural family as much as possible), remain there until the crisis was resolved, and then return home. Holding to such a model, the agencies recruited foster parents only from "typical" families. Caretakers were to be young ("suitable in age and strength to meet the demands of parenting"), religious minded ("to give him the values of living for which he could customarily look to his own parents"), and have children of their own (so he would have siblings). Working mothers ranked low on the list ("usually the foster mother is not employed except in the care of the home"), and single men and women were excluded ("it is desirable to have two foster parents—in order to provide maximum opportunities for personality development").

This definition left no room for retarded children. Foster parents told interviewers that they were most put off by the problems of retardation. The influential Child Welfare League of America pronounced that the "special needs" of retarded children prevented them "from forming emotional relationships inherent in normal family living." The belief ran so deep that even examples to the contrary did not alter policies. When one social worker reported that a retarded child in foster care had progressed "so dramatically that he was accepted by and returned to his natural parents," the incident testified to how "the 'impossible' can be achieved."

Indeed, Willowbrook itself had periodically attempted to initiate foster care, but even though it was prepared to relax standards, the program had little success. The facility considered requests for one resident or for ten residents, for residents of any specific color or religion (take your pick, black or white, Catholic or Protestant); the institution did not even object if both the husband and the wife had full-time jobs and hired a worker to care for the retarded boarder. Should a boarder prove troublesome, the family could return him or her to Willowbrook immediately and take another. Even so, between 1968 and 1972, an average of only thirty-five residents a year entered foster care, and one-third of them were returned to the institution.

This record did not inhibit Blum. She understood that no procedure could work more efficiently or effectively than foster care to meet the decree and provide residents with a normal environment. Foster care, unlike group homes, did not require complicated procedures for leasing a property or hiring a staff. It did not demand a rigorous monitoring system; the clue was to pick the right parents. Thus foster care came as close to representing an ideal solution for Willowbrook as Blum could imagine, and not surprisingly she pursued it avidly.

The program was so attractive that DMH broke with every social welfare precedent and made natural parents eligible for foster care benefits. Parents of Willowbrook residents willing to take them home would, regardless of income, qualify for the stipends. For the first time, a state was willing to pay parents to take care of their own children. But very few of the parents accepted it. Four years later, only some seventy of them had entered the program. The numbers were low because many parents had died or moved out of state or could not be located. So, too, many families had had no contact with their child since institutionalization and could not years later reinvest themselves. (A story, undoubtedly apocryphal, that the MPU staff recounted again and again was about a family in which the mother had been told that her child was born dead; because of inquiries from MPU, she discovered that the father and the doctor had secretly decided to institutionalize him.) Perhaps a generous state reimbursement policy could have altered parents' original decision to choose Willowbrook over home care. But assistance that might have prevented institutionalization could not facilitate release.

The exceptions, the seventy parents who took their children back, prove the rule. Most of them had not institutionalized their children at birth but at a later crisis—when the child reached school age and no classes were available, or when other siblings demanded extra attention, or when marital problems became severe. When the new foster parent program began, the original crisis had passed—the siblings had left home, or the mother was widowed or remarried—and with services now in place, they were ready to enroll. For the great majority of parents, however, the children had been away from the table too long to find a place at it again.*

In designing her own foster care program, Blum broke with tradition, recognizing that the retarded needed foster parents willing and able to make a long-term commitments. These clients would not return to natural parents or outgrow the placement, and so the point was not to locate a young family with children but to find a permanent setting—even if the family was older and more rigid than most foster care agencies would select.

Notes from the Field
Interview with a Foster Family

From: Barbara Rios
To: David and Sheila

The Phillips family lived on a quiet residential street in a middle-class black neighborhood. All the homes on the block were brick single-family dwellings, with front lawns the size of postage stamps, and patches of grass straining to locate the sun that periodically filtered through the trees. Mrs. Phillips, a slim and well-groomed woman, greeted me warmly. Her house was comfortably furnished and decorated with plants and lots of breakable knickknacks. She was pleased I had come, and insisted we sit in the dining room and have coffee and cookies.

Mrs. Phillips talked with animation about Bobby, her thirty-year-old white retarded foster "child." She and her husband, a government employee, had been living alone in the house since her children and her grandson, whom she also raised, had recently left. She considered going back to work—years ago she had been employed in a shop—but she really wanted "something to do and be useful at the same time." She heard about the program on a radio advertisement, and knew that New York was looking for homes for people from Willowbrook. When she saw a neighbor caring for a resident, she decided to apply.

An MPU social worker invited her to a session to meet some residents. One prospective client was a twenty-year-old man who had recently run away from a foster home and she knew immediately that this was not the type of person she wanted to take care of. Someone this age might get into trouble or have "problems

*As if to demonstrate that such a policy could prevent institutionalization, Bronx parents with retarded children at home requested these same foster care benefits, even though they were not of the Willowbrook class. DMH refused and the parents filed suit on equal protection grounds (with the cooperation of the plaintiffs' lawyers, who wanted to see the benefits extended beyond the class). The court, however, ruled that DMH's distinction between the Willowbrook class and other retarded was reasonable. It could offer sums to one and not to the other.

with sex." She was disappointed to learn that there were no children in need of homes, but nevertheless returned to the next session. There she met Bobby, who was older but cheerful and well behaved. She liked him and within a short time a trial visit was arranged and the placement completed.

Mrs. Phillips described Bobby as "low functioning," but then added that he was really quite normal. He spoke clearly, dressed himself and did simple tasks without supervision. Most important, he was generally "well tempered and never violent." She showed me the room she had furnished especially for him. It had a colorful bedspread, curtains, and posters on the walls. She kept calling Bobby "my son," and added that he called her "Mommy," and her husband "Daddy." Since he had entered Willowbrook as an infant, this was really his first home and they were his first parents.

Mr. and Mrs. Phillips take Bobby "wherever we go," shopping, to church, to social events at the Baptist church, on trips out of the city. His appearance was always neat, Mrs. Phillips explained. He is as well dressed "as we are."

Mrs. Phillips supervised Bobby very strictly. When he was not at his workshop, he did chores, from emptying baskets to sweeping the porch; only then was he allowed to watch TV. Mrs. Phillips has worked with him on puzzles, and taught him to write, count, and do simple math. She hoped that he might learn to read someday, but added that she did not want to confuse him by teaching him too much. He recently memorized his address (it took several days), but then forgot it when she started to teach him his telephone number.

Mrs. Phillips has been trying to "break Bobby of his bad habits," like having fits of laughter or becoming too babyish. He used to meow, saying "Look, Mommy, I'm a kitty," but stopped when she consistently ignored it. She noted that raising a retarded person required different approaches. When a normal child misbehaved he could be spanked, but a retarded person shouldn't be. Bobby often "doesn't understand" or "forgets" and so was not completely accountable for his actions. Bobby was not allowed to leave the house or yard by himself. He pays no attention to traffic and often "wanders in a fog." He spent time with peers only at the workshop and at the dances it sponsored on Friday nights. Mrs. Phillips was planning a birthday party for Bobby, intending to invite the other retarded residents who lived in the neighborhood because "he needs his own company." She was even considering taking a second resident to give him a companion.

Bobby, Mrs. Phillips reported, has so far shown no interest in sex and she hoped that this would continue. She was told by her social worker that masturbation was normal and should be allowed in privacy. Bobby does spend time in his room alone and she does not check on him there.

In sum, Mrs. Phillips has found caring for Bobby a satisfying experience. It was "hard work," requiring "love and patience." Only people who "like the retarded" should take on the assignment. But if they did, they would find great satisfaction in being able to help someone.

The Phillipses were typical of the families who joined in the program. The majority were black or Hispanic working-class people in their forties or fifties. What made them enroll? It was not unusual for the women to talk wistfully about "how I wanted to have a large family but I only had two," and then explain that "my children are grown and we have the room." Many of them also had had prior experience with the severely handicapped. The foster parents in Staten Island, for example, were frequently ex–Willowbrook employees; those in Queens had worked in nursing homes or state hospitals. They often had friends or relatives who cared for the disabled. In fact, the very helplessness of their charges had its own appeal. These "children" would not move away—which meant that those attracted to the assignment were likely to err on the side of overprotection, not neglect.

The foster parents often spoke about the religious sources of their commitment. The women emphasized the importance of caring for "all God's children," how God "has all kinds of flowers in His garden" which need tending. A majority belonged to a Baptist or Pentecostal church, and they, together with the foster children, not only attended Sunday worship regularly but organized their social life around church activities, singing in the choir and going on weekend retreats.

Financial motivations buttressed a family's decision to become foster parents. Many of the women defined the position as an alternative to work in a factory or an office. The monthly allowance from MPU was $291, somewhat more than the $236 from child welfare. But the burden was too great for anyone to think of the assignment strictly in dollar terms. These caretakers described their foster children not in the language of the marketplace but the family: "I am a mother to her. She doesn't need much but love and care and good food." "It's like being an ordinary mother, but retarded children are easier in many ways. They are always sweet and loving. They don't give you the same headaches."

That the clients came from an infamous institution actually made it all the more rewarding to care for them. When a black foster mother walked down a street with her white foster child, it was obvious that she was not an unfortunate parent but a skilled caretaker. Her stature increased further when neighbors learned that the child came from that place they had seen on TV where people were naked and lived in excrement. Now he was well groomed and well behaved, sitting quietly in church on Sunday morning, thanks to the benevolence and sense of duty of his foster family.

These considerations not only help explain how MPU managed to recruit some foster homes for residents but clarify why it could not recruit more. These caretakers were a minority of a minority, and even they could not handle the retarded who were incapable of toilet training or highly aggressive. Moreover, MPU set stiff requirements for care. It would not normally give a foster family more than two clients; in child welfare, three or four clients was commonplace. Each client had to have his own bedroom, no mean feat in a city like New York. The net effect was that Blum, who had originally hoped to recruit twenty foster families a month, had to settle for five. After two years, MPU had only 294 class members in foster care and had nearly exhausted the pool of potential parents.

Facing the need to open many more group homes than anyone had anticipated, and understanding that the established voluntary agencies would provide only minimal help, Blum looked for and found her most avid supporters among organizations that had never before designed large-scale programs for the mentally retarded. Failing to make alliances with those she had considered her natural allies, she courted more unconventional groups to find a warmer reception.

Among the first agencies Blum solicited were the minority-run, ghetto-based ones with which she had worked during the Lindsay administration. Aware of just how new and, perforce, inexperienced they were in retardation, she counted on their commitment to serving the underprivileged whom others avoided.

Black leaders dismayed with the disorganization and apathy of the ghetto created these local agencies in the hope that they would combat neighborhood deterioration, unemployment, juvenile delinquency, and drug addiction. The problems were well beyond their ability to solve, but their efforts attracted major assistance—first, on an experimental basis from the Ford Foundation's Grey Areas project, then from Lyndon Johnson's War on Poverty.

In the late 1950s, the Ford Foundation announced its readiness to fund innovative programs in community welfare and the most trend-setting of its grants went to New York's Mobilization for Youth (MFY). Located on the Lower East Side and directed by an unusual mixture of professional and community leaders, MFY ran employment projects for ghetto youth (finding them jobs in factories and repair shops), taught welfare recipients about their entitlements (encouraging them to demand their full benefits), and raised the political awareness of ghetto residents (prompting them to take control of institutions like the schools). These initiatives were bound to bring MFY into bitter (and losing) conflicts with vested interests (such as the board of education). But along the way, it helped to make power to the people one of the rallying cries of the 1960s.

What the Ford Foundation started on a limited scale, the War on Poverty continued on a grand scale. In New York, the results were most apparent in Bedford-Stuyvesant, a heavily black Brooklyn neighborhood with one of the highest rates of delinquency and drug addiction in the city. The district did have a Coordinating Council of some 115 small agencies, and when the War on Poverty was declared, the council moved quickly to win support. The design of a vest pocket park brought it favorable publicity, a visit from Robert Kennedy, and, with his help, substantial funding for the newly created Bedford-Stuyvesant Restoration Corporation. Between 1968 and 1976, the corporation renovated some three thousand neighborhood houses and attracted small and large businesses to the area. The corporation had a social mission as well, organizing mental health and day care centers, and rehabilitating and leasing properties to local agencies for group homes for the handicapped.

The career of Shirley Pierce demonstrates how these changes benefited the resettlement of the Willowbrook class. Raised in Bedford-Stuyvesant, she studied accounting and then worked as a bookkeeper for a local construction company. There she came to know the neighborhood politicians, the heads of the Restoration Corporation, and the agencies. In 1970, Barbara Blum interviewed her for an accounting position at the city Department of Mental Hygiene; upon learning about her Brooklyn connections, Blum instead hired her to serve as a liaison between the city and the minority-run agencies.

As soon as the consent judgment was signed, Pierce joined the Willowbrook Task Force. When Barbara Blum arrived at MPU, Pierce immediately became central to the new director's attempts to recruit minority agencies. Pierce combined the orderliness of an accountant with the dedication of a black activist. She kept meticulous files on practically every black church and social action group in Brooklyn, convinced that if blacks did not help their own, no one would help them. If they did not organize group homes, Willowbrook's black residents were likely to remain institutionalized.

Pierce had little trouble persuading black organizations of this argument. They not only shared her viewpoint but, operating on a shoestring, welcomed the contracts that MPU wrote. Thus, when Pierce contacted the Bedford-Stuyvesant Community Mental Health Center, explained the need for a residence, and discussed the architectural assistance available through the Restoration Corporation, she was warmly received. To be sure, it would take months for the center to put together a proposal, but that testified to inexperience, not a lack of will. Pierce also brought in the Colony South Settlement Houses, an antipoverty organization that ran manpower training programs. Along with many other minority agencies, Colony South grossly underestimated the difficulties of administering a group home. (If the major voluntary agencies seemed to believe that each retarded person required intensive care twenty-four hours a day, the new ones thought that lots of love would solve every problem.) But however crucial it was for MPU to explain the complexities of the task and to pace the agencies' involvement—open one home and gain experience before starting a second—Blum found these problems far more manageable than cajoling uninterested parties.

Blum also received assistance from a small number of Orthodox Jewish agencies who were outside the Jewish Federation. These splinter groups were typically organized by devout women who shared an anti-abortion belief and indeed, often had ten or twelve children of their own. They were distressed at the prospect of Jewish children, retarded or not, living in Christian group homes. Accordingly, they arranged to lease a residence in their own neighborhood and take in, insofar as MPU staff would allow, Jewish children from Willowbrook. The residences had kosher kitchens and the staff ran religious services and observed the holidays. Although state and federal policy prohibited such expressions of religious preference, MPU staff and everyone else generally looked the other way. If sectarian groups were not allowed first to care for their own, Willowbrook would never be emptied.

Blum was even more successful in cultivating the small agencies founded by parents to serve their retarded children. Here, too, cooperation was not automatic. The parents ran narrow and exclusive programs—sheltered workshops and day care centers. They rarely opened group homes—their children did not need them, at least while the parents were able to provide care. Although troubled by the Willowbrook scandal, these parents were uninterested in deinstitutionalization. In fact, they worried that the state would divert resources from existing community programs to the Willowbrook class.

Rather than try to undercut the consent judgment (which would have been futile), the parent agencies shrewdly took advantage of the situation. Joining together in an Interagency Council, they negotiated an agreement with Coughlin: They would open group homes for the Willowbrook class if half the beds in each were reserved for non-class members already in the community and the state assumed all the costs. Coughlin, needing the placements, agreed.

With the fifty-fifty deal secured, a number of parent agencies were ready to do business with MPU. The New York City chapter of Weingold's ARC soon opened the first of its seven group homes, although its executive director, Michael Goldfarb, rarely had a kind word to say for the decree and kept on his desk a list of all the mischief he could attribute to it. So, too, the Association for Children with Retarded Mental Development (ACRMD), one of the earliest parent organizations in the city, expanded its operation to run four group homes. To be sure, MPU now had to open twice as many group homes, and the parent agencies drove hard bargains, recognizing that the pressures to meet the decree gave the state little room to maneuver. But none of this troubled Blum, who was quite willing to extend the judgment's benefits to another and no less worthy group.

Blum's most notable success came with the smallest of these agencies, Young Adult Institute. Founded in 1957 by a psychologist, YAI taught mildly retarded adults social and vocational skills. Never financially secure, it limped from one fiscal crisis to another until, in 1973, it agreed to teach severely retarded adults in order to gain funding from New York City. YAI's professional staff soon discovered that even very handicapped persons could make significant progress, and once the Willowbrook decree was signed, the agency expanded. Between 1976 and 1980, YAI opened twelve group homes, becoming the second-largest provider of residential services to the retarded in the city.

Although Blum gradually learned that her greatest successes came where she least expected them, she was surprised that United Cerebral Palsy of New York State became the single largest provider of services to the Willowbrook class. In 1972, UCP did not run programs for a single retarded person. By 1979, it administered several buildings at

Willowbrook itself as well as a nearby institution, Nina Eaton, for ex-Willowbrook residents, and supervised a hundred three-bed apartments for class members in the community.

UCP was founded by parents of handicapped children to provide local workshops, summer camps, and chapter clinics. They also organized state and national bodies, which soon developed a separate interest in research, looking to do for cerebral palsy what the March of Dimes had done for polio. The result was a certain tension, probably healthy, within the group. The state and national bodies raised money very effectively (as watchers of telethons could testify), and divided the sums between the locals and the national. In New York, at least before 1970, the locals dominated. UCP State had only a small office, a budget of less than $100,000, and not much to do besides fund-raise.

In 1971, Robert Schonhorn, trained as a clinical psychologist, became executive director of UCP State and in short order transformed the agency. A man of restless energy, he seemed happiest when three conversations were going at once and his phone was ringing. Finding fund-raising too limiting and recognizing that he could not move UCP State into direct competition with service-oriented chapters, he looked for gaps to fill. The most obvious was the institutionalized retarded. Although a majority of victims of cerebral palsy suffer from mental as well as physical defects, UCP chapters saw themselves treating cerebral palsy, not retardation; doing community service, not institutional reform. Accordingly, Schonhorn had to himself the retarded who were incarcerated—just when Willowbrook was becoming front-page news.

Schonhorn was the only agency director willing to testify for Bruce Ennis on Willowbrook. And he was the only director ready to sign a half-million-dollar contract with DMH to send out "mini teams" of therapists to teach the Willowbrook staff the rudiments of care. In early 1975, Schonhorn offered to treat fifty of Willowbrook's worst cases in a unit on the grounds of the nearby South Beach Psychiatric Center. DMH was delighted, calling the arrangement "a milestone of collaborative enterprise." Schonhorn said it was "goddam time somebody ran a bang-up institution."

Having turned down Tom Coughlin's request to head MPU, Schonhorn made him and Barbara Blum a proposal they could not refuse: He would open three-bed apartments in the community for the Willowbrook class (with no 50 percent community match necessary). Schonhorn also contracted to provide the clients with transportation, day programs, and recreation, so that soon the UCP yellow vans became familiar sights on the city streets.

Schonhorn was so unconventional an agency director that he joined with Blum to set up a revolving fund to enable smaller agencies to pay their first bills. Although the state eventually compensated the agencies for the costs of renovating and furnishing group homes, the bills came due long before DMH processed the vouchers, and the agencies faced impatient creditors. Blum was urging DMH to expedite its paperwork, but in the meanwhile, she and Schonhorn opened a checking account and gave ninety-day, interest-free loans to the needy agencies. The arrangement demonstrated that Blum was never afraid to innovate in order to further placements, and Schonhorn always relished original solutions.

All told, the MPU statistics were impressive. Over its first four years (1976–79) it opened one hundred group homes. The parent-dominated agencies, with YAI in the lead, were responsible for almost half of them (forty-five); the Catholic agencies contributed another 20 percent, the minority-based agencies 15 percent. UCP added its one hundred apartments, and the Protestant and Jewish federations did their small share. In this way, well over one thousand Willowbrook residents entered the community.

Just as Blum assembled an unusual group of agencies to administer the group homes, so she put together an unusual staff to run MPU. One of the few demands she made before accepting the post was to have the right to select personnel outside civil service lists, and since all her staff was to be "provisional," Coughlin agreed. Blum then used her freedom to hire people who actually cared about what they were doing and went at it with diligence.

Some of them had worked with Blum before. Karin Eriksen, trained as a social worker, had assisted her at Special Services for Children in organizing community programs. Her first task at MPU was to compose accurate job descriptions: this position to screen caretakers, that one to monitor clients, and so on. Irene Arnold had accompanied Blum on her city tours for Lindsay's first task force and was now running Retarded Infant Services, the only private agency in the city that located homemakers for families with severely handicapped children. Trained as a lawyer, Arnold had been among the first Americans to go to Germany to resettle concentration camp survivors—and she knew whereof she spoke when she compared Willowbrook to the camps. At MPU, Arnold designed a clients' rights unit to ensure that no one took advantage of residents' helplessness.

As word of the MPU mandate spread, young professionals working in special education, particularly Catholics, applied for the positions. Perhaps in an earlier day, some of those who had been raised in blue-collar families and attended parochial schools might have joined a religious order. Although such a choice seemed out of the question in the 1970s, a career linked to doing good was not. They all had read Dorothy Day, admired her sense of social justice and shared her political sympathies. The radical Emma Goldman had found Day "a new one on me, for I have never heard of Catholics being radical." By the 1970s, however, Day had inspired a significant Catholic-left movement, which to those in retardation meant organizing alternatives to institutions. Thus Pat and Brian Dionne, who had served as houseparents in the first Catholic Charities group home, joined MPU. By experience and temperament, they were well suited to negotiate the contracts with the voluntary agencies and to oversee the quality of care.

The dirtiest job went to someone Blum and Eriksen knew from Lindsay days, Pat Pelner. Previously, she had run group homes for ex–mental patients; now it became her unenviable task to travel to Willowbrook and help select and prepare clients for community placement. She had a choice of two bathrooms, one with a sign that said shigella, the other, hepatitis B. Worse yet, the attendants took out their anger and frustrations on her. Sabotage was the order of the day, in part to get even with those who disparaged Willowbrook's employees, in part to make certain that deinstitutionalization did not proceed smoothly enough to cost them their jobs. So on the day that agencies came out to screen for group home admissions, records were lost and residents were taken off tranquilizers or anti-epileptic medication to make their behavior appear too bizarre for placement. In the Willowbrook wars, Pelner was in the trenches.

In truth, no one at MPU had it very easy. It was no fun to play hide-and-seek with Willowbrook attendants; it was not much better to negotiate dollars with an agency director who wanted a higher overhead allowance. But just when a staff member reached a breaking point, Blum provided R and R, usually at the lunch club at the top of the World Trade Center. A spirit of camaraderie pervaded the office, with in-jokes (about who Coughlin was sending down this week to make sure that

MPU did not overstep its authority), anniversary celebrations (Blum's first year on the job), victories (this month MPU made more placements than any other), and defeats (when an angry community burned down a group home about to open). Those who took part in MPU's rescue operation generally found it the most exciting and rewarding assignment they had ever undertaken.

8

Moving Minds

Anyone who doubts the convenience of institutionalizing the retarded (or other stigmatized groups) has only to examine the process of opening a group home. Persuading a voluntary agency to administer the residence turns out to be the simplest part. Locating, renovating, and securing the necessary permission to use a suitable physical structure is far more complicated, and prone to failure at any point during long and protracted negotiations. To open an institution for five thousand inmates, the state must identify one property (preferably on surplus land that it owns), one architect, and one builder; it must convince one community of the profits that will accrue to it through expenditures and employment opportunities. To open one group home for ten Willowbrook residents, the state must locate one site (in a decent neighborhood), one architect, and one builder, and convince one community of its moral duty to accept this facility and, given the requirements of the consent judgment, another four as well. It is hard to imagine officials willingly assuming such an assignment, and historically, of course, very few of them did.

In April 1975, plaintiffs and defendants alike believed that meeting the community placement provisions of the consent judgment would not be onerous. New York City had a variety of housing stock, a relatively depressed real estate market, a mobile population, heterogeneous neighborhoods, and inhabitants with a reputation for not knowing who lived next door. But it soon became apparent how mistaken both sides had been. Placement looked easy because few had tried it before.

Barbara Blum and the MPU staff actually managed the task far better than the signers of the decree had the right to expect. The review panel and plaintiffs' lawyers were never satisfied with the rate of placement, convinced that incompetence or bad faith lay behind each delay. Still, between 1976 and 1980, MPU opened some one hundred group homes for over one thousand residents.

The state's first achievement lay in revamping internal procedures so that a group home for ten could be opened more expeditiously than an institution for ten thousand. The Facilities Development Corporation was so geared to large construction jobs and time frames of five or ten years that getting quick approvals and renovations accomplished for a single brownstone was almost beyond its ability. Since FDC, for example, generally sought 200-to-500-acre locations for institutions, it had authority only to purchase properties. But for group homes, leasing was preferable, as it would bring in the greatest number of properties with the lowest expenditures, at least in the short run. So the Office of Mental Retardation and Developmental Disabilities, now separate from the Department of Mental Hygiene, requested and obtained legislative approval for FDC to negotiate five-year leases with an option to renew for an additional five years.

Locating rental properties that on initial inspection seemed suitable was not particularly difficult. Staff from MPU and the voluntary agencies contacted real estate brokers, walked the streets, and placed advertisements in newspapers and trade magazines—Wanted: One- or Two-Family Homes, or Two-to-Three-Bedroom Apartments. Probably no more than seven people ever worked at this job at one time and most of them had other major responsibilities; nevertheless, they found an ample supply of acceptable-looking homes not sandwiched in between factories and garbage dumps.

Then the problems began. First FDC had to conduct a "real property" analysis, to determine the appropriate rental for the site, and do an architectural feasibility study, to determine the extent of the necessary renovations. Both took time. The real property analyst had to compare the building with others in terms of space, conditions, and location, make certain that the title was in order, and check that no existing leases prevented MPU from occupying it immediately. This hurdle passed, the architect next reported on the structural adequacy of the building (including plumbing and heating), the necessary changes to accommodate the clients (the numbers of bathroom doors to be widened for wheelchairs), and the alterations that the various city and state building codes required. The architect also had to submit drawings of the present structure and of his proposed renovations, describe the work necessary to satisfy each building code, and offer a preliminary cost estimate for the entire job.

To fulfill these assignments, FDC had only a handful of property evaluators and architects on its staff, understandably enough, since even New York did not build institutions daily. So when MPU began submitting dozens of requests for evaluations, FDC was unable to complete them for months. More delays occurred for no one was certain whether the restrictive state building codes or the lenient city ones governed group homes. Should institutional standards apply because its residents would be very disabled or should halfway house standards apply because the structure would be in the community?

Confronting the logjam, and unremitting pressure from the review panel and plaintiffs, Tom Coughlin managed to bring authority for code approvals into OMRDD, to enlarge the FDC staff, and, together with Barbara Blum, to bring some rationality to the codes. (They decided, for example, that fire escapes obviated the need for a second inner stairway, but that the toughest fire detection and sprinkler regulations would have to be met.) Both Blum and Coughlin sent a steady stream of memoranda to FDC, alternately praising and damning it, all the while prodding it to act faster. The result was that by 1978, FDC was completing the real property and architectural feasibility analyses in six to seven weeks.

Once FDC set rental and renovation costs, the project went back to OMRDD for approval—which could be handled in about a month's time. The next step called for FDC to negotiate a lease with the owner of the property. Whether it was a private individual or a real estate company (like Lefrak) or a charitable agency (most often the Catholic Church), discussions centered on the rental figure, the extent of renovations required, who would carry them out, how the property was to be left after the lease expired, and myriad other details which anyone who has so much as sublet an apartment can well imagine. All this required three to four months to complete (that is, when agreement between parties could be reached) or negotiations might drag on for months (and never come to a satisfactory outcome). This part of the process could not be streamlined. MPU could only accumulate enough properties "in the pipeline" to maintain a steady supply of potential sites.

After MPU and the property owner signed a contract, three state offices had to review it: Budget (because dollars were involved), the attorney general's office (because a lease was involved), and Audit and Control (because vouchers and scheduled payments were involved). At first, obtaining the approvals took endless time. But after complaints from Coughlin and a court order obtained by the review panel and plaintiffs' lawyers, the process was completed in seven to eight weeks.

When all these steps had been accomplished—usually over a five-month period—renovations could begin. OMRDD was prepared to assume the costs, but for efficiency's sake, it preferred to have the owner disburse the funds and oversee the work. On the average, barring strikes and shortages of materials, it took about six months to renovate a group home, although many of the jobs went on longer.

Usually one year passed from the time MPU identified a group-home site until it was ready for occupancy, which does not seem unreasonable. But this figure is for sites that actually opened; a substantial number of others dropped off along the way. A conservative estimate would be that for every five sites that passed the initial MPU review and were sent to FDC, only one survived. Thus the process demanded such extraordinary persistence and energy that for a large number of homes to open, a department had to make deinstitutionalization its major goal.

However cumbersome it might be to satisfy regulations, streamline bureaucratic procedures, and carry out renovations, these matters were mostly under the control of OMRDD and other state offices. But opening a group home also involved external considerations: MPU might satisfy all other requirements, and then face unremitting hostility and resistance from the neighborhood in which the group home was to open.

In fact, the most prominent barrier to group homes, the obstacle most frequently cited in the professional literature, television documentaries, and OMRDD apologies for not meeting its quotas, was community opposition, the enmity of neighbors toward the bringing of retarded persons into their midst. Occasionally, in other states, officials had made an end run around community antipathy, coming in by stealth, buying a house under a fictitious name, delivering the clients at night, and in effect presenting the neighborhood with an accomplished fact. This strategy has been pursued most successfully when administrators want to open one group home for one special group (whether it be the retarded or juvenile offenders or runaways), with no plans to organize a network of residences. (After all, as supporters would have it, the retarded person and the ex-offender have as much right as anyone to live on a block, and neighbors need not be consulted about their presence.)

Whatever the rights or wrongs of a midnight strategy, it could not be used with the Willowbrook class. A department can get away with a surprise arrival once, perhaps twice, but the third time the neighborhood will be ready, armed, if not literally, then with court papers and political influence. If OMRDD was to place hundreds of residents, if it was to organize a *system* of noninstitutionalized care, it had to be candid about its plans and give the community fair notice, even if that meant allowing opponents ample time to mount their protests. Such a strategy predictably created the most volatile situation—yet it was the only one with a prospect for long-term success.

In New York City, fair notice constituted OMRDD's announcing its intentions to the neighborhood community planning board. In primitive form these boards dated back to the early 1950s, but they were really the creation of the Lindsay administration in the 1960s, part of the process of decentralization that spurred the development of agencies like the Bedford-Stuyvesant Restoration Corporation. In order to expand local participation in municipal government, New York was divided into fifty-nine community board districts, with populations of 100,000 to 250,000; the boards were composed of fifty members each, appointed for two-year terms by the borough president. The duties were threefold: to advise City Hall on budget priorities, on the delivery of municipal services, and on land use and zoning.

Performance varied enormously from board to board, but they generally never became, as some had predicted they would, rivals for power with city agencies. They had no influence on budgets and little ability to affect delivery of police, sanitation, or welfare services. However, they were of some importance in decisions on land use. To the chagrin of real estate developers, the boards could seriously delay a large-scale building project, and sometimes delay it long enough to kill it. The board on the Upper West Side of Manhattan, for example, placed so many demands in the way of a proposed Alexander's department store—including the redesign of the local subway stop—that the plans were scuttled.

In their advisory capacity on zoning questions, the community planning boards wanted to be consulted about the location of proposed group homes, and between 1976 and 1978, OMRDD extended them this courtesy (born of political necessity as it was). Then, in 1978, the New York legislature enacted the Site Selection Law, more commonly called the Padavan Law (after State Senator Frank Padavan, of Queens, who was known for his opposition to deinstitutionalization in general and to the Willowbrook review panel in particular). Under the bill, an agency sponsoring a "supervised residence for four to fourteen mentally disabled persons" had to notify the community planning board of its intentions. The board had forty days to approve the site or to suggest alternatives; it could also oppose the site if "an excessive number of other facilities" were already in the district and one more would "substantially alter the character and nature of the neighborhood and community." If the board opposed a site or if the agency found a suggested alternative site unacceptable, the agency commissioner was to hold a hearing and resolve the dispute, and his decision was, as usual, appealable to the state courts.

Controversy over the Padavan Law was fierce. Some critics believed that it forced retarded citizens to undergo a demeaning and discriminatory process. The other side objected that the department which sponsored the group homes also determined the appropriate location of the group homes. Everyone was disturbed by the bill's vague language. Even by state legislative standards it was poorly drafted, lacking a definition of what constituted an "excessive" share of facilities or what it meant to "substantially alter" the character of a neighborhood. But one thing quickly became clear: Under the Padavan Law, OMRDD continued to do what it had always done, informing the community planning board of its plans and reserving final authority to itself.

Whatever the community boards lacked in formal authority they made up for in passion (in the not unreasonable belief that passion might compensate for inadequate power). The board chairman would convene an open meeting on the proposed group home, the neighborhood residents would come to speak (or shout) their views, and then the board members would vote to approve or disapprove the proposal. If there was a classic town meeting analogy in the minds of those who designed this system, these sessions frequently demonstrated the equally classic democratic dilemma of how to protect minorities against majorities, how to secure the rights of the few against the will of the many.

Notes from the Field (David)
A Proposed Group Home at Beverly Road and East Seventh Street
Community Planning Board 12, Brooklyn
September 20, 1978

Sheila and I drove out to the Flatbush Jewish Center, a few blocks away from the proposed site, in the heart of a middle-class, heavily Jewish neighborhood. Ed Matthews of MPU expected a stormy session and we were certain he was right as we watched some four hundred people crowd into the auditorium, many still clutching the leaflet that someone (no one was sure who) distributed announcing the meeting. The board chairman, Edward Rappaport, a lawyer, called the meeting to order at seven-thirty, gave a brief description of what a planning board was ("since so many of you here probably don't know about it"), and took up, as the first item of business, whether fruit vendors on Church Avenue should be allowed to continue to display their wares on wooden stands that jutted out from their stores onto the streets. The question arose because the police had begun ticketing them for violating a sixty-year-old ordinance. Several vendors explained that if they could not display their goods to passersby, they would lose business; a lonely voice complained about the filth along the curbs of Church Avenue because the merchants failed to clean up. All this was done with applause and boos, the way a boxing crowd warms itself up during the preliminaries for the main event.

Rappaport then provided a brief account of the board's options under the Padavan Law, making several errors of fact and placing the responsibility for mandating group homes exclusively on the court. He made no mention of the fact that New York State had signed a consent decree. He then announced the rules for speaking—five minutes to elected officials, three minutes to everyone else. He was rambling a bit, for people began to shout, "Let's get started!" I hadn't been to the fights since I was a kid and we were vacationing in Atlantic City.

Ed Matthews of MPU, tie askew, jacket wide open, took the floor to explain that 628 Beverly Road was intended to house six to ten moderately retarded children with a twenty-four-hour staff under the auspices of the Jewish Child Care Association. The clients were not capable of living independently but they would do well in a supervised setting. Matthews added that after this group home opened, four or five more would be needed in this (and every other) planning board district in order to resettle the Willowbrook class.

The next speaker, State Assemblyman Miller, announced that he had "a heavy heart," for he knew how bad things were at Willowbrook. Still, he was opposed to the site. "We are a community in transition," and a group home would drive out scores of people. Echoing the language of the Padavan Law, he declared that the community was at a tipping point and this group home would change its character. As he went on, a few whispered exchanges with people sitting around me deciphered his code language. Beverly Road, on the one side of Ocean Parkway, has a white, middle-class, but increasingly older population; the young had long ago moved off to the Long Island suburbs. The blacks lived on the other side of Ocean Parkway; if the group home came in, the fear was that some home owners would sell out to blacks, the barrier would be crossed, and the neighborhood would become black.

Then a man who lived directly opposite the proposed group home talked for twenty minutes. Occasional reminders from the chairman about the three-minute limit were either shouted down by the crowd or greeted with random cries of "I cede him my three minutes." He first complained that the patients at the nearby nursing home exposed themselves to little girls and then predicted a decline in property values. He went on to complain that the home "has rats as big as cats, and a sewerage system that when a toilet is flushed the schmutz runs out onto the street." I boggled at this image in the midst of a fine middle-class neighborhood, but nobody said a word or even looked surprised.

Surviving the chairman's time limit, he insisted that the community had to fight for "the stability of this area," a fight that it was losing. Young families would not move in because their children would have to attend Erasmus Hall High School (which he did not have to remind the audience was now mostly black). No one here, he concluded, was "against the retarded," but Beverly Road was the wrong place. Just last month a young girl was hit by an automobile at a nearby corner. The audience burst into applause.

Irving Hershey, representing the Jewish Child Care Association, made a frank appeal to a "sense of justice and humanitarianism," which brought audible groans. He remarked that this would be "a Jewish home," which would do a lot for the residents. When he insisted that however dangerous Beverly Road might be, it would be much better than Willowbrook, he was loudly booed.

Jacob Gold, the state committeeman, responded that everyone had compassion for the retarded and the state was not to take them on "a guilt trip." The Beverly Road site, he insisted, was a scandal because FDC was paying outrageous sums to buy the property. Ed Matthews explained how FDC estimated property costs and said that no price had yet been set on the property. But all this got him was shouts of "Who is the broker?" whom he refused to name.

City Councilwoman Susan Alter asked rhetorically whether the group home would maintain the stability of the neighborhood and improve its social life, and her answer was an unequivocal no. Mr. Markowitz, a candidate for state senator, echoed her remarks. Signs of "decay" were to be found in the neighborhood; the facility will trigger the exodus of middle-class people. The speakers were getting repetitious, and with the meeting now almost two hours long, people started to drift away. They missed hearing Mr. Abraham, who lived next door to the proposed site, explain that although he had great compassion for the Jewish children, he would surely move. Yes, he would be "selfish" and put the house up for sale. Who would then move in but eight more retarded? Surely for the sake of a handful of retarded a community should not be ruined.

The meeting closed with a question to Matthews. Why not put the group homes on the spacious grounds of Willowbrook, where the children would have ample room to play and face no danger from automobiles? He replied with a crash course on normalization and dignity of risk, but the audience was too restless to listen.

We lingered to have a few words with Matthews. We wondered whether he got combat pay for the evening's work. Were they all like this? we asked him. Pretty much so, he answered.

Matthews was assuredly correct about the objections to group homes. The substance of the protests was almost everywhere the same, allowing only for a particularly inventive protester. Attend one hostile community planning board meeting and you have attended them all, which inevitably generates some skepticism about the validity of the community's claims. Practically every opponent prefaced his remarks with a declaration of concern for the welfare of the retarded, and cited traffic conditions, the absence of a backyard, the presence of a nearby pond, a growing crime rate, a problem with snow removal, or difficult access for fire engines as the reason this particular group home would be ill-advised. At the very same meeting, some neighbors would insist that their children, or their dogs, would be a menace to the retarded, while others would argue that the retarded would be a menace to their children, so that the only consistent image was that of a Hobbesian war of all against all, the vicious retarded pitted against cruel neighborhood children and dogs. Since these meetings took place in peaceful and decent neighborhoods and the disputes often involved the fate of retarded people in wheelchairs, the level of fantasy reached ridiculous heights.

Some of the protesters more candidly asserted their self-interest, especially when the family home represented their total life's savings. Their concern about a decline in property values was intense, fueled sometimes by real estate dealers adept at blockbusting, sometimes by would-be purchasers using the group home as the pretext to drive a better bargain. These fears were not unreasonable, even if, as we shall see, they were wrong. Neighbors assumed that integrating the retarded would be like integrating the blacks, with home owners rushing to sell their property as soon as the minority moved in. They also doubted the reliability of the state, not without reason, after the way it had discharged patients from mental hospitals. OMRDD might dump the retarded just as DMH had dumped the ex-mental patients, leaving them to make the benches along a traffic divider into surrogate dayrooms. How could a community be confident that group homes would be better maintained than Willowbrook, or that the homes would not eventually become drug rehabilitation centers for youthful offenders?

The history of New York's neighborhoods only heightened these anxieties, for change came devastatingly quickly and thoroughly. As late as 1915, Harlem was a substantial upper-middle-class neighborhood; within ten years, it was an economically depressed, all-black neighborhood. Immediately after World War II, upper Riverside Drive around Morningside Heights was still a fashionable area; twenty years later it was filled with single room occupancy (SRO) hotels that resembled almshouses. Hence residents scrutinized each real estate transaction with the same diligence that early seers devoted to animal entrails. And no omen seemed to bode worse for a community's stability than a proposed group home.

Lacking the legal authority to exclude these residences, communities resorted to various strategies to thwart MPU's plans. In truth, the rhetoric at a community planning board meeting rarely made a difference. Occasionally, a board that had demonstrated its good will by approving group homes in the past could offer reasonable objections to a new site and carry its point. (When Brooklyn's Community Planning Board 10 voted against a group home at Narrows Avenue on the basis of saturation, MPU backed off, unwilling to antagonize a neighborhood that already had several group homes.) More typically, MPU did not swallow stories of rats in the woodwork when a particular board had a long record of recalcitrance and FDC inspectors had approved the site. Yes, retarded people living in a community faced greater danger from traffic accidents than those at Willowbrook, but the consent judgment settled the issue of trade-offs and now placement quotas had to be met. Besides, adequate staffing and well-run programs would reduce risks to a minimum. (In fact, no member of the Willowbrook class was ever struck by an automobile, although one resident from Sister Barbara Eirich's home in the Bronx came close. A staff member pushed his wheelchair out of the way of an oncoming car, at the price of being injured himself.)

Communities, however, had tactics other than rhetoric at their disposal. They could, and often did, convince the owner of the property to be sold or leased to the state to cancel the agreement. In a handful of very wealthy communities, like suburban Scarsdale, neighbors would join together to buy the house themselves, thereby resolving the crisis. This suited the owner just fine; he got his price while doing his neighbors a favor. But not every community could come up with one hundred or two hundred thousand dollars, and so most of them had to resort to still other strategies. In some cases, angry residents persuaded an owner to find another tenant or buyer, particularly when he had a continuing stake in the area, by virtue of either his business, his professional practice, or his other property holdings. Thus one physician had initially been willing to lease a second house that he owned in the Cobble Hill section of Brooklyn to OMRDD so that St. Vincent's, a Catholic charity, could open a group home. But when neighbors protested, he backed off and refused to sign the lease.

At other times, community protest so prolonged the process of approval that the owner tired of waiting and found another purchaser. Take the case of 3350 Cross Bronx Expressway, a proposed group home in the Bronx. MPU located the site in June 1978 and FDC completed the inspections by September 1978; then, in mid-October, Community Planning Board 10 objected, ostensibly because the house lacked a backyard and was too near a highway. MPU devoted the next three months to investigating the alternative sites that the board proposed and found them inadequate, whereupon the board requested a formal hearing under the Padavan Law. The hearing was held on February 9, 1979, and in March the commissioner decided in favor of the site, at just which point the owner sold the property to a different buyer.

In still other instances, when the owner was unresponsive to neighborly persuasion and no other buyers were on hand, the situation could get nasty. Some opponents were prepared to use scare tactics, ranging from abusive telephone calls at all times of the day and night to outright threats of violence to the owner and his family. Mickey Marlib, associate director of the Association for Children with Retarded Mental Development, informed MPU that the home his agency wished to buy on Cropsey Avenue in Brooklyn was no longer available. "The owner/builder informed us . . . of his decision not to sell this property for use as a hostel to ACRMD. He stated . . . that his life had been threatened (by anonymous phone callers) if he were to finalize the sale with us. The threats extended to the burning of his own home as well as to threats of damage to the Cropsey property." Marlib was not able to track down the sources of the threats, for the owner would not even return his calls.

Such incidents, it is true, were not very common. Between July 1978 and September 1979, when MPU was particularly active—locating seventy to eighty sites and negotiating with numerous community planning boards—thirteen incidents occurred. Among the problems that could keep a potential site from becoming a group home, outright intimidation was never very prominent, accounting for no more perhaps than 15 percent of the failures. Nevertheless, its importance was greater than its frequency implied, first because these incidents generally occurred when MPU had cleared all other hurdles. Intimidation, as would be expected, was a last resort when the retarded were about to arrive, which meant that the staff had invested great energy in the project. (The survivor in Stephen Crane's "The Open Boat" who wonders whether the Lord could have been perverse enough to take him within sight of shore only to drown him is the fitting analogy.) Second, the recurring fear was that hooliganism would be contagious, success in scaring off an owner in one neighborhood serving as a lesson for another. Finally, these incidents were so morally outrageous as to raise the question whether integration of the retarded was possible when prejudices ran so deep.

Still other communities resisted the opening of group homes by mustering political influence. When local politicians with some clout in the city or the state actively opposed a site and had the solid support of a core of constituents, MPU would often get a word from the governor's office to back off, or it would retreat on its own, sensitive to potential repercussions. Many communities had no difficulty in prodding their representatives to write letters in protest against a proposed group home. Even so forthright a congresswoman as Elizabeth Holtzman, fresh from her uncompromising role in the Watergate investigations, told MPU that group homes should not to be located in her Brooklyn district because people did not want to live near mental patients (whom she confused with the retarded), and besides, selling a home to the state threatened property values and cost the city tax money. Michael Lottman, who saw the letter in his capacity as a review panel member, wrote Holtzman that he was certain she would "never use or condone such justifications for excluding those minorities who you consider to have more cachet, such as blacks, Hispanics, women,

Jews, gays, etc. . . . It takes guts to uphold the law when the issue is not (as Watergate was) particularly glamorous and the implementation strikes close to home." And if Holtzman acted in this fashion, imagine the lengthy roster of lesser politicians who did too.

Still, one objection was not likely to have much impact—otherwise it would have been impossible to open a group home anywhere in New York. Defeating a proposed site demanded sustained political intervention and substantial protest. As soon as the community learned that MPU planned a group home for adults in Astoria, Queens, next to the annex of the local Greek Orthodox church school, residents took to the streets. The pastor of the church supported the demonstrations and hundreds of people picketed the site, carrying such placards as NO RETARDED ADULTS NEXT TO 500 SCHOOL CHILDREN. Joining them was the president of the school's PTA, the principal of the school, and of course, the district's state senator, state assemblyman, and city councilman. As Michael Goldfarb, director of the agency that was to run the home, recalled: "The Greek community of Astoria opposed us, and I *mean* the Greek community. It was a bloc. . . . They operated very effectively. . . . Everyone who'd gotten six votes in the previous election got to Barbara [Blum] and said we oppose the site." All of them vowed not to be satisfied until the site was dropped, which it soon was.

In much the same way, State Senator John Marchi, one of the more powerful Republicans in Albany, threw his weight against a group home in his Staten Island district, for his heavily Italian constituents opposed it. In short order, OMRDD withdrew the project and in response to Marchi's charge that the district was burdened with a disproportionate number of group homes (which was doubtful), imposed a freeze on additional residences in the area.

Even where elected officials initially resisted anti-group-home pressures, determined opponents could often latch onto an irregularity, trivial or not, and so delay procedures that the state eventually abandoned the site. This was the case with 5327 Valles Avenue, in the well-to-do Riverdale section of the Bronx, the single most protracted episode in the group-home battles.

In December 1976, Young Adult Institute inspected the property and asked MPU to lease it; in February 1977, the FDC approvals were completed. At meetings that month and in April, MPU explained to the representatives of Bronx Borough President Robert Abrams its plans for Valles Avenue; in May and June, it requested a community planning board review. But the board dallied, postponing action. MPU then asked FDC to sign a lease with the owner effective August 1, which called for the group home to open September 1. MPU informed Abrams's office about the lease but neglected to tell the community board. However, YAI did not want to move clients in before the board approved and so decided to forgo the September opening.

The board finally met in October and the neighbors cried foul, charging that MPU was trying to sneak into their community. Abrams himself wrote to Blum, accusing her and MPU of proceeding in "an inept, improper, and self-defeating" fashion. If a lease had already been signed, "I am absolutely shocked since neither my office nor the community board was informed." The *Riverdale Press* quoted the Abrams letter and published editorials under headlines like TRAMPLING OUR RIGHT TO KNOW. Blum's rejoinder to Abrams that his office had been kept fully informed (with copies of all the relevant correspondence enclosed) never did get equal time or attention.

In the midst of these charges and countercharges, the board met again at the end of November and asked for time to locate alternative sites, a request that its assemblyman, state senator, and congressman all endorsed. MPU investigated some twenty sites that the board proposed, discovering that one was a thirty-room mansion not for rent or sale, another was a building with no vacant apartments, still another was a dry-cleaning store, and yet another had a landlord who was frightened to rent to retarded citizens, given the opposition to Valles Avenue (the circle rounded). By then it was May and opponents were able to complain that the owners had all along been receiving $1,200 a month rent from the state while still living in the house—and MPU's explanation that the lease had to be honored, and were the owners not there it would have had to hire twenty-four-hour guards, hardly quieted the critics.

Still MPU would not abandon the site. It was soon autumn, with elections approaching, the wrong time to antagonize a community, and then it was the start of 1979—all told, two and a half years since the site had been located. A new borough president now charged that if MPU was still unable to locate a suitable alternative, it was proof that Riverdale would never have a community residence, and OMRDD finally dropped the site. The owner received a penalty fee of a year's rent, and Valles Avenue was free of group homes.

These accumulated experiences make it relatively simple to offer prescriptions for certain failures. Look to place a group home in an ethnically cohesive area whose political representatives hold powerful positions, sign a lease or begin to make renovations before the community board holds a public discussion, let the owner of the house intend to remain in the neighborhood, and the opposition is likely to triumph. The principle holds for many collective protest actions: The greater the homogeneity of the protesters, the greater the chance of success. Thus neighborhoods whose residents were similar in terms of ethnic, religious, and class characteristics were far more capable of moving from particular dissatisfaction to effective protest. Almost inevitably, a group home generated some opposition; the family next door or across the street was bound to complain. But the critical consideration was whether its particular displeasure spread, and that depended upon the degree to which the community shared an identity of interest. In places like Astoria, with its lower-middle-class Greeks, and Flatbush, with its middle-class Jews, the answer was clearly yes. Put another way, community planning boards in such areas operated in a spirit of pure majoritarianism. Local rule paid little attention to the rights of minorities.

MPU's several years of experience with the community boards also yields prescriptions for success, strategies that can take advantage of the dynamic described here to win acceptance for group homes. The key to victory lay in discovering and cultivating constituencies within a community that splintered a united front. MPU had to find blocs that were ready to support the group home, whether for reasons of self-interest or of ideology, and thus break the unanimity of the community's opposition. At times, the attempt to mobilize such constituencies actually produced a majority in favor of a residence for the retarded. More typically, a significant minority forced prudent politicians to calculate how many enemies they might make by opposing the home, which encouraged them to keep a low profile or even to remain silent.

No one was more adept at finding potential allies than John Sabatos, a former Catholic priest who was in charge of community placement in Brooklyn. Born into a Slovak immigrant family, Sabatos had grown up in the borough, attended the local seminaries, and after ordination served in the local parish of St. Jerome. In his blue-collar neighborhood, where some 19,000 of the 25,000 residents were Catholic, Sabatos taught classes in the parochial school, conducted sessions on family life for newlyweds, and helped to oversee the construction of a convent (which, like many others, was destined to become a group home). He also encouraged parents with retarded children at home to bring them to special church services and classes. In 1970, Sabatos was asked to take over what was an essentially empty church in the heart of Bedford-Stuyvesant. The ministry was almost exclusively social service (only a few hundred practicing Catholics were in the area), and Sabatos turned the parish house into a halfway house for a dozen or so ex-offenders and delinquents.

After three years in the parish, Sabatos left the priesthood, but, let it be clear, not the church. Formally requesting and receiving a release from his vows, he continued to do as a layman pretty much what he had done as a priest—that is, practice social work with the handicapped, now at the Brooklyn Developmental Center. His personal ties to the church hierarchy remained close, a fact of critical consequence when he took over the community placement program.

Sabatos is proof that, Thomas Wolfe notwithstanding, not only the dead know Brooklyn. Sabatos knew it block by block, ethnic group by ethnic group, clergyman by clergyman, politician by politician. Ask him for a rundown on how the group-home effort was proceeding, and he will typically start with Community Board 1 (the Greenpoint neighborhood, supportive, Bishop Vicker is there and ready to help), go on to Board 2 (Father Murphy is in this very accepting Fort Greene district), and work his way through Boards 11, 15, and 18 (the list of dishonor). And all this knowledge came into play in locating group-home sites.

Between 1976 and 1981, Sabatos oversaw the opening of fifty residences. Some of his success reflected the fact that Brooklyn had more decent one- and two-family houses for rent at reasonable prices than the other boroughs; its neighborhoods were also more mixed in ethnic and class composition and more tolerant of outsiders. But Sabatos, through perseverance and political skills, made the best use of every advantage.

He worked especially effectively with the Catholic Church, a ready ally. The Brooklyn diocese had a deeper commitment to retarded persons than other dioceses; it also had available a large number of empty convents suitable for housing the retarded, and a network of bishops, priests, and agency directors ready to gather community support. Accordingly, when a Catholic agency wanted to turn an empty convent into a group home and rent it to the state for $15,000 or $20,000 a year, community approval came quickly. The two group homes in Community Board 1 were located in former convents and run by Catholic agencies; three of the five homes in Board 2 were run by Catholic agencies and two of them were housed in former convents; in Board 6, Park Slope, four of the five group homes were run by Catholic agencies and two used former convents. Of all the group homes in Brooklyn, some 30 percent were under the auspices of a Catholic agency and some 25 percent were in former convents. It would be a rash politician who would try to thwart plans that church officials and lay leaders wanted to promote.

Occasionally, a community planning board rejected one of these proposals, challenging the state's leasing of a convent as a violation of the First Amendment or arguing that by giving a convent over to retarded citizens, the Catholic Church was abandoning the neighborhood and altering its character. But the constitutional point was flimsy and John Sabatos persuasively informed a commissioner's hearing that "to bring those that are less fortunate under the [Church's] auspices . . . is the work of the Church. Rather than leave a building vacant, to do it in this manner is only to intensify the presence of the Church and its theological commitment to the works of charity to all, regardless of their state in life. So we do not view that causing the area to go down the drain, but rather as a reaffirmation of the mission of the Catholic Church."

To penetrate other Brooklyn communities, Sabatos carefully matched the sponsorship of the group home to the religious or racial characteristics of the neighborhood. Community Board 12, Borough Park, was a stronghold of Orthodox and Hasidic Jews, and so Bais Ezra and the Women's League, both under Jewish leadership, helped persuade the community to accept the Jewish retarded. In Board 16, Brownsville, the Federation of Puerto Rican Organizations administered two of the group homes and the black-run Brownsville–Ocean Hill Mental Health Clinic ran the third. Board 10, Bay Ridge, was a lower-middle-class Italian neighborhood and very distrustful of outsiders. But the Guild for Exceptional Children had long conducted an exemplary program there, and so Sabatos interested the agency in serving the Willowbrook class and then had its directors convince the neighborhood that three new group homes would not be intrusive.

All the while, Sabatos and his assistants carried on their own politicking, touching base with the local representatives and clergymen. They also visited the neighbors next door to a proposed group home and invited them to see programs in other areas. The strategy demanded time, energy, a thick skin, and a tolerance for failure, but it produced victories.

These tactics were equally effective in the other boroughs. When MPU wanted to open a group home in Long Island City (Board 2 in Queens), the agency director, Rick Kramer, worked closely with Father Walsh of St. Mary's Church to win community approval. They arranged for the public hearing to be held in the church, and the parish newsletter carried Father Walsh's admonition: "It's one thing to give money to help those less fortunate than ourselves, it's another to have them in our midst. I hope that at the meeting we can discuss this situation calmly and charitably. I hope that the feelings of some of our families are not hurt by un-Christianlike attitudes. After all, we have many loving, heroic families caring for their exceptional children, brothers and sisters. May the peace and love of Christ reign in our hearts that night." At the meeting, which Father Walsh chaired, Kramer described his agency, explained that half the residents would come from the immediate neighborhood, and suggested that the community appoint two members to the group home's admissions committee. The questions followed their usual pattern, from the home's likely effect on property values to the dangers the retarded faced from traffic. But there were also remarks that the retarded deserved decent living conditions, and the entire session was conducted with exemplary decorum. Father Walsh seemed to know everyone in the room by first name and kept reminding his audience (congregation) of its Christian duties. At the close of the meeting, seventy of the eighty people present voted to accept the group home.

Occasionally, MPU discovered a very different source of support, such as a real estate developer with extensive properties and vacant apartments. When Joel Levy of YAI was searching for a group residence, he contacted Al Moskowitz of the Lefrak organization, and Moskowitz immediately arranged to rent him eleven apartments in Lefrak City. In fact, over the late 1970s, Moskowitz became quite adept at putting together clusters of apartments and defending the arrangements before community boards.* The head of the company, Sam

*In one building, tenants opposed to the proposal convinced the woman tenant who was fourth in the string of apartments not to move. Moskowitz then wielded the stick and the carrot. He told her that MPU would settle for a string of three apartments (which meant she would be the immediate neighbor), and then offered her another apartment, several months free rent, and moving costs if she would vacate—which she did.

Lefrak, was happy to be of service, and as Moskowitz readily conceded, benevolence was also good business. MPU was a fine tenant, paying the rents on time and making few demands. To be sure, other tenants occasionally protested and used the occasion of a board meeting to try to wring concessions from Lefrak. They transformed a Board 7 (Flushing, Queens) hearing into a grievance session against Lefrak, complaining about too many roaches and too little heat. But Moskowitz calmed them down, the clients moved in, and MPU had a ready ally.

MPU's record demonstrated, first, that the process of opening group homes, like that of contracting with the voluntary agencies, created a constituency for deinstitutionalization. Once the consent judgment compelled the state to act in advance of political support, its efforts at compliance generated political support. As MPU leased former convents and rented Lefrak's apartments (at the same time encouraging not-for-profit agencies to expand their activities) the balance of interests altered. Now groups in the community stood to gain from deinstitutionalization, and often they were strong enough to neutralize, if not eliminate, opposition. When a community planning board meeting became a standoff, retarded citizens won.

Despite the many victories, the realignment in political influence ought not to be exaggerated. Although community residences had many more friends after the judgment than before, the movement could not expect to win its battles through politics alone. The Willowbrook residents remained a minority even with some well-placed friends—which raises a second critical finding about the placement effort: The class fared better when decisions were made under a system of rules than when decisions reflected unfettered public sentiment. Formal, quasi-legal procedures protected minority rights better than did plebiscites.

This explains the irony that the Padavan Law, for all its flaws, worked to the advantage of the Willowbrook class. Its procedures took time (as much as two years) and made adversarial proceedings the heart of the process for approval (giving ammunition to those who claim we are too litigious a society). Nevertheless, the process tended to increase compliance among all the parties—and when it was finished, the homes opened, and most important, remained open.

The Padavan Law did not clearly define the criteria for deciding when a group home altered the character of a community, but it did frame the conflict between the retarded and the community in very specific terms. The issue was not whether the clients were dangerous or unsightly or disorderly, but whether the neighborhood was already so saturated with other facilities that one more would make a difference. In this way, both MPU and the community had to prepare and argue their case in relatively narrow terms.

MPU asked its Community Residence Information Services Program (CRISP) to compile data on the number of social service facilities by community board, and to map their street location. MPU then decided that five blocks (or a quarter of a mile) was the minimally acceptable distance between another facility and a group home. The rule, to be sure, did not eliminate all bickering; some boards contended, for example, that not all facilities were equal and that a ninety-bed nursing home should count for more than one. But these guidelines, crude as they were, helped ensure that group homes would be dispersed throughout the city. However strong the temptation to overload one disorganized community, MPU's own procedures precluded it. In fact, MPU was so alert to saturation that it never lost a commissioner's hearing on the issue.

The community boards also found it useful to frame their objections in terms of the number of facilities. Scare stories might inflame a hearing or fuel protests, but a board that demonstrated that three large nursing homes were just outside the five-block boundary line was far more likely to have MPU cancel a projected group home.

These considerations help to account for the third and still more remarkable outcome of MPU's efforts: Communities invariably took their defeats gracefully. *Once a group home opened, it was never the object of vandalism or even picketing.* Not one group home for the Willowbrook class had to close down or transfer its residents because of the persistent hostility of local organizations. Not a single member of the Willowbrook class living in a group home was ever injured or so much as intimidated by antagonistic neighbors. Controversy preceded the opening of a residence. But once the home was in business, indifference, and even occasionally approval, took over.

Behind this achievement was MPU's readiness to back off a site when a well-organized community was incensed. Had it persisted, for example, in opening a group home next door to the parochial school in Astoria's Greek neighborhood, protest might have escalated. The location of group homes thus represented something of a compromise between the state and the citizenry. So, too, MPU was not averse to adjusting its placement plans to locate a home in the least desirable section of a highly desirable neighborhood and thus mute opposition. Brooklyn's Community Board 15, where a Save Our Community organization kept its lively vigil on would-be intruders, approved a group home for 3730 Shore Parkway, in part because the owner lived in California and could not be influenced by its opposition, but in part, too, because the block itself, although quite pleasant, was cut off from the rest of the area by a parkway.

The acquiescence of the communities also reflected the fact that group homes did not spark either an immediate or a long-term decline in property values. Widespread fears that the presence of the retarded on a particular street would create a selling panic and drop real estate prices were never realized. The state itself suspected as much, and in a moment of inspiration, asked Julian Wolpert, an urban geographer at Princeton University, to research the point. Wolpert selected forty-two communities with group homes (of which twenty-six were in Brooklyn and the Bronx and the rest upstate) and another forty-two without group homes (but matched for income and demographic features) and calculated the outcome of some 1,550 real estate transactions. He found that the property values "had the same increase (or decrease) in market prices." Furthermore, "proximity of neighboring properties to a group home did not significantly affect their market values," and the "establishment of the group homes did not generate a higher degree of neighboring property turnover than in the matched group."

The absence of a selling panic and the peaceableness of neighbors testifies to the diligence of the voluntary agencies in maintaining the group homes. The grass was mowed, the hedges were clipped, and the windows washed, which made the residences indistinguishable from the other homes on the block. Furthermore (as we shall soon see in greater detail), the residents were not left unsupervised and neighbors had no complaints about retarded persons conducting traffic in pajamas. Indeed, the residents were often too physically handicapped and too busy in programs to be on the streets very much at all. Neighbors could easily forget about them, and that dampened any impulse to sell a home or organize a protest.

The formal procedures that MPU followed contributed, too, to this successful outcome. Opponents exhausted a number of administrative and judicial remedies, and in so doing, exhausted themselves. With ample opportunity to argue their case, they were far more resigned to the home at the end of the hearings than at the beginning. To be sure, had the situation later proved disastrous, had the retarded gone about begging for food, the administrative process would have become irrelevant. But by the same token, were these procedures absent, the community might have remained so hostile as to be incapable of noticing that the lawns were mowed, the retarded cared for, and the real estate values holding firm.

Finally, these dynamics clarify the causes of the single most astonishing result of MPU's efforts: *The Willowbrook class did not end up in marginal neighborhoods.* The popular wisdom that group homes generally are located in deteriorating sections was not true in New York. To be sure, the very wealthiest neighborhoods, in Scarsdale or Sea Gate, used one or another tactic to exclude group homes (just as they kept out blacks and, in an earlier time, Jews). But these communities aside, the group homes appeared everywhere.

Investigating the typicality of neighborhoods in which the group homes opened lends itself especially well to computer analysis. Since the federal census collects and reports data on the socioeconomic conditions of households in units of several blocks each (called census tracts), one can compare New York City tracts with group homes to New York City tracts without group homes. Selecting which of the hundreds of pieces of information to use is not particularly difficult, for in measuring neighborhood conditions, one score generally confirms another. Such a figure as residents' average income correlates positively with residents' median education, which in turn correlates inversely with the percentage of female-headed households in the tract or with the number of persons on welfare. Using these very indices (and a few others, like median worth of property and percentages of blacks), and making borough-by-borough comparisons (since the city is too heterogeneous to allow for comparisons between a given tract and the city average), it turns out that neighborhoods with group homes were almost indistinguishable from those without.

In Manhattan and Queens, practically no differences emerged. The median housing value in Queens for group-home tracts (in 1970) was $25,013; without them, $25,867. So, too, 1.9 percent of the women in group-home tracts were on public assistance; in the others, 1.6. In Manhattan, white males made up 40.4 percent of the total population of group-home tracts, 34.9 percent of the population of non-group-home tracts. In group-home tracts, average educational attainments were 11.2 years and in the others 11.1 years. In the case of the Bronx and Brooklyn, the group-home tracts scored slightly lower than average on these scales, but the differences were not noteworthy to the eye or statistically significant to the computer. The Brooklyn group-home tracts had 22.1 percent female-headed households, the others, 17.5; residents in group-home tracts had completed a median of 9.8 school years; in the non-group-home tracts, 10.2 years. In the Bronx, the median family income in tracts with group homes was $8,152; in non-group-home tracts, $9,217.

So community placement was accomplished without putting Willowbrook's residents into the wastelands of the city, without altering property values, and without ruining neighborhoods. Sometimes a community's fear of change far exceeds the impact of change, at least on it. For the retarded children and adults lucky enough to move into the community, the change was momentous, in terms of both the quality of the care they received and the life chances they enjoyed.

9

Eyes On

Those who fashioned and implemented the consent judgment worried most about Willowbrook becoming synonymous with dumping, about the group homes scattered around the city turning into mini-institutions every bit as grim as Willowbrook's wards. But in fact, the deinstitutionalization of Willowbrook illustrates the possibility, even the feasibility, of establishing decent community care. In most instances, the group homes, at a minimum, offered adequate food and clothing and an environment that was free of harm. We will postpone for later the question of whether community care surpassed this level of acceptability, for without personal dignity and bodily integrity, intellectual and emotional growth cannot occur.

That the group homes achieved this standard was one of the few points of agreement among the MPU staff, the review panel, and plaintiffs' lawyers. Silent testimony comes from the absence of complaints to the court about abuse in the community; plaintiffs' attorneys appeared before Judge Bartels dozens of times about abuses at Willowbrook but never once about them in group homes. Hard evidence comes from MPU's audits, carried out under the direction of Vicki Toomey, one of Barbara Blum's most conscientious recruits. In May of 1979, Toomey and her staff inspected fifty-nine group homes and scored them on a five-point scale (excellent, good, satisfactory, poor, noncompliant). They found that the residences were in fine physical condition (thirteen excellent, thirty good, eleven satisfactory, three poor, and only two noncompliant). In management and organization—in maintaining, for example, complete medical charts and monitoring blood chemistries—forty-six of the fifty-nine homes performed in satisfactory or better fashion. Perhaps most impressive were Toomey's findings on "residents' rights," whether, for example, they controlled their own money and were free of restraints: Twelve homes scored excellent, seventeen good, twenty satisfactory, and only eight were poor and two noncompliant. As would be expected, the group homes that performed well in one category generally performed well in the others, and those that failed in one failed in others, so that the overall outcome followed a bell curve: a few exemplary group homes at one end, a few unacceptable group homes at the other, and most in the middle, altogether acceptable.

The audits that the Willowbrook Review Panel staff regularly conducted confirm that the agency was not merely patting itself on the back. Reports from its semiannual investigations of clients in the community were generally favorable. In May and June 1978, five panel audit teams (of two persons each) inspected the living arrangements and programs of seventy-three ex–Willowbrook residents (a sample drawn from six hundred in the community) and discovered that in most cases their physical and intellectual needs were being met. Over 90 percent of community residents followed a daily schedule that satisfied audit standards of normalization (going to bed after 10:00 P.M., eating dinner between 5:00 and 7:00 P.M.) and their physical environments were clean and well maintained. Perhaps most impressive, all but one of the residents received the required six hours of programming daily.

One year later, when three hundred more clients had entered the community, the panel audits reveal no diminution of quality. In a sample of 166 residents, less than ten were on inappropriate schedules or had inadequate clothing, or lived in a bedroom not up to standards; again, only one client was not receiving six hours of programs. Finally, in December 1979, in what turned out to be the last panel audit, seven teams visited *every* group home and UCP apartment and foster home to see how the 1,420 ex–Willowbrook residents were faring. "Generally all community class members," the staff concluded, "were provided with the least restrictive and most normal conditions possible when contrasted with institutional care." Two-thirds of the city's group homes were not in need of major repairs; 98 percent of the residents were enrolled in a full day program at a school or a vocational training workshop. The audit did identify problem areas—inadequacies in clothing, staff training, recordkeeping, and building maintenance. But the community system passed the test. These were homes, not SROs.

This high level of care reflected well on the voluntary agencies that administered the group homes. Catholic Charities was morally committed to helping the disabled, agencies like YAI had exceptionally talented leadership, and parent-run agencies would not tolerate abuse. Furthermore, deinstitutionalization was not undercut by a lack of funds. The court and the decree made it possible for OMRDD to command the necessary resources. To be sure, some voluntary agencies periodically suffered from cash-flow problems, but since each Willowbrook class client brought no less than $25,000 annually, the agencies could provide the necessary staff and programs.

To conclude from this experience that when voluntary agencies are well run and well funded, community placement will succeed is fair, to a point. There is no shortage of programs in (or out of) human services that have not responded well to an influx of dollars; foster care of dependent children is one (and national defense another). A community planning for deinstitutionalization ought to be aware that the more intimately involved a private agency is with the clients and the better funded its operation, the greater the likelihood of success. But if it stopped there, if it concluded that all it must do is line up the agencies and pay them their price, the results might still be unsatisfactory.

The missing ingredient is monitoring, setting the standards of care and devising mechanisms to secure compliance. In the Willowbrook story, carefully constructed audit instruments and close supervision of the group homes ensured that in most, albeit not all, instances the scandals of institutional care did not recur in the community. Surprisingly, quality control, either as an idea or in practice, has not made substantial headway in human services. Yet one cannot assume that intervention will be successful without intricate and systematic regulation.

The child welfare system in New York illustrates the point. The city typically administered foster care in a casual, almost shoddy fashion, making little effort to discover what it, or its clients, were receiving for its money. As Carol Bellamy, New York City Council president, aptly concluded in 1979: "The City approaches its foster care system like a slot machine player: It spends millions of dollars and hopes for the best."

Behind this passivity lay bureaucratic inertia about checking into the expenditure of public moneys and into the well-being of other people's children. Behind it also was an assumption that charitable agencies could be trusted to expend funds in the best interest of the children. The city did insist that agencies be incorporated and that their social workers inspect the foster homes. But these were pro forma regulations. The city rarely dispatched its own investigators to examine fiscal management or levels of care.

The neglect was not salutary. Over the years, the child care system had its share of scandals, usually uncovered by the press or by public-interest lawyers, not by city officials. But the problems were ignored or explained away. No one took them as symptomatic of the need for public bodies to monitor private agencies.

Barbara Blum, operating in the shadow of the court and the panel, instituted more rigorous oversight mechanisms at MPU. Her deputy, Karin Eriksen, created a system of monitoring to be carried out by case managers. Each of them was to supervise twenty to thirty clients living in foster homes and group homes. They were to visit the clients on a monthly basis and report to MPU on their condition and progress. If they uncovered deficiencies, they were to advise the voluntary agency on how to correct them. Should the problems persist, they were to inform MPU and then themselves arrange to obtain the necessary services.

It was an unusual design, going a step beyond child welfare but not entirely consistent. The auditing provision was more stringent than in foster care; the case managers were hired by and responsible to an outside body, MPU, not the voluntary agency itself. But initially MPU did not provide very precise guidelines. It insisted that clients have adequate clothing and that community residences be homelike in appearance and routine, but it never specified what such standards required. More, the case managers were supposed to serve as consultants to the agency, thereby blurring lines of responsibility. If the agency did not improve its performance, was the agency or the consultant to blame? Still more confusing, the case managers were to get the clients services when the agency had not, an assignment hard to accomplish and one that turned the auditor into a broker. The person obliged to detect deficiencies was to correct the deficiencies—which put the monitor in the awkward position of monitoring her own work.

To the review panel, Eriksen's plan was "not sufficient . . . to determine compliance with the Consent Judgment." Sharing none of Blum's confidence in the voluntary agencies, the panel organized its own audit teams and audit instruments—and in the process became a more vigorous monitor than even the consent judgment had envisioned. Although the decree required a semiannual panel report to the court "concerning the progress made in carrying out the provisions of this judgment," it said nothing about method or content. The panel filled in the blanks in the most exacting fashion.

The panel's insistence on conducting its own audits, collecting and analyzing data and then submitting to the court intricate and precise reports, reflected a series of mutually reinforcing considerations. Dominated by a professional and independent-minded staff, the panel was unwilling to accept the state's own findings at face value. As an arm of the court, it also believed that every piece of information it submitted had to be able to withstand cross-examination. Most important, the panel was convinced that by scrupulously auditing every stipulation of the decree, by insisting that each client receive all his or her entitlements, it was compelling the state to adopt a new system of care, community care.

Accordingly, the panel's audits first sought to measure the extent to which OMRDD was fulfilling the deinstitutionalization mandate. How many clients were moving monthly from Willowbrook and the developmental centers to bona fide community placements? How many of OMRDD's offices were being decentralized, shifting from the institution to a neighborhood location? (This change was important not only for symbolic purposes but also to increase accessibility of the staff and to encourage a reliance upon the medical and social services in the community.) Second, the panel looked to monitor the degree to which the new community residences met the requirements of normalization. Did the routines of the group homes resemble those of a normal household? Were the clients receiving both the material goods and the teaching programs that would integrate them into the community?*

The panel defined for itself an exhaustive and exhausting task, not allowing the scope of the monitoring to become an excuse for superficiality. Critics, of whom there was no shortage to begin with and who multiplied as these policies went into effect, charged that the panel gave the judgment all the sanctity of the Ten Commandments. The panel, not in the least dismayed, was prepared to demand that OMRDD

*While all this energy was being expended upon community placement, the panel was also concerned with the level of care at Willowbrook and at the other developmental centers. Were the institutionalized clients protected from harm? On the whole, the answer to this question was no, but we reserve for Chapter 13 a fuller discussion.

meet every one of the decree's 352 stipulations and it would score the outcome.

The day-to-day responsibility for this assignment went to the panel's executive director. Jennifer Howse's style matched the panel's. She was well-nigh indefatigable, ready to do business over an 8:00 A.M. breakfast or 10:00 P.M. drinks. Before joining the panel, she had developed licensing standards for Florida's mental retardation facilities, and it became her task to design and conduct audits of Willowbrook and the group homes that would be "comprehensive in scope and specific in content." Howse and her staff developed several remarkable instruments, turning an already detailed consent judgment into an even more specific checklist.

Where the decree stipulated that "residents shall be provided with clean, adequate, and seasonably appropriate clothing," Howse broke out sixteen separate questions, many with subsections, *all* of which had to be satisfied before compliance was met. Her first one read: "How many of each of the following does the resident have specifically assigned to him/her? Underpants, Undershirt, Bra, Slip, Socks, Shoes, Belts, Shirts, Blouses, Pants, Skirts, Dresses, Sweaters, Light Jackets, Heavy Jackets, Hats, Gloves, Raincoat, Galoshes, Rubbers, Pajamas, Bathrobes, Slippers, Bathing Suit, Tennis Shoes, Wallet, Handbag and other Accessories." The auditor was next to ask who selected the clothing, how it was laundered, and how often it was changed—and then to look at the client to see whether he/she was wearing "a complete outfit" which was seasonable, stylish, and age appropriate, and finally, to check whether his/her haircut was "contemporary."

Without the slightest defensiveness about so thorough a list, Howse explained to the court that dress "affects the person's self-image as well as others' image of the person." More, if a client had no bathing suit, he would never learn to swim; if he lacked a wallet, he would never learn to handle his money. Providing these items, Howse understood, did not guarantee that normalization would be achieved—but without them there was no chance of success.

It may seem surprising, but OMRDD agreed to the suggestion of plaintiffs' lawyers that it and the panel audit jointly and accept the findings as conclusive. In this way, the state accepted the panel's definition of compliance and modes of measuring it, down to the last bathing suit and tennis shoes. OMRDD assigned some of its staff to the panel to learn how to conduct such an audit and the two groups then went out as a team—with little friction between them. OMRDD might have contested the panel audit instrument, which if not a redefinition of the judgment certainly went beyond it in specificity. To be sure, the panel would probably have won such a contest, and by avoiding it, OMRDD did gain some credibility with the judge. But it was a concession that only commissioners confident about fulfilling the decree would have made.

Notes from the Field
Sheila Audits the Auditors
May 16, 1978

I met Kathy Schwaninger of the panel staff at 9:00 A.M. at the Queens Development Center (a renovated World's Fair motel on a highway). Schwaninger began reading the case record of Christine, a twelve-year-old, nonambulatory, severely retarded black girl. She explained that since it was impossible to investigate every client, the staff had worked out a sampling technique and this resident fit the various criteria—date of exit from Willowbrook, level of disability, and so on. For three and a half hours Schwaninger pored over the record to see if it contained all the requisite information. In this record the medical and dental examinations were undated and the Willowbrook exit plans did not seem to match the client's community program. Karla Perlman, who supervised the case managers, came in periodically to try to be helpful, but Schwaninger bristled and told her she'd call her when necessary. Perlman continued to hover, wanting a good grade on this test and finding Schwaninger a tough instructor.

At twelve-thirty, Schwaninger finished and we went to lunch with Perlman and Christine's case manager. Conversation was fitful. Perlman asked questions and Schwaninger replied in monosyllables, unwilling to go into details until she had a better sense of the case. The case manager was too nervous to eat. This was her first audit.

At two o'clock we arrived at Christine's school, located in the basement of a housing project. Forty children between nine and eighteen years old were in attendance, most nonambulatory and nonverbal. The school was not in an ideal setting, but the classrooms were filled with equipment and colorfully furnished. Schwaninger introduced herself to Christine, who was wearing a freshly pressed red dress and had a red ribbon in her hair. She smiled when Schwaninger told her how nice she looked but made no sounds. The teacher was instructing the children how to find their coats—each hook was marked with a different symbol (different-colored shapes); each student was given a symbol (Christine's was a yellow square) and then taught to identify it as her own and go to it for her coat. Christine, to her delight, found her coat for Schwaninger. Schwaninger next went to the school office to examine the records. She quickly indicated to the administrators that Christine's goals were not clearly defined, which meant that they could not keep careful track of her successes and failures. The school officials disagreed, convinced that they ran a good program and did not need such elaborate records. Schwaninger repeated how important these records were, in terms of both satisfying the decree and doing the best by Christine.

At three-thirty, we went to Christine's group home. The living room was clean and decently furnished. In Christine's room, Schwaninger opened the closets and drawers; the clothing was plentiful and laundered. She checked the bathrooms, noting that the adaptive equipment for nonambulatory clients was all in place and no odor was present despite the fact that most of the clients were not toilet trained. In the kitchen, she read the menus on the wall, peered into the pots on the stove, and opened the refrigerator. Everything was in order. Schwaninger examined the residence's records and inquired why outdoor recreation programs were not regularly scheduled and why the indoor recreation was not linked to the learning programs at school. The case manager, upset, complained that she could not always get the agency to do things her way. After a short discussion, Schwaninger announced that there would be a formal "debriefing" next week, at which the agency and the case manager would review the findings with the panel staff. On that note, we left.

May 18, 1978. Back at the Queens unit at 9:00 A.M. Schwaninger examined the record of Mark, a fifteen-year-old, ambulatory, profoundly retarded adolescent who had lived at Willowbrook for ten years. The record was complete, with all programs and medical examinations listed. Another lunch with Perlman and Mark's case manager, who said that the group home we would be visiting was terrific. The residents were among the most disabled, the kind that everyone said could never leave Willowbrook, and yet their progress had been fantastic.

At 1:00 P.M. we arrived at Mark's group home, a converted convent. The home, with its four floors, seemed too large for the children; the bedrooms were small and narrow, more suitable to cloistered sisters than active children. This was one of the few group homes allowed to run a school program in-house, but it was only a temporary allowance. Within eighteen months, the clients were to be out at programs, or living with foster families. We met the house manager, who was eager to describe the children's accomplishments. He explained how exciting it had been to teach children who had never walked on a sidewalk before to negotiate curbs and watch for traffic. Now staff took them shopping regularly. The neighbors had not been friendly, unwilling to talk to them on the streets and turning down invitations to come to the home. Staff told us it had tried to get the children into the Police Athletic League but was rebuffed. The house manager will try again because he does not want the youngsters isolated.

We toured the home. The bathrooms had a whiff of urine, but were clean. Schwaninger tested the toilets, all working. The house manager explained that the children threw toothbrushes and hairbrushes into them, and so daily visits from the plumber were common. Still, every client had a toothbrush and hairbrush; the staff bought them by the dozen. The living room had little furniture and no curtains. Staff explained the clients had destroyed the furniture. Now one staff member was assigned to each client to try to modify the behavior. Mark's bedroom was also sparsely furnished, but he had plenty of clothing and underwear. Although the clients were only partially toilet trained, the staff insisted upon underwear, not diapers, for it improved training.

We went next to the program rooms to see Mark and his instructor. Mark shook hands with Schwaninger but made no eye contact. He wandered aimlessly about the room, not focusing on any objects. The teacher explained that progress had been slow but she was not discouraged. Schwaninger checked Mark's records and found the goals and objectives appropriate. Mark was not on psychotropic medication; staff did not like putting even the hyperactive children on drugs. Schwaninger was delighted with what she saw, and told the staff so then and there.

Epilogue: October 1979. I received a call inviting me to a meeting at which the group home would complete the arrangements for transferring the children to foster homes. I went out, to find the home and the residents transformed. Furniture abounded; all the children were toilet trained. The staff worried that perhaps the residents were leaving too soon, not yet fully prepared for foster home life; they sounded like anxious parents sending their children off to school. The home will now be getting a group of residents no less handicapped, and the staff will have to begin training all over again. But this time they know it can be done.

Audit styles hardly varied from one panel staff member to another, or from one year to another. The occasion was always highly formal, indeed so formal that Jennifer Howse, who would remind us not to miss a review panel executive session, was initially reluctant to grant us permission to accompany her auditors. (Her fear, which we allayed, was that our presence might dilute the official character of the moment; we scrupulously played fly-on-the-wall, saying nothing as we read the case record over the auditor's shoulder or accompanied her around the home.) The auditor's demeanor was half officer of the court, half retardation expert. Carrying the thirty-page audit instrument, she scored *every* item.

Immediately before the audit, panel staff conducted a one-day training and refresher seminar. (The price of our observing the audit was to attend these sessions, which were technical to the point of boredom but useful to ensure audit consistency.) Orders were not to miss any items on the list, and we never saw auditors, even at the end of an exhausting day, take the word of an agency employee on whether a client had adequate clothing. Instead they consistently opted for an eyes-on, trust-no-one approach; they climbed the stairs, checked the supply, and in suspicious cases, examined whether the size of the clothing matched the size of the client. Without the slightest embarrassment or apology to the staff, auditors opened doors, cupboards, closets, lifted pot covers, and did about everything but look under the carpet. The only compromises were calculated ones. Better to audit one client intensively than ten superficially, and so a sampling technique was adopted. Better to give the agency advance notice about which client would be examined than have the agency claim, rightly or wrongly, that the relevant client records were temporarily unavailable. And better to make announced visits than midnight raids—for neither the clients nor the agencies lived in a police state.

All of this made the panel audit about as pleasant an experience as an IRS audit. There was little patting on the back or small talk, and the fewer the diversions, the sooner the business would be completed. No one liked the audits, neither the panel staff who performed them nor the agency staff who received them. But the panel saw them as crucial to ensuring the quality of the system, while the agencies saw them as unwarranted intrusions into their domain.

To the panel, the audits first, and most obviously, kept the score. The staff reviewed its check sheets and made its findings, stipulation by stipulation; the group home was either in or out of compliance on an item, with nothing in between. If it failed to supply galoshes or bathing suits and yet supplied everything else, it was scored out of compliance on the clothing item. This approach made the final reports almost unintelligible; even the most determined reader got lost in the details. Neither Jennifer Howse nor Kathy Schwaninger (when she succeeded her to the post of executive director) presented the audit results in more than one-dimensional terms. They never devised a weighted scale that differentiated among the stipulations, that recognized that a poorly set table was not the equivalent of providing inedible or insufficient food. In part, the panel did not think it appropriate to differentiate among the several hundred decree requirements or to grade on other than a yes-no basis. The reports were going to the court—and one either obeyed or disobeyed a stipulation, with no findings of half-guilt. In part, too, the very detail of the reports enabled the panel to identify inadequacies and frame remedial measures.

The panel staff was confident of being able to test and teach, to grade a performance while giving instruction. But the premise was doubtful. The panel was an outside auditor, and those being examined used the occasion not for learning but for presenting proof. A case manager who was too nervous to eat lunch with an auditor was not going to retain lessons about subtle procedures. An administrator who thought precise recordkeeping unnecessary was not likely to accept advice from a court investigator. Some points undoubtedly stuck. Reminding a residence counselor to check the school's goals for a client might spur greater coordination. But the pedagogic role of the audit was hardly its strength.

A much more significant, albeit unintended, benefit was the psychic reinforcement and political leverage the audit gave staff members committed to realizing the decree. Their numbers were greater than might be expected, for a dedicated group of people worked not only for Barbara Blum in the central office but in the borough offices as well. Since all of them had willingly joined as "provisional staff," they had other aims than securing their niche in the bureaucracy. Their official and admittedly contradictory responsibilities—to monitor, educate, and provide services to the clients—still gave considerable room for initiative. In effect, a cadre of staff were ready to use the panel to get the job done right.

"Right" had a very special meaning to them: to maximize the benefits for the Willowbrook class. In public welfare systems, social workers often consider the taxpayer their ultimate client. They take their assignment to be reducing tax expenditures by interpreting eligibility for entitlements as narrowly as possible. Even in child welfare, the case manager typically identifies with the foster parent or the voluntary agency and so will reinstitutionalize a troublesome child rather than insist that the caretakers devise a new plan to keep him in the community. At MPU and in the borough offices, on the other hand, the workers considered the actual client to be the ultimate client, a judgment which produced remarkable results.

Nadine Miller and the case managers she supervised in the Brooklyn unit exemplify the novel effects of this orientation. Miller would not have joined a Park Avenue child welfare agency, for her career was as unusual as her outlook. As an adolescent, she had been moved from one foster care setting to another, which left her acutely suspicious of benevolent organizations; later, as a single parent, she had been shunted from one social worker to another, which gave her an empathy for the plight of the powerless. "If you've been beaten up as much as I have," she once commented, "you'd respond this way too." When her own child was still young, Miller decided to attend college at night, and to support the two of them, she became an attendant at the newly opened Brooklyn Developmental Center. Unlike many others there, she enjoyed working with the retarded residents and arranging activities to bring a focus into their aimless lives. She had little patience, however, for the institutional regimen, even as she moved up to take charge of a ward. The isolated facility relied too heavily on drugs and too little on programs to help the residents. As soon as MPU was organized, Miller applied for the position of borough coordinator to oversee the case managers. With little competition—few others wanted to take a provisional position—she got the job.

Miller assembled a team whose interest in community placement was almost as keen as her own. Many of them had a strong religious identification and a sense of calling in serving retarded persons; at weekly meetings, crosses, skullcaps, and turbans abounded. Others on her staff were disillusioned with working in institutions and wanted to promote alternatives; still others worked for the rights of the retarded during the day and for the rights of blacks or women or gays at night. As would be expected, turnover was high and few remained for very long. But while there, they did well by their clients.

First, Miller and her case managers had to pry the residents loose from Willowbrook. Institutional sabotage never let up, even several years after the decree. When the case managers went out to identify clients for placement, they encountered hostility. "When you said you were from the MPU, you got strange looks, as if to say you would be costing them their jobs." They also encountered subterfuge. "For over a year I thought Julio was a staff member," because the ward attendants tried to hold on to higher-functioning clients who helped out with chores. Willowbrook also tried to get rid of the most difficult clients: "The first people they would refer were the behavior problems," a case manager explained. "You would say this agency is not taking acting-out people and [you] would get a name and read the record where there was a lengthy history of aggression." At times, the Willowbrook staff would launder the record or insist that the behavior problem had been resolved—and so in self-defense the case managers had to interview and observe the clients scheduled for release. When time for discharge neared, they organized the exit conference, made sure the clients had enough clothing (nervous that the voluntary agency would not accept them in rags and tags), and then were on hand on discharge day to make sure that the staff did not "discover" some ailment, like stomach worms, which had purposefully been left untreated in order to postpone placement.

The result of successfully navigating this hazard course was not only to release a client to the community but to seal a relationship between client and case manager. "You were the one that placed the person there," remarked Walt Adams, who worked for Miller and eventually succeeded her. "How do you turn off at five o'clock when you go home and you get a phone call from a caretaker or group residence staff or the police department or someone at Kings County G [psychiatric] building. What do you say? 'I'm sorry, this is my off hours'? No, you get into your car and you go over."

In this spirit, case managers tried to ensure that even the most difficult clients, those the group homes or the public schools were ready to expel, remained in the community. "When a person is thrown out of a program, you have to figure out how to get him back, how to get him services." Every client who was forced to return to Willowbrook, no matter how extreme the disability, was presumed to represent a major staff failure, and under such an ethos, defeats were rare. From 1976 to 1980, some 350 Brooklyn residents left Willowbrook or the Brooklyn Developmental Center for the community, and only twenty-two of them went back. In five cases, the fault lay with the group home or foster parents, and second placements were quickly and successfully arranged. In the other seventeen, the clients' aggressive behavior was too difficult for the group homes to handle; nevertheless, case managers were able to arrange a second placement for twelve of them. Over the years, only five clients were reinstitutionalized for long periods, an enviable record for Miller and her staff.

All this energy had not been expended to see Willowbrook-like conditions reappear in the community, and in a variety of ways the Brooklyn group worked to prevent abuse and neglect. Before a voluntary agency opened a residence, Miller and the case managers would meet with its personnel, review the disabilities of the clients, the types and number of staff required, the day programs and the evening recreational schedules—and if the larger agencies were not always receptive to such oversight, the smaller, less experienced ones certainly were. Once the home opened, the case managers visited at least monthly, more often if they suspected that levels of care were substandard. If problems persisted, Miller and the case manager would contact the agency directors and try to devise a remedy, perhaps hiring a new house manager or arranging more programs. Often conditions did improve. When they did not, Miller raised the stakes—alerting Blum's office or, by one or another means, the review panel.

To Miller, the panel "was like God." The audit questions that others found tedious in their detail she found helpful in instructing her own staff. If anything, she was disappointed that the panel was not even more active in expanding clients' rights; she wanted each client to have a key to his own locked wardrobe and would never have allowed sectarian agencies to run sex-segregated group homes. Still, she understood that the panel was "an independent body," and when problems with a group home proved intractable and MPU was moving too slowly, Miller or one of her staff got word to the panel in roundabout fashion, for state employees were not supposed to wash their dirty linen in the panel's offices. Miller also had some say in choosing which homes and which clients would be the object of intensive panel audits, and she arranged to put the weakest home high on the list. This tactic lowered her borough's scores and earned her a dressing-down from her supervisors—but she calculated that the pressures from a failing audit would help improve an unsatisfactory setting.

The panel monitoring also stimulated MPU to expand its own auditing mechanisms. Barbara Blum, in her second year at MPU, organized a system for "incident reporting" by which group homes were to notify MPU in writing whenever clients suffered injuries. The procedures were not foolproof, and some staff used them to avoid blame for client injuries. Still, they provided clues to which homes were having difficulties. Miller's staff, for example, tallied the reports, and when incidents in a particular home increased, they went out to survey the situation.

The panel impact on monitoring was even more apparent when Jennifer Howse succeeded Blum at MPU in the spring of 1978. (That Coughlin appointed Howse to the post testifies not only to her talents but to his readiness to mollify the panel and implement the judgment.) Inheriting a staff much larger than the panel's, Howse promptly established a unit to inspect every group home run by the voluntary agencies. It was this analysis, completed in the spring of 1979, that found almost all the homes to be in compliance and identified the five that were substandard.

However useful the educational and supportive functions of audits, their ultimate function is to correct abuses, to discipline or exclude incompetent agencies or malicious staff. Uncovering violations is of little consequence if no sanctions are invoked; in the end, monitoring comes down to a question of power, to the review panel's or OMRDD's ability to compel the responsible parties to meet their obligations.

The review panel's community audits did uncover deficiencies caused by the state's policies. In some instances, especially where the changes would not be costly, the review panel and MPU quickly agreed on how to resolve them. For example, when the panel learned that most group-home staffs were woefully ignorant about the methods of record-keeping, MPU agreed to initiate more rigorous training programs. In other cases, when changes would be more costly and OMRDD held back, the panel flexed its muscle and issued a formal recommendation to the court, which OMRDD then accepted. In this way, the panel was able to get the state to increase expenditures for client clothing and make its delivery more efficient.

But when panel audits located gross deficiencies and OMRDD disagreed on the remedial measures, the two sides ended up in court, and the panel almost always won. When audits, for example, uncovered a case manager-client ratio that violated the panel's understanding of the consent judgment—and given the importance of the case manager's role, the panel would not compromise—the result was a successful appeal to Bartels. To be sure, the panel could not run to court on each and every problem that an audit uncovered. It was reluctant to complain that too few OMRDD offices had moved from Willowbrook to the community—the link to client well-being was too attenuated—and even this panel husbanded its ammunition.

In much the same way, when the audits uncovered major inadequacies in a group home, everyone's first response was to bring in technical assistance. The case managers or a special MPU team or panel staff would explain, yet again, to the agency staff how to order food or arrange medical care. If problems persisted, MPU might pressure the agency's directors to revamp its procedures or hire other staff. In 1978, Nadine Miller's case managers began to hear that residents from the Colony South group home were arriving at day programs hungry and without their medications; incident reports also revealed several suicide attempts and a mounting number of physical injuries. The proverbial straw was an incident in which the Colony South staff sent a client who had just attempted suicide alone in a taxicab to a large hospital emergency room to get his wrists stitched. MPU offered technical assistance, but improvements came so slowly that Miller's staff threatened to resign if the clients were not removed from the home. ("The residence has reached such a point of debilitation that the program is no longer salvageable," it declared. To keep the home operating would compromise "the personal integrity, morality and ideals which have guided us in every aspect of our job performance.") After such protests, the Colony South board of directors hired additional staff and reorganized the home—which produced a more creditable program.

The audits also enabled MPU to cut its losses, so that an agency scoring low on compliance would not be encouraged or allowed to open a second home. Initially, Blum had been eager to cooperate with the well-established Jewish Guild for the Blind. The Guild wanted to open a group home for its own adult blind and mildly retarded clients and MPU agreed to rent and renovate a residence provided that the Guild admitted seven blind Willowbrook clients. The contract was signed but the Guild did not fit its programs to the judgment. MPU auditors were convinced that the agency had little idea of what it meant to create a homelike environment (a lounge was located in a windowless hallway) or to manage retarded clients (auditors found them sleeping on urine-stained sheets). Nor was it keen on training clients to independence. As one of the staff put it: "I'm not going to push a client off the sidewalk when he is not ready simply because I have to comply with the decree." After this experience, MPU did not want any more Willowbrook residents going to the Guild.

The audits were not adequate to every situation. Neither the panel nor MPU was very effective in imposing its way of doing things on a borough staff determined to resist their intervention. The spirit of cooperation so apparent in Brooklyn extended to Queens, where Karla Perlman, Nadine Miller's counterpart, closely monitored the group homes in a less flamboyant but equally effective fashion. But it did not reach into the Bronx, where Dr. Herbert Cohen, director of services, and his deputies adopted a variety of stratagems to avoid panel and MPU oversight.

From the day the decree was signed, Cohen diligently pursued his own goal, which was not deinstitutionalization but the prevention of institutionalization. To Cohen, Willowbrook represented "a competing priority," and he would follow his personal preferences, even if it meant depriving the class of some services mandated by the decree.

Cohen and his staff believed that the panel was composed of amateurs-outsiders-ideologues who knew little about programs and administration. The consent judgment was so petty-minded as to conceive of treatment only in terms of "a statistical norm or a staffing ratio," and to foster "adversarial relationships that disrupt day-to-day operations." Cohen's assistant, David Kligler, argued that the Bronx team should not be controlled by fiat, and Dorothy Jacobs, head of the case managers, insisted that the review panel thought it possessed a "monopoly on knowledge, truth, and the American way of life."

Practice followed conviction. Neither the central borough office nor the case managers maintained extensive written records. (Detailed documentation seemed to them just the sort of pettifogging stipulation that the panel would devise.) Cohen often divided up the case managers' assignments to give exclusive responsibility for the Willowbrook class to one person on each of the five borough-wide teams; as a result, this worker carried a heavier load of clients than the decree allowed and many class members were not visited monthly. But this division of labor freed the other team members to visit the non–Willowbrook class clients—who were more central to Cohen's agenda.

Working with the Willowbrook class seemed the least desirable assignment. Monitoring lagged and clients' rights were not vigorously advocated. The Bronx had more class members without case managers (forty-seven in December 1979) and a much larger number of case loads out of compliance with the 1:20 ratio than any other borough. The Bronx also returned fewer Willowbrook residents to the community. Staff blamed the number of bombed-out neighborhoods and the lack of cooperation from the voluntary agencies—genuine obstacles, yet other boroughs overcame them.

Neither the panel nor MPU could reorder Cohen's priorities. First Blum and then Howse prodded Cohen to increase the number of placements, but to little avail. The panel scored his operation low on their audits, but Cohen did not revamp his organizational pattern. One reason for administrative powerlessness was Cohen's ability to avoid a major confrontation. The Bronx always managed some placements and responded quickly to instances of neglect. In 1979, Tom Coughlin ordered Cohen to leave the Bronx and take up the directorship of Letchworth (the equivalent of Jack Hammond sending Bill Bronston to the back wards). Cohen, however, was able to beat back the attack, mobilizing professional colleagues, political supporters, and parents who shared his priorities.

As the Bronx experience demonstrates, audits worked best when crisis management could resolve a situation, when a specific problem of well-bounded proportions was at issue. They were less capable of turning a system around. Audits could extinguish a fire, but not guarantee that the fire department was efficient, that the alarms functioned properly, and that the buildings were up to code.

So it was with some of the group homes that OMRDD itself operated. In 1978, when Governor Carey was about to open his campaign for reelection, his staff wanted to placate the civil service unions. The unions, fearful that closing Willowbrook would cost them dues-paying members, were criticizing Carey in particular and deinstitutionalization in general. To head off the union opposition, Robert Morgado promised that over the next twelve months OMRDD would open fifty group homes and staff them with Willowbrook personnel. Although the quota was never met, a handful of homes did open. Panel audits frequently noted broken furniture and inoperative toilets and scored the homes for noncompliance, but sanctions used against the voluntary agencies could not be applied to state-run residences. Civil service regulations made it practically impossible to fire staff. And political calculations intruded. Since the homes represented the only remnant of a larger pledge, they could not be closed down.

Audits also made little impact on the way Robert Schonhorn ran his United Cerebral Palsy programs. Schonhorn had rescued the state at its moment of trial and OMRDD treated him gingerly. While the other agencies negotiated their contracts with MPU, Schonhorn dealt directly with officials in Albany. He was acutely suspicious of auditors from MPU or the panel. When Barbara Blum tried to assign borough case managers to clients living in UCP apartments, Schonhorn resisted; it was the responsibility of his staff "both inside and outside of the residence to determine and meet all client needs." He went so far as to implement an internal system of monitoring that duplicated—and therefore obviated?—MPU's, with one critical difference. The UCP case managers reported only to him, not to MPU.

Schonhorn well appreciated that only the constant pressure of the review panel had prompted New York to undertake so massive a community placement effort—and thus made it so dependent upon UCP's services. Hence he would never attack the panel publicly or stage a confrontation, such as excluding its auditors from UCP apartments. Instead he appeared to do his best to ignore them.

Neither MPU nor the panel could alter UCP policy. Were another voluntary agency to demonstrate recalcitrance, MPU could prevent it from opening additional group homes. But Schonhorn held too privileged a position and thus, even as the auditors complained that some of the UCP apartments were poorly supervised, Schonhorn wrote new contracts with OMRDD and expanded his operation.

One last monitoring failure must be acknowledged. Reforming Willowbrook proved impossible. Whatever options the Review Panel had were inadequate to the situation. Close the place down if it was so wretched? That was precisely what the suit was about. Prohibit new admissions? That had been the policy since 1972. Let someone else run the facility? OMRDD had actually transferred administrative responsibility for several buildings to UCP State, but that had the effect of posing many of the same problems in a different form. Insist that OMRDD expend greater funds and improve staffing ratios? That, too, occurred, but with only marginal improvements. Go before the court and complain? Plaintiffs and the panel did that again and again, each time embarrassing the state but not affecting the institution. In sum, Willowbrook posed every logistical difficulty that the auditors confronted with the Bronx Developmental Services, the state-run group homes, and with UCP State, and took them to an extreme.

By its negative example, however, Willowbrook does clarify some of the considerable strengths of monitoring within the community. Conditions at Willowbrook were indisputably below those in the worst group homes. Neglect and abuse thrived on the isolated and hidden character of the place, like some microbe that flourished in dark and airless locations. Few eyes penetrate an institution—more precisely, few eyes except those of a staff habituated to look away or forget what it has seen. The semiannual visits of a panel or an MPU auditor publicized what was otherwise obscured. But these visits were not sufficient to upgrade the standard of care. To audit the institution was to take its temperature and write a prescription which was not likely to be filled.

The community settings, on the other hand, were in the public eye and the consent judgment put them under a magnifying glass. A client going to a local school or workshop could not be sent in rags and tags without provoking an immediate crisis. Indeed, such a client could not be sent hungry or ill without provoking a crisis. The list of those who saw a Willowbrook class member living in the community included not only the direct care staff and house manager, but the bus driver, several teachers and instructors, other retarded and nonretarded children and adults, neighbors, shopkeepers, nurses, doctors, and dentists, and perhaps even museumgoers, churchgoers, moviegoers, and circusgoers. Then add to this roster numerous monitors, and the formal audit becomes the last in a long line of informal audits. Thus the task of supervision was simplified because it was carried out so frequently and by so many different people. The monitors had an army of assistants.

The full significance of this point is not always appreciated. Many of the voluntary agencies complained about being audited to death, that hardly a day passed without someone coming through with a checklist. Yet in protecting the helpless and dependent, the more eyes on, the better. To be sure, visibility alone will not guarantee decent care. But when it is combined with diligent monitoring, residents are more likely to be protected from harm.

To put these observations in the context of the courtroom, Judge Bartels was not omniscient. He could not reach down to ensure that each client was properly clothed or fed. Nor could he (or the panel) implement an overall reform of the system of care. The judge, maybe even more so than the panel, was a fire fighter and he could not reorganize the bureaucracy. But such concessions made (and they are not minor ones), the court (and the panel) created a climate in which the most progressive and determined administrators would come forward, at both the higher and the lower echelons, and the court helped them gain and exercise power. In the world of social policy, where the cliché is that nothing works, it is no small thing to say that courts can help correct particular abuses while encouraging a few bold advocates to put a new system in place.

10

Life Chances

Notes from the Field
The Day After Christmas at Sister Barbara's Group Home

From: Robert Zussman
To: David and Sheila

I arrived at the Lincoln Apartments in the Bronx around 10:30 A.M. The place was lousy with staff. The tree in the dining room still had the litter of the previous day's attack strewn about it, including a few unopened gifts. The kids were scattered about playing with their toys—Angie with an "XL Robot," asking him questions, Spencer with Simon (another electronic game). The staff was helping the kids figure out how the games worked and helping them play. The TV was on but no more than one or two of the kids were watching it. Kathy drafted me to help her write a letter to her grandmother; Frank and Ted were sitting at the dining room table with one of the counselors, Frank munching on an apple and helping Ted to do the same by cutting up pieces and handing them to him.

The free time did not last long, though. Marty, the residence manager, had scheduled a full round of activities for the day. Frank and Kathy headed out to lunch at Burger King with two of the women counselors. Mario and Spencer, along with one of the older boys from the apartment downstairs, went to Marty's nearby apartment for lunch. Ted and Albert, the two younger boys, joined three of the younger kids from downstairs to head off for a puppet show. I went with them.

This was my first ride in an ambulette. We brought the kids downstairs, one staff to one kid, where an ambulette had pulled up, outside the door of the building. Each kid was wheeled on by the ambulette driver, who then attached the wheelchairs to the floor of the van with special built-in pegs. Three of the staff piled in the front, I sat on the floor in the back with one other. The driver took off across the bridge and into Manhattan, then down the East River Drive. He had on the radio and this served as the main entertainment. Only once did one of the staff point out a sight, a tugboat plowing its way up the river.

We arrived at our destination—a very unlikely-looking ex-storehouse on Sixteenth Street. The ambulette driver got out to check that it was the right place, which it was. He came back and we wheeled the kids out. (No one had a very clear idea of exactly where we were going or what we would see there except that it was some kind of puppet show—which turned out to be only minimally accurate.) A woman showed us to the tiny elevator, into which we could barely squeeze two kids in wheelchairs and an attendant. We went up to the tenth floor of the building—to a loftlike area which served as the studio/playhouse for a very, very small repertory theater. In addition to the five kids, the five staff, and the various players, only four other people were present. Without any special explanations (either to the kids about what they were about to see or to the others about who we were), the kids were rolled up to the front and given programs. I sat down in the next row back, just behind the kids. The two women staff decided not to stay—despite the encouragement of one of the playhouse folk that the show was good.

The show was an adaptation of a Japanese fairy tale about a girl, her puppet goose, a samurai, and his servant, and their adventures on the way to a magic mountain in search of the demons who were ruining the fishing in the girl's village. The kids *seemed* to enjoy it—at least, Bert laughed quite a lot throughout it (I think at the right parts, although I wasn't quite sure myself all the time), as did a few of the others. Ted seemed to be paying attention, but I have absolutely no idea of whether or not he liked it or understood it. When I asked him afterwards I got no response, at least no response I could make sense out of, and so far as I can tell, no one else asked him either. In any case, the women came back from their shopping expedition and we headed out.

We got back to the apartment around five or five-thirty. The staff, slightly grumpy because they had been on longer than their normal hours, disappeared quickly, leaving the kids with the evening staff. I lingered, and wound up staying for dinner. Dinner was quite good, in fact—leftovers from Christmas dinner consisting of ham, collard greens, yams, and jello. The older kids, though, did not eat much, explaining that they had stuffed themselves at their various lunches and didn't have much appetite left. Ted and Albert ate with a bit more enthusiasm. Kathy and Frank talked, although with less animation, about their lunch at Burger King. Marty wandered through and said hello to everyone. Helen, the nurse, came in with a new gift (actually an exchange of gifts with one of the kids from downstairs because, as she explained, "Santa made a mistake")—a quick-draw, shoot-the-bad-guy, electronic game, which she claimed was good for hand-eye coordination.

I took a couple of shots, watched Ron take a couple, and, yes, even the kids had a turn, and then I left.*

For all the theory extolling the benefits of group homes for severely and profoundly retarded persons, the experts had very little data upon which to build their case. No one knew whether family living was really feasible for them, whether their multiple handicaps would lend an institutional quality to any setting. The principles of normalization envisioned that caretakers as parents and residents as siblings would follow ordinary routines; but whether staff members could assume a parental role with clients who were so deeply disabled, and whether the residents, who had lived so long in an asylum, could begin to interact with others, or whether their home could be integrated into the block and neighborhood, remained obscure. When the consent judgment was signed, community placement for profoundly and severely retarded persons was an idea still untested.

The experience of Sister Barbara Eirich in opening her first group home in the Bronx demonstrated just how novel and unpredictable the entire enterprise was. For all her familiarity with runaways and physically handicapped children, she was ill-prepared for the complications and frustrations of her new undertaking. She did have several guiding principles. First was normalization, which to her meant giving her charges the human warmth and emotional support they deserved. She took the concept as a psychological imperative to be as supportive and affectionate with the residents as with family members. Second, and almost a corollary, "Community people should care for community youth." Neighbors even more than experts were best suited to help retarded people. The first four staff members that Sister Barbara hired to serve as "houseparents" in her two apartments had no "experience working with the multiply handicapped [but] they did show interest, concern, and a willingness to learn." Third, Sister Barbara was determined to serve the most handicapped, those who traditionally seemed most in need of institutional care. All of her first twelve clients had cerebral palsy, and three also had a history of seizures; all had been diagnosed at Willowbrook as severely or profoundly retarded, and a majority had no verbal skills whatsoever. Mario, for example, was bright but severely crippled; Spencer was ambulatory but could only stammer, while Ted was just able to crawl and smile—at least, that was their level

*See the Sources and Methods section for a discussion of our approach.

of development upon leaving the institution. Finally, Sister Barbara resolved that none of them were going back to Willowbrook. "No matter what problems emerged, no matter how difficult, we had to find solutions, as no child . . . was ever to return to the institution." She even took her houseparents out to Willowbrook, ostensibly to help her select the children, but really to make them aware of its sights and smells, so that they would understand and share her mission.

The first rush of enthusiasm that came with rescuing twelve souls quickly gave way to a bewilderment bordering on panic. The disabilities of the youngsters, who ranged in age from eight to eighteen, were actually more extensive than their medical records or Sister Barbara's own observations had suggested. A new staff, with little by way of preparation, was frantically remaking twelve to fourteen soiled beds a night and no less frantically changing the diapers of eight of the residents during the day. (The Willowbrook records had indicated that most of the children were toilet trained.) Mealtime was an hour-and-a-half ordeal. Four of the children were unable to feed themselves, two required extensive supervision to prevent choking or regurgitation, and eight drooled so badly as to interfere with chewing and swallowing. All the while, three of them had frequent temper tantrums and two others cried much of the time.

The duties were so onerous and exhausting that Sister Barbara's plan of organization had to be modified. She had expected to run this home exactly as she had run the home for runaways: a two-shift staff, on three and a half days, off three and a half days, maximizing personal contact with the children. (Instead of having to adjust to new faces several times a day, the children would interact with two groups of caretakers.) But no one seemed to be able to handle the Willowbrook residents for so long without a break, especially not when they were up much of the night and shuttling from task to task during the day. Somehow Sister Barbara had to schedule shorter shifts and yet not lose intimacy—a problem rarely confronted, because few had attempted to organize a group home for such exceptionally handicapped people.

Sister Barbara devised an ingenious solution. She introduced shifts but insisted that staff share *all* (and she meant all) tasks. Usually shifts and specialization of function go hand in hand, a division of labor accompanying a division of time. What Sister Barbara wanted, and what she got, was six mothers and fathers for twelve children. She did appoint a residence manager and hire a principal cook and housekeeper, but the assumption was that every counselor helped with cooking and cleaning as well as with the residents. "I do basic child care," one counselor explained. "I give the kids basic exercise; if they do something wrong, I talk to them. I do their hair, their nails, give them baths, do the ironing, teach them how to care for their teeth. I also do washing and cooking, especially when the cook is out." In short, "I teach them to be independent, let them do what they can for themselves. It's like being a mother."

A consulting psychologist visited the two apartments weekly, but in both title and function he was an adviser to the counselors, not their supervisor. "The psychologist has ideas," one of the staff commented, "but he can only give you what he knows. Sometimes our own ideas work better. In the beginning we were blind about toilet training, jaw control. Some of his suggestions work, but if we see shortcuts, we take them."

The routine produced a special attachment between the counselors and the residents, as testified by low staff turnover. In January 1980, three and a half years after the home had opened, almost half of the original counselors remained. Their occupational histories did not predict such continuity. Most were black and Hispanic women, living in the Bronx, who had worked sporadically as factory hands or domestics. Although they did have complaints about the job—the pay was too low and the future insecure—very few of them were looking for a new position. To be sure, they did not possess the skills or credentials to get an edge in a tight employment market; none had college degrees. Still, had they been less committed to the position, they would have quit, moved on, and looked elsewhere—as they had in the past.

Hence one takes them at their word when they describe the satisfactions that they found in the assignment. "I'm never going to find another job with this atmosphere. It's more than a job, it's a way of life." Or: "You got to have care and love, that's it. Without it, you wouldn't be able to take a job like this. It's a lot of care, pain, and work." They grumbled about the household chores not because the tasks were menial but because it took them away from the children—and it was caring for them that they liked most. They delighted in "hanging around, playing with the kids, watching them progress." And the rewards came from the residents' responses. "Coming in and seeing the children cheerful, you know they care for you. Their wanting you, it makes you feel good." In effect, the staff members were being asked to invest *themselves* in the assignment. It was not their skills that counted but their personal commitment, and particularly for people with few educational advantages, the opportunity was as rare as it was welcome. "You have to keep going or the kids will stay the same. They are mirror images of the counselors. I see myself in what they do. This is the only home they have. It can't just be the job. If you're not going to make an effort, you should just get out."

This attitude did not emerge from a textbook knowledge of the principles of normalization. The staff had little idea what the term meant (although when it was explained to them, most thought it sounded "like a good idea"). Nor did it emanate from a professional awareness of the abilities and disabilities that accompanied profound or severe retardation—most counselors did not know the diagnostic label or IQ score attached to each resident's record. Rather, they had been selected for their personal characteristics (warmth and involvement) and then given ample opportunity to display them. Hence they tended to minimize the intrinsic mental handicaps of the children, and to focus on their potential for progress. Unwilling to accept a diagnosis of incurability, not caring that the mental age of the resident was scored four and a half, they did not make the label self-fulfilling.

They often ascribed the residents' difficulties to physical, not intellectual, handicaps. People who lifted youngsters in and out of wheelchairs and onto and off toilets several times a day experienced their charges as more immobile than retarded. Sister Barbara inadvertently encouraged this attitude. Soon after the children arrived in the home, she arranged orthopedic surgery for many of them, discussing with the staff the advantages of the operations. (Even if the surgery could not restore the use of a leg or an arm, it could straighten a limb, thereby giving the child a less weird appearance.) The result was that counselors' descriptions of the youngsters were positive in tone and optimistic in outlook, emphasizing strengths, not limitations.

> Mario can read a little. He pronounces clearly. Spencer has trouble in talking, but he is coming along good. They can both express themselves. They get very emotional when you can't understand them. They understand, but have trouble with speech.

> Spencer can't walk or crawl. He doesn't speak clearly. He has no fine motor coordination. But he can read, do math, remember things. One night at dinner we were discussing the dance. Spencer was sitting there

drooping and drooling. Then he suddenly looked up and said, "June 12," and he was right.

Some can't move without our assistance. We are their arms and legs. Some seem just as free as so-called normal people. They can all communicate, even the ones who can't talk. Like Spencer, he can play Simon and Maniac [electronic games] and he wins nine out of ten times. I can't beat it one out of twenty. Once I was helping Spencer onto the bus and a dude I know asked what I was doing with retards. I told him that I had taken Spencer to Alexander's and he had played Maniac. I said to the dude, "That guy you called a retard, he played Maniac and he won ten times. Now who do you think is a retard?"

To be sure, some children had more trouble learning than others. But to the staff, a slow child was "lazy or stubborn" and required "more patience." The failing became one of personality, not cognition, giving the staff an incentive to correct it. Indeed, the counselors were quick to describe each child's personality. (Mario was "a riot," Spencer "very intelligent," and Ted "affectionate.") All of this made them ready to respect the residents' preferences. They encouraged them to select their own food, games, and television programs and were pleased when residents liked different activities and different foods, for choice spoke to personhood.

Notes from the Field
Sister Barbara's on a Fall Day

From: Robert Zussman
To: David and Sheila

During dinner, a meal shared by the staff and children, the staff nurse appeared. At first she sat quietly and chatted casually with some of the kids, mostly asking them about certain things at school, particularly what they ate there. But she had another item on her agenda as well. The residents, she explained, directing most of her comments to Spencer, were the apartment lease holders. This was, of course, a fiction, as the clients had not signed the lease and their signatures would not have been accepted, even if they *could* have signed, without Sister Barbara's assurances. Nevertheless, the nurse said that since the residents were the lease holders, Sister Barbara thought it might be a good idea for Spencer and Mario to go to a tenants' meeting. "Would you like to do that?" she asked them. Mario smiled and said yes. Spencer, whose verbal skills, despite an insistence to the contrary from the staff, appear to me to be quite slight, looked up and smiled an open-mouthed smile. There was no further discussion, except an "O.K." from the nurse. No one asked, and no one offered an explanation about what it meant to sit in on a tenants' meeting.

A question: Is the normalizing effect of sitting in on a tenants' meeting enough to offset the effect of possible embarrassment that the kids will face there?

After dinner, two of the smaller boys, neither of whom can speak, were taken into the living room. One was placed on a sofa, lying in his pajamas with his head up on the armrest. The other was placed (I say placed because neither could have put himself into this position) in an armchair, head up on one armrest, feet draped over the other armrest. Both were facing the television, which was tuned to the news. Both looked extremely comfortable, but neither was watching the TV. Their eyes were directed elsewhere and certainly neither could understand very much of what they were seeing.

A question: Could these children have asked to watch TV or was this a choice made for them by the staff?

Marty, the program manager, arrived quite excited, as he had just arranged for two of the residents to go to a Mets game the following day. He explained that he had been promising to get them tickets for months. He also explained that these two were the only ones who were Mets fans rather than Yankee fans. When he told the kids about the tickets, they registered agreement but no particular enthusiasm. Later, when another staff member suggested to Mario, who was to go to the Mets game, that they do something together the next day, Mario had already forgotten about the game. Later, when Mario was about to go to sleep, the staff person came by with the copy of the Mets schedule and put it up on the wall in his bedroom. As he put it up, he turned to Mario and asked, "Is this where you want it?" He got no answer, or at least no answer that I could see or hear, but went ahead and put it up anyway.

A question: How does the staff know that Mario is a Mets fan and not a Yankee fan? Was the idea of going to a baseball game the residents' idea, or was it an idea "suggested" to them by the staff? Will the schedule of the Mets game later be referred to as an item that Mario "put up himself" on the wall?

Spencer and Mario were left sitting together after dinner in the dining room, with the stereo on and with a staff member who was bantering with them. At one point the staff member noticed that Spencer was wearing a Special Olympics T-shirt. He asked if he had been in the Special Olympics. Spencer did not answer, but the staff person realized that he had not been. He then asked, "Where did you get it?" Spencer looked up from his normal position, which is head slumped and eyes crossed, opened his mouth wide in a sort of smile, and pointed a crooked arm at Mario and said something like "e-e-e."

Question: Was this a "staged" event? That is, did Mario really give the T-shirt to Spencer, or was it a gift "negotiated" by the staff? Are the two "really" friends, as the gesture from Spencer to Mario tended to suggest, or is this a friendship created by the staff by leaving the two together on the basis of their both being males of roughly the same age? Is their friendship real in the sense of being spontaneous, or is it manufactured by the staff?

After dinner, one of the staff members asked Mario about his "girlfriend," a teacher at the school who was recently married. The staff person said that all of the kids were heartbroken when she married and asked Mario why she "broke up" with him. Mario answered that it was because he had too many other girlfriends. Later Mario showed me pictures, one of which was of the teacher with a man whom Mario referred to as her "real boyfriend."

Question: The staff member's kidding Mario about having and losing a girlfriend was clearly normalizing. Mario himself joined in. But Mario also recognized that it was a myth, as evidenced by his reference to the "real boyfriend." Does it matter that Mario recognizes the mythical quality of the normalizing process?

The staff's job is predominantly physical care—changing clothes, bathing, moving, and feeding their charges. Doing this work for other people's children is usually considered demeaning, handling urine-soaked clothes, being drooled on, and so on. Yet the staff shows no apparent discomfort with this aspect of their work, and no apparent resentment of the residents for "subjecting" them to these demeaning tasks. Rather, the staff treats the residents with considerable affection. Why should this be so?

The first impression of group-home life at the Lincoln Apartments may be of an elaborate puppet show. Normalization seems a script for the staff-puppeteers to follow as they manipulate the resident-puppets. One puppet is very bright, another very funny, another very affectionate, but all these characteristics appear to be imposed by the staff on residents who are too handicapped physically and mentally to be capable of scripting their own parts. So when one resident wears a Mets cap and has a schedule of the team's game on his wall, the staff is assigning him an interest that he does not possess. Similarly, when the residents sit in front of the TV set with their legs up, the staff is arranging a scene. When two boys of the same age are said to have exchanged gifts, once again there is the suspicion that the staff has set the stage and written the lines. The group home takes on the quality of a performance—an amiable one, to be sure. The atmosphere is relaxed and the residents well cared for; there is no bad puppet. The staff relates to everyone without making anyone into a scapegoat. So even if group homes were nothing more than elaborate puppet shows, that would justify them.

Sustained observation of the daily routine alters this initial impression. Perhaps the enterprise had begun as a puppet show, but in *Pinocchio* fashion, life had been breathed into the puppets. The residents, too, were involved in making some of the decisions. They were not simply plopped in front of the TV, but often "asked" for programs by giving the staff signals that a casual observer might miss. Albert and Ted, both nonverbal, had word boards (one with thirty words, the other with eighty). When they wanted to watch television, they would move a spastic arm until it more or less hit the character for TV. The staff would respond by positioning them in front of the set. There is no way of knowing how much they understood of the program. But they made the request, and that required effort and forethought.

The residents' imprecise gestures meant that the staff, like parents of an infant, had to listen and watch for clues. What was surprising was how many signals the residents transmitted. Sounds or flailing gestures that at first appeared random were deliberate attempts to gain assistance.

Spencer wanted me to pull him up on his wheelchair. He could not yell, "Hey, pull me up," but had to point to the phrase on his phrase board: "I want . . . to be pulled up." However, since his phrase board was on the floor during dinner rather than on his chair, he first had to get me to hand him the board. All of this required my being able to interpret a rather imprecise point of the hand from him as a sign meaning: "Let me have the board." Thus even a relatively simple message from Spencer required energy on his part and an ability to interpret his action on my part.

When I arrived, Ted was in the living room, "watching TV." I went in to say hello. He slid off his chair and crawled (something he does with only enormous effort) over to the game chest and pulled out—or rather kept shaking his head until I pulled out—a Monopoly board. We "played" for a while, until we both got bored, with some highly modified "rules." He seemed to be getting a kick out of the rhythm of the game, rolling dice, being handed properties, seeing me move his piece and give him money.

There was an unspoken contract between staff and residents, which both honored. The staff had taught that it would respond to signals by residents that expressed their own will. The residents, in turn, made the effort, knowing it would be rewarded.

Over dinner I fed Albert, who cannot feed himself. Albert, as it turned out, had a distinct preference for a tomato-cucumber salad to the peas and carrots also on his plate. But his making this preference known was entirely dependent on my asking him before each bite: Tomatoes? Peas? Chicken? and waiting for a nod yes or no.

In this fashion, residents and staff built up trust which prompted the residents to make greater efforts to communicate more complex thoughts. They were willing to risk failure, knowing it would not bring shame.

As I arrived, everyone was talking excitedly about an upcoming party to celebrate the third anniversary of the home. The residence manager came in soon after to ask some of the staff about people who might be coming. Ted, through a series of grunts and points on his word board, somehow managed to get across that he wanted an old teacher of his, Miss Greene, to come. When the residence manager realized who Ted meant, he said her name and Ted's face lit up. The manager promised to go and call her, and he did.

Later that evening, Miss Greene called back. The person who answered the phone told her about the party. Ted got on the phone and spoke in a language that I think only he can understand, but his voice followed the cadence of regular conversation. Ted remained excited about having talked to Miss Greene, and wanted to show me on his board what he did when he last visited her. He pointed to a number and to "time" to show me the hour. Then he pointed to play or eat or sleep or dress to show me what he did. He did this for fifteen or twenty minutes, while Kathy, one of the other residents, helped interpret.

The staff, perhaps unconsciously, urged the clients to communicate even more. Maybe they asked too much, at times setting goals that the residents could never reach.

At one moment in the evening, the phone rang. Mario yelled out, "Phone," and Spencer yelled out something which I, at least, could not understand. One of the staff members got up to get the phone, and as she went she said, "Why don't you get it? You guys just sit there and yell, 'Phone, phone.' If you want someone to get the phone, get up and get it yourself."

But in some instances, the residents were clearly determined to be heard.

Ted began crawling toward his room about an hour before dinner one evening. I asked him if he wanted to go into his room and he nodded yes. I asked him if he wanted to get onto his bed and he nodded yes. Then Ted, whose typical expression is a smile, puckered his lips into a frown and began to cry. One of the staff members joined me and asked him what the matter was, and of course she got no answer. Then she asked, "Are you angry?" A shake of the head no. She asked, "Are you feeling sick?" A shake of the head no. "Does your eye hurt?" (Ted had been home from school that day with a slight eye infection.) A shake of the head no. "Does your head hurt?" A shake of the head yes. She then assured Ted that she would get him an aspirin, which would make his head feel better—she did and it did—and cautioned him in a friendly tone: "Why didn't you tell me what the matter was? How am I supposed to know what the matter is if you don't tell me?"

All of which returns us to the baseball game. The youngsters may not have known batting averages or players, but they grasped essentials and, poignantly, their own limitations.

I said to Mario while we played catch that the ball he had rolled to me across the table curved. Mario was skeptical. Later he said to me in a questioning tone, "They threw it harder than this at the Mets game, didn't they?" Mario is aware of his limitations but happy that he could throw what someone could describe as a curve ball. If he had not been to a Mets game, would he even have known what a curve ball was?

I asked Mario if he wanted to take a walk. He said yes, and so we did. First we headed up 145th Street, passing a sporting goods store with a lot of sneakers in the window. Mario, who regularly asks the manager to get him a pair of sneakers when his casts come off, said, "Let's go in." He looked at the sneakers in the display case but told me he didn't want to buy any now because "they'll be old by the time I wear them."

The formal programming requirements in the home that were called for by the review panel were transformed. In the evenings, one of the staff members was supposed to work with one client, teach him a lesson, and then record the results on the chart. The counselors, however, were uncomfortable relating to residents in so didactic a fashion, and so teaching went on more casually. The dining room table became the desk, with everyone, staff and residents, joining in to applaud or groan at right or wrong answers. This home was not a classroom.

And it certainly was not an institution. There was no nursing station at the apartments, no separate space for staff that was off-limits to the residents.

The time before dinner was spent around the dining room table. Frank's grandmother came to visit and Frank, Spencer, and Mario were at the table. Conversation wandered. Frank's grandmother talked to him, but also to Spencer and Mario. One of the staff started to color in a coloring book. So did Mario, when the staff member stopped. Another staff member explained she'd just been grounded by her parents for staying out till three in the morning. Other staff members and Frank's grandmother gave her advice. ("You should never have gone home. What were you doing about so late and why? I hope you had a good time at least.") The conversation went on for half an hour. On the one hand, there was no self-consciousness about the kids' presence, no staff lounge to retreat to for privacy. It was normal conversation and anyone who wanted to could join in. But on the other hand, the kids did not. Spencer played with his robot, Frank listened, and even Mario, who usually joins in, listened too.

Indeed, no one on the staff had ever worked in an institution, or wanted to. "No one has any reason to be institutionalized," insisted one counselor. "There is no quality care in institutions. Most employees are just marking time. If someone wants to do more, he has to fight too much against the status quo." Others echoed this sentiment. "No one should be in an institution. When the kids first came here they were in bad condition. They've improved a lot, but they still talk about Willowbrook and how they were treated. If Ted hadn't been in Willowbrook, he could probably talk now."

The staff also liked the home's neighborhood location. Not only was it more convenient to walk to work, but much of the stigma that clung to institutional employment disappeared in the community. In fact, staff found friends and relatives supportive. "They say it's nice that I have the heart to do it," reported one counselor. "They encourage me. If I get discouraged, they say don't quit, stay there." Even the neighbors were accepting. "In the beginning, the local people were concerned about the residents. Now they are all friendly. In the summer, kids come over and talk to them and ask them for a walk."

Was the group home, then, integrated into the community? Yes, in a very particular way. The group home enabled the residents to become part of a community, not so much in a formal and instrumental way, by their purchases at a store, but in personal ways, by giving them contact with a range of people interested in their welfare. Thus the staff was more eager to take clients home with them than to take them around the corner for a trip to the grocery store. They were more prepared to have friends come and meet the residents than to go to the bother of pushing the wheelchair out to the elevator, then out on the street, then to the shop, and then back again. They had little urge to display the clients to the community (to deliver a message that they were not freaks) or, for that matter, to interpret the community to the clients (to teach them to cross on green). There had to be a reason for the outing—to eat at Burger King, or even to drink at a neighborhood bar.

Ever since his visit to the bar, Mario, with the apparent help of some friendly and sympathetic teasing from the staff, has grown enamored of the idea of getting drunk from time to time. In fact, his expressed wish for his own birthday was to go out to a bar and drink with some of the staff. Sister Barbara was concerned about the health risk, and asked the staff to explain to Mario that drinking is not "adult," and that the "really adult thing is to know when you can't drink." She also suggested that when they take him out (which she allowed), they buy Malta, beerlike but minimally alcoholic, and of course they did.

The success Sister Barbara achieved was so notable that she became a star witness in cases where it became important to educate a judge about group-home life. Since the residents had made so much progress in daily living skills (from toilet training to tying shoelaces to using their word boards) and since they were obviously enjoying themselves (giving reality to such unavoidably vague phrases as "increasing life chances"), something of a mythology began to spring up around her. Some claimed she had the ability to look into the eyes of residents at Willowbrook and tell which ones were not really retarded—marvelous testimony to how ordinary life at the Lincoln Apartments appeared. To others, she was a saint, capable of accomplishing any task by dint of her extraordinary sense of mission. But simpler explanations will do. This group home represented a coherent design that effectively translated normalization into a surrogate family, intimate and affectionate.

A second and radically different model attempted to translate normalization into practice by emulating the classroom. Here the direct care staff was to approximate teacher-therapists, not affectionate parents, and the group home was to approximate a school, not a family. Experts would maximize the developmental progress of the retarded.

Young Adult Institute most effectively realized the strengths of this model. Although the agency ran several hostels and workshops in the

1970s, the consent decree transformed its operations. By 1979, YAI was running fifteen hostels and employing over 150 direct care staff.

In keeping with a classroom model, YAI had a personnel director, who worked out of the agency's midtown Manhattan office, recruiting candidates with high educational credentials. It required a college degree with a major in psychology, social work, or special education, and some experience in the field of retardation (through a day program or a summer camp or an institution). To be certain that the candidate would "interact well with the residents," YAI demanded, first, a group interview, then an individual interview, and finally a demonstration of hands-on skills at the group home. It gave special preference to applicants who had worked with the agency, particularly in its college internship program. If Sister Barbara looked for patience, understanding, and community ties to bring cohesion, YAI looked to a common professionalism.

YAI's ability to recruit such a staff for direct care positions was astonishing, for the assignment involved changing diapers, cleaning up, and feeding residents—tasks most college graduates were reluctant to do. The key to success lay in the agency's internal organization. Staff understood that YAI was rapidly expanding and that it would appoint its supervisors (house managers) and coordinators (with responsibility for several group homes) from the direct care staff. Hence counselors had an excellent chance for quick promotion within the organization.

Given this prospect, loyalty went not to the individual group home or even to the clients, but to the agency. Staff at the residences turned over much more quickly than at the Lincoln Apartments, but YAI directors Joel and Philip Levy were not disturbed. They were seeking to hire well-trained personnel with interchangeable skills, clinicians capable of developing the clients' full potential.

In January 1979, YAI opened a new residence, Waterside, on the edge of East Harlem in Manhattan. The agency leased the entire floor of a newly completed apartment house and turned it into a spacious setting for ten residents, with an office, a living room, a dining area, and single and double bedrooms. The residents were all severely or profoundly retarded and many had additional handicaps, from blindness to severe behavior problems. Each required substantial assistance with ordinary tasks, from eating to dressing to finding their rooms. Most were ambulatory, but practically none of them could talk or were toilet trained. They were at least as disabled as those whom Sister Barbara cared for, perhaps even more so.

The majority of Waterside's staff were in their twenties, unmarried, with a small preponderance of women over men and blacks over whites. Many of them had come through YAI's internship program and intended to remain with the agency. ("It's a very good job in terms of career opportunities and job satisfaction.") They were oriented to graduate schools and professional organizations, not to unions.

Staff agreed that good counselors had to be well-trained clinicians, with a textbook knowledge of retardation, normalization, and behavior modification. "I think it is important," one counselor explained, "to have a good academic understanding of mental retardation. In school you learn sensitivity to certain needs. Personally, I'm glad I took special education. I'm using it." Another remarked, "You have to be sensitive to the mildest changes in the clients. You have to be observant and flexible. College education gives you this sensitivity."

Their training made the staff optimistic about prospects for teaching the residents. College education "affects the way you look at things. You develop a more professional approach, a more clinical approach. You don't see problems as insolvable, but just as work to be done." The more difficult the client, the greater the challenge. In fact, the word among the staff was that supervisors assigned the most withdrawn or aggressive clients to the most skilled counselors.

The pedagogic intensity at Waterside was markedly different from the relaxed atmosphere at Lincoln. (No one could hang out at this group home.) The counselors were looking for therapeutic strategies that might bring a withdrawn client out of his inner world or calm the anger of a disturbed one. Accordingly, many counselors found the job exhausting. "I get burned out regularly; every few months I have to take a few days to myself to recover. I don't think anyone should be a direct care worker for more than three years, because they get too burned out and the clients need someone with a new, fresh approach. It isn't fair to them."

Assignments at Waterside were more formally defined than at Lincoln. A therapist served as a therapist and not a cook (unless something untoward happened to the cook or cooking was a recommended program). But within each assignment, the direct care staff had much room for initiative. YAI gave "a lot of freedom to be creative. It's mainly up to us what we are going to work on for goals. We discuss it with the psychologist and everyone, but basically you do what you feel the client needs. Once a goal has been set, it's written down and everyone [working with the client] does it the same way.*

The daily routine at Waterside followed closely on this classroom model.

> Time is limited in the morning, but otherwise we have a lot of freedom about how we work. The guys get up at seven. As morning counselor, I'm responsible for making sure they are up, dressed, have breakfast, schedule their medical appointments, make sure their medication is on hand, and make sure they get to the workshops. We also have a morning orientation where we get everyone together and talk about how they're dressed, how we're proud of their effort, who has medical appointments, and if they're going to the workshop after. I like the evening better because I can spend more time with the guys. In the morning, everything is rushed. In the evening, I work with two clients, teaching them daily living skills. I teach sign language and toilet training. We set goals—three goals for each client. I make a list of the client's needs and choose three that are most important. With Gloria, her goals were eating, drinking, and toileting. Once she learned these, she would have goals like dressing. I think teaching is the most important.

The assignment of two clients to each counselor determined the grouping of the clients. At Lincoln, all staff worked with all residents; at Waterside, staff were assigned to clients by level of functioning. Each therapist worked with her two clients in their formal programs and recreational activities.

The clinical-minded staff described the residents by level of functioning.

> They're low-functioning and multiply handicapped. They don't have good daily living skills. Mary is verbal but she has a mobility problem, because of her gait and her seizures. Patricia is about the highest-functioning. But she has emotional problems. She rocks, sucks her thumb, makes mad dashes across the house to take something from someone. She's deficient in socialization and verbal skills. Karen has good daily

*Giving direct care staff such autonomy was unheard of at Willowbrook. Therapy aides, as they were called, were just that—aides. The job description required them to be "following suggestions of a therapist," moving the clients through "structured exercises . . . within the framework of very special instructions and guidelines." Under this formal division of authority, no professional or would-be professional would go to work as an aide in an institution.

living skills but she is stubborn. She does little without prompts. Her performance depends a lot on her moods.

Only the cook, one of the few nonprofessionals in the home, described the residents in the language used at Lincoln: "Florence sweeps the floor and sets the table. Sandy can set the table with help. Sarah loves to wash dishes, she likes to play with water, so we give her dishes to wash. Some kids empty the garbage. Mary helps wipe the table. They can all feed themselves, but some need the food cut up. They all make the sign for more."

The point of the diagnosis, however, was not to stigmatize but to treat.

> Mary has basic skills but needs improvement in keeping her voice softer, but we are working on that. We're trying to get her to realize that it's nothing to be ashamed of, that it isn't her fault. Gloria still needs assistance in basic daily living skills, and we're trying to get her to be more active. To keep her from just sitting there, we give her chores, like emptying the trash can or trying to wipe the table.

The staff was so involved with teaching clients that it made no attempt to carve out a separate private space. In fact, even during off-hours almost all the talk was about the clients.

Notes from the Field
Evening Activities at Waterside

From: Robert Zussman
To: David and Sheila

In the large open living area, one client was off in a corner, sorting plastic sticks by color. Two blind clients were sitting side by side on a sofa, listening to a Donna Summer record. (How do I know they were listening? Upon being asked about the music, one client answered, "Donna.") One of the staff handed a tambourine to a client, who then shook it a few times; another led one client's hand over a balloon with a Magic Marker to make designs, sometimes letting air come out of the balloon so the client could feel its release. I was enormously impressed by the ability of the staff to create activities for clients who were almost entirely unresponsive. Moreover, the staff seemed to be working hardest with the most difficult clients.

The residents were called for dinner by names, not very normalizing, but good programming for a population in which the ability to recognize and respond to one's own name represents an important achievement. Dinner itself was therapeutic in the same way: "Eat with a fork. Don't use your hands. If you want more, make the sign for it. Don't just shove your plate." So was clean-up after dinner, as each client took his or her plate to the kitchen and dropped it into a sudsy basin.

After dinner the entire group, clients and staff together, had a talk. Sitting in a circle, they followed a discussion led by one of the counselors. He began the meeting by saying he had some announcements. First he asked John, one of the verbal clients, to say as many of the clients' names as he could; then he called out the names of the nonverbal clients. Has anyone seen Karen? If you are here, Karen, please raise your hand. He then waited for her to raise her hand in response (sometimes with help from another counselor). After a resident responded, the counselors would call out, "Very good. Let's clap for ———," while they also helped the other residents to clap. Finally, the counselors went through all the clients, saying something good that each one had done (Graham isn't rocking as hard) and clapping again for each client.

This meeting (there is a meeting every night) was a bit long and some of the clients got restless. Phyllis in particular got up a number of times and barged out (either to go back to sorting her colored plastic pieces or to scrounge scraps of food from the garbage) and had to be brought back. Similarly, Sarah got up at one point to go sit down in a chair by herself on the other side of the room, and had to be pulled back.

After dinner and the meeting, I went out with Joe and two clients, Graham and Carl, to pick up some brownie mix that Joe would later bake, with the two clients' help, for a dessert. We went to a small store located right around the corner from the building, with Joe holding Graham's hand and me holding Carl's. At the store, they were greeted with smiles by the store manager, a matter of particular note since Carl (who is blind) made it a point to sniff at various things, and Graham (who is hyperactive) started to pick up and unwrap cookies three or four times before he got the idea (from my putting the cookies back) that he wasn't supposed to take them. Nevertheless, they were greeted with mostly good humor.

The remainder of the evening was spent much as had been the time before dinner, with some clients listening to music, others simply sitting, and the staff doing what it could with the rest.

After showering the clients and putting them to bed, staff members had roughly an hour before it was time to leave. They sat around in the living room with the TV on, glancing occasionally at newspapers but also talking. Mostly they talked about the meeting planned for the next day, griping that the agenda would be devoted mostly to Sarah, whose vomiting problem had already been the subject of considerable discussion at previous meetings. There is nothing especially remarkable in this except that it could very easily have been different; they could have spent their time gossiping about their personal lives or not talking at all. Instead they chose to talk about the most explicitly therapeutic aspect of their work.

Activities at Waterside were so structured for learning and therapy that staff minimized personality distinctions among the clients. In the classroom, it mattered little if one student was funny or another affectionate; what counted was their achievements. At Lincoln, after the clients went to bed the staff often sat around and laughed about a funny remark one of the residents had made or discussed how another had endeared herself with a special gesture. At Waterside, the staff turned on the tape recorder and replayed the tape of the evening meeting, stopping it so that everyone could hear one client say his name for the first time.

In this professional setting, rewards also came from the opportunity counselors had to review cases with other staff and with agency consultants, who visited often. At Lincoln, staff members might or might not take the advice of the expert, depending upon whether it made sense to them. At Waterside, the staff and the expert made the decision together and it was binding. Indeed, counselors respected the consulting experts, in part because they saw themselves eventually becoming experts; in return, the consultants respected the counselors: "The staff has good judgment; I wouldn't want to interfere with them."

The daily interaction changed not only the clients but the counselors. "You learn to be more open, to touch and be touched, to be more accepting of people, more flexible." Another observed: "You learn about yourself, working with the clients. It's a humanizing experience. The retarded don't play social games. You know their reactions. They are direct and honest in their feedback." Such sentiments promoted a distinctly missionary form of activity. The staff wanted not only to help the residents have "normal experiences," but to teach the community that the retarded were "just people." Sister Barbara's staff conceived of the community in terms of friends and relatives. The staff at Waterside thought of it as a formal "public" and took as one major purpose of the group home the demystification of retardation. With this goal in mind, counselors always took residents along to the grocery store, sometimes making several trips so that different residents would experience shopping—and different neighbors would experience seeing them. And they were mindful of setting the right tone for the public encounter. "It depends on how they see you act with the clients. Most of it is fear of not knowing retarded people. When they see how you respond, they ask questions. The kids in the building used to come up and visit us and told their parents about the home."

These features could not have been recreated in an institution. Waterside's staff would not have found either the autonomy or the opportunity for advancement there. Moreover, the goal that it prized most for the clients was inimical to institutional life—it wanted to maximize opportunity for independent living, by which it meant the ability to exercise choice. "Choice is a major objective of our program. Institutional clients feel they have no control over their situation, and we try to develop a sense of 'I'm a person' in them. In the beginning they need a lot of direction. We have to structure activities, take them to a movie, to the beach, etc. When we repeat these activities they can eventually make a decision. How could they decide to go to the movies if they don't know what a movie is? Decisionmaking is built into most aspects of the program—choice of food, of clothing. We work to the goal of a choice by residents."

So, too, Waterside's manager proudly explained: "We try to push choice. We give them as much choice as we can, even if they don't understand—like putting three things on the bed and asking which they want to wear. If they have to wear a sweater, we ask if they prefer a white or a blue one. When we go out to a restaurant, we ask whether they want a banana or an ice cream, or what kind of ice cream. Even if they just repeat the last word, it's a beginning. So they feel they have some control over their lives. We ask, 'Who wants to go out? Who wants to go to the park?' Mostly they have a choice, but some just like to stay in and we insist they go out sometimes."

There is something ironic, if not contradictory, in the notion of "pushing choice." The counselors would not allow the clients the option of remaining encapsulated in their own private world. Staff readily conceded (boasted?): "Clients are not allowed to spend all of the weekend in the house, or go out just one day. While in the house they must, for at least part of the day, be involved in some activity, even if it's only watching in the kitchen while we make a dessert." But no one at Waterside worried whether such an insistence involved a coercion of its own, not only because the value was too deeply held to be questioned but because they assumed that passivity and lethargy was the price the clients were still paying for their years at Willowbrook. Indeed, the counselors were convinced that they could easily distinguish between the Waterside clients who came from their own homes and those who came from institutions. Clients reared at home "are less withdrawn. They don't have the scars. They're more verbal, show more affection, both sad and happy. They're more friendly. They try to show what hurts or bothers them. They make more demands." The staff's intent was not to push the residents beyond their capabilities but to raise them to their capabilities; to compensate for the sins not of nature but of institutions.

Did the classroom atmosphere at Waterside create a theater of its own? Did Waterside live by a myth that the severely and profoundly retarded could acquire skills? No one among the counselors thought so, because progress was measured in inches, not in miles. Staff considered it an achievement if a client who never made eye contact before now did, if a client who had to be led to join a circle for a meeting now entered on his own. In sum, urging choice on retarded persons, even foisting it on them, constituted an explicit acknowledgment of their intrinsic worth. Being forced to be free brought a dignity all its own.

Still a third model emerged for group homes, one that demonstrated that a residence in the community would not automatically become either an affectionate family or a stimulating classroom. It was quite possible, in fact quite simple, to turn a group home into an institution, to duplicate its rigid and impersonal routine on a smaller scale.

A residence that OMRDD operated exemplified the process. The building, formerly a convent, was not an ideal setting for a group home, but the use of space exaggerated every structural difficulty. The dining room had two long tables with four chairs each, so that the staff could not join the clients at a meal. Similarly, the staff made the living room into a dayroom: At one end was a sofa and chairs, generally lined up in a row; at the other were two long rectangular worktables. Off this room was a smaller, more intimate one, which the staff furnished with a television set and usurped for its own use. The door to the room was frequently closed, although the staff occasionally invited a few residents in to watch a program.

Notes from the Field
A Night in the Ex-Convent

From: Robert Zussman
To: David and Sheila

The evening began routinely enough. Each staff member took three or four of the residents and did the standard state program—ten tries at a particular sign, followed by a reward consisting of a bite to eat or a drink of water. Each resident was working on different signs: one still trying to learn the sign for "eat," another trying to put together a string of five signs in a sentence, and others at various points in between. I was, and still am, curious as to why all the residents were working on signs when at least one is verbal (Marvin) and at least a few others are capable of making various sounds.

Program time was followed by dinner, spaghetti with sausages. As usual, the staff did not eat with the clients, but grabbed bowls from the kitchen as the residents were finishing up, and ate more or less catch-as-catch-can. But on this evening not even all the residents ate together. Van, the star client by virtue of his adeptness in both sign language and skills, is, like all the other residents, required to make a sign for eating before he begins his meals. This evening, he was rather slow about it; he began with a well-formed sign for "I want to," then trailed off in the sign for "eat." Greg asked him to make the sign again. Van gave the same performance. Greg asked him once again. Van gave the same performance. Greg asked him once more. This time Van's sign became even sloppier, trailing off after the sign "I." Greg said, "O.K., if you're gonna fool with me, you aren't gonna eat. Go stand in the corner. Go on—go." Van walked over to the corner and stood there, head bowed and hands to his face, as everyone else ate. He stayed there for fifteen minutes before Greg called him back and said it was all right to eat.

The staff's treatment of Marvin was even stricter. Marvin is the only verbal client in the home, but his speech consists almost entirely of curses—"bitch," "beat your ass," and so on. The staff does not enjoy this. But at the suggestion of one of the consulting professionals, they have instituted a new policy. Instead of telling Marvin to be quiet when he swears, they are supposed to ignore him—working under the assumption that his swearing is a dysfunctional attempt to get attention. The staff, or at least some of the staff, had apparently transmuted the policy into: Ignore Marvin no matter what he's doing, unless you get too angry at his swearing, and then punish him—exactly the opposite of the policy's intent. So after having ignored Marvin and his swearing for most of the afternoon, Greg lost patience over dinner. After muttering "bitch," "beat your ass," and "God damn" a few more times, Marvin was sent into the office to cool off while the other residents were eating. Like Van, Marvin was called back after a while, but (unlike Van) he was punished by a denial of his dessert, a piece of chocolate cake, which was by far the best part of the meal.

After dinner is time for the recreation program, then showers. Greg had taken his "lunch break" (the misnamed but union-won right to take one hour off in the course of a nine-hour shift) and was downstairs sleeping, so I helped Carol with the boys. They were all lined up in the corridor outside the bathroom and undressed—except Mark, who had lived at home before coming to the residence; he went into his own room to undress, but did not close the door. They then filed one by one into the shower, while the others waited in the corridor for their turn. Carol washed. I dried. After showering, the clients came downstairs for medication and Carol took her "lunch break."

Greg and I were left alone with the residents. He had asked me earlier if I wanted to see the Knicks game, which I did. We settled down in the second living room. The residents wandered about, mostly in the dayroom. Greg brought in a stack of papers, I assume with the intention of catching up on his paperwork. But he soon dozed off. While he slept:

Marvin made what I guess you could call a pass at Sarah. He kissed her hand. Sarah took his hand and placed it on her breast. She touched his groin. Greg woke long enough to see only a moment of the action and said to me: "Good. Maybe it will keep him from swearing." Marvin's mood changed fairly quickly. He began to pick at his face, making his nose and cheeks bleed. Greg either slept through it all or continued the "program" of ignoring him. Meanwhile, Edward had managed to get into a bottle of pHisoHex. When I saw him, he was sitting in an armchair, empty bottle in hand and his face covered by both the pHisoHex and an impish smile. Ira was sitting across from him on the sofa, in a huge gob of the stuff.

I will not bore you with my moral crisis at this moment. Suffice it to say that my curiosity about what would happen won out over my concern for the situation—probably the wrong decision (especially in regard to the pHisoHex), but that was the decision I made. Finally, Carol got back. She cleaned up Marvin. She cleaned up Edward. I helped her give him a second shower. She muttered a few things about Greg, asking me where he'd been, but said nothing to him. When I asked why she said nothing, she answered only, "Why stir him up? There's nothing you can do about some people." Carol did not, however, seem concerned that Willy was sitting with her pajama tops undone or that Steph was also sitting on the floor with her shirt off. Nor did she seem to be too disturbed, let alone do anything, when I reported that there was a pile of shit sitting in the upstairs bathroom. I had noticed it, or rather smelled it, during shower time after recreation, but had said nothing. Greg continued to sleep, and I left.

That so institutional a setting and routine were recreated in the community is not to be explained by the clients' disabilities. The residents were in some ways more handicapped and in other ways less handicapped than those at Lincoln or Waterside. They were considered "behavior problems"—some were aggressive, others had strange mannerisms, still others were self-abusive—but all of them were ambulatory and able to hear and see. Nor is it to be accounted for by the demographic characteristics of staff members. They resembled their counterparts at Lincoln: blacks and Hispanics, with a high school education or some college training. What did distinguish the staff and what explains the style of life in the group home was their prior work history: All of them came from a state institution and maintained its patterns in the community.

Oddly enough, they had requested the assignment, but they were soon grumbling about the all-encompassing character of the job. "I'm like a housekeeper. I clean, dress the kids, make sure they are clean when they leave, get them to do little things for themselves. We're not supposed to call them kids, the residents. It's a lot of responsibility. We're responsible for anything that goes, but the people at the top, they don't listen to us." Or: "At [the institution] we just took care of the residents, no cooking or cleaning or washing clothes. Here I wash clothes too, three times a day, and the machines are always broken."

Not surprisingly, the staff soon devised coping strategies such as calling in sick; but then the other staff would take the following day off to compensate, creating a cycle of absenteeism. "[This job] has put me through too many changes. I went to the doctor. I wasn't eating and was losing weight because I worried too much. I couldn't handle all eight residents at once and do the housework. He told me I was in bad shape. I'd get an ulcer if I didn't get rid of the stress. It was from the job. So I got an attitude if they [the other staff] don't have to work, I don't either. I ain't gonna worry about the house. I'll put down I did it. I tell the house manager, yes, I put the washed clothes all away, when I only put two, not eight. I can't kill myself for the job."

In the community, as at the institution, the staff did not report someone else's negligence, making it almost impossible to discipline even the most flagrant offender. A supervisor insisted that civil service rules tied her hands. She could write a memo to personnel, but not fire anyone herself. "No, it would have to go through personnel. You'd have to burn down the building to be fired."

The direct care staff's displeasure with their jobs was reflected in and reinforced by their relationship with the professionals. The tensions that existed in the institution reappeared here, for again the professionals issued orders to unskilled workers, ensuring that they would think of themselves as custodians. "They [the professionals] come in once in a while and tell you what to do, but they don't know; they're not with the residents all the time. They won't even let the kids touch them. They pull back if a kid touches them. They just want programs on a paper. They don't care if they're good."

The staff's indifference to programming and its problems in relating to the residents reflected a deeply held belief that the residents were, and would always be, damaged. "These kids can't be normal. Sarah makes funny noises—that's her outlet. Van goes like this [gesture] when you smoke. How you gonna stop them after all these years?" To this staff, the notion of clients making decisions seemed fanciful. "These kids can't have any choice. Maybe what to have for dessert. But they can't decide where to live." Can they choose their own clothes? "They don't know how. Van can put on a pair of pants if you tell him, but he can't pick his clothes from a store." In fact, the concept of choice was so alien that the staff instinctively tried to limit rather than expand personal preference. Mark, who had lived with his parents for many years, was different from the others. When he undressed, he went into his room and folded his clothes neatly; he had his own particular mannerisms, eating and showering very deliberately. Instead of encouraging his individualism, the staff called him "fussy" and "stubborn" and allowed the other residents to steal his food. His nonconformity was a nuisance and therefore to be discouraged.

The staff appeared so indifferent to the personhood of the residents that at times it came close to violating the minimal standard of protection from harm. Little effort was made to keep the home clean or in good repair, except for those areas that staff frequently used (the office, the adjoining bathroom, the kitchen, the dining room). The farther one went upstairs and into the space that was more exclusive to the residents, the dirtier and more disorderly it became. The residents' sleeping areas had a stench from malfunctioning toilets—although more residents were toilet trained here than at Lincoln or Waterside. None of the staff, however, complained about the odor. Perhaps years at the institution made the smells part of the occupational hazards of working with the retarded.

Client abuse also traveled from the institution to the community. At times, staff members would tease a particularly disturbed client, but usually they let the other clients do it for them. They grouped residents not to promote friendships but to even scores, a hallowed institutional tradition. The staff knew which resident would respond aggressively to another. "There's certain ones they like and others they don't. Marvin don't like Willie. He won't mess with Victoria, though, 'cause Victoria would knock him down. He didn't mess with Stephanie. Ira don't like Mark and Edward." It was Marvin who often became the pawn in the staff game, angered to the point where he injured another resident or was himself assaulted.

Act One

One evening, Marvin had just had his medications changed and was even a bit louder than usual. More, whether because of the medication or for some other reason, his bladder was also out of control. He pissed in his pants twice, something he usually does not do at all. So by the time recreation came, Carol and Dotty, the staff on duty, had pretty much had it with him. Marvin does not usually take part in recreation; he remains in the room, but only to pace around and swear. This evening, Carol and Dotty decided that Marvin would participate and take his turn crawling through the tunnel. But Marvin's only answer to their suggestions was his standard "Beat your ass." They decided they would "help" him through the tunnel. The tunnel is a piece of plastic draped over a series of metal rings and was very pliable. Carol put the tunnel over Marvin's head and with Dotty's help essentially pulled the tunnel over him until it was easier for him to stand up than to back off and resist. They got Marvin through, which he did not appreciate. He began to spit. Dotty grabbed the top of the turtleneck Marvin was wearing and pulled it over his head, using it as a mask. Marvin stopped. Dotty let go. Marvin began to spit again and they repeated the cycle. The next time, though, Marvin kept spitting even with the turtleneck over his head, essentially spitting into his own face. Eventually Dotty let go and Marvin went back to his pacing, angrier than before, spitting occasionally. Dotty and Carol both said he'd probably go for someone, meaning that he'd claw at someone's face, which he does when he gets angry. They were right; later in the evening, he dug his nails deep into Willie's cheeks.

Act Two

Sitting in the television room one afternoon, Marvin began to "act out"—cursing, slapping lightly, banging the wall, threatening to throw a pillow. I had been sitting beside him and decided to deal with the situation by moving away—all in all, still as good a tactic as I can think of. Dotty, though, had another strategy. She asked Ira to move over next to Marvin, which he did, and explained to me that if he got mad enough he'd hit Marvin back. She could not control Marvin, but she could use Ira to control Marvin.

Later, around the time of the shift changes, Marvin was sitting in the office with most of the staff. He was sitting quietly, but from the point of view of the staff, this was hardly enough to make up for the accumulation of past sins. Susan saw Victoria rocking peacefully in the kitchen and called out to her: "Hey, Victoria, come on over here and beat up Marvin." She came in, jumped up and down a bit, jabbed playfully at the air, and never got around to hitting Marvin, to her credit.

The review panel and MPU had sufficient monitoring mechanisms in place to make certain that the group home never degenerated to the level of Willowbrook. The residents always went to their day programs and were more or less adequately dressed—otherwise the teachers would complain. The staff also had to keep itself in line on special occasions, such as a dance at Roseland Disco.

Because the group home was in the community, an enterprising staff person could occasionally exercise initiative. In the winter of 1980, a highly religious forty-two-year-old woman arrived as a temporary counselor. She was eager to have "a relationship with the kids," to "take them out and do things with them," and much to the surprise of the rest of the staff, she did.

I arrived around eight-thirty, as the residents were coming home. To my amazement, Thelma, as soon as she was through with her mopping, announced that she was taking the kids out. She called for Mark, Van, and Victoria and asked them to get their coats on. Where did she go? She reported later that she had gone for a walk and that she had done the same thing with a few of the other residents on two previous days. On the walk, she had stopped with them for a soda at a pizza place. There she had run into trouble and she was indignant about it. The proprietor had at first refused to serve them, stating: "This is a place of business." She told him that he had to serve them, that the kids were citizens, and they had their rights. He relented. The other staff who were listening to the story all agreed, although not with quite so great an indignation.

Thelma's having taken the kids out may be contagious. Ira, who usually does little other than sit on the toilet, today grabbed my hand and pulled me to the coat closet, and then pulled me to the window—all as clear a message as I could want from someone nonverbal that he wanted to go outside. I accommodated him and we took a walk along the avenue. With one exception, there were no stares. As for Ira, he seemed blissful, managing a huge grin for a good ten blocks and curious to look in store and apartment windows. Only when we got back to the residence, to which he returned without any prodding, did he exhibit any "behavior problems": He pissed in his pants while we were waiting for someone to open the door. No one ever said it would be easy.

Thelma continued her behavior the following weeks. She even took out Marvin, an act which inspired a statement of ironic admiration from Alice. ("She's brave.") Alice herself took out Van and Ed after that—the first time she had ever taken any of the kids out and something she seemed a bit apprehensive about. She was relieved when I offered to go with her. The two men were quite good. We walked to a five-and-ten-cent store for the primary purpose of picking up some shaving cream but with the secondary purpose of giving Van and Ed an inside look at the store. (This could very well have been the first time either had ever been inside a store.) Alice gave them a chance to pick out something to eat and each picked a bag of pretzels. Alice paid at the counter, with Ed and Van standing beside her. No one responded to their presence in any way that I could see.

Thelma's experiences notwithstanding, the staff believed that taking residents outside was an invitation to disaster. The point of each anecdote was to explain that the community would never tolerate the bizarre behavior of the residents. One favorite story was about the time a nonverbal resident of another group home went into a grocery store and uttered his first words: he turned to the proprietor and said, "This is a holdup."

The staff was equally reluctant to have outsiders enter the group home. Each visitor was a potential spy who could report on its failures. "It's bad when the parents come and they interfere. They see you telling their kid to clean up when he's urinated on the floor. They say you shouldn't do that. It's your job and you're getting paid to clean up."

The staff's discomfort with family visits was mild compared to its dislike of review panel audits. They detested the investigations, the peering into drawers, the counting of underwear, the inspection of menus and food on hand. Since the supervisors were anxious about the ratings, they put pressure on the counselors to clean up, mend the clothing, and get the clients' records up to date—which they grudgingly did, all the while grumbling about the cause for all this bother, the absurd principle of normalization. "When we first started here, the psychologist said this should be like a home. But if it's like a home, why do they all have medication at four? Why do they all eat dinner at five? Why do they all wake up at six? They say it should be like home; it doesn't have to be neat all the time. You can have things lying around like your own home. Then why does the review panel look for straightened closets? Why do they make sure everything is neat before an inspection?" Finally, the staff was right. The residence had nothing in common with normalization. It was not a home.

Most of the group homes for the Willowbrook class followed one of these three models. Smaller voluntary agencies, operating one or two residences, tended to adopt a family model along the lines of the Lincoln Apartments. They were not large enough or experienced enough to attract professional-minded staff seeking advancement; at the same time, they often enjoyed strong ties with the local community, and taking their cue from their experiences with antipoverty programs, hired staff from the immediate neighborhood. Manhattan's Episcopal Mission, for example, recruited counselors for its two upper Manhattan residences from the CETA training program for minorities. The agency could not offer much by way of opportunities for promotion, but turnover among its predominantly black and Puerto Rican staff members was very low. As at Lincoln, counselors apparently found sufficient satisfaction in providing the residents with emotional nurture to keep them at the job.

The larger agencies, operating five or more homes, tended to follow the classroom model. They had a prior involvement in mental disabilities, already retained a professional staff, and were now expanding rapidly and offering opportunities for promotion. Thus the Association for the Help of Retarded Children, which ran eight group homes, advertised in the professional-help-wanted pages of the *New York Times*, and described many prospects for advancement within the organization. Its staff, like YAI's, actively designed and evaluated client programs and, in keeping with a professional orientation, received training in "not becoming too attached to any one resident." Since MPU increasingly preferred to deal with the larger agencies, the classroom model was the most popular among the group homes.

The third model, the group home as a transplanted institution, reappeared elsewhere besides some state-operated facilities. In fact, the single largest provider of services to the Willowbrook class, United Cerebral Palsy of New York State, fit (or fell) into this pattern. By 1980, UCP State was operating some one hundred apartments, each for three clients; yet despite the intimate scale, the programs were essentially rigid in design and character.

UCP's formative experience in delivering services came in the aftermath of the Willowbrook scandal. At the state's request, Robert Schonhorn sent in several "mini-teams," each composed of a variety of specialists. After the consent judgment, DMH and plaintiffs asked him to take over several Willowbrook buildings and to share in the running of some others. Schonhorn agreed and hired a cadre of well-qualified professionals to deliver very specific therapeutic services to the residents and to oversee the attendants. When he went on to establish community programs, he followed the same design. As distrustful of the direct care staff in the community as he had been in the institution, he recruited specialists to perform all important tasks. Indeed, his agency provided the most extensive array of professional services in the city.

The UCP design produced neither the affectionate ties of the Lincoln Apartments nor the classroom learning of Waterside. Instead a fragmentation occurred. In trying to ensure that minimal standards were met, it unintentionally put an institutional stamp on the apartments. By giving direct care staff mainly custodial chores, and leaving all the teaching to the professionals, the program minimized staff involvement and maximized staff turnover. UCP would not even allow direct care staff to purchase clothing or furniture for the apartments, supplying them instead from a central storehouse. Perhaps most disturbing, the reliance on specialization did not seem to fit with effective teaching.

Notes from the Field
At Play with UCP

From: Robert Zussman
To: David and Sheila

It was like getting a birthday gift wrapped in bright paper with elaborate ribbons tied around it, and opening the box to find another, smaller box inside, and then another box, and finally nothing but a thirty-nine-cent key ring from Woolworth's in the final box.

When I arrived at the apartment, the kids were sitting in a semicircle in the dining area, watching television. Before and during dinner, the evening's recreation team began to arrive. A bit after six, the minibus driver arrived and the four members of the team (only one of them had been there before) put the kids' coats on, wheeled them downstairs and onto the bus, and we headed out to the program. The staff talked to each other. No one talked to the kids.

In not too long, we arrived at a school, the site of the program. We wheeled the kids into a classroom where they were met by a group of students from a local college. There were about three or four students; it was hard to tell, as they circulated in and out of the room. They did seem to know the kids, but not well. We put the wheelchairs in a circle and "recreated." One of the students led a song with lyrics along the lines of "If you're happy, if you're really happy, clap your hands . . . touch your nose . . . touch your eyes," while a staff person prompted them to give the right response. This was followed by a rendition of "He's Got the Whole World in His Hands." And that was it. A man who appeared to be in charge, wearing a suit, wandered in and announced that there was a gym upstairs. The kids could use the mats up there if staff could get the kids up two flights of stairs—a more difficult task than it might at first appear, considering that these kids don't walk and there's no elevator. We carried five of the kids up, the consensus being that one was too heavy to carry, and someone stayed behind with her.

> In the gym, we placed the kids down on the mats. One of the recreation team found a basketball and wandered off to shoot hoops, soon to be joined by another of the staff. There were quite a lot of other people in the gym, all retarded or staff. Another man, who looked as much like a gym teacher as I can imagine anyone looking, came by. He had never seen the kids before but did seem to know the college students. He was, in fact, impressive, quickly making suggestions about what kinds of exercise the kids could do. But it was not personal; he referred to one of the girls as a "little boy" and persisted in calling her "him" even after one of the staff made the appropriate correction. He discussed the kids in technical language with the staff. In all, he spent about five minutes with the group and the kids spent about twenty minutes in the gym. These twenty minutes are what turned out to be inside all the boxes.
>
> We took the kids back downstairs, put on their coats, wheeled them out to the minibus, and headed back to the apartments. The kids probably spent more time in the van than in recreation. I realize that I have said very little about the kids themselves, for the kids were, in a sense, barely there. They were, to be sure, the reason the recreation staff came, but they were "dead weight." They had to be wheeled, carried, transported, but it didn't really matter much what they wanted or what they thought. Nobody, for example, asked them if they wanted to go up to the gym, a question that at least one of them is quite capable of answering. Indeed, they may not have been the reason for anything that happened. In fact, one of the team said as much: "What we care about is that we get practice."

UCP did not carry into the community all the institutional baggage, but it did carry in a collective response to individuals, which made the residents more anonymous and the programs less personal.

In examining the performance of group homes, much of the professional literature continues to think about suitability of placement in terms of characteristics of individual clients. Those returned to an institution from the community were ostensibly too aggressive or too dependent. But this formulation is analogous to blaming the worker in a factory for an accident or an illness when the lighting is poor or the ventilation inadequate. The point is to design a healthful and safe workplace—and by the same token, to design suitable community programs.

The experience of the Willowbrook class not only demonstrates the feasibility of placing even the most handicapped persons in the community (a point of major import in itself), but also illustrates some of the models that might be followed—and in this way helps us to stop thinking about the client and begin thinking about the setting as the determinative element in placement outcomes. The question is not whether the client has one or another disability but whether the group home adopts a consistent and useful model, either one described here or another of equal efficacy. There should not be *a* group home to which the client must adjust, but a variety of types of group homes that should be shaped and fitted to suit the client. If one design does not work, do not fault the client but alter the environment. However self-evident this may sound, it has to date been anything but received truth in the field.

The professional literature has also been obsessed with trying to fix on an optimal size for a facility. Strenuous debates occur on whether a forty-bed residence can create the same environment as a twenty-bed, or whether a five-hundred-bed institution can be subdivided into smaller units so as to approximate three-bedroom apartments. But the debate seems irrelevant, for in isolating size from other considerations, such as style of organization, numbers take on a magic all their own. Smallness, by itself, does not guarantee a homelike environment. Some ten-bed group homes and three-bedroom apartments can be turned into institutions; others can be made intimate, supportive, and habilitative. It is true, however, that settings larger than fifteen are almost certain to be institutional in character, no matter what administrative strategies are used. In them, the staff is bound to be rotated and the time of eating set to match shift changes; the ordering of supplies is centralized and the clothing color-coded to simplify distribution. Group activities are given precedence over individual choice—and so an institutional environment is created. This same process undoubtedly occurs in other settings: Think of the difference between a classroom of fifteen or forty, a dinner party for eight or thirty. But with the retarded, as with other dependent persons, the effects are exaggerated. Their disabilities are such that larger numbers will almost certainly produce regimentation in order to complete onerous tasks, from lining up clients for showers to setting up an assembly line for diaper changes.

It may also be time to bury the question of whether group homes are or are not in the community. If critics go on at length about the difficulty of getting normals to be friends with the retarded—as though community living is the equivalent of intimate ties—supporters get rhapsodic about the visit to the museum or the zoo—as if living in a community involves a checklist of events attended. Are group homes in the community? No, if one means choosing acquaintances by preference (not by the accident of a shared residence), or attending different functions with different social circles (basketball games with one, weddings with another). Yes, if by community one is talking about visibility (so that residents are better protected from abuse) or convenient location (so that staff would prefer to work there). And finally, yes, if one means the opportunity to exercise some degree of choice and enjoy a variety of life's ordinary experiences.

A month after a number of blind and deaf clients from Willowbrook moved into their group home, they and their staff went out for a walk. A few minutes later, it started to rain and the clients, to the staff's bewilderment and horror, started to take off their clothes. As the counselors frantically tried to keep them covered, it dawned on them that the clients assumed it was shower-time at the facility. They had never before felt the rain.

PART III

ALL TOGETHER NOW

11

Fighting the Plague

The single most unanticipated conflict in Willowbrook's many wars pitted the New York City Board of Education and Department of Health against the Willowbrook class, or at least that small segment of it that consisted of hepatitis B carriers. As more and more Willowbrook residents entered the community, and its public schools, the fact that some of them were carriers of the disease assumed a sudden significance. Everyone had known that hepatitis was endemic at Willowbrook; indeed, the institution had been the setting for research into hepatitis during the 1950s and 1960s. So long as the carriers remained confined, no one was concerned, both because Willowbrook provided a quarantine from the rest of the community and because the carriers posed no particular threat to fellow residents, most of whom had already contracted the disease and built up immunity against it. Community placement, however raised the question of whether the carriers were seeding their classrooms with hepatitis B. Did the decree pose a public health menace?

As agonizing as the question was, the effort to resolve it represented the high-water mark of cooperation among the review panel, OMRDD, and plaintiffs' attorneys. Together they tried to prevent Willowbrook's residents from being twice stigmatized, once as retarded and then again as carriers. Indeed, their joint efforts demonstrated all that an alliance could accomplish for a group long considered among the least powerful in our society.

* * *

On Thursday afternoon, September 7, 1978, three days before her thirteen-year-old son, Timmy, was to begin another school term, Janet Wheeler opened a mailgram from the New York City Board of Education. "Dear Parent," it read:

> As the Department of Health has informed you, your child is a hepatitis-B carrier. In the interests of health and safety your child will be excluded from school temporarily until appropriate educational arrangements are made. If you have questions call 596-5627.
>
> JOYCE R. COPPIN
> *Assistant Superintendent*

Although the board's terse notification surprised Mrs. Wheeler, she was by now well accustomed to events in Timmy's life taking unexpected and troubling turns.

Her own upbringing in a New York middle-class family had been uneventful. She attended a local college, married an architect, moved into a fashionable section of Brooklyn, and began to raise a family. The Wheelers' first child was born in 1963. Two years later, as planned, she became pregnant again. The pregnancy was routine, but six weeks before the delivery date Mrs. Wheeler went into premature labor and delivered Timmy. To her astonishment, he was retarded, a case of Down's syndrome.

The family physician advised immediate institutionalization, explaining that the children required round-the-clock care. The Wheelers agreed and arranged for Timmy to enter a private facility. The Wheelers rarely visited him; all the while, the costs of his care mounted. In 1971, when Timmy was six, the Wheelers separated. Facing the expenses of two households, they agreed to commit Timmy to the state's institution—Willowbrook.

The little that Janet Wheeler heard about Timmy's progress at Willowbrook satisfied her. He lived in the showpiece building, the children's unit, and had learned to walk. To be sure, his medical history was disturbing. First Timmy contracted shigella, and then he had several more bouts with intestinal parasites and diarrhea. A subsequent blood test revealed that he had also contracted hepatitis B and, worse, had not been able to shake free of the virus. He, like several hundred other residents, was now a carrier of the disease. Nevertheless, unable to cope with Timmy, she was not about to fault Willowbrook.

Janet Wheeler did not take part in the protests in 1972 or the litigation, but soon after the decree was signed, Timmy moved to the Brooklyn Developmental Center. Janet Wheeler preferred the new setting; she now was spared the opprobrium of saying that her child was at Willowbrook. But out of sight was still out of mind. Occasional letters from BDC (Timmy's birthday is coming up, would you like to come to a party? It has been a year since you have been here; would you like to pay a visit?) went unanswered.

Since Timmy was relatively high-functioning, prone to occasional temper tantrums but otherwise quite manageable, he was high in line for group-home placement. As the planning progressed, Mrs. Wheeler, for the first time since his birth, became involved. In the fall of 1977, Metropolitan Placement Unit notified her that Timmy was scheduled to enter a coed group home and attend a local public school. MPU staff was convinced that "Timmy would benefit greatly from this type of setting," but Janet Wheeler vehemently disagreed. Timmy was much too hyperactive to adjust to a more relaxed setting, and besides, the home was located "on a thoroughfare, in a severely depressed neighborhood . . . where heavy traffic of another kind is the order of the day. There is open drug dealing and junkies nodding at all hours." Surely Timmy was better off on the "grassy open space" and "varied play areas of the Developmental Center."

As it turned out, the substance of Janet Wheeler's objections was not as important as the education she received as Timmy moved through the placement process. She met frequently with the MPU staff, the group-home director, and even plaintiffs' lawyers, learning about normalization and the advantages of life in the community. The first placement fell through when the agency decided that Timmy was not a suitable candidate; in March 1978, MPU proposed another—a group home for eight boys in the heart of a middle-class neighborhood. This time, Mrs. Wheeler attended an exit conference for Timmy at Willowbrook, discussed programs with the group-home staff, and was satisfied with all she heard. Timmy made a one-day visit to the home, returned for a few overnight stays, and soon moved in.

Over the next several months, Timmy enjoyed several "firsts." He attended a public school, shopped in neighborhood stores, and went to a summer camp. And over these months Janet Wheeler also experienced several "firsts." She began to visit Timmy, to relate to him more affectionately, and to wonder whether someday she might take him home.

Hence, when Mrs. Wheeler read the telegram from the board of education announcing that Timmy was to be excluded from school, she was furious, and frightened too. She was aware that Timmy was a hepatitis B carrier and suspected that the first group home had rejected him because of this condition. But what did the board of education intend to do? Would Timmy's temporary exclusion turn into permanent expulsion? Would his group home panic and try to remove him? Would this become the first in a sequence of events that returned him to Willowbrook? Indeed, as news of the board of education action spread, others on the review panel and in OMRDD also pondered whether the order marked the beginning of the end of deinstitutionalization. With hundreds of carriers among those still remaining at Willowbrook, was something akin to a Typhoid Mary panic about to break out?

Janet Wheeler telephoned Chris Hansen, who told her that the board's action seemed illegal to him and to the attorneys for the review panel and OMRDD. They would all be in court on Monday morning to ask Judge Bartels to issue an order restraining the board of education.

The attempt to bar Willowbrook's hepatitis carriers from the public schools had a special irony to it, for from 1956 through 1971, researchers fed live viruses to children in Willowbrook in order to study the disease and attempt to create a vaccine against it.

The head of the team was Saul Krugman. In appearance, he borders on the colorless, but controversy surrounds him. Krugman's research at Willowbrook brought him fame and power. He has chaired national committees on hepatitis, directed huge federally funded projects, been the subject of laudatory editorials in the *Journal of the American Medical Association,* and won the John Russell Award of the Markle Foundation (which read, in part: "In all his work Dr. Krugman proceeded quietly and cautiously. . . . He has zealously guarded the rights and sensibilities of patients and their families. . . . Dr. Krugman has provided an example of how [good clinical research] should be done"). Yet in April 1972, when Dr. Krugman received a prize from the American College of Physicians, a line of police surrounded the podium while 150 protesters denounced his research as grossly unethical.

Saul Krugman's interest in infectious diseases began when, as a physician with the armed forces in the South Pacific, he treated many patients who contracted malaria or jungle parasites. Upon discharge,

Krugman took a residency at New York's public hospital for infectious diseases, Willard Parker, which in several ways prepared him to work at Willowbrook. Krugman recalled entering a pavilion where some sixty children lay one next to the other "with every complication of measles—encephalitis, pneumonia, everything. I could go to another area and see dozens of children with diphtheria. . . . Every summer the Parker Hospital would admit at least 50 and sometimes more than 100 children with paralytic poliomyelitis."

In such a setting, Krugman became convinced that even the most diligent efforts at treatment were not likely to bring benefits. "Therapeutics," he once remarked, "was a slender reed in those days." Rather, the goal had to be prevention, which to Krugman meant not cleaning up a water supply or sewer system, but finding vaccines.

In 1947, Krugman moved to Bellevue Hospital and joined the NYU faculty, and in 1954 he became consulting physician to the newly opened Willowbrook facility. He immediately conducted an epidemiological survey, which disclosed an amazing variety of infectious diseases: measles, hepatitis, respiratory infections, shigella, and assorted intestinal parasites.

If Willowbrook was a hell for its residents, it could be a paradise for a researcher. On these disease-ridden wards, the line between treatment and experimentation seemed to vanish. A researcher could select his disease and enjoy substantial freedom to experiment, believing that he was serving both society and the residents.

Events in 1960 confirmed the validity of these presumptions for Krugman. Every two years or so, New York City experienced a measles epidemic, and new admissions to Willowbrook invariably brought in the disease. The results were usually disastrous, with hundreds of cases and fatality rates as high as 10 percent. At the start of 1960, Dr. John Enders, working in Boston, had succeeded in growing measles virus in culture and had managed to attenuate it to the point where it might be an effective vaccine. Krugman wanted to run trial tests at Willowbrook. The disease struck there so often and so hard that findings could be obtained quickly; and if the vaccine offered protection, the Willowbrook residents would obviously benefit. Krugman contacted Enders, received twenty samples of the limited number of doses available, and vaccinated the residents of one ward.

A measles epidemic soon struck at Willowbrook, but no one among the vaccinated children contracted the disease. "Willowbrook's children," observed Dr. Krugman, "enabled us to acquire in a short time solid information about Dr. Enders's vaccine." By 1963, before the vaccine was officially licensed, 90 percent of Willowbrook's residents had been inoculated, and measles was never again a threat. The use of an experimental vaccine at Willowbrook, Krugman concluded, "was obviously beneficial to the children."

The measles study was a sideshow at Willowbrook. It was hepatitis that held center stage. Soon after completing his initial epidemiological survey, Dr. Krugman decided to explore this widespread but little understood disease. Its symptoms had been recognized for centuries, but not until World War II did medical researchers suspect that the disease was infectious and occurred in two varieties: the short, thirty-day-incubation type that we now label hepatitis A and commonly associate with eating contaminated shellfish; and the long, ninety-day-incubation type that we now label hepatitis B and commonly associate with blood transfusions. Beyond these simple categories, little was known about causes, cure, or prevention.

In this vacuum Dr. Krugman began his experiments. Between 1953 and 1957, Willowbrook had had about 350 cases of hepatitis among the residents and 76 among the staff; in 1955 alone (the year before his research began), the disease rate was 25 per thousand among the residents, 40 per thousand among the staff. (In New York State, the rate was 25 per *one hundred thousand* of the population.) And these figures included only the observable, acute cases of patients with jaundice; the number of milder, subclinical cases was still greater. To Dr. Krugman, these conditions called for an active research strategy. Scientists had not yet found a nonhuman host for the virus or succeeded in growing it in a laboratory culture. Thus experiments would have to be carried out on live subjects, and what better subjects than the Willowbrook children? The high rate of contagion in the institution meant that they were bound to get the disease and the effectiveness of intervention could be measured almost immediately.

Krugman's experiments had a logic, a simplicity, and, one would dare to add, an elegance about them. His initial project was to determine whether injections of gamma globulin, that part of the blood plasma which is rich in antibodies, protected recipients against hepatitis. The literature suggested that gamma globulin offered temporary, "passive" immunity; the antibodies in the fluid would be able to counteract the disease for some six weeks. The critical question was whether injections of gamma globulin in the presence of the virus would lead recipients to produce their own antibodies, thereby acquiring permanent immunity that would last for years.

The team first administered varying doses of gamma globulin to one group of new admissions to Willowbrook and withheld it from another. Then, eight to ten months later, it tallied the numbers from each group who had contracted the illness. The results were clear: of 1,812 residents who had been inoculated, only two cases of hepatitis occurred (a rate of 1.7 per 1,000); of the 1,771 residents who were not inoculated, forty-one contracted the disease (22.5 per 1,000). Thus Krugman confirmed that gamma globulin did protect against hepatitis and the finding "pointed the way to the practical method for the control of infectious hepatitis at this institution."

But had the gamma globulin injection stimulated active immunity? Those inoculated were protected against the disease for almost a year, but no one understood how this protection was acquired or how long it would last. Had the gamma globulin first provided a passive immunity, which then turned active when recipients came in contact with the live virus from other residents? Could permanent active immunity be acquired by injecting patients with gamma globulin and live virus at the same time?

To answer these questions, Krugman opened a separate unit on the Willowbrook grounds. Staffed by its own personnel, it admitted children between the ages of three and eleven, directly from their own homes; when their role in the research was completed, weeks or months later, they moved onto the general wards. The experiments typically involved injecting some of the unit residents with gamma globulin and feeding them the live hepatitis virus (obtained from the feces of Willowbrook hepatitis patients). At the same time, other unit residents served as "controls"; they were fed the live virus without the benefit of gamma globulin, to ascertain that the virus was actually "live," capable of transmitting the disease, and to measure the different responses. Then Krugman would calculate how many of those who had received both gamma globulin and live virus, as compared with controls, initially came down with hepatitis; six or nine or twelve months later, he would again feed both groups another dose of live virus and measure how many of those who had earlier received the gamma globulin contracted the disease as against those who had not.

As is often the case in scientific research, Dr. Krugman's most important observation came by chance. In keeping track of the hepatitis rates in the institution, he noted that 4 to 8 percent of those who contracted hepatitis went on to suffer a second attack within a year. The second attack might possibly have been caused by a very heavy exposure to the virus, which overwhelmed the immunity the body had built up after the first attack. But Dr. Krugman believed that the etiology of the disease was more complicated than researchers had recognized. The repeat attack indicated that more than one type of virus could be causing hepatitis.

To investigate this "very attractive hypothesis," Dr. Krugman in 1964 started a new series of experiments, and within three years he helped to clarify the distinction between hepatitis A and B. In this round, the Krugman team admitted new Willowbrook residents to its special unit and fed them a dose of pooled Willowbrook virus, that is, a mixture that came from a large number of hepatitis victims and, therefore, contained all the hepatitis viruses within the institution. In short order, these First Trial subjects contracted the disease and recovered from it. The team then reinfected these children with the same pooled virus in a Second Trial, and a number of them again contracted the disease. In the course of these procedures, the team drew a sample of blood from one of the boys during his first illness (and labeled it MS-1), and then another sample from him in his second illness (labeled MS-2). Next, the researchers admitted a new group of fourteen children to the unit and infected these Third Trial subjects with the MS-1 virus. Within thirty-one to thirty-eight days, all but one came down with hepatitis. Simultaneously, the team admitted still another fourteen children to the unit, and injected this Fourth Trial group with the MS-2 virus. Within forty-one to sixty-nine days, all but two contracted the illness. Now the stage was set for the final procedure. The team gave all the hepatitis victims in the third (MS-1) group and fourth (MS-2) group the MS-1 virus. It turned out that not one child in the Third Trial group came down with hepatitis a second time; six of the eight children in the Fourth Trial group again contracted the disease.

With these findings in hand, Krugman announced that hepatitis was caused by at least two distinct viruses. There was hepatitis A, MS-1, of short incubation and highly contagious (all of the controls who lived with the Third Trial group but were not fed the virus directly came down with the disease). And there was hepatitis B, MS-2, of long incubation and lower contagion (only two of the five controls living with the

Fourth Trial group caught the disease). In short, the Krugman research established the distinctive features of two strains of hepatitis.

The findings met with acclaim, and Krugman was praised not only for his results but for his methods. The *Journal of the American Medical Association* credited Krugman's "judicious use of human beings"; Franz Inglefinger, later the editor of the *New England Journal of Medicine*, went further: "By being allowed to participate in a carefully supervised study and by receiving the most expert attention available for a disease of basically unknown nature, the patients themselves benefited. . . . How much better to have a patient with hepatitis, accidentally or deliberately acquired, under the guidance of a Krugman than under the care of a [rights-minded] zealot."

Underlying these attempts at justification, and those that Krugman himself made, was the notion that the Willowbrook experiments were, in the words of Claude Bernard, the nineteenth-century French physician who was among the first to address the ethics of research, "experiments in nature." Researchers who studied the course and spread of a disease that had no known antidote were acting ethically, for no intervention on their part could have altered the outcome. But how could feeding live hepatitis viruses to children be considered the equivalent of observing a disease? Krugman's answer was that if he had not infected the children, they still would have contracted hepatitis. Had he never come to Willowbrook, the likelihood was overwhelming that entering residents would have suffered the disease. Thus his feeding them the virus did not really change anything and was an experiment in nature. Krugman also noted that he had obtained permission from the parents of all his subjects, and he had signed consent forms to prove it.

Many parents of children accepted at Willowbrook but still awaiting actual admission—a wait that could last for several years—did receive the following letter from Dr. H. H. Berman, then Willowbrook's director:

November 15, 1958

Dear Mrs. ______:

We are studying the possibility of preventing epidemics of hepatitis on a new principle. Virus is introduced and gamma globulin given later to some, so that either no attack or only a mild attack of hepatitis is expected to follow. This may give the children immunity against this

> disease for life. We should like to give your child this new form of prevention with the hope that it will afford protection.
>
> Permission form is enclosed for your consideration. If you wish to have your child given the benefit of this new preventive, will you so signify by signing the form.

Almost every phrase in this particular letter encourages parents to commit their children to the unit. The team is "studying" hepatitis, not doing research. The virus "is introduced," in the passive voice, rather than the team's being said to feed the child a live virus. Gamma globulin is given "to some," but the letter does not explicitly state that it is withheld from others. "No attack" or a "mild attack" of the disease "is expected to follow," but absent gamma globulin, a claim of "no attack" was false and left unsaid was that in some cases the attack would not be mild. Finally, the letter twice described introducing the live virus as a "new form of prevention," but feeding a child hepatitis hardly amounted to prevention. In truth, the goal of the experiment was to *create,* not deliver, a new form of protection.

To send such a letter over the signature of Willowbrook's director appeared coercive. These parents wanted to please the man who would be in charge of their child. Moreover, an especially raw form of coercion may have occasionally intruded. When overcrowding at Willowbrook forced a close in regular admissions, an escape hatch was left—admission via Krugman's unit. A parent wanting to institutionalize a retarded child had a choice: Sign the form or forgo the placement.

What of Krugman's contention that his research was an experiment in nature? The claim ignores the fact that the underlying problem was not ignorance about a disease but an unwillingness to alter the social environment. Had Krugman wished to, he could have insisted that hygienic measures be introduced to decrease the spread of the virus. Should the facility resist carrying out the necessary cleanup, he might have asked the Department of Health to close the place down as a health hazard, which it surely was. Furthermore, Krugman had at hand an antidote of some efficacy. His own findings demonstrated that gamma globulin provided some protection, and yet he infected control groups with the virus and withheld the serum from them in order to fulfill the requirements of his research design.

Finally, to introduce one more irony to this account: While Krugman was trying to discover the etiology of hepatitis at Willowbrook, Dr.

Baruch Blumberg was actually solving the puzzle in his laboratory, without conducting experiments on humans. In the course of his research on the body's immunological reaction to transfused blood, Blumberg observed that a strange band occurred when he mixed a vial of blood drawn from a hemophiliac with that drawn from an Australian aborigine. Labeling the band the Australia antigen, he investigated its properties; like a detective on the trail of a culprit, he followed several false leads and then the true one, discovering that the Australia antigen was the infective agent in hepatitis B. His first published report appeared in 1967 and Krugman confirmed the finding (the Australia antigen was in the blood of the MS-2 children but not the MS-1 children). Thus those with a utilitarian bent, who might be prepared to give Krugman leeway with his means because his ends were important, will have to consider that, however accidentally, we would have learned almost everything we needed to know about hepatitis B in the laboratory.

Once Dr. Blumberg identified the hepatitis antigen, research burgeoned. Blumberg himself reasoned that the antigen, although only part of the virus, might still have the capacity to stimulate the production of antibodies. In October 1969, he applied for and received a patent for a vaccine that could clean the antigen "coat" of its impurities. Krugman also began research into a vaccine and by trial and error learned that after he boiled serum with the antigen for one minute, the product appeared to stimulate antibodies without apparently causing the disease itself. He tested the preparation on a new group of Willowbrook residents, found that eight of his fourteen subjects did not contract the disease, and called a press conference to announce that he had created a vaccine against hepatitis B.

The publicity and praise was lavish, but the announcement was premature. Krugman's preparation actually caused a mild form of hepatitis and as such did not qualify as a true vaccine. Still, Blumberg's ideas and Krugman's near-success did point the way to other investigators, who refined their processes. As of 1975, when the Willowbrook class began to leave the institution, a vaccine was still not available but success seemed close.

Still other researchers, investigating the etiology and spread of hepatitis B, learned just how serious the disease was. The incubation period is very long, from two to six months, which makes it especially difficult to know how and where the patient contracted it. The first symptoms are fatigue, loss of appetite, malaise, abdominal pain, vomiting, headaches, and intermittent fever; then the patient becomes jaundiced, the urine darkens, the liver swells, and enzymes normally stored in the liver enter the blood (in easily measured amounts). Generally, these symptoms abate in two to six weeks, but the fatigue and malaise often persist for months. No drugs are available to quicken the recovery; doctors can only recommend limited activity and a regular diet. And complications are not unusual. The mortality figure for hepatitis B ranges from 1 to 10 percent, depending upon the age and general health of the patient. Those over the age of forty and with other medical problems are at the top of the scale, children with sound medical histories at the bottom. Put succinctly, hepatitis B is far nastier and more debilitating than hepatitis A.

The diagnostic breakthroughs also clarified that hepatitis B was far more widespread than had been thought. Many victims contract a subclinical, nonacute case; they do not turn yellow or experience the full effects of the other symptoms but do often suffer liver damage. Even more important, the new technology established that hepatitis B (unlike A) exists in a carrier state. Ordinarily, hepatitis B patients produce antibodies against the virus and rid their blood of it within six months. But in a minority of cases (particularly where a genetic defect alters the immunological system), the patient recovers from the acute symptoms of the disease but does not shake free of the virus. The carrier state is doubly dangerous: The carriers themselves are more susceptible to cirrhosis of the liver and cancer of the liver. And of course, the carriers pose a risk to the health of others.

Epidemiologists next began to investigate the characteristics of hepatitis B carriers and found the roster bewildering in its variety. It included drug users, male homosexuals, patients and technicians in kidney dialysis units, dentists, surgeons, Americans of Taiwanese or Chinese origin, and the institutionalized retarded. In New York, among 3,000 male homosexuals tested, 70 percent had had a case of hepatitis B and 5 percent were carriers; among 1,228 kidney patients on dialysis machines, 64 percent had had the disease and 15 percent were carriers. Among 666 Chinese-Americans, 81 percent had a history of hepatitis and 9 percent were carriers. Among the institutionalized retarded, 74 percent had had hepatitis B and 10.5 percent were carriers.

The groupings at first looked random. The disease correlated with occupation (health professionals), hereditary factors (Chinese-Americans), deviant behavior (homosexuals, drug users), and histories of hospitalization (kidney patients, the retarded). But the pattern became apparent as soon as the critical role of blood transmission was appreciated. Those in contact with blood or blood products have a much greater likelihood of contracting hepatitis than those who are not. So surgeons who operate are at risk: They frequently cut or prick themselves in the course of an operation, exposing themselves to the blood of a surgical patient who may be a hepatitis carrier, and, perforce, exposing the surgical patient to their blood. Dentists, too, are prone to hepatitis. Even an ordinary teeth-cleaning procedure will cause a patient's gums to bleed, and dentists, who do not so much as wear gloves, frequently scratch themselves with one or another instrument.* Similarly, drug users who share needles share blood; homosexuals who engage in anal intercourse rupture membranes. And the retarded, too, are at risk; often they receive the drug Dilantin, which controls epileptic seizures but has the side effect of causing drooling and bleeding gums. Thus the retarded who are affectionate may spread the disease by kissing or by sharing food, and those who are aggressive may spread it by biting or scratching.

Investigators also found the antigen in other bodily fluids—semen, saliva, sweat, and sneeze samples; hence sexual intercourse, kissing, and sharing food and towels might promote contagion. However, no one could be certain about the likelihood of transmission, since the disease had an incubation period of up to six months. In fact, generalizations about the communicability of hepatitis are difficult to make. If the blood of a carrier comes in touch with the blood of a susceptible, even in droplets, infection is almost certain. But what if one shared an apple with a carrier or was around when he sneezed? Here the research was not (and still is not) conclusive. Blood aside, hepatitis B spreads less easily than the common cold but more easily than tuberculosis—which leaves a considerable distance in between.

With the risks of contagion so indeterminate, one might have an-

*One research team screened 1,245 dentists at the 1972 meeting of the American Dental Association and found that about 13 percent had antibodies to hepatitis B and 1 percent were carriers of hepatitis B; both figures were "substantially above" the national averages. Another team tested physicians' blood for the presence of antibodies and found that 18.5 percent were positive. How many other physicians were carriers? The researchers did not know; antigen testing "was omitted because of practical considerations related to study acceptance by the participants." The implications of being a carrier were too devastating to a medical career for doctors to join the tests.

ticipated bitter debates about appropriate public health measures. Instead medical experts consistently minimized the dangers of contagion so long as basic hygiene practices were followed. In 1976, the Center for Disease Control (CDC) convened a task force to formulate guidelines. Its members, which included Dr. Krugman, conceded that the epidemiology of hepatitis B was "only partially understood," but then went on to urge "good personal hygiene." People in a household with a carrier should wash their hands frequently and avoid sharing razors, toothbrushes, towels, and other personal items. Hospitals did not need to isolate hepatitis B carriers on special wards, but staff should remember to wear gloves in handling blood or blood-contaminated clothing. In laboratories, technicians should wear protective clothing and not mouth pipette blood.

The CDC provisions concerning carriers in institutions for the retarded replicated those concerning ordinary households. Insisting that "It is important to avoid placing unwarranted limited restrictions on antigen positive retarded persons," it emphasized the need not to share toilet articles and to wash carefully after contact with blood or blood-contaminated items. CDC expressed no misgivings about the community placement of retarded carriers. To the contrary: "Antigen-positive persons should be given the same consideration for placement programs or nursing homes as those who are negative."

That the guidelines adopted so integrative an approach reflects, first, that the risk of contagion was being considered in the abstract, not against the background of an outbreak of hepatitis B. More important, CDC never really considered excluding carriers from hospital settings. The dangers that patients posed to staff were assumed to be normal to health care; indeed, since health professionals were at risk, CDC was confident that recommendations on hygiene would be faithfully followed. Finally, no CDC committee would recommend penalizing carriers when such a policy might deprive surgeons or dentists who were carriers of their livelihoods. This was a matter not simply of self-interested professionals protecting each other, but of a shrewd calculation of costs and benefits. To levy penalties against surgeons or dentists who were carriers would undoubtedly prompt health professionals to screen their patients and, perhaps, to refuse to treat carriers. The CDC policy opted for risk taking on both sides. Patients would not know whether their doctors were carriers—and in turn, doctors would not discriminate against carrier patients.

Ethical considerations counted as well, and no one formulated them more forcefully than Baruch Blumberg. Awarded the Nobel Prize in 1976 for his research, he addressed the complex problem of "bioethics and the carrier state." Insisting that science was not a discipline of "facts" which could ignore "values," he noted that some one million hepatitis carriers lived in the United States alone, and public policy faced an unavoidable "conflict between public health interests and individual liberty." Carriers could be denied the privilege of donating blood. But should all carriers be penalized when "the extent of the hazard to the public is not clear?" Should a new diagnostic technology be used "to regulate the risks inherent in people living together?" To Blumberg, the answer was no; he found the risks of contagion considerably less than the costs of state intrusion and hoped that "carriers who have already been identified will not be jeopardized." Had New York's board of education and department of health followed his advice, the judiciary would have been spared still another intervention.

Since those who suffer from one social injustice do not build up immunity against another, the members of the Willowbrook class almost became the victims of hepatitis B for a second time. The new diagnostic procedures revealed which Willowbrook residents were carriers, but at first, under the 1976 CDC guidelines, community placement was unaffected. Between 1976 and 1978, the state sent some forty carrier children to group homes and public schools without arousing much concern. Occasionally, a voluntary agency would balk at accepting a carrier, but it would back off under a threat to cancel all its contracts. So, too, the city teachers' union formally requested the exclusion of all carriers from the schools; its real purpose, however, was to make certain that teachers' assignments to a class with a carrier were voluntary and compensation would be forthcoming if they contracted the disease. A few school officials worried about the "very explosive possibility of a 'hepatitis scare,' " but the CDC guidelines inhibited any action.

In the summer of 1977, the explosion occurred. A pregnant teacher of a carrier in a special education class at P.S. 69 in Staten Island contracted hepatitis. The incident might have escaped notice but for two coincidences: hepatitis is especially dangerous during pregnancy, and P.S. 69 borders on Willowbrook. Word of the teacher's illness spread quickly through the district; the parents, learning that there were three carriers enrolled in the school, contacted their local representatives and the board of education, some asking about the risks of contagion, others demanding that the carriers be expelled. While the number of inquiries and protests mounted, the teacher's doctor learned that she actually had hepatitis A, not B, and the carriers, therefore, were not implicated. But the news of the diagnosis did little to quiet the furor. The questions of risk, once raised, had to be answered. What was the likelihood that a carrier would transmit the disease to other children or teachers? This time it was hepatitis A, but next time might it be B?

As soon as classes opened in September, a group of irate parents forced the principal to ask the city Department of Health to evaluate the situation. On September 26, William Goldman, a physician, and Edward Galaid, an epidemiologist, observed the classroom behavior of the carriers and were distressed by what they saw. The retarded children were a hygienic nightmare. They embraced, kissed, and drooled on each other's toys; they shared each other's drinks and food. Some of the children had bleeding gums (from taking Dilantin) and one of the carriers was a fourteen-year-old girl whose frequent menstrual "accidents" soiled the bathroom and the classroom. Goldman and Galaid were also disturbed when they visited the pride of the school's special education program, the woodshop. Where the teachers found an excellent opportunity to teach manual dexterity, the doctors identified a "high potential for cuts" and transmission of the disease.

Goldman and Galaid immediately reported to Dr. John Marr, chief epidemiologist at the department's Bureau of Preventable Diseases, that because of "numerous potentials for transmission . . . we feel that the three [carrier] children should be excluded from their present classroom arrangements [and placed in] a special classroom where all known hepatitis B carriers could be instructed." Marr was uneasy about the recommendation and circulated it with a covering letter quoting from Blumberg's 1976 Nobel Prize speech—"All members of the carrier class should not be stigmatized because some can transmit hepatitis." For a moment it appeared that the department, in keeping with the CDC guidelines, might recommend against exclusion. But Goldman adamantly argued that the CDC guidelines were not based on direct observation of the retarded and he challenged his colleagues to deny the possibility of contagion under such classroom conditions. As is so often the case, the public health official who raised the possibility of a risk that could not be conclusively refuted carried the day. Just as CDC endorsed the swine flu vaccine because it could not rule out an epidemic, so the Department of Health endorsed carrier segregation because it could not rule out contagion. On September 29, Marr informed Lloyd Novick, the deputy commissioner, of the exclusion decision and Novick concurred. The department then telephoned the board of education with the recommendation and the board implemented it the next day.

The decision left everyone unsatisfied. On the evening of September 29, some two hundred parents crowded into the P.S. 69 auditorium; furious that the carriers had been admitted to the school in the first place, they were now fearful that segregation did not go far enough. "Can this [disease] be transmitted from a water fountain to a child who might have just lost a tooth?" demanded one parent. Others wanted to know about the possibility of contagion on the school bus, in the lunchroom, or in the auditorium. The health officials considered the prospects "remote," which led parents to declare that "remote possibility does not mean non-existence. We parents are not gamblers in the risk of a child's health."

The board of education was no more pleased with the decision. Was it now obliged to give each carrier student in city schools a separate classroom and teacher? Such action might be not only expensive but also illegal, violating Federal Law 94-142, which explicitly required schooling for handicapped children in the least restrictive environment. As one state education official informed the city, "The segregation . . . at PS 69 cannot be construed as being within the requirements of the law. . . . Their environment appears to be very restrictive indeed." To be sure, the board might avoid penalties by citing Department of Health orders, but to the board's puzzlement, the department was reluctant to deliver in writing the advice that it had given over the telephone. Segregation may have brought a temporary respite in the P.S. 69 crisis, but it seemed an awful precedent.

Lloyd Novick and John Marr at the Department of Health were probably the most uncomfortable of all. As things stood, the department had full and exclusive responsibility for the segregation of the carriers. Any opposition to the policy, because it seemed either too restrictive (violating the rights of the carriers) or too permissive (endangering the susceptible students and teachers), would be directed at the department, a position that prudent administrators generally avoided. Even more unsettling, the department did not have a creditable defense against either attack. In the heat of the moment, it had abandoned the safe territory of the 1976 CDC guidelines—no outsider could have faulted a policy in line with a national standard—merely on the strength of two investigators' spending a few hours in one classroom. At the same time, by taking the possibility of contagion seriously, the department was now obliged to evaluate all the other risks posed by the carriers, from the use of common water fountains to school buses. Small wonder, then, that it sought a way to come back off the limb.

By mid-October, the department managed the feat and sent its long-awaited letter to the board of education. Its first official communication not only omitted all reference to the Staten Island incident and its own recommendation for segregation; it also announced that the risk of contagion from hepatitis B carriers was "unknown but certainly slight," and had to be balanced with "the recognized need of the carrier pupils for normal educational and social experiences." The letter went on to explain that the department was appointing a task force to examine the entire question of risk; in the meantime, it told the board to provide hand-washing facilities in or near each classroom and to assign an aide to every teacher of carriers. If the board observed these precautions, the department believed that the carriers could remain in mixed settings pending the task force report.

It was a shrewd strategy. By not mentioning the P.S. 69 decision, the department kept the official record clean and obviated the need to do anything more about the incident. Appointing a panel of experts would both distribute the burden of responsibility and provide much-needed guidance; meanwhile, the schools were on notice to improve their hygiene, so if a case of hepatitis B occurred, it was the fault either of the board (for not providing sinks and aides) or of CDC (for issuing permissive guidelines). The Department of Health was safely out of the direct line of fire.

To prepare for the task force, the department needed more information about the number of student carriers and their classroom behavior. Accordingly, John Marr turned to Dr. Curtis Bakal, a graduate of Yale College and Harvard Medical School, at the department for a one-year residency in public health. Bakal's inclination for social medicine may have been inherited—his father had practiced in New York's garment district—or it may have reflected his own liberal politics. Either way, he was intrigued by the novel policy questions that the carriers raised and the prospect of rewriting CDC guidelines. This intense, energetic, and widely read young physician may also have had a little of Ibsen's Dr. Stockman about him. Was the release of the hepatitis carriers into the community the equivalent of discovering a contaminated public water supply? To engage in a scientific inquiry and a crusade was an irresistible combination for someone beginning a public health career.

Over October and November, Bakal contacted MPU, received its list of known carriers in the schools (which numbered thirty-six), and then, with the help of four assistants, visited their classrooms. Before going out, the team members were briefed by Dr. Goldman, and he or Dr. Galaid joined their initial tours to be certain they would "know what to look for." Armed with checklists and sheets with rows of columns ("drools," "bites," "responsible toilet habits," and the like), they watched children and questioned the teachers. Basing his conclusions on some firsthand observation but even more on teachers' recollections, Bakal said that a majority of the carriers "indulge in frequent close contact with their classmates, some kissing, some putting their fingers in the others' mouths." A significant number also had bleeding gums, lacerations, nosebleeds, or menstrual accidents, which produced "a considerable potential for spread of hepatitis." Those who did not hit their friends kissed them—just like ordinary children in ordinary classrooms, one might say, only these were carriers.

While Bakal was collecting the data, Marr and Novick organized the task force. Although they briefly considered putting together a group that would include not only physicians and researchers in hepatitis, but other interested parties as well (civil libertarian lawyers, academics, and community representatives), they decided, without much debate, to limit the group to experts in the disease. In this way, they expected to formulate guidelines that were scientifically sound and seemingly above controversy. But evaluations of risk inevitably involve social and political considerations, and by limiting the group to medical experts they were guaranteeing that the decision would give primary consideration to eliminating health dangers.

Of the experts selected, two were in public health—John Maynard of CDC and Donald Lyman from New York State's Department of Health. Robert Purcell was a bench researcher working on the hepatitis vaccine. Wolf Szmuness of the New York Blood Bank, Robert McCollum of Yale Medical School, and Saul Krugman of NYU were also involved with testing the vaccine, and all of them had conducted hepatitis research on institutionalized subjects. Who was not invited? For one,

Baruch Blumberg—whose Nobel Prize acceptance speech counseled against penalizing the carriers. For another, clinicians who might think in more individual terms. For still another, any professional in retardation who might have examined the issues from the perspective of the carriers.

Notes from the Field

Excerpts from Curt Bakal's Report of the Proceedings of the Advisory Committee on Hepatitis B,

December 20, 1977

The committee met to discuss the issue of placement of known hepatitis B carriers in the New York City public school system. Dr. Marr detailed the events that initiated the Health Department's involvement. Dr. Novick then posed two related questions to serve as a framework for the ensuing discussions:

(1) What is the approximate risk engendered by secretion exchange among students?

(2) What constitutes adequate precautions?

Dr. Maynard stated that we are clearly dealing with an infectious agent and may be now "seeding" classrooms with it. Dr. Krugman stated that we could group carriers and "immune" students [with antibodies against hepatitis] together. Dr. Maynard noted that since the majority of children in special education classes are not and were never institutionalized, they are probably susceptible and their environment is being seeded by carriers. Thus what was formerly a contained problem now has the real potential for spreading amongst the general population. In fact, the rate of hepatitis B in the U.S. appears to be increasing. The only way to contain the spread of the antigen lies in the testing of high-risk groups and subsequent special placement of carriers.

Dr. Szmuness agreed that some form of separation is unavoidable. Dr. Pitkin [from the board of education] stated that there is a real advantage for hepatitis carriers who are separated from the susceptibles. There would be fewer restrictions placed on their activities since contacts with other children would not have to be minimized.

Dr. Novick then stated that the consensus of the group appeared to be in favor of initiating special placement for the carriers, but that the extent of separation would have to be delineated.

At this point the reluctant consensus of the meeting appeared to be that (1) separate placement of carriers is desirable and that ideally they could be placed in classes with immune peers; and (2) serological [blood] testing of pupils and teachers might have to be performed in order to effect this change. Dr. Pitkin stated that only one Willowbrook student has been fully mainstreamed into a normal classroom; therefore, the need for testing exists only in the special education classroom. Perhaps parental objections to sero-testing could be minimized if testing was publicized as a means of protecting and placing susceptible students. Participants agreed that with good public education and maintenance of a government low profile, there should be minimal objection to blood testing.

Most of the committee felt that placement should be made on the basis of epidemiologic criteria [whether the student was a carrier]; individualized judgments based on behavioral criteria [whether he was aggressive] would be hard to make and would lead to problems. Therefore, any child from an institution for the retarded which has endemic hepatitis B who is placed within a neighborhood school would be screened, and separate placement would be based on the results.

The committee agreed that our best recommendations would be based on medical and educational considerations; political considerations would have to be dealt with by politicians.

Dr. Krugman noted that the sequelae to any actions taken might be devastating to certain individuals and that political controversy would follow any course of action. Perhaps, he pondered, we should do nothing. Dr. Lyman noted that precedents set by this committee on hepatitis B might possibly be applied to other transmissible diseases in the future, and therefore might necessitate a whole set of unwieldy, unenforceable guidelines and placement arrangements, so perhaps our best course of action is to continue existing arrangements. (These questions were phrased rhetorically. The consensus was that existing arrangements are not sufficient and that each problem should be dealt with as it arose; we must act to minimize disease transmission.)

It is not surprising that experts in hepatitis recommended blood tests to identify and segregate the carriers. Public health and research-oriented physicians were most likely to move to reduce contagion, even if they were uncertain just how serious the risk was. To them, even one case of contagion through a carrier was one case too many. But what is more surprising is the tenacity and self-confidence with which the task force held to this premise and considered its decision the only legitimate one. Those who disagreed had to be acting "politically." Any course other than isolation represented partisanship.

The only tense moment in the task force meeting came toward the end of the day, when Saul Krugman and Donald Lyman momentarily backed off the consensus and raised the possibility of doing nothing. But the group closed ranks quickly, reaffirming the public health credo: "We must act to minimize disease transmission." An unknown risk had to be judged by the maximum potential damage.

But apparently not all unknown risks, for no one in the meeting so much as raised a query about the threat of contagion from other hepatitis carriers, whether homosexuals or surgeons. To be sure, only the retarded were on the agenda. But if a group was about to revise the CDC guidelines for one category, it might well have pondered, however briefly, the necessity of revising policy for other categories. If firsthand observation of the retarded in classrooms revealed the inadequacy of existing policies, might not firsthand observation of homosexuals or surgeons also reveal inadequacies? Perhaps yes, perhaps no—but the question never surfaced.

The Department of Health was delighted with the work of the task force the way that an autobiographer might be pleased with his own book. It now had retrospective approval for its September segregation decision and a prospective procedure that seemed realistic and enforceable. Over January and February 1978, Drs. Novick, Marr, Pitkin, and Bakal worked out the details (with Bakal spending every spare minute reading the hepatitis literature). They decided to do blood tests only on those students who were now in the same classrooms as the known Willowbrook carriers (the number would total some three hundred), to determine their epidemiological status (carrier, immune or susceptible) and to recommend that the carriers, the immunes, and anyone who refused to be tested be segregated in one classroom; the susceptibles could mix with everyone else. The department recognized that the design was not perfect, but it did solve the immediate problem. Individual classroom assignments based not only on blood findings but on behavior might have been preferable—so that a carrier who was high functioning, able to follow hygienic rules, and well behaved would not have to be isolated—but such classifications seemed too complex or subjective. So, too, it might be useful to test the blood of all retarded students enrolled in public schools (or even all nonretarded students) to identify the carriers among them, but such a procedure was well beyond the scope of available resources. In the best of all worlds, one would also test a matched sample of another three hundred retarded children, not in contact with the Willowbrook carriers, and see if their antigen results were any different. But again the department decided no, on the grounds that finding a matched control group would be near impossible. Besides, it was not conducting research but trying to solve a public health crisis.

On February 27, 1978, the department sent its recommendations to

Irving Anker, then chancellor of the board of education. Unless the blood tests became the basis for classroom assignments, "there is a real potential for a considerably increased incidence of this sometimes serious and even fatal disease." It explained its proposed testing procedures, and in very carefully phrased language, declared that "*susceptible* children should be taught in separate classrooms and use separate equipment and toilet items from the carrier children." (Whoever devised this ploy and phrased the policy in terms of isolating the susceptibles, not the carriers, must have wondered why Southern states did not claim that whites were excluded from black schools.) The department invited comments and suggestions, anticipating "continued cooperation for the benefit of the City's school children."

The chore of doing the testing went to Curtis Bakal, and so he was the first to learn that cooperation was not to be the hallmark of the project. His task had the quality of a dungeons and dragons game about it. The treasure was the blood samples of all pupils in contact with the Willowbrook carriers and the skill was to avoid the many dragons blocking the route. Bakal needed an updated list of carriers, so he would have to do combat with MPU; he needed the help of its staff and the tacit approval of the Willowbrook Review Panel to persuade parents to cooperate. Closing in on the treasure, he needed permission to perform the tests from the parents of children in classes with carriers, and, to come to the chief dragon, he needed the full assistance of the board of education. For his weapons, Bakal had the findings of the task force, the certainty that he was protecting the public health, and the prestige that accrues to a doctor. It was not necessarily the most powerful arsenal, but Bakal deployed it well.

Like any novice to the game, Bakal was unprepared for his first challenge. He telephoned Karin Eriksen at MPU to ask for the updated list of carriers and readily agreed to meet with a few of her associates to discuss procedures. When he arrived at her World Trade Center office he was surprised to find nine people, including Dr. Philip Ziring, director of medical services at Willowbrook (and one of its most dedicated professionals), ready to pounce on him. "We were 'set up,' " Bakal reported back to Novick. "I was besieged by a very angry group . . . [who] began to display an unusual degree of rancor towards me." They accused the department of "singling out three Willowbrook children," and repeatedly wanted to know why it had not been concerned with contagion from nonretarded hepatitis carriers. They were also annoyed that the department had acted unilaterally, failing to consult MPU about the guidelines.

Bakal recovered quickly and demanded an apology, for he had come "in good faith, not wanting or expecting to tangle with anyone." The department was only "concerned with protecting the public health" and so had framed the guidelines on its own: "It seemed proper that we abide by public health principles which are best worked out by the people most familiar with these principles." Moreover, the estimate of contagion was "not mine alone, but is part of a consensus of nationally recognized hepatitis experts and epidemiologists." All of them agreed that "the poor hygiene and particular types of social relationships between retarded schoolmates make the retarded classroom a much higher risk situation." To ignore such a situation, Bakal concluded, "would be irresponsible."

Although the confrontation did not change anyone's mind, MPU still gave Bakal his list of carriers. Eriksen and Ziring were convinced that the department was discriminating against the retarded, but since they could not deny that some element of risk was present, withholding information seemed unreasonable.

Bakal's meetings with the MPU borough staff were still more adversarial, but this time he was prepared. The case managers in Brooklyn wanted to know why the department did not improve the hygienic conditions in the classrooms instead of isolating the carriers—to which Bakal responded that this "structural approach" was not compatible with a "public health approach." Since the best way to reduce a health risk was to eliminate it, the department preferred isolation. When the case managers seemed reluctant to encourage parents to sign the release form for the blood tests, Bakal overpowered them by suggesting that the department might declare a health emergency, which would permit it to test anyone it pleased but would also spark public hysteria.

Bakal's call on the review panel, from which he wanted nothing but its silence, was the most volatile of all the encounters. The panel insisted that "Either a person is a hepatitis B carrier or he is not; his mental handicap and previous place of residence are irrelevant to this determination." It was also troubled that the department had taken it upon itself to decide risks and benefits. As Murray Schneps declared (to Bakal's amazement), "The Health Department does not have a right to eliminate risk." To Bakal, the statement was a contradiction in terms;

the very job of the department was to eliminate risks. But to Schneps, the department was no less an interested party than the panel; the carriers' potential risk to the health of others was only one consideration. Their entitlement to a public school education was another—and therefore, the department could not act unilaterally to resolve a public policy dispute.

Bakal left the meeting all the more convinced that the department had to decide policy exactly as it saw fit. The panel, he reasoned, had "the task of jealously guarding the right of the [Willowbrook] group," which turned it into a "single interest" party with a "situational cost benefit analysis [that] differs from the general community." Furthermore, it had an ideological commitment to deinstitutionalization, which he himself believed "may not always be in the client's interest although the party line states it is so." The department, on the other hand, was not bound to a "party line." Its charge was "to impartially protect the public health," which elevated it above particular interests to represent the general welfare.

The moral advantage that came with such a self-definition may explain how Bakal and the department went about getting permission from the parents to give the children blood tests. Even by standards of dungeons and dragons, this was a tricky maneuver. If the information in the department's request to the parents maximized the risk of hepatitis contagion, the parents might agitate for the immediate exclusion of all carriers from the schools. If it minimized the dangers, they might be too complacent to approve the tests. Even more exquisite was the question of what to say about the purpose of the tests. If the department supplied full information on the proposed isolation of carriers, the parents might balk at the prospect of discovering that their children were carriers and having them penalized. (Even the task force recommendation to cohort those who refused to be tested with the carriers would have to be scrapped if, say, two hundred of the three hundred parents refused permission.) And yet the parents had to receive some indication of the department's plan.

Whatever the legal or ethical requirements of informed consent, the department opted for vagueness. After discarding several preliminary drafts, including one that described the proposed cohorting arrangements in detail, it issued a misleading four-page communication. A covering letter signed by Bakal noted that parents had been worried that hepatitis carriers "might be hazardous to children around them."

Hence the department and the board of education "have worked out a program to help eliminate some of the possible problems [and] to help all children, carriers and non-carriers." There followed two pages of "Questions and Answers." "How can I as a parent or guardian help?" By giving consent to test your child to see if he is a carrier or immune, or a susceptible. "What does the testing involve?" A simple blood test, free of charge. Then to the heart of the matter: "How will the test results help my child?"

> The results of all the tests will be used to determine more exactly the hazard in the classroom. Once this is done, programs can be planned to best protect the health of the children in these classes.
>
> We think that parents, guardians and teachers should know if their child is susceptible to hepatitis, or if their child is immune. Also, some children who were carriers in the past may no longer be carriers, and it would be nice for parents, guardians and teachers to know this, too!

Parts of the letter were obviously intended to minimize panic. The carriers "might" pose hazards, the problems were merely "possible"—this after the department and the task force had decided that the carriers were hazardous and problems did exist. But the letter disguised the purposes of the tests. The text declared that the results were to "determine more exactly the hazard" of contagion so that "programs can be planned"; what it chose not to say was that plans had already been made for segregating the carriers. It mentioned that everyone would want to know whether his or her child was susceptible or immune—but it did not add that the tests might also reveal carrier children, who would then be isolated. Finally, the letter did not allude to the price of noncooperation, that children whose parents refused permission to test would be grouped with the carriers. The procedure was ostensibly voluntary—"the decision is up to you"—but only because the consequences of refusal were not acknowledged. Inevitably, then, one distortion produced another. Since the department was unwilling to say why the children were being tested, it could not say what would happen if they did not agree to be tested.

In the short run, the document accomplished all that Bakal and the department wanted: Practically every one of the three hundred parents consented. A few parents, it is true, did grasp the implications of the department's plans, but Bakal handled them smoothly. Typically, the protesters had a retarded child in the same special education classes as a Willowbrook carrier, and they were worried not only about contagion but that the parents of normal children at the school might try to eliminate the entire program. The public school in Floral Park, for example, was located in a substantial middle-class, almost all-white neighborhood in which the number of children had been steadily declining (by virtue of a simultaneous drop in the birthrate and rise in the cost of homes). With classrooms becoming empty, the school board and the PTA faced a choice: Accept black children bused in from other sections of Queens or accept mentally retarded children for special education classes. They opted for the retarded, either because their prejudice against blacks was stronger or because they knew that the retarded would be in their own classrooms. The parents of the retarded, aware of the nature of the trade-off, sensed the precarious nature of their children's position in the school. They felt vulnerable and militant, scared and aggressive—and these contradictory emotions made them pliant to Bakal's tactics.

Thus, at one hastily convened meeting, the Floral Park parents demanded of Bakal why their children had been placed in jeopardy and threatened to sue the board of education. Bakal calmly informed them that the risk of contagion from the carriers was low; besides, they could not win such a suit, for they would never be able to prove transmission from a Willowbrook carrier. When the parents then wondered whether they should consent to the tests, Bakal told them that a carrier child posed serious risks to the rest of the family; however, he added, few children would be carriers (which was true) and those who were would probably recover in a few months—which was unlikely, for among the retarded with Down's syndrome the carrier status persists for years, even for life. Whether because of confusion about the danger itself or calculations on the safest political course, the parents signed the consent forms.

The board of education, the one quarter from which Bakal expected no difficulty, turned out to be his most formidable adversary. Not that the board qualifies as a dragon—it was too slothful for that. A dinosaur would be more like it. (The analogy is not ours. We began an interview with one of the board's attorneys by asking him to give us a feel for the board. Without hesitation, he responded, "Did you ever see a dinosaur run?") Had Bakal an even nodding acquaintance with the history of the board, he would have been far less complacent. It was so poorly managed that 110 Livingston Street has become a synonym for bureaucratic ineptitude. In the late 1970s, the board administered 900 schools with staff of some 100,000, but no one could be precise about the numbers. New York's comptroller complained that the board had no central file of names and school addresses for its employees.

It was Progressive reformers, determined to remove school appointments from the hands of the ward bosses, who created a central and professional administration to provide educational leadership. Unfortunately, centralization had no such effect. The board administrators have been so keenly sensitive to political pressures, whether from the mayor's office or the teachers' union, that they are usually incapable of acting. As the community's involvement in the schools has mounted, so has the intensity of the conflict—which has made the board still more reluctant to reach decisions.

Minority groups discovered this truth in the early 1960s when attempting to promote desegregation. Because such a change would have transformed every element in the system, from teacher and student assignments to allocation of financial resources, the board dodged (let us appoint a committee and await the results), appeared to give in (advocating centralized school "parks"), backed off (it was not feasible), found excuses (the problem is with residential segregation, not school policy), and by one tactic or another avoided action. One researcher who tried to chart the board's steps charged it with "cautious, minimal action, deliberate delay and vacillation, ineffective planning and preparation." He came away convinced that "conditions will probably get worse before they get better."

Ignorant of this record, Bakal, in his first encounter with the board in February 1978, actually felt optimism. The Division of Special Education and its director, Helen Feulner, treated him courteously, providing him with a desk and access to a secretary and a telephone. From here he contacted all the principals whose schools had Willowbrook carriers, informed them of his testing plans, and asked for a list of students in classrooms with the carriers. He also wrote to the board requesting permission to begin the testing. However, he got no response. As the days turned into weeks, Bakal began to understand that the dinosaur was not going to run.

Part of the problem was that Chancellor Irving Anker was battling for survival against Mayor Abraham Beame's plan to reorganize the board and eliminate the chancellor's office. Furthermore, various constituencies within the school system were divided about the Department of Health's plans. Advocates of the disabled believed the fuss unwarranted; others were more concerned about the administrative headaches that would follow upon such a reorganization. (How was a carrier in Brooklyn to be cohorted with a carrier from Staten Island?) As usual, conflict bred inertia, and Bakal's letter lay unanswered.

As March turned to April, Bakal made charges the board's critics had been making for decades. In its "many layers of bureaucracy," "vital information" was often lost and "consideration on vital issues pigeonholed." Sounding like disappointed black activists, he complained: "It has been said that . . . any programmatic change which disturbs the inertia of a massive agency will . . . be resisted. So it was with the Board of Education and hepatitis B."

Bakal soon managed to locate several pressure points. Hoping to prod Anker to action, he contacted the lawyers from the chancellor's own office. Bakal explained his need for formal approval of the testing program, and by way of background described the unknown but potentially serious risks of contagion from the carriers. As he spoke of illness and disease, some lawyers heard lawsuits and liability. Suppose a parent whose child contracted the disease sued the board; whatever the difficulty of tracing the contagion to the carrier, the board might be found culpable for not following the suggestions of the department. (One lawyer present thought otherwise, but of his views in a moment.) Hence, to protect their client, the board lawyers urged Anker to approve the testing. So did Gordon Ambach, the state commissioner of education. Concerned that HEW might find the Staten Island situation a violation of Federal Law 94-142, he warned Anker that it might withhold all educational funds from the state system.

This combination of pressures moved Bakal's request to the front of Anker's desk, and the chancellor now discovered that the testing plan bought him time. The results would not be available until the summer, and in the interim the board would be free of liability. On April 14, 1978, Anker gave permission to the department to do the blood tests in the schools.

Had the board followed its time-honored habit of doing nothing, it might actually have been in a stronger position. The hepatitis issue, as the Department of Health well understood, was controversial and hence, with a refined instinct for self-protection, all department correspondence with the board took the form of suggestions and recommendations. At no point did the department *order* the board to do anything —which veterans of bureaucratic warfare knew would mean that final responsibility rested with the board. One of Anker's legal advisers appreciated the tactic and urged him to sit tight; if the Department of Health objected, well, let it do the testing outside the school, or if it preferred, let it invoke its statutory authority, declare a health emergency, and thus compel the board to cooperate. But the board ignored the advice. Dinosaurs apparently not only run poorly but do not know when to sit still.

On May 1, Bakal began the testing, and by the end of June he had data on some 452 students, the 44 known Willowbrook carriers and their 408 classmates.*

Of the 408: 87 were ex-Willowbrook residents who had already had their blood tested in the facility:

69 were immune (antibody positive)
18 were susceptible (antibody and antigen negative)

Of the remaining 321, whom Bakal tested for the first time:

20 were immune
235 were susceptible
60 refused to be tested
1 was a suspected new carrier
5 were confirmed new carriers (antigen positive)

Translating these findings into classroom assignments, the department wanted the 253 susceptibles in one cohort and the remaining 199 (immunes, carriers, and unknowns) in another. But the most intriguing question was what to make of the five new carriers. Were they proof of the potential for contagion that so concerned the department? Medical and family histories of the five revealed that none of them had ever been institutionalized and only one had been at risk for hepatitis (because of a blood transfusion as an infant), which led Bakal to pin responsibility on the Willowbrook carriers. Conceding that "the current study cannot be used to statistically assess the risk attributable to the presence of carriers in the classroom," he still insisted "that the test program may have detected a larger number of hepatitis B carriers than would be expected in the general population, and that the most significant risk factor for all but one of them appears to be contact with the carriers in classrooms." Of course, Bakal had no way of knowing whether testing

*Bakal noted in his report that "all figures are approximate"; in one draft he had 44 known carriers, in another 45, and this confusion would persist right through the court testimony that was to come.

another group of several hundred retarded students would uncover just as many new carriers, but he remained convinced that the new cases vindicated the department's position.

On July 20, the department sent the board an analysis of the results, and then on August 2 it submitted a final report, with updated but essentially unchanged guidelines. By now Frank Macchiarola had replaced Anker as chancellor (the bureaucratic structure survived Beame's challenge, only the leadership changed). "It is our recommendation," the department told him, "that . . . this Fall . . . the children be separated into classes of susceptible and non-susceptible to eliminate any possibility of transmission of this disease." Segregating the carriers within the schools would resolve the public health risks.

The recommendations alarmed the new administrators, and they quickly devised their own plan. Those now in charge of special education decided not to follow the department's recommendation to isolate the carriers in the schools, but to exclude all the carriers and their classmates from the schools. The carriers would remain at home until some plans could be made for them;* the susceptibles and those untested would be assigned to the borough developmental centers. Only the immunes would be left in their classes. Finding the administrative chore of implementing the department's policy cumbersome, the board took what it thought to be the path of least resistance.

The board did attempt to get the Department of Health to order the exclusion as a health necessity. But when the department refused, the board proceeded on its own. On August 16, Macchiarola informed the department of its decision, and the vehement protests from Bakal and others that "the approach you suggest is not in keeping with the spirit of our recommendations" had little impact. The board did back away from penalizing the susceptibles, but it remained adamant about excluding the carriers. On September 7, it sent telegrams to the parents of carriers, stating that their children could no longer attend school.

There is a folk wisdom among attorneys who litigate against New York City: Always sue the city on Friday and schedule the court hearing for Monday, because corporation counsel does not work on weekends.

*It appears that the board reasoned that since the susceptibles had been exposed to the carriers and hepatitis had up to a six-month incubation period, contagion was still possible. In a way, the policy demonstrated the extremes to which a "risk-free" position could be taken.

In this instance, the timing was fortuitous, but still effective. The board of education telegrams went out on Thursday, Janet Wheeler called Chris Hansen that same day, and the lawyers immediately prepared and filed a motion on Friday for a restraining order against the board so the children would not miss any classes. The city's lawyers did not work over the weekend, confident that the court would dismiss plaintiffs' motion out of hand. Only vaguely aware of the events that had culminated in the telegrams or that a consent judgment, a review panel, a team of lawyers, and a judge were determined to protect the Willowbrook class, they assumed that the Department of Health was fully cooperating with the board of education; hence they had only to inform the court that the carriers posed a health risk to other students, that the board was taking the precautionary step of temporarily excluding the carriers, and the judge would rule in their favor. Moreover, the papers that corporation counsel had received from the plaintiffs seemed very thin, encouraging the idea that the attorneys for the class were only going through the motions. (Later they would discover that the full set of papers had been delivered to the chancellor's office, but since it was Friday afternoon no one had bothered to send them over.)

On Monday morning, the attorneys for the board found Judge Bartels's courtroom jam-packed with lawyers, state officials, and observers. The size of the crowd did not disturb them. Making their way to the defendant's table, one of them remarked to the other: "There must be an interesting case on the docket this morning, after ours."

For the first (and last) time in the history of the case, the state, the review panel, and the class lawyers were seated together at plaintiffs' table, which had an almost holiday air about it. Their position was that the retarded carriers had been singled out for discriminatory treatment. Dr. Philip Ziring, the lead witness, testified that the schools did not screen other students for the hepatitis antigen and Willowbrook carriers would be the first antigen positive group anywhere ever penalized. "We are aware," Ziring declared, "of some physicians and dentists who . . . have themselves become identified as carriers, and to my knowledge, these individuals have not been restricted from their practice either, despite the fact that they have their hands in the mouths of patients, or their bellies in the case of surgeons." Ziring explained that sound hygienic practices (described in CDC's 1976 guidelines) were adequate to prevent contagion. The Willowbrook carriers, for example, had been attending classes for several years and yet "there hasn't been a single clinical case of hepatitis B among any of the children who have been in contact with the carriers." Conceding that the carriers did pose "some risk," he concluded that it was "quite small, if not easily manageable, and certainly one which I don't think called for this kind of drastic response on the part of the Board of Education."

Plaintiffs' lawyers also demanded to know by what authority the board of education had excluded the carriers. The Department of Health, after all, had only suggested cohorting in special classes. Moreover, expulsion violated not only the terms of the consent judgment but also Federal Law 94-142, which entitled the handicapped to an education in the least restrictive setting. The case against the board seemed so open-and-shut that plaintiffs rested after one morning of testimony.

The board of education counted on Department of Health officials Lloyd Novick and Curt Bakal to refute Ziring, which they were prepared to do up to a point. Novick contended that since the tests had uncovered new carriers, procedures that minimized contact were justified. Bakal (who had just returned to Harvard to continue his public health studies and had to be flown down to New York) insisted that although the risk of contagion could not be quantified, it was "not a remote possibility." Citing his classroom observations of the retarded, he argued that their unhygienic personal habits justified segregation. But neither he nor Novick supported the board's removal of the carriers —which left the board in the peculiar position of calling witnesses who agreed that the risk of contagion was real, but exclusion was not justified.

The only defense that the board mustered was administrative necessity. To organize separate classes for fifty carriers scattered all over the city was too burdensome; besides, not enough classrooms had sinks to implement the necessary hygienic measures. And what was wrong with sending the carriers back to the developmental centers? Retarded students did not often mix with normal students in the public schools—which was the board's way of conceding that it was not fulfilling the principles of mainstreaming.

Even before the two days of hearings were over, Bartels made it clear that the Department of Health's recommendation to segregate the carriers in the schools was not before him. Rather, he had only to pass on the board's exclusion order, and no testimony suggested that the risk posed by the carriers was grave enough to justify such a measure. Immediately after the hearings closed, he ruled that "The Board of

Education adopted the present course of action which none of the medical experts countenance. . . . It is not necessary to close the schoolhouse door to these children." As for administrative convenience: "These obstacles, real as they may be, cannot be allowed to vitiate the right of these handicapped school children." And in his footnote he cited *Brown* v. *Board of Education.*

The board of education returned the carriers to their regular classrooms and then convened all the parties to see whether a compromise could be fashioned. Surprisingly, the board did not simply decide to drop the matter then and there; it now had a federal court order that carriers were to remain in their classrooms, an order it could cite should future liability claims arise. And yet the board pressed on. Perhaps it gave too much weight to the pronouncements of the department of health; perhaps it was too sensitive to political considerations, more frightened of parental and union protests than of OMRDD and the review panel. In all events, the board was determined to get itself off the hook, not perceiving that it was already free.

The meetings that the board organized in October replicated the courtroom encounters. The Department of Health smugly announced that its guidelines had just been endorsed by the Northeast section meeting of epidemiologists—but who this group was and what their endorsement meant was never made clear. When the board of education explored the possibility of modifying the stipulation that a sink be installed in every classroom with a carrier (since many schools had antiquated plumbing), the department would not yield. The panel and OMRDD were no more flexible, seeing no reason to penalize the carriers in light of Bartels's findings. Everyone soon recognized the futility of the sessions, at which point the board proposed another plan.

Following the essential points of the department of health guidelines, it proposed that the carriers be reassigned to nineteen classrooms in five schools, one in each borough. Brooklyn's eleven carriers, for example, would travel to one special school, where they would be divided into four groups, each group with four teachers and four paraprofessionals. The fifteen carriers from Staten Island would make up four classes, the ten from Manhattan another four, and so on. Neither OMRDD nor the panel nor the class lawyers would agree to the scheme, and thus Bartels now had another dispute before him, in effect, the department of health guidelines.

But he did not have the department of health before him. The board of education remained the lone defendant, a position that reflected the department's skill in keeping out of the line of fire. Under these circumstances, the board's counsel argued that the department guidelines were "presumptively valid"—that is, that once the department issued recommendations, the board, and the court as well, had to assume their correctness, and if plaintiffs disagreed, the burden of proof rested on them. As Charles Schonhaut, acting director of special education, put it: "If the city agency that has that responsibility tells us that there is risk then we have to act accordingly. We have to follow their recommendations so as to reduce the risk." The board's plan "best meets the needs of the individual children consistent with the Department of Health recommendations. . . . It's the best . . . plan we could develop given the circumstances." The two administrators who designed the plan emphasized that the carriers would have smaller classes, more teachers, and groupings consistent with their educational skills. But even they conceded: "We don't think this is educationally what we would like to do, but we have no choice. We are being told we have to isolate these kids. Isolation to us is not what we would do if we have a choice."

Plaintiffs were convinced that the board did have a choice. Using the considerable expertise of William Bitner, of the review panel, and Kathy Schwaninger, its executive director, they demonstrated that the board's claims notwithstanding, cohorting lumped together students with widely divergent skills, putting into one class those who were just learning the simplest forms of pronunciation with those starting to construct sentences. Bitner and Schwaninger also reported visiting carriers in their classrooms and not seeing the drooling, biting, and kissing that Bakal had described. What was more, the teachers seemed entirely comfortable with the carriers.

The second trial closed with a day of medical testimony, from John Marr of the Department of Health for the defendants, then from Cladd Stevens, of the New York Blood Bank, for the plaintiffs. Marr insisted that although the risk of contagion from the carriers was indeterminate, it had to be contained. "We felt," he explained, "that even though we did not have all the answers, it was preferable to recommend separation of the classrooms. . . . We did not want to attempt to assess the magnitude of the risk by conducting what would have been a natural experiment, by allowing the carriers and the susceptibles to stay in the same classroom as we observed them over months or years. . . . In our classroom observations we felt that those factors do exist that would promote the spread of the disease. . . . I believe [the risk] is small, but it is real and I believe as an epidemiologist that we could not afford to ignore it."

Cladd Stevens countered that infectivity depended on so many factors (from the strength of the antigen in the carrier to the receptivity of the susceptible) that she was unconcerned about carriers in the classrooms. In fact, she found the test results obtained by Bakal to be "reassuring." She noted that in earlier tests, when the blood of black children in the city schools had been analyzed for exposure to hepatitis, some 8 to 13 percent revealed either antibodies or the antigen; the comparable figures for Hispanic children was 16 percent, and for Chinese, 20 percent. Thus, to find five carriers and twenty immunes among the 270 classmates of the carriers was just about right, an average exposure of 9 percent. "To my mind," Stevens concluded, "it's not particularly alarming. . . . I should say that there is no evidence at all as to the risk of hepatitis B infection from among classroom contacts." With that the plaintiffs rested.

The issues confronting Bartels were much more difficult than in the first round of litigation, for here the board of education seemed to be in accord with the Department of Health. Segregation, unlike exclusion, was supported by some medical experts. Thus what had taken him one day to resolve in September now took three months, and not until February 28, 1979, did Bartels deliver his decision. He was convinced that the board's plan would adversely affect the education of the carriers; the smaller class size would impose "a limitation on the opportunities which these children would otherwise have for peer interaction. . . . The potentially devastating impact of the stigma caused by isolating these children as hepatitis B carriers may traumatize them and impair the continuity of their learning process." But however serious the disadvantages, the question remained whether "the proposed segregation of carrier children . . . is justified to protect the health and welfare of the non-carrier retarded children." Did the risks of contagion justify isolating the carriers?

Bartels was skeptical about the extent of the danger of contagion. He had little patience with circumstantial epidemiological arguments, particularly when no single case of *acute* hepatitis had been reported from anyone in contact with the Willowbrook carriers. In the courtroom, the question of contagion turned into a question of liability; whether party

A infected party B became a matter of whether party A injured party B—and framing the issue this way shifted the burden of proof from the carriers (where the Department of Health placed it) to the victim. The public health officials assumed the carriers were guilty until proven otherwise; since they had the antigen, it was up to them to demonstrate conclusively that they were not (and would not be) responsible for increasing the incidence of the disease. To the judge, the carriers were innocent until proven otherwise. The fact that someone else in a carrier's class turned up with the antigen was not dispositive unless it could be shown that it was the carrier that had actually transmitted the disease.

Given the six-month incubation period for hepatitis B and the fact that research was only a few years old, the department could not satisfy Bartels on the precise threat that the carriers posed. It did not help their case that the uproar had begun with a mistake, that the Staten Island teacher had contracted hepatitis A, not B, for the judge noted again and again that the controversy had its roots not in the laboratory (with an unimpeachable case of a carrier transmitting hepatitis) but in public agitation based on error. Without stretching the civil rights analogy too far, here again was a majority (susceptibles) unfairly excluding from the schools a minority (carriers), whose rights the court scrupulously safeguarded, at least after *Brown*.

Bartels was also disturbed by the Department of Health's readiness to segregate *all* the Willowbrook carriers, regardless of their particular behaviors. He could appreciate that biters and bleeders might need extra surveillance, but well behaved students able to respect hygienic measures should not be penalized. It seemed as if the department, like the board, had taken the easy way out. A judge, unlike an epidemiologist, thought in terms of individual, not collective, responsibility. Thus, concluded Bartels, "The proposed segregation seems an unwarranted and unnecessarily restrictive reaction to the purely theoretical risk of transmission that the Board has shown."

Up to this point, Bartels's opinion remains open to dispute. The health department officials were persuaded that if one classmate of a carrier had had visible manifestations of disease (e.g., turned yellow), then the judge would have been on their side. Because the illness was subclinical, he discounted its seriousness. But Bartels's decision then went on to display the powerful advantages of the legal mind-set. Cutting through a morass of procedural law, he came (even more clearly than plaintiffs' lawyers) to the crux of the matter, to the failure of the Department of Health to enact its proposals in the manner prescribed by the New York City Charter so as to make them binding. "The Health Department's recommendation," the judge noted, "did not carry with it the full panoply of trappings traditionally considered essential to insure the trustworthiness of a valid regulation. For example, no public hearings were held, no notices of proposed rulemaking were published, and only limited opportunity was provided for input by interested persons." Under such circumstances, the guidelines could not be given "presumptive validity," and for the board of education then to exclude the Willowbrook carriers amounted to denying handicapped individuals public education. "We conclude," ruled Bartels, "that the segregation of retarded hepatitis B carriers without imposing a similar restriction on non-handicapped [carrier] persons would constitute unlawful discrimination."

This procedural point was not some technicality in administrative law that allowed the court to do what it wanted to do anyway. Rather, if the risks posed by the retarded carriers were as grave as the Department of Health insisted, then why did it refrain from exercising its legal authority to frame a regulation, to hold a hearing, and to issue guidelines under its statutory authority? Why did it have the board of education bear the burden of the case instead of taking the lead itself?

The answer rests in the fact that the department was too unsure of its evidence on the risks of contagion to issue a regulation, which by its very nature would have had to treat all carriers, not only retarded carriers. A health department could no more write a code about hepatitis carriers and address only the retarded than it could issue a regulation about legionnaires' disease that addressed only whites or males or legionnaires. A regulation on hepatitis B carriers governing school attendance would have to be general: *All* students would have to be tested, and *all* teachers as well. Whatever distinctions were to be made about the carriers would have had to be made for all of them or on the basis of some rational and coherent standard.

The predicament was even worse, for regulations covering carriers could not be limited to schools. If carriers posed a health risk, if saliva or perspiration contained the antigen, then how could a health department write regulations without addressing hepatitis B carriers working in food establishments? Should not every cook and waiter be screened for the antigen, retarded or not? And a code could not stop at food establishments. What about the dentist whose ungloved hands were in his patient's mouth, whose chapped hands or cut finger might transmit the antigen? And what of the surgeon? Or the nurse? To pose these questions is to make obvious why the department backed off a code. It had neither the audacity nor the evidence to take on the general problem, to regulate not only the retarded but the surgeons. In effect, one has only to go through the exercise of writing a formal department of health regulation to see why it stayed in the background.

But then why did the department, astute enough to realize that it could not address the general problem, try to affect the specific problem? Why did it take on the retarded at all? In part, public health considerations did count; give an epidemiologist a situation in which contagion seems likely and he will move to correct it (without necessarily thinking about larger issues). But more important, the story makes sense only if one appreciates the stigma that the retarded bear. They could be penalized on the basis of evidence that was not compelling enough to penalize surgeons.

In the end, when it is difficult or impossible to know where the public interest rests, particularly when the rights of minorities as against the majority are at stake, then a reliance upon a mechanism like the court may bring us closer to an equitable decision. Whatever commitment Bartels had to protecting the Willowbrook class, his most notable attribute was his commitment to playing by the rules, to treating minorities the same way as majorities. This quality speaks not only to his character but to the character of the court. We may not agree on what is best for us all, but at least we can insist on fairness for us all—which is what courts are especially well suited to do.

PART IV

COMING APART

12

Politics, Politics, Politics

In the winter of 1980, the Willowbrook wars entered a new phase, the third in their almost decade-long history. The first stage, from 1972 to 1975, had been a time of high drama and intense constitutional debates. Public interest was keen and participants shared a sense of a crusade; good and evil were clear-cut and no cause seemed more worth fighting for than closing Willowbrook. A second stage came with the signing of the consent judgment, a time of remarkable innovation when the life style and life chances of the Willowbrook class were being revolutionized. Indeed, had the Willowbrook wars ended in 1979, they would have seemed an unqualified victory and the lawyers, the OMRDD administrators, the judge, and the review panel all deserving of decoration.

The campaigns continued, however, with strong counterattacks and reversals, never to the point where all the first hard-won gains were lost but with major defeats nevertheless. It is tempting to attribute the decline to energies running dry and crusading spirits dissipating; to be sure, some of the participants did burn out or move on, including Barbara Blum, Bruce Ennis, and, as we shall see, Tom Coughlin and Jennifer Howse. So, too, it had been easy to capture public attention when institutional conditions approximated those in concentration camps; it was near impossible to keep interest alive when the issues involved the quality of the physical therapy program or the ratio of case managers to clients.

All this acknowledged, the reasons for change go deeper. Over the period 1976–79, the implementation of the consent judgment had proceeded with surprisingly little interference, not only because of pressures to satisfy the court decree but because the new departures, from organizing the Metropolitan Placement Unit to contracting for group homes, seemed exceptional, special to this one case and not worth bargaining about even to those with designs on OMRDD's fiscal resources. For example, no one knew what funds the decree would command, or how regularly they would be expended, or how they might be tapped for other purposes. By 1980, with the flow of dollars substantial and predictable, the Willowbrook appropriations became integral to the system of political horse-trading—contracts for powerful supporters, jobs for would-be voters, favors for constituents—chips to be negotiated and exchanged in the course of doing business with the state. The implementation of the consent judgment was secure enough to command attention and yet vulnerable enough to be undermined.

The turning point came in the wake of the review panel's attempt to ameliorate the condition of the class members confined in Gouverneur Hospital. In the early 1960s, some 160 of Willowbrook's most disabled children had been moved into empty wards of this antiquated hospital on Manhattan's Lower East Side, and two decades later it was hard to decide whether the residents or the buildings were in worse shape. The youngsters were all bedridden, their body weights roughly matching their ages—twenty years, twenty pounds. After decades of neglect, their limbs were too contracted to allow them to sit, let alone walk; few could understand speech, none could talk, and all were highly susceptible to infections. As for Gouverneur, originally constructed in 1898, it had never been thoroughly renovated. Layers of lead paint peeled off the walls; rotten window sashes let in rain; the incinerator leaked foul gases and the electrical wiring allowed only an eerie half-light on the wards. In February 1976, the New York City Fire Department recommended that due "to the deterioration . . . as well as the complete absence of fire safety provisions, this building should be condemned." A few months later, HEW disallowed some $84,000 a month in Medicaid payments for Gouverneur.

Under these circumstances, DMH began to search for another facility. In the days before the consent judgment, it would simply have scattered the Gouverneur residents to other developmental centers, but the review panel was certain to block such a move and the newly politicized Gouverneur Parent Association was demanding that either the building be renovated or all the residents be transferred as a group: "Together we came, together we leave!" Convinced that family care or group homes for such disabled residents was, for the moment, impossible, officials located another vacant city hospital building, Delafield, along Riverside Drive adjoining Columbia Presbyterian Medical Center. Since the building needed only a minimum of renovation and the medical center might be willing to provide services, Coughlin happily informed the panel of his intention to move the residents there. The panel was disturbed that he had not made specific plans for community placements, but it allowed the transfer "only because of the immediacy of the life-threatening situation which existed at Gouverneur."

No sooner was this done than Coughlin announced that the Delafield scheme had fallen through, but he now had an even better arrangement. The Mental Retardation Institute (MRI), nationally known for its clinical services, had agreed to run a facility for the Gouverneur clients. As part of New York Medical College, it would operate the top three floors (or twelve wings) of the college's Flower and Fifth Avenue Hospitals. Flower Fifth, Coughlin explained to the panel, had agreed to phase out its acute care service and admit instead chronic and long-term-care patients, essentially the retarded and the elderly.

The panel went along. The need to remove the clients from Gouverneur was urgent, and the panel did win a commitment that placement in Flower Fifth would be transitional; its residents were to go into the community no later than March 1981. Moreover, MRI enjoyed a first-rate reputation and was promising to organize an elaborate, perhaps too elaborate, service system, with 216 nurses, 10 on-duty physicians, 50 psychologists, 27 teachers, 14 occupational therapists, 5 music therapists, and 5 art therapists. This staffing pattern almost justified the exceptionally high cost of services—MRI had negotiated with OMRDD a reimbursement rate of $245 per day per patient, for a total of $14 million annually. Although the panel rarely concerned itself with the cost of services when entitlements for the class were at stake, it did question this expense. "We urge you," it wrote Coughlin, "to carefully review the cost data . . . before finalizing a contract." Coughlin, however, responded that Flower Fifth would be a showpiece, habilitating the retarded the way Rusk Institute rehabilitated the physically handicapped. The panel also took comfort in the fact that the facility was to be used exclusively by the Gouverneur residents "until such time as a complete wing had been emptied through their placement in the community," which might promote a high quality of care.

What Coughlin did not tell the panel was that New York Medical College was in serious financial trouble and that the $14 million arrangement was part of a bail-out. Between January 1, 1975, and December 31, 1977, its expenses had exceeded its income by $9 million, and even after dipping into capital it still owed significant debts, including a half-million dollars to the state's Facilities Development Corporation. Back in the early 1970s, the college, on behalf of MRI, had built a twenty-four-bed unit in Valhalla, Westchester County, and borrowed $4 million from FDC under a "leaseback" arrangement, the equivalent of a mortgage. The debt was supposed to be repaid in monthly installments of $31,000, but by May of 1976, MRI had fallen behind on payments, and by the fall of 1977 it was deep in arrears. To compound problems, Westchester County was insisting that MRI had overclaimed $729,000 in patient reimbursement and wanted the money back. At the same time, Flower and Fifth Avenue Hospitals was in trouble. It had lost an estimated $3.7 million in 1977, and was anticipating further losses in 1978. To be sure, FDC did hold title to the Valhalla facility and in case of default could take it over. But what it wanted most was cash, not another building.

To avert bankruptcy and default, the state comptroller's office together with DMH, Budget, FDC, and Westchester's Community Health Board negotiated a solution in which the linchpin was the reimbursement rate for the Gouverneur residents. First Westchester agreed to reduce its claim against MRI; then DMH raised the reimbursement rate for the twenty-four-bed Valhalla unit from $134 to $249 a day, retroactive for six months. Finally, and most important, the Gouverneur residents moving into Flower Fifth would bring along their $14 million a year. Thus, courtesy of the Willowbrook class, FDC would get its money back and the New York Medical College would become solvent.

The arrangement seemed so satisfactory that still another change took place: The New York Archdiocese fulfilled a long ambition to acquire a medical school by taking over New York Medical College. In February 1978, a few months after the Gouverneur arrangement was completed, the archdiocese agreed to pay $10 million for the college and its health-related facilities, and to assume their outstanding debts, a step it dared take only because of the income that Flower Fifth would be generating. Now the resources following the Willowbrook class were becoming part and parcel of the network of wheels and deals in New York State. It was big dollars and big business.

It was big politics too. These events took place right before the 1978 gubernatorial election, and AFSME, the civil service union, already angry over the phasing down of Willowbrook, was furious that the state should give $14 million to the archdiocese via Flower Fifth. The union started to attack not only deinstitutionalization but the Flower Fifth arrangement as well, which made it all the more important for the administration of Governor Hugh Carey to pledge to open fifty state-run group homes and staff them with Willowbrook employees. Thus one deal generated another, so that by June 1978, everybody had something—the archdiocese its medical school, the union the promise of jobs, FDC the prospect of payment—everybody, that is, except the residents who had just been moved into Flower Fifth. For all the lavishness of reimbursement, their care was not merely less than promised but less than satisfactory. It fell to the panel to investigate and to condemn the outcome, in the process earning for itself a number of powerful enemies.

The panel could hardly have escaped giving the Flower Fifth program the most exacting scrutiny, for within six weeks, four of its residents died suddenly. The panel dispatched a team of two physicians and a nurse to investigate and their August 18 report confirmed that quality of care bore no relation to quantity of dollars. The most serious problem was "grossly improper positioning of residents during feeding and medication administration." Flower Fifth's residents spent most of their time lying on their backs, and if healthy individuals would have difficulty swallowing in such a position, "for those with neurological impairments . . . strangulation by food or development of devastating pneumonia is a constant day-to-day peril. . . . In three out of four deaths occurring in residents since the facility's opening [staff could not find the records on the fourth], respiratory problems or factors relating to feeding were directly responsible." The team noted other deficiencies: "There is no systematic provision for routine laboratory and other testing . . . of those in need of annual examinations; nor for laboratory monitoring of clients taking medications with potential toxic effects. . . . There are no provisions for insuring adequate fluid intake. There are no provisions for control of infectious diseases. There is inadequate control of environmental temperature."

The team offered a long list of recommendations (a physician should examine each client in a recumbent or semirecumbent position daily; a registered nurse or physical therapist should certify in writing that prior to feeding, the resident was in a proper position), and at the panel's request, reexamined conditions in mid-September and mid-October. Although it found that life-threatening deficiencies had been "substantially alleviated," it remained dissatisfied with the lack of progress in laboratory techniques and temperature control. The team recommended that the panel continue to monitor Flower Fifth closely —which the panel had every intention of doing.

At just this time, the panel learned that Flower Fifth was planning to admit a new, non-Willowbrook group of sixteen residents, referred by the city's Department of Special Services for Children. The panel objected, doubting "the wisdom of expanding a program which was already out of control." Jennifer Howse, now head of MPU, concurred. "The MRI program was still woefully inadequate," she wrote Coughlin (with a blind copy to the review panel). "We should move very carefully on any proposed expansion of beds. . . . The program has a bad reputation and before OMRDD sanctions any additional unit, MRI/Flower Fifth should be able to demonstrate that their program is sound." But Coughlin and the archdiocese both disagreed. The debating point was that the panel had no jurisdiction over the movement of non-class members into a separate part of Flower Fifth. The sticking point was that the archdiocese was discovering that even with a reimbursement rate of $245 a day, the facility was not on budget. Either Flower Fifth would increase its daily census to 165 clients or the whole operation might collapse.

Over the winter of 1978 and well into the spring of 1979, the review panel, Flower Fifth, and OMRDD went round and round these issues. The panel was acutely dissatisfied with the level of care; Flower Fifth anxiously watched its resident population drop from 156 to 126 as some children were placed in the community—so that even less income was becoming available to make the requisite improvements. Tom Coughlin, masterful compromiser that he was, tried to conclude a treaty by following the well-worn principle of giving each side what it wanted most. He promised that if the panel allowed Flower Fifth's census to go up to 151, all its Willowbrook class residents would be in group homes by October 1980, six months ahead of the original schedule. The panel, still smarting from having sanctioned the mass transfer in the first place, drove a hard bargain. It would permit the census to reach 151 only on condition that it found the quality of care at Flower Fifth sufficiently improved to warrant new admissions, and if residents were to enter community settings of no more than three beds.

By the end of May, with negotiations at a stalemate, the panel restated its demands as a formal recommendation to the court. Coughlin objected, contending that the panel had no right to control non–Willowbrook class admissions to Flower Fifth and that the consent judgment allowed community placement in settings up to ten beds. His first point seemed to Judge Bartels straightforward and valid, but the second raised the complicated issue of what was in the best interest of the class —and thus once again the parties went back to court to resolve a major dispute.

The five-day trial had little of the excitement of previous confrontations. There were no photographs of maggots, no debates on public health versus civil liberties. The spectators' benches were practically empty and the press coverage nonexistent. Yet the courtroom provided a forum in which postulates that seemed commonsensical were overturned. However traditional the notion that medically frail individuals required large, hospital-like settings, the testimony proved quite otherwise.

Not for the first time, the state's case supported plaintiffs' arguments. Many of OMRDD's experts, while not enthusiastic about a three-bed limitation, were not happy about ten beds either. Richard Scheerenberger, head of a Madison, Wisconsin, facility that placed very handicapped youngsters in group homes, had little patience with the panel's three-bed limit. But he was convinced that the best arrangements were intimate ones and he himself placed only two retarded children in a setting—"the little guys, they can't compete for attention." Explaining further that numbers had no magic, he would allow teenagers to live in groups of two to six (depending upon their personalities and disabilities). By the time Scheerenberger left the stand, Judge Bartels was uneasy with both the panel's fix on three and the state's insistence on ten.

Other OMRDD witnesses reinforced the judge's misgivings. Karen Greene, from Nebraska's innovative ENCOR program, testified that three-bed homes were best for highly disabled clients. Her problem with the panel's position was that the voluntary agencies in New York seemed reluctant to operate such small units. Left to her, the Flower Fifth residents would enter three-bed placements. But unlike the panel, she was prepared to let agencies first do it their way.

The agencies themselves had trouble explaining to Judge Bartels why they preferred the larger settings. Sister Barbara Eirich declared that she would be unable to go home and sleep at night if Flower Fifth clients were placed in an apartment setting serving only three. But when the judge asked her why she would sleep better if the setting served ten, her response trailed off into irrelevancies. On cross-examination, Michael Lottman established that half of Sister Barbara's board of directors had resigned in opposition to her opening a ten-bed apartment for Flower Fifth clients. Thus given even less reason to rely upon her arguments, the judge confessed, "Ten beds bothers me. I cannot conscientiously say that I could sleep very well for you to have Sister Barbara's program of ten. . . . With all lack of evidence one way or the other, [it] is too much of a risk for these people and I am unwilling to take it."

Testifying for the panel, Linda Glenn and Kathy Schwaninger explained that deeply disabled clients needed "an opportunity to interact with a few staff." "We have learned in this field," noted Glenn, "that we have gone exactly backwards. We have said the more handicapped you are, the larger the group you can live in." Only in intimate settings could the handicapped receive the attention necessary for development.

The point impressed Bartels not only because it seemed to him correct but also because it came from the panel—and the panel's work had just been warmly endorsed by the court of appeals. The state had appealed a minor ruling by Bartels (upholding the panel's recommendation to give the Consumer Advisory Board additional staff) and the court of appeals affirmed, endorsing the panel's powers so emphatically that even its most devoted admirers were astonished: "We treat the organizational structure established under the Consent Judgment, a Review Panel with the power to recommend interpretation of the Judgment and methods of implementing it, as analogous to the powers granted, say, to Congress under Section V of the Fourteenth Amendment to effectuate the matters and substance and procedure contained in the first four sections of that amendment." If the panel was akin to Congress, Bartels was not about to override its recommendation.

Yet its insistence on three beds, he repeatedly complained, was "too inflexible." "Your problem is you have taken an arbitrary position. . . . I mean a fixed position . . . whereas after listening to the testimony one is inclined to believe that there must be some flexibility." While three beds might be best in some or even most cases, it might not be best in all cases. Why lock the program into one mold?

Even for an active judge, Bartels outdid himself in the course of this hearing. He supplied a running commentary to the testimony, not only dominating the examination of witnesses but announcing which arguments did or did not satisfy him. The court of appeals ruling seemed to give him an extra touch of confidence and he was sufficiently impressed with OMRDD's efforts at implementation to think that cooperation among the parties was possible. He was also concerned that the new team that had just taken charge of OMRDD might not share its predecessor's commitments. In August, Coughlin had gone on to head the Corrections Department and his successor, James Introne, came from Budget. Quite self-consciously, Bartels lectured Introne on his expectations for this case. Commissioner Coughlin had not only been pleasant, courteous, and intelligent, but "at all times he did not consider this an adversary proceeding because he realizes, as we all do, that this is an effort to help helpless people. The point is not how strong an adversary we can be. . . . You must always have in mind the poor people and what they are going through and the great necessity for the humane treatment of them. . . . The saving of money should not be the object but to most efficiently serve these helpless people. . . . As long as the Commissioner of the State and old and new counsel realize that, we will be able to make progress."

In the short run, Bartels had his way. Aware of his dissatisfaction with their solutions, the two sides agreed to another round of negotiations, and on the last afternoon of the trial, the attorneys managed to frame a compromise. Over the next twelve months, OMRDD would place half of the Flower Fifth clients released to the community in settings of six beds or less, and the other half in settings of three beds or less; then, together with the panel, it would evaluate the results, determine which settings functioned better, and report the findings to the court. Thus the trial ended with a settlement that Bartels found innovative. "I must say that I do enjoy these proceedings," he announced right before adjournment. "It is difficult to decide some of these cases. But it is a marvelous thing for me to see such dedicated people before me. I don't often have that pleasure when I am dealing with bank robbers and drug dealers."

In the long run, Flower Fifth became the rallying point for opposition to the court and to the panel. Judge Bartels may have thought that he was devising a novel way to conduct social research, but to the new leadership at OMRDD and to the state legislature, Flower Fifth was the proverbial straw. Something had to be done about a panel that considered costs irrelevant, that could upset arrangements involving millions of dollars and in the process rewrite and toughen the terms of the consent judgment.

At about this time, and as part of the process of bringing the wild card that was the consent decree back into the deck, Budget reasserted its authority over OMRDD's expenditures. It disliked the funding arrangements for group homes, the combination of "620 funds" and Purchase of Service dollars that Coughlin and Blum had patched together in 1976, not only because of the amounts expended but also because of the way they were expended. OMRDD enjoyed enormous flexibility in shifting appropriations from one account to another; it could also write a more lucrative POS contract with one agency and a more modest one with another. To Coughlin, this latitude was a necessary flexibility. To Budget, it was a blank check.

Confronting the combined pressure of the panel, the judge, and HEW, Budget had initially acquiesced. But three years into the decree, as the number of group homes and the size of contracts mounted, it helped persuade the legislature to revoke OMRDD's right to transfer unexpended funds into POS contracts, and it tightened its own control over the use of 620 funds, no longer permitting OMRDD to transfer leftover dollars to group-home contracts. Deprived of this discretion, OMRDD might not be able to maintain its fiscal commitments to group homes and the entire community system would be jeopardized.

The crisis was more apparent than real, for Budget was fully aware that OMRDD had an alternative source of funding available, albeit one that it had, until now, been reluctant to tap, the Medicaid dollars for Intermediate Care Facilities for the Mentally Retarded. Federal funding for ICFMRs dated back to the late 1960s, part of an effort to substitute less intensive, and seemingly less costly, modes of care for hospital stays. The program had not established a minimum or maximum size for ICFMRs, but HEW assumed that they would be mini-institutions for hundreds, though not thousands, of residents. Not until 1976 did mental retardation planners take advantage of this lack of specificity and begin tapping ICFMR funds to reimburse half the cost of group homes of fifteen beds or less. Skillfully working their way through and around the regulations and getting waivers for the most cumbersome requirements on the amount of staff and space, Minnesota administrators were the first to use Medicaid dollars for community residences.

Word of their success spread quickly, and no sooner was Barbara Blum installed at MPU than she and a team from Budget went to Minnesota. To their surprise, they returned reluctant to copy the Minnesota system. Robert Norris, one of OMRDD's senior analysts, was convinced that "it cannot be said that an ICF/MR . . . is cost advantageous" for New York. Minnesota had the benefit of staffing and space waivers from the regional HEW office, but it was by no means certain that New York could obtain waivers or that Washington would approve them.

Norris was not alone in his opposition. Coughlin and the review panel were afraid that the regulations would medicalize the group homes. Inspired by a hospital program, the ICFs required much more intensive nursing supervision than New York's group homes used; adopt ICF and nurses in white might carve out a station area in the living room. The voluntary agencies were also reluctant to handle HEW's forms, face its audits, and negotiate about cost allowances and disallowances. Finally, as the state's watchdog agency, the Commission on the Quality of Care for the Mentally Disabled, calculated: "While conversion of community residents to ICF-MR's eliminates significant costs from the State's budget, it simultaneously raises the overall costs." ICFMR codes would practically double group-home costs; if the state was now paying 100 percent of a $20,000 charge, it would not enjoy substantial savings by paying 50 percent of a $38,000 charge.

Such considerations kept OMRDD out of the ICFMR program until 1978, when Budget's restrictions forced the agency to seek federal dollars. What made Budget precipitate the change? One reason was that HEW was now prepared to grant the ICFMRs many of the necessary permissions; another was that the state's deinstitutionalization program was large enough to make even small savings on each group home add up to a significant total; multiply $2,000–$3,000 per year by 1,000 clients, and the sums became considerable. To be sure, the state reduced its own costs only by almost doubling the total price of the program—but Budget was interested not in how much money was spent but from whose pocket it came. To Budget, federal dollars were not real dollars; they were Other People's Money, to be tapped whenever it would bring New York an advantage. Thus, if a $20,000 or $30,000 expenditure by the state alone turned into a $38,000 or $48,000 expenditure that could be divided evenly with Washington, there was a net saving.

Hence, beginning in 1979, OMRDD converted the group homes into ICFMRs, at once reducing the program's flexibility while securing its place in the system. Because the conversion came late, well after the residences had established their own styles of care, the homes did not become mini-hospitals. The shift did raise costs and compel the agencies to become far more businesslike in keeping records and books, but such alterations were not especially difficult for experienced providers. What might have happened had Barbara Blum been forced to follow ICFMR regulations from the start is a very different question. She might have been precluded from contracting with new and small agencies unable to cope with HEW regulations, and the residences might have become far more institutional in style. In 1979, however, the impact of ICFMR on the Willowbrook class was minimal.

Perhaps its most important effect was on OMRDD itself. The ICFMR conversions regularized the funding for community programs and thus made the group homes permanent in the state. Coughlin, already a proponent of deinstitutionalization, hardly needed such encouragement. But his successor, James Introne, seemed to share little of his enthusiasm for an extensive network of small group homes. Instead, the new commissioner of OMRDD was pleased that under the ICF program Budget had enlarged its control over expenditures.

Notes from the Field
James Introne Attends His First Panel Meeting (David)
Evening of September 14, 1979

I was convinced that it was dislike at first sight, and within minutes Jim Introne and Jim Clements had each other for enemies.

I knew that at the end of August, Introne had written Clements the obligatory "new commissioner" letter, promising that the decree would remain "a priority concern of OMRDD" and hoping that they could avoid "any disagreements which may lock us into the position of adversaries." He suggested an early meeting with the panel "to seek accommodation and mutual understanding," and Clements offered it. "We would welcome the establishment of open, authentic communication," Clements replied, and then spelled out what authentic meant. The panel had several concerns (which really covered most of the judgment). They ranged from "funding adequacy, security, and timeliness for both client basic needs and community residence contract and lease payments" to "securing a process of attentiveness to audit recommendation implementation." Introne's visit with the panel was not going to be a social call.

The panel had just completed some housekeeping chores when Introne entered, flanked by several associates, new faces to Willowbrook's front lines. Although I knew that he was only thirty-four, I was still surprised by how young and baby-faced he looked; he wore his jacket and tie the way my teenage son used to, collar askew, knot down and off center, as though this dress was someone else's idea of what was required. After brief introductions all around, Introne, seeming very ill at ease, spoke first. He said he wanted a positive relationship with the panel, avoiding legal battles and court confrontations. Too much time had been wasted in each side's trying to win minor points; OMRDD and the panel had been so caught up in details as to lose sight of the larger picture, the "spirit" of the decree.

Introne went on to insist that implementing the decree must not provoke a political reaction. Public opinion had to be reckoned with, even at the price of going a little slower. Since most legislators did not know much or care about mental retardation, they were especially susceptible to constituent pressures. Indeed, they did not like courts ordering them about. To tell the legislature "this is the way it has to be" was not appreciated in Albany.

Although OMRDD would continue to make community placements, Introne concluded, it faced important constraints. He wished that the judge and the panel would appreciate the climate in which OMRDD had to operate, for then they would be more amenable to compromise.

Clements showed no such inclination. He knew all about power and politics, he remarked, but the panel was the arm of the court and its job was to see that the decree was implemented. The judgment was a contract, and if Introne believed that the panel was impatient to see it fulfilled, wait until he got to know the judge better. The panel had no desire to be adversarial; in fact, at various times it had warned that the state was being unrealistic in setting goals for community placement. Still, if OMRDD ignored the advice, the panel had no choice but to insist that obligations be met.

Introne interrupted to argue that OMRDD often promised too much because the panel was never willing to accept what could be done. OMRDD, for example, was now having difficulty in making three-bed placements for the Flower Fifth residents, but nevertheless, it had been forced to agree to the condition. Moreover, the panel concerned itself only with New York City. The department had to worry about the whole state as well as the price tag.

The two sides then reviewed eight of the panel's concerns, during which Introne frequently turned to his aides for information. His answers to questions seemed to me to be vague generalities. What would he do about cash-flow problems to the agencies? He was reorganizing the department. How would he deal with the slow pace of community placements? He was launching an education program and reorganizing FDC. After an hour of this, it was 10:00 P.M. and Clements brought the session to a close by declaring that he was "discouraged by the meeting." Introne, taken aback, asked why, and Clements responded that he had heard all this four years ago, that many of the same problems were still unsolved, and now the panel would have to wait until a new administration learned the ropes. Introne apologized for not being better informed, but he hoped to cure that in the next six months, which discouraged Clements more. The panel, he told the commissioner, can only report to the court on what it finds, not on what it hears—and with that the encounter ended.

The panel members remained for a few minutes to share impressions. They seemed to think Introne was not a very astute politician; the real pros would take him over. They commented that unlike Coughlin he had little experience with retardation and would be likely to follow Budget. Everyone agreed that hard times were coming.

Introne's presentation to the panel made it apparent that his agenda bore little resemblence to Coughlin's. Arriving at OMRDD after an apprenticeship as deputy director of Budget and part of Carey's circle of advisers, Introne had a very different sense of his task, indeed of his constituency. For him, the consent judgment did not seem a means to expand resources; rather, he wanted to get the court and the panel off the back of the state as quickly as possible. Coughlin had uncorked the genie of the decree. Introne would secure his reputation by stuffing it back into the bottle.

The new commissioner believed what he told the panel about the near omnipotence of the legislature and public opinion on so marginal an issue as mental retardation. Confident that he was already witnessing a backlash, he may have assumed that a confrontation with the panel would be disposed of in a short and splendid little war, not in months of trench warfare. He appeared convinced that satisfying the decree meant essentially getting the number of residents at Willowbrook down to 250, and seemed determined to reach that figure by one or another means, as though the language about least restrictive alternatives or quality of life were incidental. He probably believed that he was advancing his case by telling the panel it was bogged down in excessive detail.

Introne had another, equally compelling reason to reduce Willowbrook's population to 250. He had to satisfy the latest HEW regulations or possibly lose some $80 million in federal support. In 1979, as in 1975, the twists and turns in OMRDD strategy reflected Medicaid reimbursement policies. Analyze them and one knows which way the wind is blowing.

Back in 1975, New York had faced a 1977 HEW deadline for relieving the overcrowding at Willowbrook. Reasoning (not altogether correctly, as it turned out) that the proposed consent judgment mirrored HEW's demands, the state signed it and set about satisfying both plaintiffs and HEW. But as 1977 approached, and the rundown from Willowbrook proceeded too slowly (in part because the panel would not allow mass transfers to other institutions), OMRDD was once again fearful that HEW might halt funding because Willowbrook, and its other facilities as well, remained overcrowded.

New York was only one of many jurisdictions in this bind. All over the country, states with antiquated and inadequate facilities for the retarded could not meet HEW standards and their administrations had begun lobbying for a relaxation of the 1977 deadline. They were joined by some of the most dedicated proponents of deinstitutionalization, who reasoned that if HEW stuck by its regulations, many states (particularly those not restrained by a court order or consent decree) would pour thousands of dollars into institutional construction so as to protect the flow of millions of federal dollars—rather than attempt the slow and difficult task of placing the retarded in the community. Hearing all these arguments, HEW backed off and agreed not to halt reimbursements to substandard institutions, with one proviso: A state would continue to receive funds for "non-complying beds" if it designed a deinstitutionalization plan that won HEW approval and was implemented by July 1982.

New York was delighted with this compromise; if nothing else, dealing with the review panel had taught it how to draw up plans. It became the first state to submit one to HEW, promising to reduce the population of its institutions for the retarded from 14,000 to 10,300 by 1982. Willowbrook, as provided for in the decree, would drop to 250 and other facilities would decline between 10 and 20 percent. HEW agreed to continue funding, Budget breathed a sigh of relief, and the state went about its business, making some but not sufficient progress toward the new quota. When Introne took over as commissioner in August 1979, OMRDD was releasing 93 residents a month statewide; to satisfy the

HEW requirements, it would have to release 155. So Introne had three years to finish the job or occupy the commissioner's chair when the funding stopped.

This accounting may help explain why Coughlin left OMRDD. After four years on the job, he had every right to want another assignment. (When we saw him six months later, he not only looked younger but told us that compared to OMRDD, Corrections was a piece of cake.) But the move was not entirely his idea. Years of forcing Budget to do his bidding had made him enemies enough in Albany—and although he had done remarkably well by the decree, critics charged he had neglected the rest of the state. Perhaps most important, Coughlin had a well-earned reputation for insisting upon a level of community care that might not fit well with a need to release 155 clients a month. It seemed time for new blood, which just might be thicker when it came to moving clients first and worrying about the quality of services later.

In December 1979, Introne released his first projections on community placement and they were ambitious. By March 1981 (when the judgment fell due), he intended to place in the community all 1,700 residents remaining at Willowbrook by moving out 120 class members a month. MPU had averaged thirty placements a month; once, under Howse, it reached fifty and the entire office stopped to celebrate, with Barbara Blum sending over a basket of apples tied with a gold ribbon. None of this deflected Introne, whose desire to be rid of court oversight and concern about HEW deadlines may well have kept him from designing more realistic placement plans. Over time he reassigned some of his staff to take charge of community placement, replaced several of the borough directors, and shifted primary responsibility for monitoring the group homes from MPU to the directors. Those who appreciated administrative necessities would accomplish 1,700 placements on schedule.

The first casualty of these changes was Jennifer Howse, who resigned as head of MPU to accept a commissionership in Pennsylvania. Her letter of resignation, which she shared with Judge Bartels and the panel, stated that although she had intended to remain in New York until the decree was implemented, she was leaving now because of a "fundamental disagreement with the massive placement goal you set for the next 18 months, together with some of the methods you have chosen." Over the past four years, MPU had a "track record for real quality . . . based on a carefully planned foundation and incremental growth." She thought Introne was about to undercut it. "To jeopardize that record . . . seems pointless. I sincerely hope you will find reason to reconsider your approach."

A few of Howse's friends had wanted her to remain and wait Introne out, believing that so disastrous a scheme was bound to result in a very brief tenure. But Howse was not one for guerrilla warfare. She did tell Bartels privately of her distrust of Introne, but more a professional than an agitator, she took no other action. Indeed, besides the judge and the panel, who could she turn to?

The panel tried its best to talk Introne out of his plan. "You can do it only by dumping," Murray Schneps told him, "and it will destroy the entire fabric of OMRDD. The whole system will come down. The staff won't stay. The voluntary agencies can't do it." Failing in this, the panel issued a formal recommendation that OMRDD "renounce and abandon" its "irresponsible and dangerous plan." But Introne persisted. "I intend, as do all defendants," he responded, "to follow . . . all the relevant requirements of the judgment," and he would decide what was relevant. If a facility of fifty beds could be used to house ex–Willowbrook residents, then the requirement to get the institution down to 250 would be relevant, and the ten-bed limit would not.

Over winter 1979–early spring 1980, the conflict between Introne and the panel intensified. Introne, for example, forbade the MPU staff to talk with panel staff unless it notified his office in writing of the substance of the conversation. In December 1979, OMRDD and the panel conducted what would turn out to be their last joint audit, and barely managed to get through it. OMRDD now tried to dispute whatever findings there were of noncompliance. Perhaps thinking in terms of a future courtroom confrontation, it was not ready to give any ammunition to the enemy.

Just as a major confrontation was imminent, the panel was suddenly and unexpectedly dealt a death blow. On Friday afternoon, March 31, 1980, as the legislature was about to pass the governor's budget, the panel learned that the state senate's Finance Committee had deleted the appropriation for the panel. It did grant Carey's requests for all other Willowbrook-related expenditures and expressed its "support of the efforts of the Executive to meet the community placement mandates of the Willowbrook Consent Decree," but it reduced the

OMRDD appropriation by $342,000 "to reflect denial of funding for the Willowbrook Review Panel."

It was a brilliant preemptive strike; just how brilliant would become apparent as the panel and Chris Hansen, in charge of the plaintiffs' case, tried to recoup. It turned out that Albany had followed a very carefully composed script, its every word precise, its every action plotted. Everyone in the governor's office and in OMRDD publicly expressed shock and dismay at the legislature's action. Many observers blamed Frank Padavan, chairman of the Mental Hygiene Committee and author of the site selection bill, insisting that his hostility toward the decree in general and the panel in particular was so great that he had contrived singlehandedly to eliminate this item from the budget. They even claimed to be doing everything possible to rectify the situation. But in private, they competed with each other to take credit for the maneuver and to make certain that nothing went amiss. It was reminiscent of Agatha Christie's *Murder on the Orient Express.* Who killed the panel? Everyone on board.

Under the terms of the consent judgment, the governor and his aides were obliged "to take all actions necessary to secure [its] implementation . . . *within their lawful authority.*" Specifically, the decree required them to "take all steps necessary to ensure the full and timely financing of this judgment, including, if necessary, *submission* of appropriate budget requests to the legislature." (italics added.) In these terms, the governor and OMRDD had fulfilled their legal obligations. They had asked the legislature to fund the panel; it was the legislature, following on the Finance Committee, that refused. On March 31, Introne notified Clements that "it is my understanding that it is beyond my lawful authority to authorize payment for the Panel members or for Panel staff for work performed past March 31, 1980." For someone caught unawares, he knew just which words to use in telling the panel that insofar as payment was concerned, it was out of business.

The events of the next few weeks made still more apparent how well designed the entire maneuver was. Hansen moved immediately to bring the issue before Judge Bartels, aware that the panel staff could not afford to work without pay. He was even confident that the court would, and could, act. After all, this was not the first time a legislature had tried to subvert a federal court order by withholding appropriations. Federal courts had responded to such ploys with firmness, and Hansen expected no less from Bartels.

The judge was at first baffled by the legislature's action. At the start of a two-day hearing, he asked the state's attorneys: "What goes on up in that Finance Committee? It is so irresponsible that it is shocking." He blamed only the legislature, disbelieving that the governor had anything to do with it (Carey was "an innocent victim of some stupid accident of the Finance Committee in the legislature") or that Introne was involved ("I think he is a much brighter man than that . . . and he certainly would not attempt to do that sort of thing"). Insofar as he could fathom, the problem resulted from a misunderstanding: The legislature had not realized that "they cut my right arm off. . . . It's odd that they should pick on the Review Panel item because without the Review Panel I couldn't operate." That the amputation was not accidental did not dawn on Bartels, at least not immediately.

His enlightenment, or disillusionment if you will, came only toward the end of the hearings. Until then, he had been calmly exploring how the governor might free up four to five thousand dollars to tide over the panel staff until the legislature would mend its ways. Only when he discussed with the OMRDD attorneys the specifics of an order directing the executive to supply the funds did he recognize that more was at issue than a misunderstanding. First, the state's attorneys asserted categorically that the governor could not lawfully divert even a few thousand dollars to the panel; he had no right to override the legislature's deletion. Second, they asked Bartels to stay the implementation of his court order, so that "we might seek review in the Circuit Court." Bartels misinterpreted the request, thinking the delay was to enable the governor to come up with the money. It was Chris Hansen who gently interjected: "The remarks you have just made, Your Honor, lead me to believe that you did not hear what [counsel] said. He was asking for a stay of 24 hours to appeal this court order." At that moment, Bartels perceived that the state's strategy was not cooperation but confrontation. Without the panel, he declared, there was every good reason to expect that conditions at Willowbrook would quickly deteriorate. "If you are going to run a place like this, which Senator Kennedy said back there in 1965 was a snake pit, I am not going to permit it to degenerate that way into a snake pit." With that, he closed the hearings and sat down to draft a document ordering the governor to fund the panel.

Both the governor's staff and the OMRDD leadership were pleased with the legislative initiative. Who said precisely what to whom is buried in denials and boasts, but more than the idiosyncratic behavior of a committee chairman was at stake. For one thing, it was no accident that the executive budget had exposed the appropriation for the review panel in a line item. Although much, but not all, of the budget is laid out into specific units, it would have been simple to include panel expenses in a more general category (like consultants, or other court-related expenditures) and thereby protect it. For another, the governor did have a choice about appealing Bartels's order; instructed by a federal court to expend money, he could have made the appropriation and waited for someone else to take him to court for usurping legislative prerogatives. To be sure, his attorneys insisted that the state constitution prohibited his acting, but he might well have chosen to find money for the panel, cite the federal court order, and see what, if anything, would happen.

Why do in the panel? The question had almost as many answers as there were participants in the Willowbrook venture. Introne was determined to reduce the facility's population to meet HEW quotas in the most rapid manner, and he wanted to be free of panel quibbles about the size or the quality of the alternative settings. Moreover, once it seemed that the commissioner's constituency was not the retardation bloc but the inside players at Budget and the governor's office, then the panel became nothing other than an obstacle.

Members of the legislature had their own gripes. The court, the panel, and the consent judgment had forced constituents to live next door to the retarded and brought a stream of irate letters to politicians' headquarters. The judgment had also committed resources to the Willowbrook class in disregard of the priorities of the legislators themselves. Worse yet, the panel was composed of carpetbaggers, such as the chairman, from Georgia, who were ideological fanatics; in the words of Frank Padavan, the panel was so absurd as to place "non-ambulatory severely retarded clients . . . in high rise city apartments." Only a "narrow-mindedly legalistic" group could be so foolish, a view with which many fellow legislators concurred.

Or to turn the question around: Was there anyone who wanted to keep the panel alive? Not the voluntary agencies—which could do without its audits. Not the Catholic Church—which could do without its meddlings on Flower Fifth. Not the unions—which could do without its critiques of direct care staff incompetence. Not the board of education, or the Department of Health—which could do without its advocacy of the rights of the retarded. Not the community planning boards, not the directors of the developmental centers. It is a good thing the panel never threw a birthday party; no one would have showed up.

Except the judge and plaintiffs' lawyers. Bartels unequivocally ordered the governor and OMRDD to fund the review panel or be found in contempt of court. When the state appealed his order, the Edna McConnell Clark Foundation, under the leadership of John Coleman, gave NYCLU a grant to pay panel staff while the hearings went on. Hansen and his co-attorneys, with good reason, anticipated a victory. Only a year before, the Second Circuit had endowed the panel with powers akin to those of Congress; surely, its judges would not now allow the legislature to abolish it.

Going to court is never free of risks. The Second Circuit is an eleven-judge body (with some senior judges eligible to hear cases too), and attorneys have no way of knowing which three judges they will draw for their particular case. In 1979, plaintiffs had faced three of the circuit's most liberal members. In 1980, they drew, as presiding judge, its single most conservative member, Ellsworth Van Graafeiland; he was joined by the former chief judge of the circuit, also of a very conservative bent, Edward Lumbard, and the court's only woman judge, a new Carter appointee, Amalya Kearse. Two of the panel were known to be hostile to judicial oversight of institutions, and a two-one decision in favor of the state became a distinct possibility.

Oral argument went badly for Hansen. The two senior judges had little understanding of the nature of the review panel; their questions confused the panel staff with the panel members. Nor were they particularly interested in the broader issues of the case; at no point did they ask about the conditions in the institutions or the rates of placement. Indeed, in a footnote to their decision, the two judges gratuitously remarked that "nothing in this opinion should be construed to agree with the view that a federal court properly exercises its function when it takes upon itself the supervision of a state institution like Willowbrook."

Whatever the judges' inclinations, the case itself posed some of the most difficult constitutional questions about the separation of powers. Hansen's argument was that when constitutional rights were at stake, the court had the duty and authority to compel a state to respect them, regardless of cost. Drawing essentially upon school desegregation decisions, he cited Chief Justice Burger to the effect that "State policy must give way when it operates to hinder vindication of federal constitutional guarantees." He also cited precedents from litigation on prisons and institutions for the retarded. The federal court in Minnesota, for example, had ruled that "the obligations of the defendants [the Office of Mental Retardation] to eliminate existing unconstitutionalities does not depend on what the Legislature may do, or indeed, upon what the governor may do, or indeed, upon what defendants may be able to accomplish with means available to them. . . . If Minnesota is going to operate institutions . . . their operation is going to have to be consistent with the Constitution of the United States." A legislature's power of the purse could not be allowed to undercut the Constitution or render ineffective the law of the land.

But the court of appeals was not ready to fit the facts before it to this level of principle, and unanimously (with Kearse writing a concurring opinion) overruled Bartels. Lumbard and Van Graafeiland insisted that the governor had fulfilled the exact terms of the consent judgment; required only to request funds from the legislature, he had done so and could not be penalized for its refusal to agree. Moreover, the two judges emphasized that the legislature (ever so shrewdly, we should note) had not withheld funds for all implementation of the decree but for only one (and in terms of dollars relatively minor) item, the panel itself. Had the legislature taken the first course, Hansen would have had an easier time of invoking the constitutional rights of his clients. But as matters stood, he could only make a predictive argument, that is, that the panel was necessary to prevent future harms; he could not, at least yet, point to actual constitutional violations that his clients were suffering, precisely because up until now the panel had been doing its job effectively. Hansen was in a classic Catch-22 situation, the very success of the panel eliminating the justification for its continuation. From the perspective of the court of appeals, with Kearse emphasizing the point most, the district court and the state ought to be able to devise alternative mechanisms for monitoring the judgment.

Finally, the court of appeals was not impressed with the precedents that Hansen marshaled, for it took seriously the idea that the only proper judicial intervention in institution cases was to close down a facility that was violating constitutional principles. In Minnesota, for example, the court had ruled that *if* the state chose to run a facility for the retarded, then the facility had to meet constitutional standards. But this finding did not, at least theoretically, coerce the legislature, for the state always had the option of avoiding all new expenditures by closing the institutions. "This remedy," the court of appeals insisted, "leaves the question of the expenditure of state funds in the hands of citizens of the state, not in the hands of the federal judges." (Of course, the state had already agreed to close down Willowbrook, but the court of appeals ignored that fact.) On June 4, 1980, the reversal came down, with a closing line of advice: "Those organizations and citizens who are properly concerned with the supervision of conditions at Willowbrook must seek to convince their representatives in the New York State Senate and Assembly, who control the purse strings . . . that funds for the Review Panel should be provided." The defenders of the panel and the class should enter politics.

13

Willowbrook Revisited

Notes from the Field
The Morning After the Court of Appeals Decision (David)
June 9, 1980

A meeting at NYCLU of the plaintiffs' attorneys—partly a wake, partly a reunion, and partly a strategy session. Chris Hansen chaired it and Bruce Ennis attended, along with his old boss from NYCLU days, Aryeh Neier. Lucy Thompson represented Justice, Murray Schneps the review panel.

As would be expected, the first go-round focused on just how the "lawful authority" clause had entered the decree in the first place. Both Hansen and Ennis insisted that the phrase was innocuous, in no way permitting the governor or the legislature to violate the constitutional rights of the Willowbrook class. But clearly the court of appeals had not read it that way and they were angry and embarrassed about being defeated by their own language. Everyone agreed that a lack of funds was not a justification for violating constitutional rights; still, there was not much optimism about petitioning the court to meet en banc, that is, with all its judges attending, to rehear the case. It rarely granted such a motion and the likelihood in this instance seemed minuscule.

It took no time to dispose of the idea of appealing to the Supreme Court. Not only was its majority giving unmistakable signs of being unhappy with the right-to-treatment doctrine, but it was increasingly hostile to the lower courts' involvement with institutional cases. Lucy Thompson also noted that there was still no way to link the abolition of the review panel to a constitutional violation. At the moment, no data existed to demonstrate that the state was incapable of doing its own monitoring and protecting the rights of the class.

As the group came to recognize that without full documentation of constitutional violations no court was going to do anything about refunding the review panel, the need to sit back and wait for things to get worse became apparent. Hansen talked with some enthusiasm about raising the stakes and, after a time, asking Bartels to appoint a master with fuller authority over OMRDD than the review panel. Neier liked this idea and so did Schneps. When the residents at Willowbrook returned to rags and tags, the lawyers would return to court and ask for relief. To cure a situation by first allowing it to degenerate was hardly appealing to anyone with the dimmest hope for rational policy planning. But at this juncture, no other option was available. If you were going to win by the Constitution, you had to be prepared to lose by the Constitution; and however logical it might seem to ask for the panel's reinstatement in order to prevent a decline in the quality of care, sound policy and constitutional interpretation operated in different spheres.

Some of my frustration with this predicament must have been shared by the others, for once the "sit-back-and-wait" posture was accepted, the group moved directly to consider persuading the governor and the legislature to restore the panel funds. The discussion, to be sure, was brief and not very specific—how could it be when no one in the room knew much about the legislators or Carey's executive assistants, apart from the most prominent ones? Still, it was the first time I had heard this group so much as mention politics or the possibility of lobbying. They were looking—squinting would be more accurate—at the capitol instead of the courtroom, a new phase in the Willowbrook wars.

The Next Day, with the Review Panel (Sheila)

The meeting was at the Summit Hotel and the cigarette smoke that pervaded the lobby irritated me, probably because I was uneasy about the coming session. David had told me about yesterday's wake/strategy meeting at NYCLU. I was anticipating something worse—a full-fledged funeral.

The panel gathered as usual in a windowless room on the second floor, completely dominated by a long conference table and decorated with plastic plants. The suffocation of the lobby continued unrelieved, for most of the members smoke cigarettes and David Rosen puffs continuously on acrid cigars. Today, in addition to the conference table there were three rows of chairs, a pew section at the services. At the table sat the panel members and staff and plaintiffs' lawyers. Bruce Ennis took his seat in the pew just before the session started.

Clements called the meeting to order, asked Hansen to summarize the court of appeals ruling (which he did by emphasizing the disastrous consequences of the "lawful authority" language). Clements then announced that he had telephoned Bartels's law clerk two days before to ask the judge to meet with the panel, but the judge had refused, thinking it inappropriate. At Clements's insistence, Bartels did have a long telephone conversation with him, and he finally agreed to issue the following statement:

June 5, 1980
To: Willowbrook Review Panel

The Review Panel over the years has been responsible for a great number of improvements in the custody, care, and health of retarded clients. . . . Without such a Review Panel, the Court would never know to what extent the State is performing and what extent the State is not performing its legal obligations under the Consent Judgment. The Review Panel, in my opinion, over the years, has acted impartially and intelligently and with great expertise. . . . I sincerely hope the Panel will continue in the future the same services it has so well performed in the past.

Accordingly, I would definitely request that every effort be made by the plaintiffs and any outside or public-spirited organization to continue this independent Review Panel . . . by continuing their attempt to have the Legislature restore to the budget the relatively small amount necessary to finance the Panel. Politics is one thing; proper assistance to the helpless retarded another thing. Strong efforts should continue to obtain the support of the media in this respect. At the same time, efforts should be made to obtain from foundations, or otherwise, the necessary funds.

(The above statement by the Honorable Judge John R. Bartels was made at the request of Dr. James Clements)

Although the words were kind and deeply felt, it was obvious to me and to everyone else in the room that the judge was not going to be much help. He had written a perfect letter of recommendation to the press, to the foundations, and to the legislature. But, overruled on appeal, he felt unable to do anything himself.

Over the next hour, a variety of strategies were discussed, recapitulating the NYCLU meeting. Most attention went to the idea of replacing the panel with a master, which did not prompt any protest from the panel itself. As Schneps put it, you win some and lose some, and it was now time to plan the next step in the campaign.

Professional to the last, the panel spent the closing hours reviewing its formal recommendations, particularly disturbed at the prospect of OMRDD trying to move hundreds of residents into twenty-five-to-fifty-bed community facilities. As I listened to the discussion, I found myself getting increasingly annoyed at the lack of appreciation for the panel. Although I understood the politics of constituencies well enough, something rankled. As of last July, the panel had been in operation for five years; its members had all come to New York at least once a month to discharge their responsibilities—from organizing the audits and riding herd on OMRDD to making unannounced visits to Willowbrook. (Only those who had never been to Willowbrook could imagine that a $200 honorarium would compensate for such efforts.) They had taken on the burden of monitoring the fate of some of the most handicapped people alive—and here they were, casually dismissed, without even a gold-plated watch. Bartels had to be prodded to make his statement and could not bring himself to meet with them face-to-face. His right arm had been cut off, and yet he could not say thank you in person. Nor did the parents whose children now lived in first-rate group homes; nor did the voluntary agencies whose opportunity to expand their services had in good measure come about because of the panel's unrelenting pressure on the state. Nor did the ex-commissioner or the MPU staff, who had been so expert at using the panel to capture resources and bureaucratic territory. Maybe conscience is its own reward, but I still wished that some of those who had benefited from the panel's labors could have expressed a degree of gratitude. It was not a eulogy I was after, but a death with a bit more dignity.

For the next year and a half, in keeping with the court of appeals' advice, the organizations and citizens concerned with the welfare of the Willowbrook class did channel their energies out of the courtroom and into the political arena. Behind the shift was, first, the need for Hansen and his co-counsel to bide their time, to let the conditions at Willowbrook degenerate to the point where the lawyers had the ammunition to go back into court. In the interim, why not try negotiating? Even more important, plaintiffs were deeply divided among themselves as to the likely outcome of another court contest. Hansen was relatively confident that after Willowbrook deteriorated (and everyone agreed that it would), Bartels would approve a motion for a master and his decision would be upheld by the court of appeals. But others were less sure.

At the start of 1980, the prestigious firm of Paul, Weiss, Rifkind had joined the case on a pro bono basis (taking over the obligations of the Legal Aid Society), and two of its associates, Jonathan Siegfried and Helen Hershkoff, were now participating in the strategy sessions. And so was Lucy Thompson from the Justice Department, for much of this time under the control of the Reagan administration. The three of them constantly reminded Hansen of what he already knew well enough: that several of the Supreme Court justices (most notably Burger and Rehnquist), along with many others on the federal bench (like the three judges who had sat on the review panel case), were leading a retreat from the social reform orientation of the Warren Court. While the change in attitude did not affect all issues (abortion rights and civil rights, for example, were for the most part well protected), it certainly did have a bearing on institutional reform cases. Already, in actions on prisoners' rights, the Supreme Court had reversed lower court rulings designed to reduce prison overcrowding. (Rehnquist's majority opinion sarcastically noted that he could find no one-man/one-cell principle lurking in the Constitution.) So, too, the Court had reversed lower court rulings limiting the power of parents and psychiatrists to commit children to mental hospitals. ("Although we acknowledge the fallibility of medical and psychiatric diagnosis," wrote Burger, "we do not accept the notion that the shortcomings of the specialists can always be avoided by shifting the decision . . . to an untrained judge.") And closest to home, the Court was demonstrably uneasy with lower court rulings in the Pennhurst case (Pennsylvania's Willowbrook), which ordered community placement for its residents. Although no definitively negative decision came down from the Court (in part because plaintiffs' attorneys relied upon federal and state statutes and kept the constitutional questions in the background), still the majority evinced an unmistakable hostility to court-appointed masters for institutions and a skepticism about a "right to treatment" for the mentally disabled.

With the court so unpredictable in its actions, co-counsel urged Hansen to pursue the political gambit. Michael Lottman and Murray Schneps strongly disagreed, convinced that OMRDD in particular and the legislature in general would never promote the best interest of the class. But in the end, Hansen, who was among the most fair-minded and conciliatory of people and who disliked presiding over these war councils, was willing to give politics a chance.

An accidental meeting of Bruce Ennis and Jim Introne at a party in Albany started the maneuvering. Introne told Ennis that he was interested in resolving the panel crisis but needed significant concessions in order to persuade the legislature to restore the funding. Ennis, in keeping with the new resolve, responded that Introne would find plaintiffs ready to talk. The upshot was a letter in mid-August from Introne to Ennis, outlining his demands: Clements and Schneps were to go off the panel, which was to be reduced to five people. Introne also sought assurances that the case would be closed once Willowbrook's population reached 250 (thereby establishing the principle that the "least restrictive alternative" would not keep the court involved until every last resident of a borough developmental center had been suitably placed). Finally, he wanted the right to place Willowbrook residents in "transitional" settings larger than the decree's ten-to-fifteen-bed limit (thus running down the institution's population quickly).

Ennis sent the letter to Hansen, who responded that a five-person panel without Schneps or Clements would represent "serious concessions for us but maybe not insurmountable" so long as plaintiffs kept a three-to-two majority. He had no problem in agreeing to discuss the panel's future role, although what Introne perceived to be nitpicking he found of utmost importance. He would never agree to end the case once Willowbrook dropped to 250—for tomorrow OMRDD could rent buses, remove everyone from the facility, put them in another wretched institution, and the suit would be over. But if Introne wished to define more precisely the closing moment, Hansen was ready for discussion. As to increasing the size of community residences to fifty, it was "not acceptable and I intend to be very hard-line on that." Yet, he conceded to Ennis, even here there might be room for a few exceptions.

Ennis communicated Hansen's views to Introne, and as an intermediary, softened the tone. The commissioner responded positively, "encouraged to find that we have a closer, shared view." Where Ennis had said that "everyone would also agree that the panel should not become involved with extremely detailed issues of operation and management," Introne heard substantial agreement with his position that the panel had been much too rigid. Where Ennis had allowed for "a few reasonable waivers" to the ten-to-fifteen-bed limitations, Introne heard permission for several large transitional institutions. "We have maintained," he told Ennis, "that the Judgment focus more on [Willowbrook] in terms of the institutional reform for the residents. . . . The enormous attention given [by the panel] to the community placements . . . moved away from the recognition that residents in Willowbrook require equal amount of attention." In other words, Introne thought he could do business with the practical attorneys like Ennis, once he was rid of intractable panel ideologues like Clements and Schneps.

Whatever reservations plaintiffs had about Introne's position, it still seemed sensible to arrange face-to-face meetings and to do so quickly, for the legislature might restore panel funding in its supplementary budget in mid-November—or at least so Introne promised. On October 16, the two sides got together and staked out general positions. Introne, doing most of the talking, insisted that the legislature rejected a community placement ideology and was tired of panel recommendations that ignored all fiscal considerations. Warming to his attack, he argued that the panel offered simplistic and unworkable solutions to complex problems because it did not understand New York State or its government. Hansen defended the panel and in the debate attention came to focus less on the criteria for closing the case or even the allowable size of community residences than on the powers of the panel. With both sides expressing an eagerness to continue negotiations, they adjourned to draft new rules that ostensibly would pacify the legislature and restore panel funding.

Hansen was ready to concede that a five-person panel "shall avoid excessive involvement in extreme details." He was also willing to stipulate that the panel "establish priorities for implementation of the various [judgment] orders." Introne, for his part, had his counsel draft a "Proposed Mission Statement for the Willowbrook Review Panel." Serving as "a neutral body . . . [to] assist the parties in resolving disputes that may arise between them," it was to respect such principles as: "Specific provisions of the Judgment are *subordinate* to achievement of the basic goals and objectives of the Judgment." "The Panel . . . will assist the parties to achieve the specific provisions of the Judgment, *if possible.*" And "The mission of the Panel is . . . to assist in establishing a service structure that *upgrades institutional standards* and provides a *range* of appropriate alternative living arrangements." (Italics added.)

Over the next several weeks, the two sides did not so much negotiate these points as agree to negotiate them, although even this small measure of progress led some participants to expect that the legislature would reverse its anti-panel stance. But the mid-November supplementary budget made no provision for the panel. "Neither Senator Padavan nor Assemblywoman Connelly," Introne's counsel wrote Hansen on November 20, "was willing to include . . . funding for the Review Panel. . . . Their reaction is that Review Panel 'supervision' of the state's effort . . . using the existing Consent Judgment as the standard . . . is unacceptable. Without substantial modification of the Consent Decree so that it describes a system of service which is attainable . . . they are unwilling to fund the Panel. . . . Each believes that the prerogative of the legislature to appropriate funds as it sees fit was reconfirmed by the Second Circuit decision and is unwilling to fund the Panel without substantial additional progress in our negotiations. . . . Commissioner Introne remains willing to continue the efforts. . . . This is far preferable to a destructive cycle of litigation, followed by strong legislative reaction and possible cuts in the funding of services, followed by more litigation."

It was as opportune a moment as any to break off negotiations, for the prospect for success was minimal. Hansen was not going to abandon the fundamentals of the decree to fit Introne's Mission Statement. Nor was he about to allow the availability of financial resources to determine class entitlements or turn the entire case into one of upgrading Willowbrook. Introne himself had little interest in breathing life back into his vanquished enemy. And even if by some chance the two sides did reach an accord, there was slim prospect for winning legislative approval. Given the Second Circuit decision and the Supreme Court's new attitude, the legislature would be disinclined to change its mind.

Nevertheless, the negotiations continued for another full year, less to Introne's displeasure than to Hansen's. Introne had every reason to keep the NYCLU lawyers at the bargaining table—for not only were they out of the courtroom but the fact that negotiations were in progress enabled the Carey administration to claim that it was doing everything possible to reverse the legislature's wrong and to honor the decree. (The press bought this line; the numerous editorials that urged the legislature to restore the panel exonerated Carey of blame.) What kept Hansen at the table? Why was it so difficult to break off negotiations? Because Hansen was under unremitting pressure from co-counsel to try again. The latest Supreme Court decisions were enough to give pause to even the most confident proponent of a sue-the-bastards strategy. The dynamics of the negotiations also made it difficult to know exactly when to call a halt. At each point that an impasse seemed to be reached and Hansen would not budge, OMRDD backed off, and thereby sparked a debate among the plaintiffs about joining one more negotiating session.

Moreover, Hansen was being urged by NYCLU to keep negotiating. Governor Carey had proven himself to be a good friend to civil liberties —think of his stand against capital punishment—and several of his aides were telling NYCLU lobbyist Barbara Shack that the organization owed the governor continuing negotiations. In fact, Shack was soon drawn into discussions; she knew the major players in Albany well and was confident that she would be able to arrange an agreement. Hansen had to educate her from scratch (explaining just why fifty-bed group homes were not terrific), while she kept pushing for just one more round of talks.

Discussions continued sporadically through the winter of 1980–81, although they produced nothing other than legislative inaction and hurried calls from OMRDD to plaintiffs to keep at it. By March, Hansen was disgusted and threatened to resign from the case unless he was free to file his motion immediately; co-counsel and NYCLU officials persuaded him to hold off until the legislature passed its April budget. When the budget deadline came and went with no mention of the panel, Hansen started getting his papers ready even as OMRDD continued to insist that a court contest would ruin the excellent chances for a negotiated settlement. But this time Hansen stood firm, whereupon, to the deep embarrassment of its NYCLU friends, the state beat plaintiffs to the punch by filing its own motion first. On May 22, OMRDD asked Bartels to modify the consent judgment to allow the placement of the Willowbrook class, including those from Flower Fifth, in settings of up to fifty beds. For reasons of pride, Hansen rushed to file a preliminary version of his motion for appointment of a master that same day.

Just when it appeared that litigation was under way, settlement talks began in earnest. Maybe OMRDD calculated that plaintiffs would get their master; maybe it did not want to usher in a reelection year for Governor Carey with another Willowbrook trial. In any event, the two sides came closer than ever before to a substantial agreement.

It took two months of steady discussion and five drafts, but at the end of September, OMRDD and most, but assuredly not all, of the plaintiffs' lawyers had a document they could live with. Hansen got the right to a master to be appointed by the court for a three-and-a-half-year term, with unlimited renewals and guaranteed funding (to come from the executive budget as part of litigation expenses). He also won agreement that Willowbrook would not only be down to 250 residents by 1984 (three years later than scheduled) but be completely closed by 1986. If it failed to meet the 1986 deadline, OMRDD was to pay a fine of $1,000 per day per client to a fund for the benefit of class members. For its part, OMRDD could place the Flower Fifth residents in settings of up to eight beds, thereby nullifying the three bed–six bed agreement. Finally, and among the plaintiffs most controversially, the agreement declared that "the parties recognize that variance from the facility size requirements of the Consent Judgment shall be the exception rather than the rule and shall be permitted only on a temporary, transitional basis. . . . Plaintiffs reserve the right to challenge the creation of any transitional facilities." The appendix to the document spelled out the practical implications of this concession: twenty-seven group homes might be affected; nine of them might go from ten to fifteen beds, five might go to nineteen beds, and thirteen might go to twenty-four beds.

Each side considered the settlement a victory. OMRDD believed that it now had the right to use twenty-four-bed residences. Hansen, along with the lawyers from Justice and from Paul, Weiss, Rifkind, was certain that he had given nothing away. The consent judgment, after all, was silent on the size of transitional facilities. In allowing a two-step process of transfer, Judd had permitted the movement of clients to other large institutions; in the case of the Bronx Developmental Center, Bartels had not. Hence, by declaring now that plaintiffs maintained the right to challenge the use of large facilities, and by stipulating that the state would have to demonstrate that the new settings were "the least restrictive currently available" and capable of meeting all the clients' program needs, Hansen believed he had erected sturdy barriers against twenty-four-bed residences.

Others in his circle disagreed, and vehemently. Lottman and Schneps were convinced that language recognizing an "exception" would compel the court to allow at least some twenty-four-bed residences—otherwise what was the document about? One simply could not make a category central to a settlement and then insist that it was a null category. Hansen, they insisted, had made an egregious blunder and the state would now be free to use mini-institutions to fulfill the community placement requirements of the decree.

Arguments among the plaintiffs' attorneys became increasingly shrill until Schneps was no longer on speaking terms with the Paul, Weiss, Rifkind lawyers and Justice was threatening that unless the proposed settlement went through, it was joining OMRDD's side. Hansen, looking more and more like a general with no troops behind him, wavered, not entirely confident of the correctness of his interpretation. Still, on September 28, 1981, he joined with OMRDD to ask the judge to postpone the opening of the trial because a tentative agreement had been reached. He explained that he would be meeting with his clients over the next two weeks and would then report to the court their views on the settlement.

Notes from the Field

The Clients Review the Proposed Settlement (David and Sheila)

October 6, 1981

We arrived at NYCLU to find some forty people crammed into the library-meeting room. The purpose of this session seemed straightforward—lawyers asking their clients to review a proposed settlement. But since this was a class action suit with some five thousand clients and it was the first time in the decade-long history of the case that their collective advice had been solicited, an air of unreality pervaded. Clearly, the meeting was the result of objections among the lawyers, particularly Schneps, to the settlement. And just as clearly, it demonstrated that there was no existing body or committee to represent the class. In every sense, this was an ad hoc gathering.

Nevertheless, as we looked around the room, it was apparent that those present had earned the right to give counsel. They were the ones who had picketed at Willowbrook in 1971 or served as the named plaintiffs in 1972 or were on a consumer advisory board or chaired one of the parent benevolent societies. In effect, the veterans of the war would now sit in judgment on the settlement.

Hansen opened the meeting, outlined the agreement, noted the differences of opinion, and declared that the session was not for show but for substance. He made his points matter-of-factly, never raising his voice above a conversational tone. He liked the provisions for appointing the master, for closing Willowbrook by 1986, for setting the penalty of the fines in case of delay. He regretted that Flower Fifth residents would go into settings of up to eight beds, but he emphasized that the heart of the controversy was whether the settlement helped or hindered OMRDD in building large facilities. He was still convinced that the arrangement impeded such an effort. Since the decree said nothing about the issue, the state was free of any limit on the size of transitional institutions; by this agreement, the state accepted a twenty-four bed limit and the need to defend placement in them by demonstrating a fit with clients' needs; Hansen was certain OMRDD could never manage that, and besides, he retained the right to contest each and every enlarged facility. Were the agreement to be rejected and the case to go to trial, he would win it. But many months later, all he would get from the judge was what he had already gotten from the state. Under the proposed settlement, plaintiffs would have a master in place immediately to clean up Willowbrook and breathe new life into community placements.

Schneps spoke next. He began formally, reciting his credentials (from named plaintiff to review panel member), but quickly launched into an attack on the lawyers who had fashioned the settlement, Hansen excepted. They had been gutless and ignorant, negotiating with the state when they should have been suing it for contempt. Either because of inexperience or in a rush to get back to their private clients or out of a need to satisfy Reagan-appointed superiors in the Justice Department, they were selling out the class. ("Whose face will you see ten years from now? Whose face did you see ten years ago?") Admitting that he was "bitter and very angry," he insisted that the document was a total disaster, canceling out the decree and all the favorable rulings that had been won from Bartels. The state wanted one thing only, the right to build institutions, and this agreement gave it to them. The state's lawyers said so, the lawyers he consulted with (like Lottman) said so; the only *experienced* lawyer who disagreed was Hansen, and this time he was wrong. Sure it was a gamble to go to court, but the consent judgment was a contract, and conservative judges did not like to upset contracts. Anyway, it was better to go down fighting than surrender.

Then those round the table had their say:

Ida Rios, a plaintiff and a member of the Consumer Advisory Board: In the Bronx, we know what a transitional facility is. The Bronx Developmental Center is taking up millions of dollars. There is little community placement because all the money goes to the institution.

Bernard Carabello, ex–Willowbrook resident, friend to Michael Wilkins, and one of the celebrities of the 1972 scandal: How can we compromise with the state? If we agree to twenty-four-bed facilities for a short period, the state will come back and ask for double that number for double that time.

Diana McCourt, mother of a Willowbrook resident and an organizer of the 1972 protests: I am terrified about trusting to the state. I am more afraid of taking my chances with the state than with the court. My child is out of the institution and we should do all we can to get others out too.

Jerry Isaacs, father of a Willowbrook resident and member of CAB: We have a consent judgment which the state has failed to live up to. The state will never give up anything; we have to go to court. This paper sells us down the river. We've given in too many times in the past. This is not the time to run scared.

Jose Rivera, brother of a Flower Fifth resident: When my brother moved from Gouverneur to Flower Fifth, he did not eat for days. Transfer him again and he could die. I stand with Murray Schneps. He's been there. Put these kids in transitional facilities and many of them will never see a final placement.

Willie Mae Goodman, head of the Gouverneur Parent Association: The state told us when our kids moved into Gouverneur that they would stay there only two years; they stayed fourteen. We are getting old and can't keep fighting the state year after year. Fifty-bed places are terrible. Under no condition should we have to go backwards. Chris, you're going backwards.

Periodically, one of the lawyers from Paul, Weiss, Rifkind, or from Hansen's staff, broke in to defend the settlement. Courts these days were not like the courts of the early 1970s. Bartels would be overruled on appeal; the Supreme Court would likely strike down a court-appointed master. These arguments, however, made little impact and Schneps took the occasion to denounce the proponents as self-interested, cowardly, and ignorant.

Three hours into the meeting, with people starting to drift away, Hansen called for a vote. After a brief discussion on eligibility—with so ad hoc a group, it was an impossible issue to resolve, so everyone present was to vote—Hansen asked who wanted to accept the settlement as it now stood, and received not a single aye. Then he asked who wanted to renegotiate the document, as opposed to moving right back to court, and moving right back to court carried by more than a two-to-one majority.

The meeting broke up with lots of good will among the participants (although not among the lawyers). Going into battle was exhilarating, particularly when the enemy was so disliked. On the way out, Raymond Silvers, the parent who had so poignantly described his visits to Willowbrook, came up to say hello. Although he used to tell us how much he hated Willowbrook, and how much he distrusted group homes, he now had a different message. He and his wife had just agreed to have Paula, their daughter, enter a residence run by a Catholic agency. The rabbi had cried when he heard about it, but they were confident they had made the right decision. Paula would be well cared for, even after they were gone.

The overwhelming rejection of both the present settlement and future negotiations was essentially a vote of no confidence in the state. Parents who had lived through not only the troubled times at Willowbrook but the disasters at Gouverneur and Flower Fifth were not about to give OMRDD the slightest benefit of the doubt. If reasonable (or unreasonable) lawyers disagreed on the potential of the document to do mischief, then the only prudent course was to nullify it. Assume that the state would act in the worst possible manner, and then plan strategy accordingly.

At the same time, the vote represented a surprisingly strong endorsement of community placement, surprising because it came from parents who in 1972, and for a long time thereafter, had been acutely suspicious of group homes. Their original quarrel was not with institutions but with bad institutions, and many of them had joined the lawsuit not to bring their children back to the community but to make Willowbrook a better place. Then, slowly, they changed their minds. Either as CAB members or as officers in the Benevolent Society or as parents, they toured the group homes and saw residents not only decently clothed and fed but, for the first time, treated with dignity. Not believing for a moment that transitional facilities would become anything other than permanent institutions, they were determined to give those still in Willowbrook these advantages. They had traveled too far to go backward now.

One more nasty round of debate took place when plaintiffs' lawyers discussed whether to respect the parents' advice. Those committed to the settlement argued that forty self-selected people did not represent the will of the class, and besides, as court-appointed attorneys, their responsibility was to decide what was in the best interest of the class. But by now Hansen had lost confidence in his own reading of the settlement proposal and would no longer go along with the compromise.

One last futile round of negotiations followed, spurred by the Justice Department, which was still opposed to a courtroom confrontation. Cleverly, albeit to no avail, Justice rewrote the document to omit all reference to transitional facilities; since Hansen conceded that the consent judgment did not prohibit them, why not avoid the issue entirely, and when the state decided to open them, let the sides have at each other? This solution, however logical, made the document simply provide for the appointment of a new master, which gave the state no victory to show the legislature. Still, before all this became clear, several more sessions and several more weeks went by. It was now the end of October, the trial on plaintiffs' motion for a master and defendants' countersuit for the right to use fifty-bed facilities was rescheduled to start in early December—and it was nearly ten years since Geraldo Rivera had filmed his Willowbrook exposé.

Plaintiffs might have taken it as an omen, television broadcasters as a warning against sequels—but Geraldo Rivera's decision to do an anniversary program, to take the measure of Willowbrook a decade later, turned out to be a fiasco. This time, the state knew precisely what to do before the cameras arrived.

In 1971, as a young and obscure reporter, Rivera had raided the institution to get his story. In 1981, as a media celebrity, he opted to play by different rules. One of his staff telephoned OMRDD to work out the arrangements for filming weeks in advance. Perhaps he had changed, perhaps television news had become more cautious. Rivera insisted that the network lawyers, sensitive to lawsuits over violations of privacy, would not allow him to broadcast footage obtained without the permission of the facilities' directors. He took it to be a choice between going in the front gate or not going in at all—and thus OMRDD had ample opportunity to prepare for his visit.

It took advantage of every day. The first stop on Rivera's announced itinerary was Letchworth, Westchester's institution for the retarded where in 1972 he had filmed conditions every bit as awful as those at Willowbrook. His staff went out for a preliminary tour, noting that many of the grimmest features of the place remained much in evidence. The graveyard, for example, still had rows upon rows of tombstones marked only with numbers—a shot that Rivera had used very effectively in his earlier broadcast. But in the three weeks between this scouting trip and Rivera's arrival with the film crew, Letchworth received and expended a $450,000 special allowance from Albany. A team of maintenance workers replaced all the numbered tombstones with tombstones engraved with names; one wonders whether, in the rush, they matched names to numbers very carefully. A crash effort at landscaping went on, in which crews planted rows of evergreens during a weekend sleet storm. Deputy director Maurice Halifi, to his superiors' chagrin, told Rivera on camera about the appropriation, explaining that "we wanted to put our best foot forward in terms of your visit."

Numerous phone calls alerted Rivera to the hasty cleanup, and in an effort to keep the story newsworthy, he arrived at Letchworth two days *later* than scheduled. Interviews with Halifi and with parents established the fact of the cosmetic changes. But the images of Letchworth were of freshly painted walls and decently dressed residents. Yes, a cleanup had occurred, but for whatever reason, the place looked acceptable.

The preparations at Willowbrook were even more extensive. Painters, plasterers, and repairmen were specially assigned to Buildings 6 and 7; because the 1972 exposé started with Building 6, OMRDD officials accurately guessed that Rivera would return to film there; and since the ex-resident Bernard Carabello was likely to be along, a visit to his old Building 7 was predictable. Someone was even camera-wise enough to order a repair for the signpost at the gate, figuring that Rivera would want a shot of it.

Believing that rumor around OMRDD offices had it that he would go to Willowbrook two days after his Letchworth visit, Rivera, in another modest effort to get behind the cover-up, went out to Willowbrook the very next day. The result was that his cameras captured the maintenance men at work, with lots of footage of the painters and plasterers, of piles of mattresses arriving on top of automobiles, of the signpost being fixed. Surveying this scene of mad bustle, Carabello pointedly asked the latest Willowbrook director, Ella Curry, whether all this activity was typical, and she answered that it was. Murray Schneps, who also came out to tour with Rivera, told viewers that in all his years, he had never seen these Willowbrook buildings so clean.

Rivera and his crew then went to the Bronx Developmental Center.

Again, the diligence of OMRDD in preparing for the visit emerged on camera, with frames of electricians repairing wall sockets. And again, one of the facility's administrators explained what was happening. "I have been arguing for eight to ten months for new furniture. It was not until the news media showed up that I got the new furniture." He had been awaiting new shower heads for two months. "It was the day that Mr. Rivera showed up that we finally got new shower heads." That same day, "carpenters finally came to fix up the holes in the walls that had been there for several months. . . . Also on the day that Mr. Rivera showed up, we received larger supplies of pajamas on the unit than I had ever seen."

When he aired the program on *20/20* several weeks later, Rivera made the theme of the broadcast how the state had tried "to fool our cameras," but had been caught in the act. Caught or not, the state had managed to neutralize his report. Rivera and many of those who were interviewed *spoke* about a reality that was often grim, about a suction pump at Willowbrook that had not functioned and so a resident choked to death, about a balcony at the Bronx Development Center that lacked a proper railing and so a resident fell to death. His camera, however, showed no such abuses. The voices may have recounted instances of gross negligence, but all the images on screen were innocuous. The figure of a repairman intruded between the lens and the exposed wires. Everywhere the camera turned, staff hovered about, enclosing it in a circle of officialdom.

OMRDD took enormous satisfaction in being one step ahead of the media, even if the cost ran to some $2 million. But if it concluded from the episode that conditions at Willowbrook were such that a fast clean-up and staff alert could make the place presentable, then it drew the wrong conclusion. What it failed to appreciate was that a trial by camera was very different from a trial in a courtroom.

Rivera operated on a tight schedule—one day for Letchworth, one day for Willowbrook, and the days not even very long when one subtracted coffee breaks and lunch. Moreover, even in an era of high technology, moving a film crew about was cumbersome. Rivera traveled in a caravan, making each visit to a Willowbrook building something of a procession, and officials had no difficulty racing ahead of it. And Rivera's moves were predictable for he followed his 1972 script faithfully; had he varied his tactics more, he might have been able to film on a less prepared stage. Finally, Rivera had a greater stake than he would care to admit in showing an improved Willowbrook. If nothing had changed, if the facility was as much of a horror in 1982 as it had been in 1972, then what had his exposé amounted to?

With evident relief, the plaintiffs left the negotiating table and plunged frantically into the task of preparing for trial. The pressure of time and the prospect of taking on OMRDD in the courtroom dissipated the tensions that had built up over the past several months. It helped, too, that there were no arguments over the strategy for the case. Everyone agreed that the aim was to justify the appointment of a master by offering vivid evidence of the horrors at Willowbrook and the other large facilities. After one and a half years without the panel, OMRDD had proven itself incapable of clothing, feeding, or teaching the residents. Hansen did intend to touch on the community placement part of the decree, but only briefly. He would make the obvious points that OMRDD had fallen well behind the agreed-upon placement schedule and that the experts in the field still considered group homes the preferred setting for the retarded. He was not, however, going to spend much time on the quality of the residences. The point was to get a master by revealing Willowbrook's many inadequacies.

Preparing the case took energy and perseverance, but the task itself was simple enough. Wake Hansen up in the middle of the night and he could deliver a lecture on how to collect data on institutional conditions. Hence the calls went out to the usual experts to come tour and testify. Indeed, Hansen had not been idle while the negotiations stretched on; immediately after the November 1980 fiasco with the legislature, he hired Marnie Loomis, a former panel staff member, to analyze panel and OMRDD documents and draw up charts demonstrating lack of compliance with various requirements of the judgment. The steps to be followed were all so familiar that the only problem was that boredom might breed sloppiness. But there was more than enough hostility to OMRDD to maintain diligence. OMRDD, for example, tried again, as it had in 1973, to prevent plaintiffs' lawyers and experts from touring Willowbrook on their own—which only had the effect of generating acrimony between the two sides and forcing Bartels to write one more order protecting the right of discovery.

And yet it was the state that actually had the easier case. Since 1975, it had put into place an exemplary network of group homes (which plaintiffs would not contest); now was the time to take the credit and cash this chit by asking the court for a minor modification in the decree. OMRDD did not require a master but needed permission to use transitional facilities of up to fifty beds. The team that brought you over one hundred group homes will bring still more—it just requires a temporary waiver of the size limit. The problems at Willowbrook needn't be denied; they merely prove the necessity for transitional facilities. Your Honor, despite our best efforts, Willowbrook remains below standard; a special curse clings to the place. The solution is to close it down as quickly as possible. In short, let every nightmare story that plaintiffs present verify the need for fifty-bed units.

But OMRDD adopted a more conventional strategy, defending conditions at Willowbrook and arguing that community placement now faced insurmountable barriers. Perhaps the new team in Albany, having played no part in the accomplishments and having little appreciation for them, could not imagine building an entire case around the virtues of the group homes. So, too, the fiscal orientation of Introne and his deputies may have riveted their attention on HEW reimbursements; to give up on Willowbrook in the courtroom just might prompt a cutoff of the multi-million annual federal contribution. Finally, and by no means least important, OMRDD was convinced it could prove its assertions. Everyone knew that the real estate market in New York was exceptionally tight, and while Willowbrook was not a model institution, it had declined in size and improved in quality to the point where OMRDD felt comfortable that a one-day scheduled tour of the place would not prompt another scandal. And anyone who thought otherwise had only to see what happened when Geraldo Rivera went to film his program.

The opening day of the trial, December 10, 1981, realized OMRDD's every fantasy. In his brief opening remarks, defense counsel let drop, rather casually, the suggestion that the judge should go out to see Willowbrook for himself, a suggestion that neither Bartels nor Hansen picked up. But all morning long, as plaintiffs were beginning to examine their lead witness—Jim Clements, of course—they nervously debated how to respond. Should they do nothing and give OMRDD more time to erect a Potemkin village for a later visit by the judge? Or should they suggest that Bartels go right out today, on the assumption that OMRDD was not expecting an immediate visit? Since several of the attorneys had been to Willowbrook just three days before and found conditions bordering on the disgusting, they decided to move quickly. Right before lunch, Hansen stood up to suggest that "in the interest of insuring Your Honor can get a fair portrayal of what the facility looks like rather than a show tour," the court should adjourn immediately for a tour of Willowbrook. Defense concurred and so did Bartels. Car rides were arranged on the spot, and off they went.

The institution that they saw was barely recognizable in its good order. They visited five buildings—some of them those that Clements had begun to testify about, the others chosen by Hansen himself—and found the maintenance and sanitation quite acceptable. The floors were freshly mopped, the walls clean of feces, the residents clothed, and the staff very much in attendance. To be sure, some of the bathrooms had piles of debris (left there after a hasty sweep-up?), and some gaping holes still marked the walls. But the place was altogether presentable.

Defendants ended the tour exhilarated, plaintiffs in a state of shock. Hansen and the others had guessed wrong. OMRDD had prepared the bait, dangled it, and they had swallowed it whole. The cleaning teams had done their job, staff had been on the alert, and for three hours, Willowbrook passed scrutiny. Now how were they to prove that the three hours were atypical and that what the judge had seen with his own eyes was exceptional?

Plaintiffs' answer was to bring to court a battery of experts to describe what they had seen and learned over repeated tours and analyses of state reports. Clements set the style. In a resigned, almost depressed manner, he told the judge that "nothing had changed" at Willowbrook, except that it had become smaller. Life inside was as degrading and dreary as it had always been. He recounted seeing a resident sitting in the lunchroom, his clothing soaked, a puddle of urine at his feet. When a staff member was asked to clean it up, she replied that it was not her job. Meanwhile, the resident dropped his spoon into the puddle, picked it up, and continued eating with it.

Clements had with him 126 photographs, taken by NYCLU attorney Robert Levy, who had accompanied him on the tours of Willowbrook. He reviewed them one by one. Here were partially clothed clients, there piles of feces on the shower floor. Bartels listened attentively, examined each of the photographs, and took extensive notes. At one point, a state official's beeper went off in the courtroom, much to the judge's annoyance. "This is to me a very important session," he remarked. "I want everyone to be able to hear the testimony as well as myself." On another occasion he remarked quite matter-of-factly that the photographs showed conditions that he had not seen, which gave plaintiffs the chance to remind him how brief his tour had been.

The witnesses who followed Clements corroborated and amplified his testimony. Raymond Watts, a sanitation expert, testified that he found twenty-five violations of Food and Drug Administration standards at Willowbrook's food services. "When [insects] are walking through and on and over people's clothing, people's food, people's eating and drinking utensils," he explained, "they are doing two things: they are tracking filth from one place to another and if the filth happens to be a pathogenic type of filth, they can spread disease." Marnie Loomis took the stand to summarize what she had discovered as an investigator for Hansen: "I have never recalled seeing so much dirt, filth, feces and urine as I have seen in the last nine months at Willowbrook."

Loomis, together with Kathy Schwaninger and Margaret Sullivan (of CAB), reviewed OMRDD's own reports to document inadequate programs and chronic staff shortages. This many years into the judgment, the state was actually monitoring its own performance closely, and thus was in the unenviable position of having its findings cited against it. Plaintiffs got much ammunition, for example, from OMRDD's March 1981 audit report on Willowbrook. Over 95 percent of the residents, it had found, did not have adequate evaluations of their program needs; the few residents with adequate plans often did not receive the required six hours of instruction. And even an occasional program that was properly run, like toilet training, met frustrations of its own. Its coordinator testified that his graduates regressed when they went back to the wards, not because they forgot their lessons but because bathrooms were frequently kept locked and ill-fitting clothing, held together by pins, could not be undone.

Staffing ratios, perhaps the best indicator of the overall quality of an institution, also fell below decree standards. Loomis testified from detailed charts, with data drawn from OMRDD reports, that over the past eleven months only 4 percent of the shifts had the requisite number of direct care staff in each building, and only 25 percent had the requisite number of midlevel supervisors. Willowbrook was so dirty and the clients so neglected because staff was not on hand to make it otherwise.

Lest Bartels think Willowbrook particularly egregious and consider ordering a mass transfer to the other developmental centers, plaintiffs brought in equally damaging testimony on them. OMRDD's August 1981 survey of the Bronx facility, for example, found "a pervasive need for maintenance and housekeeping on all units. . . . In every apartment, there is one toilet stall with no door or curtain for privacy. . . . Individual towels and washcloths and drying racks were not seen in any of the living units. . . . Most of the units had holes in the walls and mildew in the shower stalls." Loomis told of seeing a sink filled with vomit and a floor covered with urine. Schwaninger recounted killing several roaches about to crawl into a resident's dinner plate.

Finally, plaintiffs described conditions at Nina Eaton, a fifty-bed facility that might be a prototype of the new and enlarged transitional facilities that OMRDD wished to use. Loomis declared that she was "shocked at how filthy it was." Clements testified that in one dayroom "the floor was so filthy that my shoes actually stuck to the floor and popped as I walked." Both of them told of seeing clients in various stages of undress or lying unattended on the floor or staring vacantly at TV sets.

As planned, plaintiffs gave little attention to the community. A few witnesses reported a general satisfaction with the group homes that they had visited, reiterating what Bartels had already heard dozens of times: Retarded people progressed better in small and intimate settings. But most of the testimony went not to refighting the group home versus the institutions battle, but to letting the judge know that the institutions were awful, his own brief visit notwithstanding. With the panel now gone, he had better appoint a master or else the entire institutional system would soon be indistinguishable from Willowbrook in 1972. How would that stand as a memorial to Judge Judd or as the outcome of his own six years of work on behalf of the poor unfortunates?

This court case was one that defendants were desperate to win. Not only did the private law firm of LeBoeuf Lamb—hired by the state at rates up to $135 an hour—seem tired of being defeated by the young, jeans-clad lawyers of NYCLU, and not only was the use of larger facilities critical to the state's plans, but it appeared intolerable that a victory so carefully crafted in the legislature should come apart in the courtroom. OMRDD had not abolished the review panel only to be saddled with a master.

Throughout the trial, the defense table was the scene of frenetic activity. No sooner would a plaintiffs' witness make a charge about deficiencies at a building or the plight of a client than heads would come together, whispers would begin, and someone, slip of paper in hand, would dart out of the courtroom to make for the nearest telephone. Enough information was forthcoming for the state to take more than two weeks to present its case.

Its first task was to oppose the motion for a master by demonstrating that conditions at Willowbrook did not require so drastic an intervention. Fresh from its success with Rivera and its tour with the judge, its attorneys aggressively and even confidently cross-examined plaintiffs' witnesses. Thus the defense closely reviewed Clements's photographs, claiming that he had focused on the exceptional, not the rule, on the one client who was poorly dressed, not the many clients who were adequately dressed. Moreover, it argued, a photograph was intrinsically a static image pulled out of context. If one saw a snapshot of a resident sitting in urine, there was no way of knowing whether a few seconds before he had moved away from his attendant and a few seconds later she would come over to clean him up. Indeed, the defense presented its own photographs, which, unlike the plaintiffs', were taken in color. In this Willowbrook, there were no puddles of urine and no holes in the wall. Attractive spreads covered the beds and colored curtains framed the windows.

The defense next sought to invalidate the staffing charts that Loomis had presented. Over the better part of two courtroom days it maintained that she had erred in not measuring compliance on an institution-wide basis. She had also failed to count nurses as midlevel supervisors, had not factored in instances of 1:1 staff coverage, and had taken her data from the less accurate daily compliance forms, not the sign-in sheets. The testimony was tedious, but OMRDD was determined not to let Loomis's accusations stand unanswered.

For all its aggressiveness, OMRDD could not deny some instances of negligence and incompetence at Willowbrook. Too many experts told too many horror stories to suggest that this was a problem-free institution. Accordingly, it offered two lines of defense: one, that management plans were coming into place to resolve the difficulties; two, that in any institution holding several thousand very handicapped people, one had to expect less than optimal conditions. Yes, "certain clients of the more than 2000 institutionalized members . . . were dressed in tattered clothing. . . . [But] many of the clients constantly disrobe or engage in clothes-ripping behavior." Moreover, OMRDD was working hard to correct the problems. Between 1976 and 1981, its expenditures on clothing rose from $235 per client to $582, and it instructed staff to check each client's clothing at the end of every shift. OMRDD had also contracted for the design of a new line of adaptive clothing which the state's prison industries were interested in manufacturing.

So it went, inadequacy by inadequacy. Conceding occasional staffing shortages, defendants explained that they were the result of "problems like job uncertainty and a nationwide shortage of physical . . . and occupational therapists. Besides, it was now introducing a "cluster concept" for staffing that would resolve the issue. Admitting that parts of the institution were filthy, it insisted that "it is unlikely that any institution housing 2000 people, whether hale or disabled, would at all moments be clean in every respect. Besides Willowbrook had clearly changed for the better and 'maintenance is a never-ending task.' " Plaintiffs, therefore, were not justified in asking for a master just because conditions were not always optimal.

On the other hand, defendants were justified in asking for fifty-bed facilities, for in no other way could community placement proceed. It is never simple to mount an "impossibility" argument; opponents can always inquire whether strategy A or strategy B has been tried, and the burden then falls back upon the defense to explain why they would not work. In this instance, however, the predicament was even worse, for OMRDD had to call as witnesses those who, against the odds, had managed to accomplish a significant number of community placements. People who had done what others thought impossible now were to confess to failure—a posture which did not suit them very well.

First to testify was Ed Matthews, who had survived bitter attacks from community planning boards to locate many of the sites that MPU had opened. Under direct examination, he said what he was supposed to: that the real estate market in New York had dried up and that the search for residences of ten beds or less for nonambulatory and very handicapped residents "has been routinely unsuccessful." But cross-examination wrung major concessions from him. For one thing, Matthews worked now with only a single assistant; previously he had had up to six. Matthews conceded that he had been under strict instructions to look for sites for nonambulatory residents within a quarter-mile radius of six named hospitals in Manhattan and the Bronx, and that guideline was difficult to satisfy. If the guidelines were relaxed, would placement become simpler? Clearly, yes. Matthews explained that he had "in the pipeline" eighty-eight sites with real potential to become group homes. Apparently, he confronted a hard but not an impossible task.

Testimony from Cora Hoffman, who had spent her time trying to pacify local politicians about group homes, was so evenly balanced on direct examination that plaintiffs did not bother with cross-examination. She readily described the ferocity of community opposition to the retarded, and just as readily described how she overcame it. She related that community boards frequently appealed a group home's location to the commissioner, and how the commissioner regularly ruled in favor of the home—an outcome Bartels ironically professed to find "startling."

Perhaps to give the court a firsthand experience with legislative obstinacy or to get on the record the claim that the legislature should have final say in making appropriations for the Willowbrook class, the defense called State Senator Frank Padavan to the stand. Recounting how much New York had done for the handicapped, Padavan insisted that the legislature should decide on services for the retarded so as "to spend money wisely, prudently, and productively." Bartels listened politely, but reminded the senator: "This is a court proceeding. I am bound by oath . . . to follow the law as I see it. I am not bound to follow the findings or conclusions of a committee of the legislature."

OMRDD ended its case by asking to be free of artificial numerical restrictions, to make placements based "on the individual needs of the clients, rather than an inflexible rule limiting the number of beds." Its experts argued that current research could not distinguish among the merits of serving "more than 3 people or 6 people or 10 people, etc.," that the size of a facility was only one factor to be reckoned with in placement. Zygmond Slezak, acting commissioner for OMRDD (while Introne served in the governor's office), insisted that fifty-bed settings would provide quality care and Castle Hill, with fifty-three residents, was a case in point. Indeed, its clients included Barbara Blum's son, and she would testify to its virtues.

Blum's appearance in court on a bitter-cold January morning was the most dramatic moment in the twenty-five-day trial. Plaintiffs were at once bothered and puzzled by her willingness to testify—bothered because they knew that Bartels admired her and would give great weight to her observations, puzzled because they could not figure out why she would be willing to help OMRDD. Surely she had not performed so magnificently at MPU only to repudiate the decree now? Was she paying off a political debt to Carey or an emotional debt to Castle Hill? The most likely explanation was also the most obvious: Blum, at heart, was a firm believer in the art of the possible and it was not her style to lead a right-minded but hopeless crusade. "In government, timing is everything," she insisted. "If you go past a certain point, sometimes the pendulum swings the other direction. . . . We are in a period of federal cutback. We're going to have fewer resources. It becomes very important to finish the task that we've begun." If the only way to do this was by using transitional facilities, at least more people would leave Willowbrook immediately, and perhaps someday enter the community.

On the stand, Blum reviewed at length her record at MPU, describing the various obstacles she had overcome to serve the very retarded. By implication, her successors had an easier time of it because a wide network of providers was now available. But instead, Blum contended that she would have been able to depopulate Willowbrook sooner had larger transitional facilities been available to her. Now, with housing in New York more "at a premium" and the remaining Willowbrook clients more handicapped, the state certainly required added flexibility.

Blum told the court that she and her husband were "very pleased" with the care that Castle Hill gave to their twenty-seven-year-old son, Jonathan. Its staff and programs were "very helpful when an individual requires as much service as Jonathan does and when an individual is as unpredictable as Jonathan is."

Hansen assigned Murray Schneps the task of cross-examination; since Blum was going to testify as a parent of a handicapped child, she would be questioned by another parent of a handicapped child. Schneps performed deftly, never attacking such a favorite of the judge frontally. (He did not ask what she knew about the treatment of other residents at Castle Hill or residents at the other fifty-bed facilities in the state.) Rather, he approached her as one steadfast friend of community services to another, and in this fashion obtained significant concessions.

Was the task of moving people into the community while you were at MPU difficult too? "Yes." Should difficult tasks be shunned? "No. I think most things worth doing are difficult to accomplish." For all the references to a more handicapped population now at Willowbrook, weren't the overwhelming majority of residents that you placed out severely and profoundly retarded? "That is true." Has the task become more difficult over the past several years? "Nothing is really impossible that we are talking about." Did you confront the hostility of community planning boards and still manage to open group homes in those very areas? "The answer to that is yes." As for your son, would you like to see him placed in a community residence? "At the time he is able to move into a community residence, there is nothing that I would rather see."

Blum did hold firm to one defense contention: The services that people like Jonathan required could only be provided efficiently and relatively inexpensively in larger settings. "There are certain of our Willowbrook class members who are almost imprisoned now in the institution because we can't break through and take the next step quickly for them." But her testimony led Bartels to remark that he could understand that Jonathan's special needs might be best met at Castle Hill; but how many others at Willowbrook fit into Jonathan's category? "Has anyone ever been able to decide whether there are a number of Willowbrook residents who need such a scale of medical, psychological, and psychiatric assistance that they could be best served in a larger institution or facility than just a ten-bed?" In fact, OMRDD had never conducted the individual evaluations that would have answered Bartels's question. Indeed, if OMRDD had had the competence to collect such data, it probably would not have been in court in the first place.

The trial closed with two days of testimony elicited by the attorneys from the Department of Justice. Once the negotiations had failed, the department adopted a new posture of neutrality, and its attorneys, who had customarily sat at plaintiffs' table and taken their cues from them, set up a separate table against one wall of the courtroom and presented their own evidence. They refused (or were unable) to take a position on the question of a master. What they did argue, however, was that fifty-bed facilities would be disastrous, and they offered powerful reasons why.

One witness for Justice not only confirmed Bartels's observation that OMRDD did not really know the needs of Willowbrook's residents, but argued that 95 percent of a sample of residents he had examined could easily be served in group homes. Another witness recounted how Sweden, in the 1960s, had constructed expensive seventy-bed facilities in order to empty its larger institutions. Now, however, it was stuck with them and not very happy about it.

Justice also put on the stand George Gray, an architect who had worked for many years for FDC. Gray explained that opening group homes in New York was not nearly so impossible as defendants contended. OMRDD had only to use imagination to locate a variety of sites, and the life safety codes it complained about were not nearly so restrictive as it suggested. OMRDD had also limited itself to one source of funding, the ICFMR program; several others (specifically the 1981 Omnibus Budget Act) could also be tapped to good effect. And why hadn't OMRDD hired additional staff and searched for residences in the four-to-seven-bed as well as the eight-to-ten-bed size? By the time Justice was finished, OMRDD seemed ignorant about the clients, the federal regulations, and the city's real estate market.

Plaintiffs left the courtroom confident that Bartels would rule in their favor; however badly they had fared in politics, they had done superbly in litigation. Within three months, their optimism was rewarded. In April 1982, Bartels handed down a sixty-nine-page decision that gave the class everything the attorneys requested. The issues posed by the twenty-five-day trial—the longest in the history of the case—were relatively simple for the judge to resolve. Having a precise definition of the aim of the case—community placement—he had a clear criterion by which to measure claims and counterclaims. He also had the distinct advantage of seven years of implementation. Since OMRDD had in place a relatively reliable system of monitoring, he had a useful mechanism for gauging the accuracy of courtroom testimony and his own observations as well.

Expert testimony and OMRDD's own reports convinced Bartels that the Willowbrook of 1982 was dangerously close to the Willowbrook of 1972. "According to the State's own auditing teams, Willowbrook's maintenance deficiencies are extensive." So, too, "the court accepts the testimony of . . . the administrator of the Willowbrook toilet-training program, that his efforts are seriously hampered by the frequent unavailability of clothing changes and ill-fitting clothes that are pinned shut." Bartels also found staffing ratios out of compliance; if more employees showed up on payday or were in abundance in one building but absent from another, the averages might work out right but the clients would be poorly supervised. Aware of just how important the planning of client programs was, he especially regretted that "defendants have been remiss in developing and implementing individual development treatment plans." The cause of all these deficiencies was obvious to him: Once the legislature abolished the panel, "as might have been expected, conditions at Willowbrook have materially deteriorated." And the diagnosis carried the cure: "the appointment of a special master to protect the class members from harm."

Bartels's decision went on to reject the state's request for fifty-bed settings. Having already ruled (in the case of the Bronx Developmental Center) that transitional facilities merely slowed the process of community placement, he could find no reason to reverse himself. Professional opinion had not changed; "the trend throughout the country is toward smaller residences." Conditions at the borough and upstate developmental centers also demonstrated that larger facilities "fail in important respects, to provide class members with the most basic services mandated by the Consent Judgment."

Perhaps most telling, the state's own performance demonstrated that transitional settings became permanent ones. The court had actually permitted some Willowbrook class admissions to the Bronx facility, provided that the parents approved of the step. However, of the ninety-three class members who had entered since 1977, sixty-three were still there, despite OMRDD promises to place them in six to eight months. Moreover, Bartels gave no weight to the argument that residents remaining at Willowbrook were too medically precarious to enter small group homes, for "defendants have not offered any individualized medical evaluations . . . to justify this statement." Rather, "As defendants admitted, class members with these types of physical handicaps already reside in the community."

Bartels was impatient with the claim that placements had now become impossible to make. The court did take "judicial notice of the current housing shortage in New York City," and he was prepared to postpone the deadline for reducing Willowbrook's population to 250 from 1981 to 1985. But he saw no reason to modify the consent judgment. Defendants had "in the pipeline" over 150 potential sites; besides, "the only real crunch in housing is located in Manhattan and the Bronx." Defendants should ignore clients' "county of origin" and place them in the other boroughs. They should also hire more site selection staff, explore the use of equivalency adjustments to resolve problems with life safety code regulations, and investigate a variety of funding sources. In sum, Bartels concluded, decrees should only be modified in the case of a "grievous wrong evoked by new and unforeseen conditions," and the record before him had not demonstrated that such a wrong existed.

It would have been convenient to close this account with the Bartels decision. Ten years after Michael Wilkins introduced Geraldo Rivera to Willowbrook, a major experiment in court-sponsored social change had reached an appropriate stopping point for analysis: A new master, replacing the review panel, would oversee the implementation of an unmodified decree. Seemingly, politics had reared its head but plaintiffs were able to return to court and secure their victory. But such was not the outcome.

To no one's surprise, the state appealed Bartels's ruling. Hansen was not especially concerned, for the judge had documented his findings meticulously and the court of appeals rarely reverses a lower court on the facts. The decision itself, to say nothing of the record established in the trial, was replete with evidence of Willowbrook's gross inadequacies, and both noted specific strategies that OMRDD might have adopted to make ten- and fifteen-bed community placements. Indeed, plaintiffs were all the more pleased upon learning which three judges of the court of appeals would be hearing the case. Judge Henry Friendly, a conservative in the tradition of Learned Hand, was known to be insightful. Judge Jon Newman had compiled a distinguished, and liberal, record as a district judge in Connecticut. Charles Wyzanski, on special assignment from Massachusetts, also enjoyed a reputation for intelligence and sympathy for the underdog. It was unlikely that this panel of judges would disagree with Bartels.

And yet it did. On March 31, 1983, the unanimous opinion, written by Friendly, came down, upholding Bartels in part and reversing him in part, but in effect casting a long shadow on the prospects for institutional reform through court intervention. The court of apppeals gave plaintiffs their master, citing inadequate conditions at Willowbrook. But then it gave defendants the right to modify the consent judgment by making community placements in facilities of up to fifty beds.

The substantive implications of the ruling are serious enough. Fifty-bed units are mini-institutions, not group homes, and neither the model of a family nor that of a classroom fits with them. The emotional ties between house staff and resident and the intellectual commitments of teacher to student are not likely to survive in such settings. One need only consider the difference between a group of three eating around a table or playing in a living room and a group of fifty eating cafeteria-style and going through activities in an auditorium.

Even more portentous is the reasoning the appeals court adopted in reversing. Both in tone and in substance, the decision demonstrated a fundamental discomfort with judges as institutional reformers. Such an activity, the court found, was properly left to politics, to the conflict and compromise of competing interests, not to judicial decisions or consent decrees. In a courtroom, in an adversarial setting (as the Friendly opinion referred to it several times), the full complexity of issues that face an agency like OMRDD cannot be fully appreciated. If a facility represents what might be considered a stage-one horror—the Willowbrook of 1972—then courts would be forced to intervene. In the face of massive deprivation and degradation, judicial intervention in the ordinary course of politics would have to occur. But once conditions improve, once it becomes a question of fifty-bed versus ten-bed settings, judges have no business substituting their judgment for that of elected officials.

Hence the court of appeals faulted Bartels because "the district court lost sight of third parties and the complex environment in which OMRDD must operate. On a less narrow and adversarial view of the evidence, OMRDD's difficulties in stemming neighborhood resistance and securing federal funding take on a real and formidable aspect." Bartels had not (and in the opinion of the appeals court could not have) adequately evaluated and appreciated the political forces shaping OMRDD's decisions. By the same token, Bartels was so loyal to the precise language of the consent decree that he had lost sight of the economic constraints that influenced OMRDD policy. He did not reckon with the fact that "to obtain community placements of 8 to 10 beds, OMRDD often must purchase vacant sites that could accommodate group homes above the 15 bed/10 bed limit at little additional cost." Bartels did not (and judges inevitably would not?) give enough weight to the fiscal imperatives under which the state had to operate.

In this same spirit, the court of appeals instinctively adopted OMRDD's, not the plaintiffs', definition of what the Willowbrook case was ultimately about: to erase a scandal by reducing Willowbrook's size. How this was accomplished and where the ex–Willowbrook residents went was of no pressing concern so long as one scandal did not beget another. Whether it was fifty-bed settings or ten-bed settings was truly irrelevant; courts were not obliged (or even permitted) to enforce normalization principles. Hence, when Bartels disallowed the fifty-bed units, he was allowing one not especially critical provision of the judgment "to override the more comprehensive goal of transferring the population of Willowbrook . . . to facilities of more human dimension as quickly as possible." The modification requested by defendants "is not . . . in derogation of the primary objective of the decree, namely to empty such a mammoth institution as Willowbrook. . . . To be sure, the change does run counter to another objective . . . to place the occupants of Willowbrook in small facilities bearing some resemblance to a normal home, but any modification will perforce alter some aspect of the decree." Plaintiffs and judge had believed that establishing group homes was the essence of the suit. To the court of appeals, it was merely "some aspect" of the decree.

From these premises, the court of appeals delivered what may be a death sentence to this consent judgment (and perhaps others as well). The decree, it found, was not a contract, whose every detail should be enforced by the court, but rather a guideline, a goal, a target to be reached. The decree did not stand above politics but was very much within politics; its purpose was to stimulate change, to encourage the state to adopt a new approach. But its every provision was not carved in stone. In the decision's most telling line, Judge Friendly declared: "In institutional reform litigation such as this, judicially imposed remedies must be open to . . . accommodation of a wider constellation of interests than is represented in the adversarial setting of the courtroom." What plaintiffs had assumed to be the total universe—a judge, two litigators, and a decree—was not the sum at all. Courts had to make room for the "wider constellation of interests," and in making the room, judges themselves should move out of the way.

The court of appeals decision, then, brings the Willowbrook story to an ambiguous close. Reform through litigation may turn out to be a more transitory phenomenon than its proponents anticipated. But the lessons to be drawn from the Willowbrook experience and the policy implications that flow from it are of a greater variety and demand fuller explication.

Leaving the Field

Christmas 1983 (David and Sheila)

As we review the decade-long struggle to fashion and implement the Willowbrook consent decree, the complexity of events allows no simple or unqualified conclusions. Often, as we researched, we would be asked for a quick tally of victories and defeats. Was the decree being fulfilled? Was the court capable of reform? Were the clients merely going from one back ward to another? It is not modesty but pride that dictates our first answer: we kept our account purposefully intricate so that readers could draw their own conclusions. And undoubtedly they will. For example, some are certain to come away persuaded that the court was so bogged down in detail and so frequently called upon to adjudicate minor disputes that the entire episode illustrates why judges should stay out of institutions. Others will define the court's ability to keep abreast of the most minute developments and resolve conflicts as the best evidence for judicial intervention on behalf of minorities. But even as we anticipate widely divergent interpretations, a number of findings may well achieve a general consensus.

First, the deinstitutionalization of Willowbrook did not recapitulate the deinstitutionalization of the state mental hospitals. Dumping was not the end result. From 1976 to 1982, 2600 of its 5400 residents entered living arrangements in the community that, with a handful of exceptions, were decent, safe, and even habilitative. Despite obstacles, real and imagined, to fulfilling such an agenda, the consent judgment appreciably enhanced the life's chances of a full 50 percent of the

Willowbrook class.* Thus, future debates about deinstitutionalization will have to reckon with the fact that even the most handicapped and long-term institutional residents can be returned to the community and benefit from it.

Indeed, future debates on the proper role of the judiciary will have to reckon with the fact that the court was equal to the task of institutional reform. Neither the initial size of the facility nor the intractability of the state bureaucracy nor the handicaps of the clients prevented the court from carrying out structural change. Fact-finding was not beyond its ability; at a relatively modest cost (some $350,000 annually) the review panel kept the judge fully informed about conditions. And if its reports were never a model of clarity, if precision all too often substituted for an articulate overview, still, the judge did have eyes and ears in the field.

By the same token, enforcement was not beyond the court's ability. Not that Judge Bartels ever had recourse to formal sanctions. Contempt was a threat frequently raised by plaintiffs' attorneys, but not once levied by the judge. Instead, the court's orders were implemented through both direct and indirect means. Direct, because OMRDD officials took the threat of contempt seriously, not merely because they were worried about the potential fall-out (no one wanted to show Governor Carey the headline announcing he might go to jail), but also because they shared a deference to the court that would not allow them to be comfortable in violating its edicts. They would denounce the decree as rigid, hair-splitting, and mindless—and then grow apprehensive about the court's response should they fail to fulfill its stipulations. To be sure, as the events post-1980 showed, respect went to the letter, not the spirit, of the document. Even so, adherence is adherence, and a ruling that could not be overturned on appeal would be carried out.

The court also exerted indirect influence, for the state bureaucracy proved more responsive than would have been predicted. The Willowbrook case altered the bureaucracy's ordinary way of doing business, so that a Thomas Coughlin or a Barbara Blum came to exercise power and new units like the MPU were created to avoid traditional stalemates. Courtesy of the court, Budget did not always have the last word and protecting one's turf was not necessarily a successful tactic.

The import of this achievement becomes all the more apparent

*As of September 30, 1983, 50 percent of the class was in community placement, 38 percent was in Willowbrook (1024) or other institutions (1003), and 12 percent had died.

when one recalls that the commonplace dilemma for twentieth-century governments is to locate levers of change within bureaucratic structures. It was the function of Max Weber's celebrated charismatic leader to unsettle permanent administrations. Charisma was necessary precisely because bureaucracies were so hostile to innovation. In this sense, the court approximates the function of the charismatic leader, for it, too, has the ability to break through stalemates.

Almost all the literature debating the proper role of the judiciary in a democratic society frames the issue in terms of the court versus the legislature, appointed judges as against popularly elected representatives. But it would be no less accurate to understand the conflict as between the court and a bureaucracy dominated by a civil service that may be impervious to both the legislature and the executive. Put another way, many of the most essential decisions affecting the delivery of governmental services are made in administrative offices by tenured officials who are far less known to the general public than judges, indeed whose decisions will be made without public knowledge or participation. For example, it is not clear that the traditional tilt of the department of mental hygiene to mental health as against mental retardation represented more than the personal preferences of its staff; and to suggest that constituents might have had the legislature instruct the department otherwise is naive, because elections are not going to turn on mental hygiene policies. The problem confronting modern societies may be not how to divide authority between legislatures and courts, but between the bureaucracy and all other bodies.

The court fulfills many of the same functions of Weber's charismatic leader with considerably less challenge to democratic values. The charismatic leader, by definition, is above the law; he wins his following in order to pursue an unprecedented, autonomous, truly unregulated path. The court, on the contrary, depends for its authority upon established norms and shared goals. Its ability to shape bureaucratic decisions comes through an appeal to underlying principles and values. (That this fact is not lost on the American public is well demonstrated by the furor that our most charismatic president, Franklin Roosevelt, provoked when he unveiled his court-packing plan.) Hence, for much of the Willowbrook case, the court was not so much ordering the legislature about as ordering the bureaucracy about, and if eventually the point got lost in the rush of events, it should be prominent in a general overview.

The fit of the judiciary with a democratic polity is reinforced by yet another unnoticed effect: the ability of the court to create constituencies for change *after* the fact. It has often, and correctly, been noted that in institution cases, the court acts on behalf of a minority, be it the mentally retarded or convicted criminals, who because of stigma or prejudice is systematically excluded from the political process. The well-known argument, first set forth in the famous footnote four of the Carolene Products decision, suggests that "discrete and insular minorities" who are denied access to the political process (think of blacks as well as the institutionalized) cannot trust to the legislature as against the courts. But less appreciated is the fact that court action on behalf of such minorities may bring into existence constituent groups who come to have a felt interest in perpetuating or extending the innovation. Thus, few people or organizations had a stake in community services prior to the consent judgment. But the dynamics of implementation fostered a coalition that included voluntary agencies, religious organizations, parent groups, and even some real estate agents. Although the coalition was far from cohesive, its very presence testifies to the court's ability to work back into the political process. Decisions made on behalf of a minority will not spur an endless chain of seemingly autocratic rulings but enhance political involvement, reducing the insularity of the minority that caused much of the problem in the first place.

All this noted, the idiosyncrasies of the Willowbrook case must be recognized. The outcomes reflected not only structural considerations but individual characteristics as well. Although it is convenient to refer to *the* panel, *the* court, *the* plaintiffs' attorneys, these were not pieces in a chess game but people with distinct personalities and goals. Most obviously, each of them were determined to make all necessary sacrifices to fulfill the decree, a commitment that might not (and has not) reappeared in other cases. It made a difference that Judge Bartels was a senior judge who was at once able and willing to arrange his calendar to give priority to the well-being of the class members. It mattered, too, that James Clements, Murray Schneps, Michael Lottman, and Linda Glenn turned the Willowbrook Review Panel into an active, interventionist, and uncompromising body. Imagine how different the story might have been had panel members been looking for political advancement or careers in state administration.

By the same token, plaintiffs' counsel, most notably Bruce Ennis and Chris Hansen, were dedicated to protecting the welfare of the class. Regardless of how time-consuming the preparation or the supervision of the decree, their energies did not flag. And in this same spirit, the personal interest of the governor in these proceedings had its impact. Other executives have responded to institution cases with barely disguised hostility, dipping into a bottomless bag of political tricks to block the implementation of court orders. Hugh Carey cared about the handicapped, and if he was not always in control of the legislature or his own administration, his lieutenants understood that the governor really did want the decree fulfilled.

In Willowbrook, then, four of the principal parties—judge, panel, attorneys, and governor—supported the decree. Would success have come with only one or two of them? If plaintiffs in another jurisdiction face a divided line-up, say an apathetic judge or an angry governor, can they anticipate success? The combination required for victory cannot be calculated from the Willowbrook experience, but as each actor drops off, the odds grow worse.

The pressures generated by the court and the decree, the necessity to satisfy the judgment, turned out to be the mother of innovation. The helping professions learned, often to their astonishment, that practices deemed impossible by conventional wisdom were quite feasible. The long-standing belief, for example, that the retarded could not be placed in foster care turned out to be incorrect. Administrators compelled to recruit foster parents located older and experienced caretakers who were both competent and eager to accept the assignment. So, too, voluntary agencies that had traditionally shunned the retarded (either because they seemed too difficult to manage or demonstrated too little progress) learned that their staffs were capable of serving this group, and, no less important, that this group could benefit from their services. And once the agencies assisted the Willowbrook class, they became involved with other retarded persons. To be sure, the agencies had other incentives to respond to the retarded—the number of normal foster children was dropping dramatically. But without the consent judgment, it is doubtful if they would have moved so quickly or so ably. The clue was to stop thinking about fitting the client to the services and begin thinking about fitting the services to the client. If foster care did not seem suitable for the handicapped, redesign foster care. If group homes did not seem suitable for the disabled, redesign the group homes. The dictum is obvious, and yet it had rarely been followed.

These experiences also helped to alter other postulates that guided professional thinking. Post-Willowbrook, it is doubtful whether psychiatrists will be able to invoke triage language automatically. The retarded fared too well in the community, normalization was too effectively translated into practice, to make battlefield metaphors meaningful. Nor will it be so simple to equate the retarded with the chronically ill. The success of family models and classroom models in community residences subvert medical models. The once entrenched notion that retardation is essentially a medical responsibility, with physician-directors in charge of retarded patients, has been undercut. Just recently, the physician in charge of Flower Fifth told us that among his 120 charges, the most handicapped of the Willowbrook class, 100 could function perfectly adequately in community residences. Even a few years ago, such a conclusion would have been unthinkable.

In more practical terms, did the decree change the state's *system* of care? Were the victories won by the Willowbrook class isolated and contained, or have they promoted reforms elsewhere? Much of the evidence comes down on the side of containment. The court was best able to correct particular and well-defined problems, which is another way of saying that OMRDD reacted with crisis management, solving one headache and then confronting another.

Despite the promises Governor Carey made in 1975, non-class members do not enjoy the privileges afforded the class (and not all members of the class enjoy all the entitlements of the decree). Many of New York's institutions remain overcrowded and understaffed, with residents (including those at Willowbrook) lacking programs or even diagnostic studies that would identify the appropriate programs. Normalization is certainly not a byword in Albany, and parents of severely and profoundly retarded persons have great difficulties in obtaining community services. Still, it is striking to see how far state policy has shifted toward community placement. In 1976, New York's institutions for the retarded held 20,000 residents, and only a handful of state charges were in the community. In 1982, institutions had 12,000 residents, while 13,000 of OMRDD's clients were living in the community, no less than 80 percent of them in group homes of fifteen beds or less. In other words, of OMRDD's present 25,000 clients, almost half are in bona fide community residences, which by the standards of 1972 comes close to constituting a revolution.

All uncertainties conceded, the turn of the wheel is not likely to bring OMRDD back to 1972. Too many procedures are in place for doing efficiently and effectively what seemed nearly impossible ten years ago. The techniques for opening and funding group homes are well established, and it is apparent that the cost of delivering good community care is no more expensive than (and by OMRDD's own calculations may be less than) running bad institutions. Moreover, many of the critical medical, educational, and recreational services that are essential for deinstitutionalization, or for that matter for the prevention of institutionalization, are now available. There may even be a significant change in the public perception of the retarded. Enough handicapped people have been seen in museums, playgrounds, zoos, and neighborhood streets to make their presence less threatening.

Despite these accomplishments and all the benefits that accrued to the class and to some others, the court as caretaker is not without its problems. The case was incredibly time-consuming. The parties were back before Judge Bartels again and again, and neither he nor anyone else could find a way to limit a commitment once made. However logical the idea that judges in institution cases should only concern themselves with issues of major import, it turns out there is no way to draw a line between vital and minor matters. A judge will not want to ignore persistent nudity among residents; yet, to bring improvements, he will have to become involved with seemingly trivial details about ordering, laundering, and designing clothing, to say nothing of setting staff ratios (to make certain that enough people are on duty to dress the clients) and supervisor ratios (to make certain that staff fulfills its assignments). Add to the roster adequate medical care, diet, cleanliness, and temperature control, and even without including community placement, it is apparent that reforming an institution requires a submersion in details that can come dangerously close to drowning a judge, or anyone else.

Furthermore, these contests by their very nature have something of a runaway quality about them. Plaintiffs' lawyers become the self-appointed guardians of the public interest, but by whose say-so and to what aims is never altogether resolved. Ennis and Hansen, understandably enough, defined the public interest as what was in the best interest of their clients. But what entitled them to define the best interest of their clients and to link it with societal interests? These questions, let it be clear, are structural; in practice, Ennis and Hansen made efforts to consult with the parents of the class members, especially when tough points of settlement arose during negotiations with the state. But the consultations were ad hoc—no formal mechanisms exist in a class action suit for ensuring representation of the class. Indeed, no mechanisms exist, beyond the court itself, to ensure that the public interest is being served. Ultimately, plaintiffs must take refuge in a narrower and legalistic position that they are doing the best for their clients and others should worry about the larger social agenda. Which, of course, brings us back around to the question of democracy and court reform.

During the course of our research, we noticed a marked shift in the skeptical questions put to us. At first, we were most often asked about the likelihood of dumping; was the decree creating a hundred mini-Willowbrooks scattered around the city? As time passed and the question was answered in the negative, we were asked to justify the expenditure of so many resources on this very handicapped group when money could be going to . . . (and different people completed the sentence in different ways, from bag ladies living on doorsteps to black youths in need of job training to elderly couples driven to shoplifting in supermarkets). Five years into implementation, the accusation was that the Willowbrook class was too privileged. Critics charged that the pity was that one had to be retarded to join it—otherwise membership would constitute a windfall.

There is no disputing that reform through litigation determines the allocation of social resources in an ad hoc and idiosyncratic manner. Neither the attorneys nor the judge in this suit (or any other) were in a position to ask whether devoting millions of dollars to community placement was in society's best interest. They had neither the inclination nor the capacity to reach conclusions about priorities. Social change through court intervention is guaranteed to be haphazard, hit or miss, with resources expended on problems that capture the imagination of a litigator or a judge.

Although it is small consolation, we must remember that American society does not acquit itself very well in resolving allocation of resources. Where is the logic, or equity, in a system that upon discovering a homeless man shivering and incoherent on a subway platform will expend $15,000 on him for three days in an intensive care unit and then release him penniless to suffer who knows what fate? Inequities are all around us, and perhaps courts should not be judged by standards rarely applied elsewhere.

Furthermore, to frame the question in terms of whether Willowbrook class members or, say, bag ladies ought to receive support presupposes not only that resources are too limited to serve them both but also that if the class were less favored, the bag ladies would be more favored. But in politics, such trade-offs do not occur. It would be no less accurate to assume that if the class went unsupported, the federal tax dollars saved would go to building another missile silo or rescuing a bankrupt corporation.

The best tactical answer to those concerned with other deprived groups is to recommend that they scrutinize Willowbrook's successes and failures in order to inform their own efforts. To sit back and wait for social conscience to bestir itself would be to let the underprivileged go hungry. To be sure, more advocacy will not introduce greater rationality or even equity into the system. There will still be winners and losers, not by virtue of some standard of merit but by the energies of the advocates. Yet, rather than envy the Willowbrook class its victories, it would be better to emulate its winning strategies.

Still, the issue is not so easily resolved. An element of unfairness clings to the notion that social resources will go to those with the best legal talent. Even more important, a court that would determine allocation of resources does appear to be usurping a legislative function—and however fiercely one wants to debate whether the action is justified, many legislators, and judges as well, define it as usurpation.

A dialectic appears to operate in judicial reform in which action sparks reaction. A court may ably serve in the first instance as an antidote to politics, rectifying obvious legislative failures, like Willowbrook in 1972. But to the degree its interventions are successful, to the degree that it reorders priorities to correct wrongs, it sooner or later generates a hostile political response. Nor is there much prospect that courts will learn to (or choose to) short-circuit these negative reactions. Judges and court monitors are not adept at politics, not by temperament and not by definition of proper behavior. If the class has a constitutional right to services, cajoling legislators seems unnecessary or inappropriate, or both.

Nor can one expect that what friends a court decree may have in a state capital, even when they include the governor or heads of committees, will take the initiative to bring the judiciary and the legislature closer together. Hugh Carey or Tom Coughlin would not for a moment have considered inviting the review panel to Albany for a chicken dinner, let alone a champagne supper, although they personally admired what the panel was doing and the cause it was advocating. From their perspective, to introduce its members to the political leaders or budget directors would have reduced their ability to use the panel as leverage for resources and at the same time violated their definition of separation of powers.

Thus an inescapable tension separates elected officials from court officials, and one must anticipate both a legislative backlash against the courts—witness the death of the review panel—and then just as predictably, a judicial backlash against more reform-minded colleagues. It includes a marked reluctance among judges to appoint masters in institution cases, and to define a broad right to treatment or habilitation. In short, the court is pulling back from the fray.

But it is a pullback, not a wholesale retreat, and so conflict between the judiciary and the other branches of government is not eliminated so much as reduced. Two recent decisions convey the nuances of the change. In the first, *Youngberg* v. *Romeo,* decided by the Supreme Court in June 1982, the justices ruled that the institutionalized retarded had a constitutional right to safe conditions and to "training related to safety and freedom from restraints." (In the case at hand, Nicolas Romeo's sixty-three injuries and long periods spent in restraints were unacceptable.) But at the same time the court not only refused to decide whether the institutionalized residents had "some general constitutional right" to training per se, but insisted that the rights it found could be overriden when a "qualified professional" believed it appropriate. "The decision, if made by a professional, is presumptively valid," and therefore "interference by the judiciary with the internal operations of the institutions should be minimized."

The *Romeo* decision is not easily characterized. The Supreme Court is clearly looking to circumscribe judicial involvement in institution cases and just as clearly it is setting minimum standards that must be respected. At the least, Stage One horrors, the Willowbrook that Judge Judd visited in 1973, are within the ken of the court. Stage Two conditions, those which disturb but do not shock the conscience, apparently are not.

But predictions of more modest court activity may be premature. In a case brought by Murray Schneps and Michael Lottman against the Suffolk (New York) State School, a facility that was in every sense not far from Willowbrook, Judge Jack Weinstein, in August 1983, found in the *Romeo* standards a constitutional right to community placement.

He had no difficulty at all in ruling that Suffolk's epidemics of shigella and its infestations of cockroaches violated *Romeo*'s safety standards. More interesting yet, he found that: "Some residents are unduly physically restrained by living in the Center. They are capable of much freer and more productive activities in small group homes, and hence are constitutionally entitled to them. The Constitution mandates community placement for those who have been adjudged by qualified professionals to require a community setting in order to exercise basic liberty interests."

Before brushing aside the decision as evidence of why plaintiffs' lawyers in Willowbrook always wanted to draw Judge Weinstein, or, on the other hand, concluding that *Romeo* was a great victory for normalization, one must reckon with Judge Weinstein's remedy in the Suffolk case. Despite the shigella in the institution and the shortage of group homes in Suffolk, he rejected the motion by Schneps and Lottman for a court-appointed master. He was hopeful that the Suffolk director, indeed New York's executive and legislative branches, would not flout the court order to improve conditions and arrange community placements. Noting that institutional reform is not an easy assignment for an administrator, Weinstein decided that "having lawyers and the court constantly looking over his shoulder is one burden that should be minimized." The administrator was to make biannual reports to the court and plaintiffs' lawyers, and they would all await future developments.

Is the Weinstein decision all bark and no bite? Is *Romeo* a victory for institutional reform through court action or a disaster? Is the judiciary alive for social change or dead? To each query the only appropriate response is yes and no. Ambiguity reigns. Or put more broadly, the balancing act between judicial, legislative, and executive prerogatives continues, not to be resolved once and for all in definitive fashion but to be kept in a state of perpetual adjustment and readjustment, each one nudging and poking at the other like commuters on a crowded platform trying to win a little more space. It may be the glory of our constitutional system—or its major flaw—that the several branches of government are constantly skirmishing with one another, in a condition of perpetual stress. Whatever the verdict, it is clear that no one can set a reform strategy for the ages. Here, too, one must anticipate adjustment and readjustment—now a move to the court, now a shift to the executive, perhaps a return to the legislature.

* * *

Finally, the Willowbrook experience has greater relevance to a wider range of public issues than we could have anticipated at the outset. Here we will touch on only two of them, one drawn from a traditional concern in the field of human services, the other drawn from a novel concern in the field of neonatology.

If the retarded are able to live with dignity in group homes, it should be possible to design alternatives for the elderly and frail to uncaring, congregate, and profit-minded nursing homes. Indeed, it should be possible to arrange for many among them to remain at home and out of nursing homes (or even hospitals) altogether. If responsible caretakers can be found to serve the profoundly retarded, they can be found for the aged—if we look for them and compensate them. If there are ways of successfully monitoring group homes, there are ways to protect the well-being of the elderly in apartments or other scattered settings.

What holds true for the elderly holds true as well for the homeless. They may make greater demands upon services, and on public space, but after Willowbrook we have a better sense of the feasibility of alternatives to neglect on park benches or indiscriminate confinement in state armories. By an irony that is not unusual in the history of institutions, the Keener Unit was ordered closed by the review panel as grossly inadequate for the Willowbrook class, only to be reopened recently by the city as a men's shelter. We are unwilling to learn that herding the dependent into such places will inevitably generate yet another scandal. We seem even less prepared to grapple with the fact that crowding such a population into one area is to guarantee substandard conditions and neighborhood opposition. Three homeless men can evoke a sympathetic response. Four hundred will only produce fear and disgust. It would be a pity to have to await the appearance of a television camera in one of these shelters and the ensuing lawsuit before addressing the problem.

A still more unusual and broader connection exists between the Willowbrook experience and the questions now facing neonatology. Over the past decade, physicians have made remarkable progress in keeping babies with low birth weights alive. Because of advances in medical technology, the greater majority of infants born between 800 and 1500 grams now survive. But this very achievement creates a predicament. Many of these babies are at risk of suffering severe brain damage or other crippling deformaties, making the decision of when to use and not to use the new technology agonizing. What is the relevance of this crisis to Willowbrook? It turns out that in the debate, the eventual fate of the handicapped babies takes on critical importance. Many commentators are prepared to give parents and physicians the exclusive right to decide whether these infants shall live or die because of the nightmarish conditions existing at institutions for the retarded. Some, for example, would not allow the state or an advocate for the infant to override a parental choice to let a mildly retarded infant die precisely because the state's intervention would only mean that another soul would suffer the hell of Willowbrook (which is often named specifically).

But we are now in a marvelous position to affect the debate. The existence of humane alternatives to Willowbrook, the knowledge that the very handicapped can live a life with dignity in a group home, has immediate import to decision making in the neonatal nursery. The issue is not one that we can pursue here (although we may pursue it in the future). Our point now is to demonstrate how little distance separates the highly sterile, almost futuristic infant intensive care unit from the filthy and decrepit wards of Willowbrook. The belief that by isolating a few thousand people on its grounds we could isolate the problems of the handicapped is a fantasy that should have been dispelled years ago.

Are these findings likely to be heeded? We are too familiar with the history of reform to carry more than a faint hope. But an analysis of a decade in Willowbrook's history confirms old maxims about institutions and teaches new ones about alternatives, and perhaps these maxims will inspire and guide changes in our systems of care.

Afterword to the AldineTransaction Edition: A Look Back on the Field

I

Since the 1984 publication of the *Willowbrook Wars*, the changes that we traced in the care of the developmentally disabled, especially the movement from institution to community, have not only proceeded on course but in many ways, accelerated.

Willowbrook itself is history. In 1984, then Governor Mario Cuomo made closing Willowbrook a priority, and he and the Office of Mental Retardation and Developmental Disabilities (OMRDD) set a 1987 deadline for transferring all of the residents. They considered a variety of proposals for how to use the site, from relocating state agencies from the World Trade Center to constructing housing for senior citizens. But from the start, the College of Staten Island (CSI), whose facilities were scattered over the borough, had the inside track. On September 1987, the state transferred ownership of the property to the CSI. Groundbreaking ceremonies occurred two years later, and in 1994, the CSI campus opened, with fourteen renovated Willowbrook buildings serving as classrooms, laboratories, and offices.[1]

The transfer of residents from Willowbrook was not without points of conflict, several of which had to be resolved in federal court, but the process did go forward and the 1987 deadline was met. In 1984, 2,291 class members had been living in group homes or in independent housing; 721 members still resided at the facility and another 1,085 were in other institutions around the state. [2] By February 1987, the last residents had left Willowbrook and their departure became the occasion for the class lawyers to to reach a final settlement with New York officials. The agreement provided that by 1992, all Willowbrook class members would be in group homes, not other institutions; however, it did allow for placement in group homes of more than six beds. Once these placements were complete, the case would be closed. Judge John Bartels approved the settlement and considered it "the best protection we could devise." A few parents demurred on the grounds that the state should not be permitted to place class members into quasi-institutional settings of twenty to thirty beds.[3]

The state met the terms of the 1992 agreement and on March 11, 1993, Judge Bartels, then ninety-five years old, signed a permanent injunction to supercede the 1975 Willowbrook consent decree. After eighteen years of federal court oversight, more than fifty orders and opinions, and over a hundred court hearings, Bartels ceremoniously closed an era of disability litigation. Signing the Injunction and invoking civil rights language, he declared: "The retarded have really overcome.... Social justice has prevailed."[4]

The injunction itself was an odd document but from plaintiffs' perspective, a highly desirable one. Typically, the issuance of a court injunction looks to stop an action; in this case, it served to continue an action, that is, to perpetuate the active supervision of the Willowbrook class. Entitled "A Document for Dignity," it recognized that the mentally disabled were now living in the community– what the 1972 consent decree had fought for had been achieved. The challenge that now had to be confronted was how best to insure that the class members, scattered throughout the city in small and separate settings, would be protected against harm and receive the services they needed. When the consent decree expired, the monitors from the office of Special Master and the Review Panel were gone. But the Injunction provided that the Consumer Advisory Board (CAB) would continue serving as guardians for Willowbrook class members who had no families or were unable to advocate for themselves. It also required the establishment of an OMRDD Commissioner's Task Force to be composed of consumers, parents, professionals, and the class lawyers, that would monitor the well-being of the class. Finally, it mandated OMRDD to conduct periodic audits of the class, a long form for a sample of them, a short form for the remainder.

How good a job have these bodies done? In 1997, the OMRDD audit chief and an "independent evaluator" appointed by the Task Force, reported the findings from 350 long form audits.[5] The survey covered many of the salient features of caretaking, from the caliber of the housing to the quality of the day programs.[6] Overall, the findings were good but not excellent. The general level of compliance with the standards reached 88 percent. However, case management services– including assessments of clients' needs and the integration of these needs into a treatment program– were inadequate for between a quarter and a third of the group. Recreational and social activities were poor for half of them. A little over a quarter lived in homes that were "not homelike, individualized, comfortable or aesthetically pleasing." Although "community integration" was a stated goal, 92 percent were in segregated day services. The audit concluded with the need to design a systematic plan of corrective action with ongoing follow-up.[7]

The findings sparked a battle between OMRDD and the advocates for the class, which persists to this very day. The Willowbrook wars continue as the plaintiffs' lawyers, now based at the New York Civil Liberties Union, tenaciously prod OMRDD. They are demanding a better audit instrument and insisting that OMRDD is obligated not only to complete the audits but to take all appropriate measures to correct the deficiencies. OMRDD takes the position that the audit instrument is more than adequate and it is doing its best to improve the programs. Developing mechanisms to remedy deficiencies is a difficult and lengthy process, complicated by the fact that the class is aging and posing new caretaking problems to resolve. It has developed some new report forms and the latest audit results show vast improvement.[8] Plaintiffs are skeptical of the claims.

What conclusions can be reached? Although much depends on whom you ask, something of a consensus does emerge. The horrors of Willowbrook are certainly gone. The worst is over. That said, there remains ample room for improvement.

According to the long-term chair of the CAB, Rita Martin: "Although a large percentage of people are getting appropriate care and treatment, there are still a large number of people who have not received the 'high quality' of care promised by the permanent injunction. On the issue of group homes, the promises have been fulfilled. But on the issues of community integration and environmental attractiveness, quality is still lacking."

To the NYCLU, whose legal team is now headed by Beth Haroules: "The folks in the Willowbrook class are probably better off today than they were in the past. But advocates and attorneys have to remain ever vigilant to ensure that the today's quality does not deteriorate. There is a real risk that the same atrocities can happen, and so we have to keep as many eyes on as possible. Certainly, we won't ever have the same atrocities of medical experimentation of history's past; but we still must remain vigilant, because without us, the class is basically helpless, and therefore at constant risk of abuse."

From the perspective of the statewide Commission on Quality Care, as expressed by Tom Harmon: "The class is much better-off, but nothing's perfect. I walked through Willowbrook, pre-consent judgment, and I have never seen or smelt anything as bad. But wherever you place vulnerable people in the hands of fallible people, there is always the chance for problems."

To the independent evaluator Ronnie Cohn: "Clearly the class members are better off than before. But despite the audit reports demonstrating 1,000 percent better compliance, there are still issues of getting people involved in the community. Certainly, community involvement was not something that we would have been looking to do thirty years ago. Today, protection from harm are not the primary concerns, though they are still concerns. What's important now are rights issues and participatory issues." Or as a consultant to the Task Force, Jim Thigpen, concludes: "From what I've seen visiting homes, OMRDD is not complying with the class' entitlements, specifically in healthcare and community inclusion. The class is better-off than it was in the past, but it's just not enough."[9]

II

The progress that New York made in bringing Willowbrook residents into the community has benefited other developmentally disabled persons in the state. In 1993, New York, belatedly, took advantage of the Home and Community Based Services (HCBS) Waiver established under the Medicaid program and tapped into new streams of federal funds. The result was a notable increase in community-based care. In 1991, 6,165 people lived in group home settings of 1-6 persons, 21,916 in settings of 1-15, 6,489 still resided in institutions, and 17,812 lived in smaller but still institutional Intermediate Care Facilities (ICFs). In 1995, two years after the waiver program started, the number of people in settings of 1-6 persons increased by 50 percent (to 9,014), the number in settings of 1-15 was up 20 percent (to 26,647); residents in institutions declined (to 4,161), and so did those in ICFs (down to 12,386). Because of this shift, New York was able to close eight of its large institutions, including Letchworth and O.D. Heck.[10]

Parents with a developmentally disabled child now enjoy many more service options than they had thirty years ago. In the days of Willowbrook, they had only two choices: institutionalize the child at the state's expense or assume themselves all the burdens of emotional and financial care. Very few day programs or rehabilitation services were available, except for a handful that the parents themselves organized and supported. Today, community-based programs are much more extensive. Parents are eligible to receive personal care assistants (PCAs) and respite care. Developmentally disabled infants receive early stimulation exercises; as children, they participate in special education classes and are entitled to support services. When they turn eighteen, they are eligible for New York's array of residential and vocational support systems, social security funding, and individualized case-management. Of course, shortfalls persist: the waiting list for group homes is long and financial support levels are not generous. But a once stark choice–Willowbrook or nothing– has become far more nuanced.

The trends evident in New York are even more apparent around the country. The number of residents in all state institutions has shrunk from 150,000 in 1977 to 40,000 in 2003, while residents in small group homes rose from 20,400 to 264,240. At the same time, the percentage of residents in state institutions below the age of twenty-one has dropped from 36 percent in 1977 to 5 percent in 2002. In short, the group home is now the setting not only of choice but of reality for persons with developmental disabilities. The battle for deinstitutionalization that the litigators and the Willowbrook Review Panel fought and won in New York helped promote a new national standard.[11]

None of this should suggest that this change, however dramatic, has successfully surmounted all the complexities of caring for the mentally disabled. Some institutions have managed to hold out against the trend and continue to deliver substandard services. An investigation, for example, by the civil rights division of the Justice Department in November 2004 of institutions in the neighboring state of New Jersey found abuses reminiscent of Willowbrook in its early days: staff members at the Woodbridge Developmental Center were guilty of physically abusing some of the 500 residents; record keeping was shoddy, staff training inadequate, rates of release to the community low, and supervision weak. One resident who had difficulty swallowing choked to death on a piece of bread.[12]

No less important, the group home system is confronting new types of problems. Turnover among caretakers is mounting, with the result that trained personnel is getting more difficult to find, and to keep. At least one reason is that wages are low and benefits limited. In state institutions, budget-minded legislators keep appropriations levels low; in private facilities, which make up the great majority of group homes, staff is rarely unionized and managers are free to set wages without the pressures of collective bargaining. Indeed, salaries in community facilities are considerably lower than in state institutions. According to a University ofMinnesota study, the average hourly wage rate in state facilities is $11.67, compared to $8.68 in non-state community services.[13]

To complicate matters further, the developmentally disabled are living longer, putting new stresses on group home management and increasing the overall demand for group homes (In the 1970s, people with mental disabilities lived on average to age fifty-nine; now they live on average to sixty-six, closer to the average for the general population.) As a result, waiting lists for placements will grow longer as new clients outlive their family caretakers and more states phase out their institutions. At the same time, developmental disabilities have to become a sub-specialty within geriatrics.[14]

However challenging these demands, let one final research finding make clear that the price of success is well worth paying. Numerous studies were conducted over the 1980s and then again over the 1990s to analyze the impact of community living on the adaptive behaviors of persons with mental disabilities (including communication, self-care, and vocational skills). A review of general research findings in the 1980s, when the community movement was still young, found "benefits very consistently accrue more to the people who leave institutions to live in small community homes." The outcomes for the 1990s were even stronger as the movement matured. Benefits were "more positive and more consistent." And all this was achieved at average expenditures that were much lower for the community compared to the institution ($30,000 per person per year as against $104,000). As Sheryl Larson and Charlie Lakin of the Research and Training Center on Community Living (University of Minnesota) aptly conclude: "The individuals who left institutions used significantly more community places, engaged in significantly more social activities, experienced significantly more personal integration, had significantly more family contacts.. .at an adjusted expenditure that was 66% of that of their counterparts who remained in institutions."[15]

III

This movement of mentally disabled people into the community is evidence of a broad and dramatic shift in both public policy and public attitudes. The most visible and important manifestation of the change was the enactment in 1990 of the Americans with Disabilities Act. Its impact on daily life is everywhere apparent, from the reserved parking spaces for the handicapped in shopping centers to the city buses equipped with moving platforms to facilitate access for persons in wheelchairs. To be sure, many of changes have greater relevance to persons who are physically, not mentally, disabled and the relationship among advocacy organizations representing each group is not always cordial. Nevertheless, the ADA has enhanced opportunities for all disabled persons, and nowhere is this fact more evident than in its support for deinstitutionalization.

The 1999 decision of the Supreme Court in Olmstead v. L. C. forged the crucial link between the ADA and community care. The case was brought on behalf of two mentally retarded women, J.L. and E.W., one of whom was also diagnosed with schizophrenia, and the other, with a personality disorder. They were first institutionalized at the Georgia Regional Hospital in Atlanta and although their physicians soon concluded that they could be appropriately cared for in a community setting, they were not discharged. Their guardians brought suit against the state to force a community placement, citing the anti-discrimination provisions of the ADA: "No qualified individual with a disability...shall be excluded from participation in...the benefits of services, programs, or activities...or be subjected to discrimination." They also relied on the ADA's stipulation that all public programs had to be administered in "a setting that enables individuals with disabilities to interact with non-disabled persons to the fullest extent possible."

Georgia resisted their claims and the case wound its way through the lower courts, finally making its way to the Supreme Court. Justice

Ruth Ginsburg wrote the majority opinion. It held that the ADA gave persons a right to community placement when treatment professionals believed the transfer appropriate, provided that movement to a less restricted setting "is not opposed by the affected individual," and the "placement can be reasonably accommodated, taking into account the resources available to the State and the needs of others with mental disabilities." Dismissing Georgia's claim that institutional care did not constitute "discrimination," the court found that disabled persons had a right to be treated in a setting that was the least restrictive of their liberties. As for the state's assertion that it could not "reasonably accommodate" community placement, the decision remanded the case back to the lower court for a finding of fact whether community care could be arranged through "reasonable modifications," or necessitated a "fundamental alteration" of services. In effect, the court ruling made clear that unless a state could demonstrate that community placement could not be reasonably accommodated, mentally disabled persons did not belong in institutions.[16]

The implementation of Olmstead has been mixed, with notable successes in some states offset by resistance in others. The decision did prompt the Bush administration in June of 2001 to issue an executive order on community-based alternatives for individuals with disabilities. "The Federal Government," the order declared, "must assist States and localities to implement swiftly the Olmstead decision." To this end, it would provide technical assistance to help states design and evaluate programs, and would investigate and resolve complaints by individuals "who allege that they have been the victims of unjustified institutionalization."[17]

By 1970s standards, even the announcement of such an initiative seems astonishing, but its impact goes well beyond rhetoric. An independent February 2004 analysis found that twenty-nine states had issued Olmstead-related plans or reports, twenty-seven states had received federal grants in 2003 to help the transition from institutions to community services, and the program had dispensed a total of $158 million over the period 2001-03. Although progress has been impeded by state budget shortfalls, it is evident that cost-neutral or low cost community programs are being implemented, including efforts to insure consumer-directed care (allowing people with disabilities or their guardians to decide what type of services they want) and to dispense information to consumers about community care options.

Although all persons with mental disabilities come under the executive initiative, the developmentally disabled have received most of the attention and resources. Most states have used these funds to expand community-based services. The Olmstead decision together with the federal initiative, the report aptly concludes, "have kept the momentum alive for serving people in the most integrated setting." Conceding that implementation has sometimes been "sluggish," it found good reason to believe that "incremental reform will continue."[18]

IV

Since the driving force in closing down Willowbrook was public interest lawyers, it is appropriate for us to leave the field with observations on how public interest law has fared over the past twenty years. In terms of recruitment and sustainability, it is assuredly flourishing. There is no shortage of law school graduates seeking the positions with these organizations, and no shortage of organizations that want to harness their talents and use the courts to accomplish socially desirable ends. The prime difficulty may be that the market for such positions is tight; many groups have limited budgets and cannot hire all the staff they could use. It may well be more difficult to land a job with an outstanding rights-oriented public interest law firm than to get a position on Wall Street.

That said, the very concept of class action litigation has changed. In the 1970s and well into the 1980s, class action lawsuits were mostly the preserve of not-for-profit, reform-minded groups who were attempting to use the courtroom as an engine for social change. By contrast, after the 1990s, commercial law firms turned to class action suits as a way of collecting tort damages for clients and, not incidentally, extraordinary fees for themselves. The process began with class action suits for asbestos and lead damages, went on to tobacco, and now is poised to take on pharmaceutical products and food. It is too soon to know whether this change will spark a backlash against all class action suits but such a possibility is not out of the question.

Despite the fact that the judicial appointment process has brought more conservative judges to the federal court, the roster of accomplishments for public interest litigation has been impressive in the field of mental disability, and, as well, in criminal justice, schools, housing, and police. As Columbia Law School Professors Charles Sabel and

William Simon recently argued, there has been "no reduction in the volume or importance" of judges holding underperforming institutions accountable. They go on to note that the intimate, and intricate consent decrees that plaintiffs won in cases like Willowbrook are giving way to less detailed court orders which allow for more policy discretion.[19] Judge Bartels did not say to New York State what one of his colleagues in the District of Columbia declared in a similar type case: "The final decision about the policies and procedures and training programs will remain with the defendants, understanding that if they fail to address serious concerns raised by plaintiffs...this may result in compliance issues down the road."[20] Rather than intervene more directly in what policies and programs should be accomplished, judges now may be more willing to spur negotiations between parties. The point granted, legal interventions to correct the substandard administration of public institutions, be they custodial or caretaker, and to expand the life chances for persons with mental disabilities, is certain to continue.

Taken together, the events described in *The Willowbrook Wars*, the extraordinary impact of dedicated lawyers, compassionate judges, diligent review panel members, responsive state officials, and a host of community organizations and leaders, from the Catholic Church to community planning board members, are a model for advancing the rights of the developmentally disabled. They may also serve to inspire change in other areas as well.

Notes

I am indebted to Chris Hansen and Robert Levy for reviewing an early draft of the afterword and to Christopher Sales for his research assistance. I am also grateful to the people quoted in it for giving of their time and sharing their insights.

1. On the transition from Willowbrook to CSI, see Staten Island Advance, Jan. 4-Jan. 5, 1984, Sep. 18, 1987; CSI website, http://www.csinews.net/MediaRelations/historyofcsi.htm.
2. On the discharge of residents from Willowbrook, see Staten Island Advance, Apr.-May 1985 series on tenth anniversary of the Willowbrook Consent Decree.
3. On the Final Settlement, see Staten Island Advance, Mar. 3, 1987.
4. On the signing of the Permanent Injunction and Judge Bartels, see New York Times, Mar. 12, 1993; Staten Island Advance, Mar. 12, 1993.
5. On the Permanent Injunction, see Willowbrook Permanent Injunction, U.S. District Court Eastern District of New York, 72 Civ. 356, 357.
6. On the auditing instruments, Willowbrook long- and short- form audits, courtesy of Ronnie Cohn (independent evaluator).

7. On the audit results, memorandum, June 30, 1997, from the Director of the OMRDD Internal Audit Unit and Ronnie Cohn (Independent Evaluator) to the Members of the Commissioner's Task Force on Willowbrook DDSO Directors.
8. On the ongoing negotiations between Plaintiffs and OMRDD, conversations with Beth Haroules, June 1, 2004, June 14, 2004.
9. Conversations with Rita Martin (CAB), Beth Haroules (NYCLU), Tom Harmon (CQC), Ronnie Cohn (independent evaluator). To all of these individuals, we asked the question, "If you had to sum up the state of the Willowbrook class today, what would you say?"
10. On the HCBS waiver and its effects on community-based care, see Charlie Lakin et al. (2002). Chapter 8 (Background and Summary of Medicaid Long-Term Care Programs) and Chapter 9 (Utilization of and Expenditures for Medicaid Institutional and Home and Community Based Services), and p. 156 (NY State Profile). In R.W. Prouty, Gary Smith & K.C. Lakin (Eds.), Residential Services for Persons with Developmental Disabilities: Status and Trends through 2002. Minneapolis: University of Minnesota, Research and Training Center on Community Living, Institute on Community Integration.
11. On the national trends in institution- and community-based care, see Services for Persons with Developmental Disabilities: Status and Trends through 2002. Minneapolis: University of Minnesota, Research and Training Center on Community Living, Institute on Community Integration.
12. On the investigation by the civil rights division of the New Jersey Justice Department, see *New York Times*, November 16, 2004, B7, Ronald Smothers, "Developmental Center Criticized in Study."
13. On low salaries and benefits in community facilities, see Polister, B. et al. (2003). Wages of Direct Support Professionals Serving Persons with Intellectual and Developmental Disabilities: A Survey of State Agencies and Private Residential Provider Trade Associations, Policy Research Brief. Minneapolis: University of Minnesota, Institute on Community Integration.
14. On the aging of the developmentally disabled, see David Braddock et al. (2004). Conclusion (Aging Caregivers and the Growing Demand for Services). The State of the States in Developmental Disabilities: 2004. University of Colorado: Department of Psychiatry and Coleman Institute for Cognitive Disabilities. American Association on Mental Retardation, Washington, DC, second printing, revised.
15. On the benefits of deinstitutionalization, see Charles Lakin et al. (1999). Behavioral Outcomes of Deinstitutionalization of People with Intellectual Disabilities: A Review of Studies Conducted Between 1980 and 1999, Policy Research Brief. Minneapolis: University of Minnesota, Research and Training Center on Community Living, Institute on Community Integration.
16. Olmstead v. L.C., 527 U.S. 581 (1999).
17. Executive Order 13217, "Community-Based Alternatives for Individuals with Disabilities," issued by President George W. Bush June 18, 2001.
18. The States' Response to the Olmstead Decision: A 2003 Update, Wendy Fox-Grage et al., Feb. 2004. From the National Conference of State Legislatures website, www.ncsl.org/programs/health/forum/olmstead/2003/olmstead_main.htm.
19. Charles F. Sabel and William H. Simon, Destabilization Rights: How Public Law Litigation Succeeds, February 2004. *Harvard Law Review*, vol. 117, 1016-1101.
20. Destabilization Rights: How Public Law Litigation Succeeds, 1032.

Acknowledgments

In the course of this project, we received such extraordinary assistance from so many individuals that we are acutely conscious of the limitations of formal acknowledgments. Without participants' willingness to give of their time and of themselves, we would never have been able to research or complete this analysis. We have formed friendships that are lasting, one of the unanticipated bonuses of leaving the archives for contemporary research.

In our order of incurring debts, we must first thank Bruce Ennis and Chris Hansen. No request we made of them was turned down, whether it involved going on a retreat of several days to review the story from beginning to end or providing access to all documents in plaintiffs' files. We next met the review panel, and over the course of six years, Jim Clements, Murray Schneps, Michael Lottman, and Jennifer Howse were generous in sharing information and perspectives. Finally, we came to know and rely upon two remarkable state officials who set a standard of cooperation with researchers that cannot be surpassed: Barbara Blum and Tom Coughlin.

Tracking the performance of OMRDD and MPU was at the core of the project, and we piled debt upon debt as we moved from the central office to the borough offices. At the MPU we depended heavily on the counsel of Michael Mascari, Ed Matthews, Allen Schwartz, Pat Dionne, Betsy Crowell, Vicki Toomey, Dottie Rowe, Joyce Roll, Irene Arnold, and Pat Pelner. We are especially obligated to Jill Comins for so patiently and clearly explaining the financial byways of contract making.

In Brooklyn, John Sabatos and Nadine Miller taught us about community placement; meetings with Shirley Pierce and Walt Adams were frequent and informative. In the Bronx, Herbert Cohen was always open and frank with us; in Queens, Karla Perlman and Judy Diazi were our guides; in Manhattan, Erwin Friedman did all he could to facilitate our research, particulary in the group homes.

From the voluntary sector, Sister Barbara Eirich, Joel and Philip Levy, and Robert Schonhorn were especially helpful, whether we wanted information, files, or the opportunity to observe group home life.

Other review panel members who assisted us included Linda Glenn (who shared with us her thinking about outcome measures), Clarence Sundram (who wanted to make certain we understood Albany politics), William Bitner, and David Rosen. That we were welcomed at panel audits and had all necessary access to panel files is testimony to the assistance of Sue Gant, Marnie Loomis, and the late Jerry Gavin. Kathy Schwaninger, during her stint as executive director, maintained the same level of cooperation.

At the NYCLU office, we became accustomed to plaguing Robert Levy and Diana Tanaka with questions on legal and political developments. Both at ACLU and NYCLU, Ira Glasser and Aryeh Neier were never too busy to stop and fill us in on some past or present Willowbrook development or to argue a point of law or policy.

As fortunate as we were in the field, so fortunate were we with those who supported our research. We began our work under a grant from the Field Foundation and we looked forward to annual visits with its executive director, Leslie Dunbar. Reporting to him was not a requirement of the grant, but more than he could imagine, it was meaningful to us. In its best tradition, the National Institute of Mental Health supported a project on deinstitutionalization that was broadly defined. Dr. Howard Davis understood our goals and did all he possibly could to see that we had the opportunity to reach them. The Field Foundation grant was administered through the Hastings Institute, and Daniel Callahan and Willard Gaylin not only donated the institute's administrative services but also gave us a stimulating forum at which to play out ideas. Our work on hepatitis B was especially relevant to the Hastings agenda and we are in their debt for sharpening our arguments. The NIMH grant (5R01-MH29300) was administered through the Center for Policy Research. Its director, Amitai Etzioni, assisted us in formulating the approach of the research and provided useful counsel along the route. We also had good advice from Leslie Scallet, then of NIMH, and Clara Shapiro of the Center for Policy Research.

Research trips to other jurisdictions were more meaningful courtesy of the efforts of Gunnar Dybwad, Lyn Rucker, and Dan Yohalem. On the role of public interest law and mental disabilities, we profited from regular discussions with Herman Schwartz, Stan Herr, Norman Rosenberg, Andrew Von Hirsch, David Ferligher, Tom Gilhool, and Carla Morgan. Our research into hepatitis B was encouraged by Curt Bakal; Saul Krugman and Baruch Blumberg were prepared to answer all our questions. Two days spent with William Bronston were as much fun as they were enlightening. The same is true of our time with Geraldo Rivera.

Over the past several years we have had several opportunities to discuss the Willowbrook case in seminars and public forums. Some of the most useful dialogues took place at the Bryn Mawr School of Social Work (courtesy of Joanna Weinberg), at the Van Leer Institute in Jerusalem (courtesy of Aryeh Goren and Dan Krauskopf), and the Columbia University Center for the Social Sciences (courtesy of Jonathan Cole).

We had crucial assistance from several staff members. Jay Kaplan, the first on board, taught us a great deal about Albany budgetary matters; he was diligent in helping us map the players and understand their stakes in implementing the decree. Susan Wick was responsible for analyzing census data and group home locations, and to our delight made her research into a Ph.D. dissertation. Barbara Rios interviewed Willowbrook parents, foster parents, and group staff in insightful and systematic fashion. Robert Zussman not only turned a vague assignment about group home life into meaningful research, but was a constant source of new ideas.

We imposed the manuscript on several good friends. Arlene and Robert Rifkind kept prodding us to rethink basic assumptions; Harold Edgar, Mitchell Ginsberg, and Sherry Brandt-Rauf made certain that we did not go too far astray on legal and social work matters. The only participants in the story whom we asked to review the manuscript were Jill Comins, Chris Hansen, and Michael Lottman, and though they will still disagree with some of the arguments here, their observations were of critical importance. We owe a very special debt to Flora Kimmich, who went through the text line by line, point by point, both for substance and style. It was an act of friendship for which we are deeply grateful.

Once again our children, Matthew and Micol, experienced the pleasures and pains that come when parents collaborate on a project and we ask some measure of forgiveness for late meals and forgone holidays. Our consolation is that a warning often delivered, that if we did not finish they would each have to devote a few years of their adulthood to the Willowbrook story, is now obviated. More important, we hope that they will have learned not only about conflict but also about caring from the participants in this story whom they have met, and from the three people to whom this book is dedicated.

Sources and Methods

Our narrative and analysis rest upon a variety of documents. We followed the implementation of the consent judgment intensively for a four-year period, 1978–1981, although we observed events both before and after these dates. Because of the cooperation we received from all parties, we enjoyed access to the principal actors, events, and documents. Thus we were observers at private meetings, both regularly scheduled and ad hoc, to address a sudden crisis. We attended the monthly review panel meetings, with the understanding that we would be silent observers. (On occasion, one or another member of the panel would look over to us, see that we had not taken a note on a remark he thought terribly important, and we would be told to get that down and not to miss it.) We attended panel meetings that were closed to all outsiders, including, on occasion, plaintiffs' lawyers. We were also present at the monthly meetings of the MPU staff with the borough directors and the intermittent planning sessions of community placement officials and case manager teams (particularly at MPU and in the Brooklyn office). We were also at sessions designed to resolve unanticipated problems. Thus, one or the other of us was present when Dr. Curt Bakal met with parents and other interested parties during the hepatitis B scare and when plaintiffs' lawyers met with OMRDD representatives to negotiate a settlement after the panel's death.

Access also meant a run of the files, which was a constant source of bemusement to various staffs. They could never quite get over the fact that we would arrive, begin opening file drawers, and spend the day reading their, and their superiors', mail.

That we enjoyed such freedom of movement, even when the various parties might be plotting court tactics against each other, is testimony, first, to each party's pride in its efforts. We made the obvious promise to keep the records and the deliberations in confidence until eventual publication, a promise which we scrupulously kept, to the point of not publishing preliminary findings. Indeed, we can think of no time when anyone asked us, even jokingly, to divulge what we knew about the other side. The teasing we received was to the effect that one day we would take over MPU or the panel and run the show, while the incumbents got the chance to be historians.

Over the course of the research, we conducted both formal and informal interviews. Some were structured to obtain biographical information or to learn about funding streams or monitoring practices; others were open-ended. Conversations over lunch or dinner about how things were going and gossip about who might succeed whom in Albany kept us attuned to upcoming developments. We had to learn that an older distinction between research time (spent in a library) and leisure time (spent at a party or a meal) was no longer relevant. Researching Willowbrook made the lines between work and relaxation disappear. It also made the assignment fascinating and exhausting, much more intense and personal than any other research we had ever conducted.

Even so, the best worked-out arrangements could, temporarily, be put in jeopardy. About a year into our research, when David was attending a meeting at the Hastings Institute, he was called to the telephone not once but several times because of a crisis. Amitai Etzioni, director of the Center for Policy Research, which administrated our NIMH grant, had published a piece highly critical of deinstitutionalization; state officials had read it and were angrily demanding to know whether this also represented our view of things. The better part of a morning went to explaining some of the basic principles of academic freedom, that Etzioni as director of the center would not dream of imposing his views on us, and that no, we had no preconceived bias against deinstitutionalization. By the lunch break at Hastings the fire was out, but he was tired and annoyed. Robert Michels, a good friend and head of the Department of Psychiatry at New York Hospital and Cornell Medical School, came up to ask what was the matter; here he was, head of a major department with broad responsibilities, and he had not been called to the phone once. David took the occasion to complain about doing research with live sources and how he missed the archives, whereupon Michels observed: You are convinced that what will make your book special is the analysis that you and Sheila will perform, and you interpret every activity that is not directly analytical as the drudgery part of the assignment. But, he went on, as confident as he was that the analysis would be fine, even terrific, we should not be most proud of that. Anyone could do the analysis. Our talent lay in getting and maintaining access, a feat we should not trivialize. Michels may not have been altogether correct—surely the proof has to be in the analysis—but he supplied us with no small measure of comfort as we continued our research.

On several occasions, we arranged what might be considered mini-conferences or very elaborate interviews to question participants on a broad range of issues. In September 1978, we held a two-day session with Barbara Blum and her staff on the occasion of her stepping down from MPU. We reviewed her term with some eight to ten of her staff present; on the second day, we had Chris Hansen and Tom Coughlin join the session to add their views and sharpen debate. The taped record of the session was an invaluable document. We also held a two-day meeting with Bruce Ennis, Chris Hansen, and Aryeh Neier that opened with Ennis in law school and ended with the latest court fight. And on occasion we prompted MPU to hold a retreat of its own, which we helped organize, to review where it was and where it was going.

All the while, we observed those parts of the deinstitutionalization effort that most concerned us: the public meetings of the community planning boards, the court hearings, the panel-MPU audits of the institutions and group homes. We could never be certain which issues would become critical, and so inevitably we covered too much ground; not knowing the end of the story is not conducive to efficiency in research. For a while it appeared as if union activity at Willowbrook would have a major impact, and we made considerable efforts to meet union officials—only to have the union elements weaken and disappear with little trace. On the other hand, we had not anticipated that the research would force us to become knowledgeable about hepatitis B. But there we were following Curt Bakal around and interviewing Saul Krugman and Baruch Blumberg.

Were we really allowed everywhere and permitted to read everything? On the whole, yes, but with a few qualifications. No request of ours to the review panel, to plaintiffs' lawyers, or to MPU officials—whether it was for a document, an interview, or permission to attend a meeting—was ever refused. However, there were limits to our ability to cover events, and we were certainly not invited to or told about all major encounters among state officials. By the same token, we doubt that anyone deliberately lied to us; but particularly with some state officials, we had to know the right questions to ask. People were much freer in giving us information about things we knew something about than in being the first to bring us into a new development. From our perspective, our greatest protection was that with good access to so many different participants we were bound to get wind of an issue and, since each side knew the other was talking to us, each wanted to give us its perspective on events.

Even as we conducted the research, and now more clearly in retrospect, we recognized that our most helpful sources were those who wanted to see the decree fulfilled. We became identified with the judgment the way biographers become identified with their subjects. In this guise, we were sought out by the decree's opponents as well as by its friends—but its friends sought us out more diligently. Toward the end of the project, as we began pulling back from the field to go to the typewriter and a new cohort of state officials started rotating through OMRDD, we found ourselves much less involved with them than we had been with Tom Coughlin and his team. Our access to OMRDD after October 1981 was reduced, a fact that should be acknowledged, although it had little consequence. We were still welcome in all the other settings (including the MPU), and the key developments were occurring in the courtroom and in negotiating sessions where we were present.

Despite our internal dialogue about how different field work was from archival work, we come away persuaded that much of the reason participants trusted us was that they defined us as historians. We were, if you will, for the record, and this was a record participants wanted preserved. We learned that historians have a position in the public world that is to be guarded and treasured: it is recognized that we are interested not in breaking a scandal or capturing quick publicity but in understanding a dynamic so that others will learn from it. Ironically, then, credentials derived from the study of the past facilitate an analysis of the present.

Finally, the question that anyone trained in the social sciences must ask: did our presence alter the events we studied? Our own rule at the start was to remain as unobtrusive as possible, with one exception. Should we or our staff observe a client in a condition that could be dangerous to his safety, we would report it. In fact, only a handful of such incidents ever occurred, and they were resolved with little ado. Still, we were not as silent as we expected to be. The longer we remained in the field, the more we became the repository of tradition, practice, lore, and data. Accordingly, we would occasionally be asked to attend a meeting to advise on how to open group homes or change a monitoring procedure, and we complied with such requests. People who had spent hours making sure we understood one or another facet of implementation were entitled to something in return.

It is doubtful if these occurrences had any lasting impact. Rather, our most important influence may have been the simple fact that we were present. At times we would get the feeling that our attending a meeting seemed to render it more important for participants, because we made them aware of the crucial nature of their enterprise. That we were studying the events may have given participants a keener sense of the significance of their assignment. In this fashion, we may have elevated by a degree or two an enthusiasm for fulfilling the decree. Did we tilt the outcome? Hardly. But we are prepared to suggest, somewhat seriously, that it would not be a bad idea to attach historians to major efforts at social reform.

One of the most difficult questions that we confronted was how to measure outcome. What difference did it make that the retarded were living in group homes and not institutions? Quickly enough, we broke the question down into two parts: What difference did it make to their safety, which seemed the easier part, for we could rely upon audits to confirm our own observations. The criteria were clear (abuse, personal rights, and so on) and the evidence (now in Chapter 9), not difficult to collect or evaluate. But what of quality of life, the intellectual well-being of the clients, or, with all due embarrassment, their happiness?

At first, we considered doing a quantitative analysis. We would analyze outcome by taking a measure (an IQ or one more sensitive to distinctions at the lower end of the scale) of the clients right before they left Willowbrook and then six and eighteen months later when they were in the community. Hard data had its appeal not only to professionals but to casual observers as well, who would ask us whether the retarded became less retarded in the community, whether normalization was a cure. So we met with consultants, worked out an elaborate methodology, secured our computer time—and then, a number of barriers (intrinsic and extrinsic) made us rethink the decision.

In practical terms, the process of deinstitutionalization as it went on in New York was too chaotic to allow for a satisfactory research design. To answer the question: did the retarded do better in the community? demands that "the retarded" be broken down into their respective categories (do severely retarded do better in the community than moderately?), and that "the community" be broken down into its respective categories (ten-bed group homes, foster homes, fifteen-bed group homes) and then divided again into the quality of the settings (good, bad, indifferent—do mildly retarded do better in poor group homes than in the institution, or do they only do better in first-rate group homes?). Yet, to fulfill such a design demanded matching characteristics of clients to group homes that were beyond our control. We could not know who was leaving, where they were going, or the eventual quality of the setting.

Still more troubling, Willowbrook was so deprived an environment that every expert agreed massive regression had taken place and that a comparison of Willowbrook with group homes would prove little. If one tested a client's skills in the institution and then again a year later, all that is demonstrated is that progress can occur if someone is transferred from an absolutely wretched setting to a better one. Put an effective teaching program into Willowbrook and the outcome might be identical.

We soon found ourselves looking for measurements not of program effectiveness but of quality of life. Did living in a group home offer the client a different experience? Did it enhance his life chances in a way that an institution could not? To answer these questions we would have to look beyond the clients' cognitive progress to the environment that the home provided. We began to think about analyzing happiness, eager to know whether clients were enjoying group home life more than institutional life.

Obviously, the best way to answer the inquiry was to talk to the clients, to conduct long open-ended interviews over time and record their reactions. But hardly any members of the Willowbrook class could tell us what it meant to be deinstitutionalized. Severely and profoundly retarded, they were unable to express themselves verbally. If we wanted to get their story some other techniques would have to be used.

Hence, we returned to one of our formative intellectual experiences in this field. We reread Erving Goffman's *Asylums* and decided to try to explore, more or less in his style, how group home life differed from institutional life. We sent Robert Zussman, a Columbia-trained sociologist, to observe life inside the home. He was completing a study of engineers (based heavily on direct observation), and we asked him to capture, insofar as he could, the residents' experience of the world. Did they have an opportunity to express their personal preferences in group homes? Did they function as something other than damaged human beings? We also wanted to know about the staff and its behavior. Did the same distancing occur as in the institution? Did counselors set up a nursing station, play favorites, and the like?

We had little idea of how different observing a group home would be from observing a workplace or an institution. "I did not realize," Zussman informed us later, "that the degree of involvement must of necessity be greater in a home setting, even a group home setting, which we think of as encompassing and expressing one's 'real' self, than a work environment which asks of people not so much of their selves as their skills." The intensity of the experience and the intimacy of the setting altered the role of the observer. Zussman became almost as much a participant as an observer, a sharer of duties as well as conversations and responses.

This intensity led him to add another dimension to the study. He wanted a check on the accuracy of the reality he was perceiving. Hence, he and others interviewed the direct care staff in the homes to understand their orientation to their work and their attitudes toward the clients. We devised a questionnaire to see if their attitudes and observations fit with his.

Zussman's observations, and later the interviews, began at the group home that Sister Barbara Eirich was running in the Bronx. From there Zussman moved on to observe other group homes. He concentrated on seven residences, three serving those mildly and moderately retarded, four serving those severely and profoundly retarded. For our purposes, however, the distinctions in disabilities appeared not as important as the models of care that emerged. Hence, our analysis devotes less time to client differences and more time to explicating the models.

We were all, to one degree or another, feeling our way through this part of the research. But courtesy of Zussman's abilities, we now have a record of group home life that at the very least starts to translate such a phrase as "life chances for the retarded" into elements that can be further investigated.

To understand what community placement meant to the clients' families, we pursued a number of techniques, all the while respecting the right to privacy of class members, their relatives, and foster parents. To interview foster parents, we first requested permission from Jennifer Howse, then head of the MPU, and borough coordinators. The borough offices sent each foster parent a letter explaining the study and asking if they would grant an interview. They enclosed a stamped postcard, addressed to us, and refrained from follow-up if no response was received.

We developed a long questionnaire on why a woman chose to become a foster parent, how she found out about the program, and her family background. We also explored performance as foster parent, from the obstacles encountered in finding services to the rewards received from the program. A staff member, Barbara Rios, MSW, who spoke both Spanish and English, conducted the interviews. She called each foster parent who returned a card and arranged an interview at their convenience, which usually took place in their home. The interview generally lasted one to two hours, after which Rios filled out an interview sheet and added general remarks. We interviewed 30 foster parents, from a group that totaled 220.

Many of the first responses were from natural parents who had become foster parents. We realized that this group was different from the foster parents that the case managers recruited, and so we analyzed their reactions separately. We also compared the socioeconomic status of the group that responded with the total group of foster parents with the MPU and did not find differences.

We followed a similar procedure with natural parents. The MPU staff sent a letter explaining the study, again with a stamped postcard addressed to us. Since the MPU never had a complete list of parents or guardians, we sent out approximately 700 letters and received 65 responses. Of that number we interviewed 35 whose children were still in institutions and 20 whose children were now in the community. Once again, a long, semi-structured interview was developed and Barbara Rios conducted the interviews.

Notes

As the notes that follow make clear, our analysis rests not only on direct observation and interviews but on a number of files. The most important ones include the New York Civil Liberties Union files, some twenty cabinets of plaintiffs' correspondence, material uncovered through discovery, and the legal papers of all parties. The Willowbrook Review Panel files, of roughly the same size, contained its correspondence and investigations of implementation. The Metropolitan Placement Unit files were our best source for following the workings of the state bureaucracy. We examined, too, relevant material in the files of the Board of Education and Department of Health on hepatitis B and some administrative files at OMRDD and Budget.

The present state of these files is, put gently, chaotic. The NYCLU files are complete, intact, and in storage. When the panel went out of business, its files were sent over to NYCLU and are now in storage as well. The MPU files would be periodically "cleansed"—that is, file cabinets would be emptied to give a new official space for her correspondence and the materials dispatched to Albany to suffer who knows what fate. Hence, boxes were not numbered, correspondence was not in order, and so on.

The saving grace in all of this was, of course, the copying machine. We have copies of all the documents used in this book in our files and we will in the near future arrange for their deposit for those who may be interested in studying the events. We made a self-conscious effort to collect information not only for our own purposes but for future researchers as well.

pages **Going Into the Field**

1–11 The literature debating the normative role of the court is voluminous. Some of the writings we found most useful both at the start of the project and thereafter include Abram Chayes, "The Role of the Judge in Public Law Litigation," *Harvard Law Review* 89 (1976): 1281–1316; and his

pages

sequel piece there, "Public Law Litigation and the Burger Court," 96 (1982): 4–60. Chayes's position is joined and elaborated on by Owen Fiss, "The Forms of Justice," *Harvard Law Review* 93 (1979): 1–58. See too, John Ely, *Democracy and Distrust* (Cambridge, 1980). For quite different views begin with Alexander Bickel, *The Least Dangerous Branch* (Indianapolis, 1962), and *The Supreme Court and the Idea of Progress* (New York, 1970).

Among the law review articles on institution cases, see especially "Special Project: The Remedial Process in Institutional Reform Litigation," *Columbia Law Review* 78 (1978): 788–929; in that same volume consult too Curtis Berger, "Away from the Court House and Into the Field: The Odyssey of a Special Master," 707–38. Colin S. Diver, "The Judge as Political Powerbroker," *Virginia Law Review* 65 (1979): 44–105; Note, "Implementation Problems in Institutional Reform Litigation," *Harvard Law Review* 91 (1977): 428–63; Gerald Frug, "The Judicial Power of the Purse," *University of Pennsylvania Law Review* 126 (1978): 715–94.

The social science literature on implementation includes Donald L. Horowitz, *The Courts and Social Policy* (Washington, D.C., 1977), and Nathan Glazer, "Should Judges Administer Social Services?" *Public Interest* 50 (1978): 64–80. More positive views of the outcomes may be found in Michal A. Rebell and Arthur R. Block, *Educational Policy Making and the Courts* (Chicago, 1982). See also Howard I. Kalodner and James J. Fishman, *Limits of Justice* (Cambridge, 1978). Helpful too were the chapters by Charles Johnson (chap. 6) and Lawrence Baum (chap. 7) on judicial impact in John A. Gardiner, ed., *Public Law and Public Policy* (New York, 1977).

The best starting point for exploring the problems of legal change and mental disability is Michael Kindred, ed., *The Mentally Retarded Citizen and the Law* (New York, 1976). A recent symposium that debated many of these issues was edited by Joanna Weinberg and reprinted in *Law and Human Behavior* 6 (1982). See also the symposium, "Mentally Retarded People and the Law," *Stanford Law Review* 31 (1979). Additional citations to the legal literature are found in the notes below to Chapters 3, 4, and 5.

The literature on institutions and their alternatives properly opens with Erving Goffman, *Asylums* (New York, 1961). In the notes to Chapter 9, below, we cite some of the material that debates the pros and cons of deinstitutionalization. In addition, see Andrew Scull, *Decarceration* (Englewood Cliffs, N.J., 1977); and John A. Talbott, *The Death of the Asylum* (New York, 1978). The best beginning for a history of institutions for the retarded is Robert Kugel and Wolf Wolfensberger, eds., *Changing Patterns in Residential Services for the Mentally Retarded* (Washington, D.C., 1969). References to the rich literature on normalization appear below, in the notes to Chapter 2. The best beginning point is Robert J. Flynn and Kathleen Nitsch, *Normalization, Social Integration, and Community Services* (Baltimore, 1980). A useful guide to the issues in general, now somewhat outdated, is Leona Bachrach, *Deinstitutionalization: An Analytic Review and Sociological Perspective* (National Institute of Mental Health, 1976). For an overview of substantive issues, see U.S. General

pages

Accounting Office, *Returning the Mentally Retarded to the Community* (Washington, D.C., 1977).

Our writings mentioned in the text include, for David Rothman, *The Discovery of the Asylum* (Boston, 1971) and *Conscience and Convenience* (Boston, 1980); for Sheila Rothman, *Woman's Proper Place* (New York, 1978).

1. Welcome to Willowbrook

15–17 Geraldo Rivera, *Willowbrook: A Report* (New York, 1972), pp. 3, 9–22; interview with Elizabeth Lee, Oct. 2, 1980. Myron M. Levine et al., "Shigellosis in Custodial Institutions," *Journal of Pediatrics* 83 (1974): 803–5.

17–22 Material here is drawn from interviews with Raymond and Ethel Silvers (pseudonym), February 1979; Francis Jensen (pseudonym), Feb. 27, 1979; Mrs. Becker (pseudonym), October 1978; Murray and Vicki Schneps, Nov. 30, 1981. The Schneps letter to Jack Hammond is Aug. 11, 1970. Testimony of Benjamin Rosepka is from the *Hearing on Preliminary Relief*, Dec. 18, 1972, pp. 32–34. *Staten Island Advance*, May 2, 1955, and interview with Jerry Gavin, Dec. 13, 1978.

22–23 New York State Department of Mental Hygiene (DMH), *Annual Report*, 1963, pp. 117, 119; Joint Legislative Committee on Mental Retardation and Physical Handicaps, *Confidential Report*, Sept. 12, 1964, pp. 1, 4. On the deaths at Willowbrook, see the *Staten Island Advance*, May 15, 18, 24, 1965, June 23, 1965, July 22, 1965. It covered the visit of Robert Kennedy, Sept. 9, 10, 1965. See also, Congressional Record, *Proceedings and Debates of the 89th Congress*, 1st Session, Sept. 17, 1965.

24–26 The statistical data are compiled from information in the DMH Office of Statistical and Clinical Information Systems, *Selected Statistics for Willowbrook State School*, 1948–1971; and its *Selected Statistics for All New York State Schools for the Retarded*, 1948–1972 (NYCLU Files). See also the annual reports of DMH over the period 1960–1972 and Gerhart Saenger, *Factors Influencing the Institutionalization of Mentally Retarded Individuals in New York City* (New York, 1960). On triage, interview with Lawrence C. Kolb, Aug. 12, 1980. See also D. Herential, *Diagnosis in Clinical Psychiatry: The Lectures of Paul H. Hoch* (New York, 1972); Nolin Lewis and Margaret Strahl, *The Complete Psychiatrist: The Achievement of Paul H. Hoch, M.D.* (Albany, 1968); Lawrence C. Kolb, "Some Important Concerns for Psychiatry," a lecture delivered at the New York Academy of Medicine (n.d.); David J. Rothman, *Conscience and Convenience* (Boston, 1980), pp. 293–324.

26–30 New York State Planning Committee on Mental Disorders, *A Plan for a Comprehensive Mental Health and Mental Retardation Program*, vol. 1 (Albany, 1965); on the results see State of New York, Legislative Commission on Expenditure Review, *Construction of Mental Health Facilities* (Albany, 1973), pp. 7–22; New York State DMH, *Appropriateness of Continued Institutionalization of the State School Population in New York State* (Albany, 1969), p. 16. Interview with Giovanni Pasanella, Nov. 18, 1982, the architect who designed the infant therapy center. See also

pages

Staten Island Advance, Sept. 9, 10, 1965; *New York Times* Op Ed article by Jack Hammond, May 6, 1972.

30–31 American Association on Mental Deficiency, ***Final Report of the Professional Evaluation Team*** (October 1967), pp. 2–3, 6, 10, 21, 26 (NYCLU Files).

31–34 Legislative Commission on Expenditure Review, ***Mental Health Facilities,*** pp. 39–43; Edward Jennings to Frederic Grunberg, "Reevaluation of Critical Priorities at Willowbrook State School," Dec. 9, 1971 (NYCLU Files). *New York Times,* Oct. 5, 1971, May 20, 1971. Lee L. Landes to Nelson Rockefeller, Nov. 3, 1971 (NYCLU Files). New York State DMH, ***Annual Report,*** 1971. Perry B. Duryea, Jr., to Dear Constituent, sent between Apr. 1, 1971, and Mar. 31, 1972. Interview with Frederic Grunberg, July 3, 1980.

34–44 William Bronston, ***Public Ransom, Public Hostage: Inside Institutional America*** (unpublished ms., 1979), pp. vi, 15, 18, 105, ii, 102, 103, 22–23, 55. Interview with William Bronston, Sept. 23, 24, 1983; with Elizabeth Lee, Oct. 21, 1980; with Eugene Eisner, Jan. 9, 1984. Deposition of Mrs. Lena Steuernagel, June 13, 1972 (NYCLU Files). Rothman, ***Conscience and Convenience,*** pp. 340–43. On Bronston's transfer see Alan Miller to Bronston, Feb. 16, 1973, reprinted in ***Public Ransom.*** See the ***Staten Island Advance*** over November and December 1971 and the testimony of Bronston at the 1973 ***Hearing on Preliminary Relief,*** Dec. 18, 19, 1972. On the Kansas incident see the *New York Times,* July 15, 16, 23, 1968; personal communication from Roger Hofmaster to authors, Mar. 28, 1984. "Dr. Bronston was terminated . . . because he failed to devote sufficient time and attention to his psychiatry training and, instead, continued to spend much of his time and energy on various social-political issues which pre-occupied him at the time."

2. The Litigator as Reformer

45–46 The *New York Times,* January 1972; Geraldo Rivera, ***Willowbrook,*** pp. 43, 69. Hearing before State of New York Joint Legislative Committee for Physical and Mental Handicap, Testimony of William Bronston, Feb. 17, 1972.

47–50 Policy and Action Conference for the Handicapped, "Report of the Proceedings," Mar. 4, 5, 1972, pp. 2–3, 12 (NYCLU Files). Wolfensberger's views are presented in ***The Principles of Normalization in Human Services*** (Toronto, 1972). On normalization generally see Michael Kindred, ed., ***The Mentally Retarded Citizen and the Law*** (New York, 1976); Robert J. Flynn and Katheleen E. Nitsch, eds., ***Normalization, Integration, and Community Services*** (Baltimore 1980); Erving Goffman, ***Asylums*** (New York, 1961).

50–52 Much of this material came from a two day interview with Bruce Ennis, Chris Hansen, and Aryeh Neier, Apr. 8, 9, 1980, Seven Springs Conference Center. Thomas S. Szasz, ***The Myth of Mental Illness*** (New York, 1961); Richard Kluger, ***Simple Justice: The History of Brown*** vs. ***Board of Education and Black America's Struggle for Equality*** (New York, 1976); H. N. Hirsch, ***The Enigma of Felix Frankfurter*** (New York, 1981); David

pages

J. Rothman, "The State as Parent," in Willard Gaylin et al., *Doing Good* (Pantheon, 1978), pp. 67–96.

52–55 David J. Rothman, "Decarcerating Prisoners and Patients," *The Civil Liberties Review* 1 (1973): 8–30; Albert Deutsch, *The Mentally Ill in America: A History of Their Care and Treatment from Colonial Times* (New York, 1949), chaps. 16, 17; Seymour B. Sarason and John Doris, *Educational Handicap, Public Policy and Social History* (New York, 1979). Bruce J. Ennis, *Prisoners of Psychiatry: Mental Patients, Psychiatrists and the Law* (New York, 1972); Morton Birnbaum, "The Right to Treatment," *American Bar Association Journal* 46 (1960): 499–505.

55–57 Tinsley E. Yarborough, *Judge Frank Johnson and Human Rights in Alabama* (University, Ala., 1981), pp. 153–82. *Wyatt* v. *Stickney,* 344 F. Supp. 387 (1972). Note, "The Wyatt Case: Implementation of a Judicial Decree . . . ," *Yale Law Journal* 84 (1975): 1338–79.

57–60 Edward I. Koch to Aryeh Neier, Feb. 16, 1972; Bruce J. Ennis to Philip Roos, Mar. 2, 1972 (NYCLU Files). Policy and Action Conference, "Report," 1. *Wyatt* v. *Stickney,* 344 F. Supp. 391 (1972); interview with Bruce Ennis, Apr. 8, 9, 1980.

60–63 Herbert J. Lerner, *State Association for Retarded Children and New York State Government, 1948–68* (privately printed, NYARC, 1972), pp. 24–30, 50–51. The retainer is dated Mar. 17, 1972 (NYCLU Files).

63–65 *New York Association for Retarded Children* v. *Rockefeller,* Class Action Complaint 72 Civ., Mar. 17, 1972, pp. 2, 12, 20, 35–37. "Post-Hearing Memorandum for Defendants," Feb. 15, 1973, especially pp. 2–3, 6, 10, 13, 16; on nurses, pp. 35–38; physical therapists, p. 50; heating units, p. 59; cockroaches, p. 61. "Plaintiffs' post-trial memorandum," Feb. 2, 1973; "Problem Areas at Willowbrook" were described on pp. 44–156. Quotes are from p. 44.

3. A Keen Intellect and a Love of Man

66–68 Interviews with Bruce Ennis, Apr. 8, 9, 1980; Louis Lefkowitz, June 8, 1981; Alan Miller, Aug. 26, 1980; Brenda Soloff, June 5, 1981. Ennis to Robert J. Hodgson, New York State Association for Retarded Children, Apr. 19, 1972; Soloff to Ennis, Nov. 1, 1972; Ennis to Ira Glasser, May 12, 1972 (NYCLU Files).

68–71 "Proceedings of a Memorial Service for Judge Orrin Judd," July 15, 1976, Remarks of Judge Murray Gurfein, p. 57, and Daniel Eisenberg, p. 14 (NYCLU Files). *New York Times,* Aug. 2, 1975; *Holtzman* v. *Schlesinger,* 361 F. Supp. 553 (1973); *Holtzman* v. *Schlesinger* 484 F. 2d 1307 (1973). Learned Hand, *The Bill of Rights* (Cambridge, 1958); Alexander Bickel, *The Least Dangerous Branch* (Indianapolis, 1962). *Hearing for Preliminary Relief,* Dec. 18, 1972, pp. 13, 16, Dec. 20, 1972, p. 239, Jan. 9, 1973, pp. 129–30. (Unless otherwise noted, all hearings are Willowbrook hearings.)

72–73 Bruce Ennis to All Persons Interested in the Willowbrook Lawsuit: Report of a Mar. 15, 1972, Tour of Willowbrook State School, pp. 6–7; Mary Stewart Goodwin, M.D., Report on a Visit to 17 Buildings at Willowbrook State School, Mar. 30, 31, 1972, p. 7 (NYCLU Files). (The quotations have been excerpted from her longer report.) Robert B. Kugel, M.D., Report

pages

of a Consultation Visit to Willowbrook State School, Apr. 17, 1972, pp. 5, 11 (NYCLU Files).

73–74 *New York State ARC* v. *Rockefeller, Memorandum and Order,* June 28, 1972, pp. 4, 6; Bruce Ennis to Orrin Judd, Nov. 2, 1972 (NYCLU Files).

75–77 *Hearing for Preliminary Relief,* Dec. 18, 1972, pp. 111, 123, 125, 174, 175, 178, Dec. 20, 1972, pp. 158, 168–69; John Bowlby, *Attachment and Loss* (vol. 1: *Attachment,* New York, 1969); S. Provence and R. C. Lipton, *Infants in Institutions* (New York, 1962).

77–82 *Hearing for Preliminary Relief,* Dec. 18, 1972, p. 232; Dec. 20, 1972, pp. 557, 570, 572, 585, 674, 834, 838, 862, 877, 953–54, 1013, 1098, 1126.

82–84 "Memorial Service for Judge Judd," p. 6; Bill Moyers Journal, "Judge, the Law, and Frank Johnson," Part 2, July 31, 1980, p. 10 (transcript); David J. Rothman, "Decarcerating Prisoners and Patients," pp. 8–30.

84–89 Robert J. Feldt, "Memorandum from a Willowbrook Tour with Judge Orrin Judd, February 12, 1973" (NYCLU Files); *New York State Association for Retarded Children* v. *Rockefeller,* No. 73-C-55, 73-C-113, U.S. District Court E.D. New York, Apr. 10, 1973. Judd reported on his Feb. 12 visit in his opinion but omitted the report when he published it in the federal supplement (typescript opinion, pp. 19–25, U.S. District Courthouse, Brooklyn, New York). *New York State ARC* v. *Rockefeller, Order for Preliminary Relief,* Apr. 12, 1973, F. Supp. 357, pp. 764–65, 759, 770.

4. The Numbers Game

90–93 Interview with Alan Miller, Aug. 26, 1980; United States Department of Health, Education and Welfare, *Report of the Special Federal Team to Assist New York's Retardation Program,* October 1972, pp. 7, 12, 13 (NYCLU Files); Willowbrook State School, *Federal Grant Request, Exodus Project* (n.d., n.p., MPU Files). Willowbrook State School, *Exodus—Diagnosis and Evaluation of Institutionalized Retardates, Progress Report,* June 30, 1972–June 30, 1973, Grant number 56-P-10302/2-01, pp. 6–7 (MPU Files). The Exodus Team reported weekly to Department of Mental Hygiene officials on forms entitled "Project Exodus Transfer Reports." The figures in the text were taken from these reports in the MPU files and matched against other documents collected by the plaintiffs' lawyers from the Department of Mental Hygiene for the 1974 trial. Reducing the population at Willowbrook became such a priority that Robert J. Patton, Second Deputy Commissioner at DMH, wrote Norman Hurd, Secretary to the Governor, a weekly letter informing him of the number of residents moved from Willowbrook. In these letters the obstacles to placement were also cited (MPU Files).

93–96 Frederic Grunberg to All State School Directors, "Guidelines for Transfers," Memorandum No. 72-26, July 7, 1972; Dr. Kamins to Mr. Kaplan, "A Visit to the Williamsburg Training School," July 22, 1968; Alan Miller to Directors of State Hospitals and State Schools, "Movement of Patients between State Hospitals and State Schools," Jan. 18, 1974; Douglas Dornan to Mary Reichsman, "Exodus Transfers to Broome County," July 22, 1974; Anonymous, "Family Care Upstate," June 15, 1973; Mattie Perry to Sidney Lecker, "Meeting on Upstate Transfers," July 30, 1973; Albert

pages

Robidoux to Miodrag Ristich, "Broome County State School," Aug. 1, 1973 (MPU Files).

96–97 Herbert Cohen to Sidney Lecker, Oct. 23, 1973; Mary Reichsman, "Notes of a Bronx Task Force Meeting," Sept. 14, 1973 (MPU Files). *Van Ness* v. *Shore Manor Ltd,* Superior Court of New Jersey, Atlantic County Chancery Division, June 7, 1976. Arthur Arnold to David Woogen, Feb. 12, 1973 (MPU Files). Interview with Fred Markowitz and Helen Gross, May 11, 1979. See also Helen Gross and Fred Markowitz, "Collaboration: The Development of a Service Network in a Community Residential Setting" (n.d., n.p.); Arnold Birenbaum and Samuel Seiffer, *Resettling Retarded Adults in a Managed Community* (New York, 1976), pp. 30–31, 38–47. New York State Moreland Commission on Nursing Homes and Residential Facilities, *Political Influence and Political Accountability: One Foot in the Door,* February 1976 (copy in Columbia University Law School Library); Island View Care Center and New York State Department of Mental Hygiene, "Memorandum of Agreement," Apr. 2, 1974.

97–100 New York State Advisory Council on Developmental Disabilities, *Report of the Council on the Willowbrook State School,* February 1973, pp. 1, 17, 18, 19 (NYCLU Files); Willowbrook State School, *Preliminary Proposal of the Geographic Unitization Council,* October 1974 (MPU Files). Although the title indicates a preliminary proposal, the document was actually the final report of the Council. Reports of its deliberations can be found in the typescript reports of its weekly meetings (MPU files). Herbert Cohen, Bernard Tesse, Calvin Michael, Walter Martin, and Miodrag Ristich to Stuart Keill, Aug. 23, 1974; James Forde to Keill, Oct. 25, 1974 (MPU Files); Olga Defelippo to Jerry Weingold, Mar. 27, 1974 (NYCLU Files).

100–102 "Brief in Support of Plaintiffs' Motion for Modification or Clarification," May 7, 1973 (NYCLU Files). The increasing involvement of the Department of Justice in institutional litigation is described in Department of Justice, *Annual Reports of the Attorney General of the United States;* see especially 1973, pp. 91–95; 1974, pp. 73–75, 78. See also U.S. Senate Committee on the Judiciary, "Hearings on the Department of Justice Budget Authorization (Civil Rights Division)," 95th Congress, 2nd Session, May 8, 1978, pp. 683ff. Interview with Michael Lottman, May 7, 1980. Louis M. Thrasher to David Norman, May 1, 1972; Thrasher to J. Stanley Pottinger, May 10, 1973; Diane Dorfman to Jesse Queen, "Enforcement of Decrees," Mar. 6, 1974. (These memos are in the U.S. Department of Justice, Civil Rights Division Files.)

102–5 Bruce Ennis to Brenda Soloff, May 30, 1973 (NYCLU Files). Quotations from the FBI instructions are condensed. (They are in the Justice Department Files, Civil Rights Division, "Unknown Subjects at Willowbrook State School—Victims," DSD158-52.) *New York State ARC* v. *Rockefeller, Order,* July 27, 1973, Oct. 17, 1973. On the State's opposition to the FBI see "Memorandum in Opposition to Motion by the United States," Oct. 2, 1973.

5. Uninformed Consent

106–10 Bruce Ennis to Willowbrook Lawyers and Expert Witnesses, "Willowbrook Strategy," Aug. 2, 1974 (NYCLU Files). *Hearing for Permanent*

pages

Relief, Testimony of Earl Butterfield, Oct. 2, 1974, pp. 13, 41, 71, 73, 29, 69; testimony of Linda Glenn, Oct. 3, 1974, pp. 232–63; testimony of James Clements, Oct. 30, 1974, pp. A36-A37; testimony of Juanita Hutter, Oct. 7, 1974, pp. 575–81; testimony of Paul Dokecki, Oct. 29, 1974, p. 37.

110–13 Kluger, *Simple Justice*, pp. 315–45. Roy D. King, Norma V. Raynes, and Jack Tizard, *Patterns of Residential Care: Sociological Studies in Institutions for Handicapped Children* (London, 1971); David A. Balla, Earl C. Butterfield, and Edward Zigler, "Effects of Institutionalization on Retarded Children: A Longitudinal Cross-Institutional Investigation," *American Journal of Mental Deficiency* 78 (1974): 530–39; Edward Zigler, Earl Butterfield, and F. Capabianco, "Institutionalization and the Effectiveness of Social Reenforcements," *Developmental Psychology* 3 (1970): 255–63; *Hearing for Permanent Relief*, testimony of Herbert Grossman, Dec. 11, 1974, pp. 68, 110; testimony of Stephen Zoltan, Dec. 12, 1974, pp. 421–22.

113–18 Executive Chamber, Albany, New York, "Press Release, Willowbrook Consent Decree," Apr. 21, 1975. The NYCLU Files contain several drafts of "Appendix A" of the Consent Judgment, with notations of First Draft, Second Draft, Third Draft. The HEW guidelines were promulgated by its Social and Rehabilitation Service, "Medical Assistance: Intermediate Care Facility Services," *Federal Register*, vol. 39, no. 12, Part 2, Jan. 17, 1974. The quotations from the proposed consent judgment are in the First Draft, pp. 47–48, p. 29 (on speech), p. 38 (six hours of programing, pp. 20–21 (on class size), p. 68 (on community placement); the Second Draft, p. 62 (DMH plan), p. 73 (on the Review Panel); the Third Draft, pp. 76–77 (the Review Panel). The Wyatt decree also relied on JCAH and provided no additional guidance. A copy of "Appendix A" is most conveniently found in the *Mental Disability Law Reporter* of July–August 1976, pp. 58–68. Deposition of Alan Miller, Oct. 23, 24, 1974, pp. 200–323. Bruce Ennis to Hugh Carey, Dec. 4, 1974; Carey to Ennis, Dec. 6, 1974 (NYCLU Files). The observations on Scandinavian practices grow out of a three-week visit we made in July 1979.

118–24 Peter Goldmark to Hugh Carey, Feb. 13, 1975 (MPU Files). Interview with Carey, Oct. 26, 1983. On the results of the negotiation, we compared the several drafts and corrections of the text of the proposed Consent Judgment enclosed in Bruce Ennis et al. to Ann Lewis and Bob Tierney, Mar. 18, 1975. Ennis kept extensive handwritten notes of the negotiations (NYCLU Files), and we reviewed them with him, Apr. 8, 9, 1980, and again June 20, 1980. Interview with Peter Goldmark, June 22, 1983. In 1976, DMH prepared a "matrix of JCAH ICF/MR and Willowbrook Consent Judgment Requirements for Individual Plans of Care" (MPU Files). This analysis demonstrates the similarities of the standards set forth in the three documents. On Mar. 5, 1975, Ennis informed Joseph Weingold (in a hand-delivered letter) of the progress of the negotiations and some of Goldmark's objections. Goldmark's views on the document are also expressed in a letter to Stanley Steingut, July 1, 1975 (MPU Files). On the institutional directors see Bernard Tesse to Barbara Blum, Sept. 21, 1976 (MPU Files). Judd's remarks are in *New York State ARC* v. *Carey, Memorandum on Final Judgment on Consent*, 393 F. Supp. 715–19 (1975).

pages **6. Ready, Fire, Aim**

127–31 "The Quinlan Quagmire," *New York Times,* Nov. 11, 1975; Murray Schneps, To the Editor, *New York Times,* Nov. 13, 1975, unpublished (WRP Files). Joseph Weingold to Bruce Ennis, June 23, 1975; Max Schneier to Jack Bernstein, Dec. 5, 1975 (NYCLU Files). See also Joseph Weingold, "Reply Affidavit," Feb. 23, 1976; Weingold to Elliot Aronin, June 19, 1975 (NYCLU Files). *New York State ARC* v. *Carey, Memorandum of Order,* Mar. 5, 1976.

132–33 Michael Lottman to James Clements, Feb. 6, 1976; Murray Schneps to Panel Members, Jan. 15, 1976 (WRP Files). Willowbrook Review Panel, *Report to the Court, July 1, 1975–December 31, 1975,* p. 1.

133–34 Hugh Carey to Peter Goldmark and Lawrence Kolb, "Implementation of Willowbrook Consent Judgment," May 15, 1975; Goldmark and Kolb to Carey, July 10, 1975; Sylvan Furman to Directors of Developmental Centers, Aug. 27, 1975; Mary Reichsman to Stuart Keill, Aug. 22, 1975; Ed Jennings and Jarvis Tabor to Hugh Butts, Sept. 4, 1975 (MPU Files). Interview with Samuel Ornstein, Oct. 21, 1981; Harold Piepenbrink to Keill, Sept. 10, 1975 (MPU Files). Willowbrook Review Panel, *Report to the Court, July 1, 1975–December 31, 1975,* pp. 2–3.

134–36 *New York Times,* Dec. 30, 1975; David Oberhausen, "A Report on the Ramirez Incident and Related Issues," Jan. 22, 1976; Willowbrook State School, "Hearing on Luis Ramirez Death" (transcript), Dec. 30, 1975; James Clements to Thomas Coughlin, Jan. 23, 1976; Murray Schneps to Lawrence Kolb, Jan. 28, 1976; Kolb to Schneps, Feb. 11, 1976; Schneps to Orrin Judd, June 8, 1976; Coughlin to Schneps, June 30, 1976 (WRP Files). See also *Hearing,* Feb. 10, 1976, pp. 77–100. New York State DMH, Willowbrook Task Force, "The Organization of a Placement Program," Nov. 24, 1975; New York State, Division of the Budget, "Draft Memorandum on the Status of Willowbrook Consent Judgment" (n.d., MPU Files). Hugh Carey, "Statement on Mental Retardation," Sept. 22, 1975.

136–38 Sterling Forest Conference with Barbara Blum, her staff, Tom Coughlin, and Chris Hansen, Sept. 15–16, 1978. Interview with Tom Coughlin, December 1975, Oct. 26, 1982. *New York Times,* Dec. 11, 1975; Lawrence Kolb, "Affidavit," Dec. 4, 1975, quoting the Department Directive.

139–41 Samuel Ornstein to James Clements, Aug. 27, 1975; Murray Schneps to Review Panel members, Aug. 29, 1975; Willowbrook Review Panel, "Minutes, October 4–5, 1975"; Clements to Lawrence Kolb, Oct. 6, 1975; Kolb to Clements, Nov. 3, 1975 (WRP Files). On one-step versus two-step placement see *Hearing,* Feb. 10, 1976, pp. 3–76. For an understanding of DMH's determination to use the decree to comply with federal regulations, see J. Robert Hendrick and Robert Kerker to Franklin White, Oct. 22, 1975, "State Compliance with ICF and ICFMR Regulations," Oct. 22, 1975; Hendrick and Kerker to White, "ICF/MR Compliance Issues," Dec. 2, 1975 (Bureau of the Budget Files, Albany). Interview with John Bartels, Oct. 25, 1979.

141–44 New York Institute for the Humanities, Conference on Confinement Architecture: The Bronx Development Center, Nov. 28, 1979 (transcript). Interview with Richard Meier, Jan. 29, 1980; Eugene Kupper, "Meier's Typeforms," *Progressive Architecture* (1977): 57; John Hejduk is quoted in Paul Goldberger, "Masterwork or Nightmare," *New York*

pages

Times, May 3, 1977. On Huxtable see *New York Times,* Dec. 25, 1976; Mental Hygiene, *News,* Aug. 12, 1977. See also Richard Meier, *Architect: Building and Projects, 1966–1976* (New York, 1976).

144–46 Jennifer Howse to Ada Louise Huxtable, June 21, 1977; Consumer Advisory Board, "Site Evaluation: Bronx Development Center," Dec. 29, 1976; H. David Sokoloff to Donald Canty, May 25, 1977 (WRP Files). For a discussion of moral architecture see David J. Rothman, *The Discovery of the Asylum* (Boston, 1971), pp. 134–37. Murray Schneps to Lawrence Kolb, Apr. 19, 1976; Kolb to Schneps, Sept. 6, 1976; James Clements to Thomas Coughlin, Mar. 11, 1977; Willowbrook Review Panel, "Minutes, February 6–7, 1977," p. 6; "Moving Papers in Support of Motion to Confirm Departmental Rejection of Formal Recommendation of Willowbrook Review Panel" (WRP Files).

146–50 *Hearing on the Bronx Developmental Center,* May 10–May 13, 1977. Cohen testimony, May 10, 1977, pp. 24, 76–77, 79–80, 63; Coughlin testimony, May 10, 1977, p. 176; Bartels comments, May 13, 1977, pp. 186, 39, 208–9; Clements testimony, May 12, 1977, pp. 71, 205, 200; *New York State ARC* v. *Carey, Memorandum, Decision and Order,* June 10, 1977, pp. 10, 11, 12.

7. Who Cares?

151–55 Samuel Ornstein, "The Organization of a Placement Program," Oct. 24, 1975, pp. 3–4 (MPU Files). Interview with Ornstein, Oct. 21, 1981. DMH, *Metro Manual Guidelines for the Metropolitan Placement Unit,* Oct. 20, 1970 (MPU Files), describes in detail the structure and functions of the unit. Much of the material in this section came from interviews with Barbara Blum, Apr. 20, 1980, June 8, 1981; interview with Tom Coughlin, June 27, 28, 1980; interview with Alvin Mesnikoff, Oct. 16, 1981. The Sterling Forest Conference was of great assistance here. The temporary nature of the MPU was made clear to the panel; see Willowbrook Review Panel, "Minutes, Jan. 24–25, 1976," and "Minutes, March 14–15, 1976" (WRP Files).

155–58 Interview with Mitchell Ginsberg, Apr. 14, 1981. See also Rothman, *The Discovery of the Asylum,* pp. 155–80; Rothman, *Conscience and Convenience,* pp. 205–36. Interagency Council Meeting, "Minutes," Mar. 30, 1976; Barbara Blum, "Review of Willowbrook Placement Problems: A Strategy for Resolution," Mar. 4, 1976; Barbara Blum, "Cost of Services for Willowbrook Class in Community Placement," September 1977 (MPU Files).

158–59 Metropolitan Placement Unit, *Six Month Report,* Sept. 4, 1976, sets out the problems of placement. See also "MPU Problem Statement," Aug. 26, 1976 (MPU Files). Jerry Gavin to Jennifer Howse, "Report of a Meeting of Barbara Blum with Voluntary Child Care Agencies," Apr. 1, 1976 (WRP Files). Jacob Trobe to Barbara Blum, July 9, 1976; Saul Hofstein, "Giving Jewish Retarded a Chance to Be Individuals," Mar. 16, 1978; see also Federation of Jewish Philanthropies, Agency Committee on Services for the Jewish Retarded, "Minutes," Jan. 26, 1977, and Feb. 23, 1977 (MPU Files).

159–61 Leonard Albert Stidley, *Sectarian Welfare Federation Among Protestants* (New York, 1944), 67. Claire Stone to Barbara Blum, Mar. 3, 1977; Sister

pages

Mary P. Garter and L. Casals, "The Ghetto as a Source of Foster Homes," *Child Welfare* 49 (1970). Federation of Protestant Welfare Agencies, *Annual Reports,* over the 1950s and 1960s were also useful.

161–64 Helen R. F. Ebaugh, *Out of the Cloister: A Study of Organizational Dilemmas* (Austin, 1977), pp. 68, 70, 109; interview with Sister Bernadette Downs, June 2, 1981, and Sister Barbara Eirich, June 6, 1981. On Catholic Charities of Brooklyn see Rev. Thomas Cribben to Isabel Sklar, Apr. 14, 1975 (MPU Files). Interview with Rev. Thomas Cribben, March 1978.

164–65 David Fanshel, *Foster Parenthood: A Role Analysis* (St. Paul, 1966); Joseph E. Paull, "Recruiting, Processing, and Assignment of Foster Homes" (doctoral diss., Columbia University School of Social Work, 1977). Child Welfare League of America, *Standards for Foster Family Care Services* (New York, 1959), p. 8; Dorothy S. Goldblatt, "Foster Family Care for the Mentally Retarded Child," *Child Welfare* 48 (1969): 423–24, 426.

165–66 Albert Robidoux to Robert Hayes, "Placement of Patient or Residents in Family Care Homes," Sept. 18, 1973; Thomas Coughlin to Regional Directors, "Placement of Willowbrook Class Minor Children in Their Own Homes," Dec. 4, 1975 (Memo No. 75–37). Gerald Dunn to Regional Directors, "Family Care Payments," July 6, 1976 (Memo No. 76-11, MPU Files).

166–69 Interviews with Karin Eriksen, May 5, 1978, Feb. 27, 1980; Eriksen to Grace Peterson, "Draft of Proposal for Family Caretaking Training Program," Nov. 19, 1976; New York State, Office of Mental Retardation and Developmental Disabilities, *Annual Report on Family Care Homes,* February 1979; Carolyn Ward to Eriksen, July 22, 1977; Metropolitan Placement Unit, "Summary of Recruitment to Foster Care, January 1977 through June 1977" (MPU Files). See Sources and Methods for details on research procedures with foster parents.

169–71 Richard Cloward and Lloyd Ohlin, *Delinquency and Opportunity: A Theory of Delinquent Gangs* (New York, 1960); Allan Easton, "Poverty and Self-Help and the Community Development Corporation," *Hofstra Yearbook of Business* 3 (1976). On the MFY experience see George Brager and Francis Purcell, *Community Action Against Poverty* (New Haven, 1967), and Francis Fox Piven and Richard Cloward, *Regulating the Poor: The Functions of Public Welfare* (New York, 1971). We profited, too, from discussions with George Brager, the late Charles Grosser, and the late Melvin Herman of the Columbia School of Social Work. See too Bedford Stuyvesant Restoration Corporation, "The Achievements of the Bedford Stuyvesant Restoration Corporation, 1967–1981," April 1981; interview with Curtis Wood, December 1980. Interview with Al Cooley of Federation of Puerto Rican Organizations, Nov. 28, 1971; interview with Carol Washington, Director of Training Programs at Colony South, May 25, 1978. Interview with Shirley Pierce, Apr. 16, 1981.

171–72 Interview with Michael Goldfarb, Apr. 17, 1978, Jan. 22, 1980; interview with Joel Levy, Nov. 16, 1979, Feb. 16, 1980; interview with Bert MacLeech, November 1979. See also Susan C. Wick, "Providing Social Services in an Urban Environment: The Case of New York City's Mentally Retarded" (doctoral diss., Boston University, 1984). Young Adult Institute, *Annual Reports,* 1973 through 1980 (at YAI offices, NYC).

172–74 Interview with Robert Schonhorn, May 3, 1978; United Cerebral Palsy,

pages

Annual Reports 1952 through 1979 (at UCP state offices, NYC). On the parent agencies, interviews with Joseph Harris, Mar. 3, 1981, Samuel Wallach, February 1978, and Ida Rappaport, March 1979.

174–76 On the MPU staff experience, we profited from frequent discussions with Karin Eriksen, Brian Dione, Pat Pelner, and Pat Dione. See also William D. Miller, *A Harsh and Dreadful Love: Dorothy Day and the Catholic Worker Movement* (New York, 1973). *New York Times,* Dec. 1, 1980. Barbara Blum, "The Return of Willowbrook Class Members from Community Placement: A Brief Note," Nov. 30, 1977; Metropolitan Placement Unit, *Setting a Standard of Quality, First Annual Report,* Mar. 4, 1976–Mar. 4, 1977 (MPU Files).

8. Moving Minds

177–78 The problems of community placement were well understood by participants. Some of the best analyses are in the letters reprinted in the Willowbrook Review Panel, *Report to the Court,* July 1, 1976–Dec. 31, 1976, including James Clements to Barbara Blum, Oct. 22, 1976; Blum to Clements, Oct. 25, 1976; Arthur Arnold to Blum, Oct. 6, 1976; Thomas Coughlin to Jennifer Howse, Oct. 26, 1976.

178–80 Isabel Sklar to MPU Staff, "M.P.U. Leasing Procedures," Aug. 10, 1976; Lawrence Kolb to Arthur Levitt, Dec. 15, 1976; Edward Curley to Dolores Pascarelli, "New York City Building Codes," Mar. 8, 1977; Thomas Coughlin to Arthur Arnold, "Physical Plant Standards," Nov. 12, 1976. Barbara Blum, "An Analysis of Community Placement Problems," Aug. 9, 1976; Anonymous, "M.P.U. Functions and Procedures" (n.d.); Blum to Leonard Gelberg, "Obstacles to Community Placement," Nov. 20, 1976; Coughlin to Recipients of OMRDD Policy Manual et al., "Community Residence Policy," Transmittal Memo No. 7, Sept. 29, 1978; Joyce Roll to George Haggerty, "F.D.C. Turn-Around Time Study," July 6, 1979; Anonymous, "F.D.C. Activity: MPU Leasing Program, April 1, 1978–February 1, 1979." (All these materials are in the MPU Files.) The Sterling Forest Conference explored these issues; innumerable conversations with Ed Matthews of the MPU and John Sabatos of the Brooklyn office were equally helpful.

180–83 Interview with Frank Padavan, Apr. 24, 1979; New York State Senate Mental Hygiene and Addiction Control Committee, *Site Selection of Community Residences for the Mentally Disabled: Historical Perspective and Legislation* (April 1979). George Hallett, "Budget Responsibilities of Community Boards" (April 1976); Benjamin Lorick, "Summary and Comparison of Current and Approved Charter Revision as They Affect Community Boards" (May 1976). League of Women Voters of the City of New York, *You and Your Community Board* (New York, 1978). We profited from the summer research assistance of Amrita Basu, "Study of the Role of Community Boards in New York City" (July 1978). William Carnahan to Regional Directors, "Legal Aspects of Establishing Community-Based Alternatives for the Mentally Disabled," Memo 77-6, July 1, 1977 (MPU Files).

183–87 Interviews with Ed Matthews, Oct. 13, 1978, Jan. 21, 1980; interview with Ed Hassett, Feb. 2, 1978; interview with Pat Stickney, May 25, 1978;

pages

New York Times, June 18, 1977. The MPU did try to educate the community planning boards; it held formal and informal meetings with members, and printed pamphlets; see, for example, New York City Long Island County Service Group, "The Role of the Community Planning Board in the Development of Group Residences for the Retarded," Dec. 14, 1978; The Community Residences Information Services Program, "Community Residence Program for New York City," Oct. 1, 1979 (MPU Files). U.S. Department of Health and Human Services, *New Neighbors: The Retarded Citizen in Quest of a Home* (Washington, D.C., 1980). Some voluntary agencies sent staff door to door distributing pamphlets about the agency and the proposed group home. For example, a YAI pamphlet provided "Answers to the Twelve Most Frequently Asked Questions About Community Residences." *New York Daily News,* Nov. 10, 1977; One to One, "Selected Case Histories of Progress and Problems in Developing Community Residences for the Retarded," Jan. 6, 1978.

187–90 Mickey Marlib to Shirley Pierce, June 30, 1976 (MPU Files). Michael Lottman to Elizabeth Holtzman, June 9, 1977 (WRP Files). *Staten Island Advance,* July 30, 1979; interview with Ed Matthews, July 26, 1978; interview with Oliver Koppell, Sept. 3, 1978; interview with Senator Flynn, Aug. 15, 1978; interview with Bert Weinert, Aug. 22, 1978; interview with Catherine Clarke, Aug. 2, 1978; interview with Grace Belkin and Marty Wolport, Aug. 8, 1978; interview with Mr. and Mrs. Eugene Smilovic, Aug. 7, 1978. Robert Abrams to Barbara Blum, Nov. 17, 1977; Blum to Abrams, Nov. 23, 1977 (MPU Files). *Riverdale Press,* Jan. 5, 1978. Michael Mascari to Thomas Coughlin, "On Valles Avenue," June 8, 1978; Brian Dionne to Timothy O'Brien, "A History of the MPU Involvement in Valles Avenue," Jan. 17, 1978; Dionne to Catherin Heavey, Jan. 22, 1978; Eugene Smilovic to Rabbi Menachem Shayowitz, Jan. 30, 1978. A copy of this letter was sent to Thomas Coughlin, Feb. 3, 1978 (MPU Files).

191–95 Interviews with John Sabatos, Mar. 21, 1978, Feb. 2, 1979, June 9, 1981; interview with Father Thomas Cribben, Apr. 14, 1978; interview with Alvin Moskowitz, Apr. 25, 1978. Especially useful was Jay Kaplan's memorandum to us, "Public Hearing in Community Planning Board Two Queens at St. Mary's Church," Oct. 19, 1980, and his "Report on a Meeting of Community Planning Board Seven, Flushing, Queens," Mar. 27, 1978. At this meeting Alvin Moskowitz, director of marketing for the Lefrak organization, spoke about its role.

196–98 Julian Wolpert, "Group Homes for the Mentally Retarded: An Investigation of Neighborhood Property Impacts," Aug. 31, 1978 (MPU Files).

198–99 The statistical data was compiled and analyzed by Susan C. Wick and a fuller report can be found in her "Providing Social Services in an Urban Environment: The Case of New York City's Mentally Retarded" (doctoral diss., Boston University, 1984).

9. Eyes On

200–202 There is a large literature critical of deinstitutionalization. See, for example, Henry Santiestevan, *Deinstitutionalization: Out of Their Beds and Into the Streets* (Washington, D.C., 1975); Joseph Halpern et al., *The Illusion of Deinstitutionalization* (Washington, D.C., 1978); H. R. Lamb

pages

and V. Goertzel, "Discharged Mental Patients: Are They Really in the Community?" *Archives of General Psychiatry* 24 (1971): 29–34. Vicki Toomey to Jennifer Howse, "Community Residence Quality Rating," May 16, 1979 (MPU Files). Willowbrook Review Panel, "Community Placement Audit, November 1977–April 1978"; "November 1978–May 1979"; December 1979. Sue Gant, "Memorandum Re Institutional Returns," Apr. 4, 1980 (WRP Files). We profited, too, from frequent conversations and meetings with Vicki Toomey.

202–3 Carol Bellamy, "Press Release," May 1, 1979; Office of Council President Carol Bellamy, "Good Money After Bad: An Analysis of Expenditure and Performance in Private Sector Foster Care," May 1979, p. 18. Blanche Bernstein, "Foster Care Needs and Alternatives to Placement: A Projection for 1975–1985," New York State Board of Welfare, November 1975; Willowbrook Review Panel, "Community Placement Plan," 1976, p. 319 (WRP Files). For Eriksen's plan, see New York State DMH, *Metro-Manual Guidelines for the Metropolitan Placement Unit,* Oct. 20, 1976 (MPU Files).

203–4 Interviews with Jennifer Howse, Oct. 11, 1978, Feb. 20, 1979, Mar. 16, 1979, June 8, 1979. Willowbrook Review Panel, "Community Placement Audit, April 30, 1975–April 30, 1976," particularly Appendix G.4.

204–13 The analysis here is based on observations of the audit teams. Interviews were held periodically with the chief of the case managers and their staff. Also, we regularly attended the meetings of case managers in Brooklyn, the Bronx, and Queens. Of especial importance were interviews with Nadine Miller, Apr. 4, 1979; Karla Perlman, Dec. 4, 1979; Dorothy Jacobs, Oct. 26, 1978. We conducted a half-day conference (taped) with all the Brooklyn case managers on Dec. 12, 1978. On incident reporting see Barbara Blum to Directors of Day Programs and Community Residences, Nov. 3, 1977; "Guidelines for Incident Reporting," Feb. 12, 1979 (MPU Files).

214–15 The Brooklyn case managers kept a file of all their correspondence with the agencies. On Colony South see particularly, Nadine Miller et al. to Thomas Shirtz, May 8, 1979. Metropolitan Placement Unit, "Evaluation of Jewish Guild for the Blind, January 1979"; Patricia J. Sira, "Annual Recertification Evaluation: Jewish Guild for the Blind," Dec. 12, 1978; John Heimerdinger to Jennifer Howse, Nov. 7, 1978 (MPU Files).

215–17 Interview with Herbert Cohen, Mar. 30, 1978; see also, Herbert J. Cohen, "Practical Problems in the Development of Community Services for the Mentally Retarded," April 1974; Herbert Cohen, "The Context and Politics of Service Development and Discussion," in Cohen et al., *Urban Community Care for the Developmentally Disabled* (Springfield, Ill., 1980), pp. 22, 82–83. Interview with Dorothy Jacobs, May 3, 1978. On Dorothy Jacobs and the Review Panel debriefing session, see Sue Gant to Cohen, Mar. 20, 1979; Willowbrook Review Panel, "Bronx Case Manager Ratio Summary, December 1979" (WRP Files).

217–19 Robert Morgado to Howard Miller et al., "Implementation of Major Mental Hygiene Initiatives," June 13, 1978 (MPU Files); Civil Service Employees Association Task Force on Mental Hygiene, "The Exile of the Mentally Ill in New York State: Nowhere and Back Again" (n.p., 1978). Interview with Robert Schonhorn, May 3, 1978. Barbara Blum to Schon-

pages

horn, Oct. 18, 1977 (MPU Files). When our final draft of this chapter was completed, the New York State Commission on Quality of Care for the Mentally Disabled published its findings on the group homes: "Willowbrook: From Institution to the Community," August 1982. Its conclusions are in full agreement with ours, including its dissatisfactions with the state-operated homes and the UCP apartments. See pp. xiv–xxv for a summary.

10. Life Chances

220–53 The material in this chapter was primarily drawn from the observations of Robert Zussman and the semi-structured interviews that he and Barbara Rios conducted with group home staff members. (See Sources and Methods for a fuller description.) We also relied on Sister Barbara's accounts of her experience. In addition to interviews with her, relevant material was drawn from GLIE, *First Annual Report*, Mar. 14, 1979–Dec. 31, 1979; GLIE, "Manual of Policy and Procedures" (n.d.), and Sister Barbara Eirich, "Group Homes in the Inner City," in Cohen et al., *Urban Community Care*. Interviews were also conducted with YAI personnel and Erwin Friedman, of the Manhattan borough services office.

There are now more studies that explore the effects of deinstitutionalization on retarded persons. The best starting point remains the classic analysis of Robert B. Edgarton, *The Cloak of Competence* (Berkeley, 1967). For more recent findings see, R. H. Bruininks et al., *Deinstitutionalization and Community Adjustment of Mentally Retarded People* (Washington, D.C., 1981). See also Elinor Gollay et al., *Coming Back* (Cambridge, 1978), and our review of it in the *American Journal of Orthopsychiatry* (1980). See also J. Conroy et al., "A Matched Comparison of the Developmental Growth of Institutionalized and Deinstitutionalized Mentally Retarded Clients," *American Journal of Mental Deficiency* 86 (1982): 581–87. Valerie J. Bradley and James Conway, *Third Year Comprehensive Report of the Pennhurst Longitudinal Study* (Philadelphia, 1982). On size and outcome, see D. Balla, "Relationship of Institution Size to Quality of Care: A Review of the Literature," *American Journal of Mental Deficiency* 81 (1976): 117–24; and S. Landesman-Dwyer et al., "Affiliation and Friendship of Mentally Retarded Residents in Group Homes," *American Journal of Mental Deficiency* 83 (1979): 571–80.

11. Fighting the Plague

258–60 The following material was shared with us by J.W.: Joyce R. Coppin to J.W., Sept. 6, 1978; interview with J.W., Nov. 9, 1978; Priscilla Wyman to J.W., Sept. 21, 1977; J.W. to Karin Eriksen, Oct. 15, 1977; Eriksen to J.W., Dec. 2, 1977; Wyman to J.W., Mar. 15, 1978.

260–67 Interview with Saul Krugman, Feb. 22, 1979; *New York Times*, Apr. 18, 1972; Daniel S. Gillmor, "How Much for the Patient, How Much for Medical Science?: An Interview with Dr. Saul Krugman," *Modern Medicine* 30 (1974): 30–35. Krugman's research design, justifications, and findings are traced in Robert Wark, Saul Krugman, Joan Giles, et al.,

pages

"Infectious Hepatitis: Studies of Its Natural History and Prevention," *The New England Journal of Medicine* 258 (1958): 407–16; Saul Krugman, Robert Ward, Joan P. Giles, and A. Milton Jacobs, "Infectious Hepatitis: Studies of the Effects of Gamma-Globulin and on the Incident of Inapparent Infection," *Journal of the American Medical Association (JAMA)* 174 (1960): 823–30; Saul Krugman, Joan P. Giles, and Jack Hammond, "Infectious Hepatitis: Evidence for Two Distinctive Clinical Epidemiological and Immunological Types of Infection," *JAMA* 200 (1967): 365–73; the Inglefinger quotation is in the same issue, p. 406. Saul Krugman and Joan P. Giles, "Viral Hepatitis: New Light on an Old Disease," *JAMA* 212 (1970): 1019–29; Saul Krugman, Joan Giles, and Jack Hammond, "Viral Hepatitis Type B (MS-2 Strain): Prevention with Specific Hepatitis B Immune Serum Globulin," *JAMA* 218 (1972): 1665–70; "Editorial: Is Serum Hepatitis Only a Special Type of Infectious Hepatitis," *JAMA* 200 (1967): 136–37; interview with Baruch Blumberg, Oct. 4, 1979. A xerox copy of the Berman letter and the original consent form were given to us by Robert Veatch from his file on the Willowbrook experiments. On the work of Baruch Blumberg, see an interview with him in *Modern Medicine* 41 (1974): 41–44; his crucial finding was published in *Annals of Internal Medicine* 66 (1967): 924. On the ethics of carriers, see his article on "Bioethical Questions Related to Hepatitis B Antigen," *American Journal of Clinical Pathology* 65 (1976): 848–53. The best contemporary discussion of the controversy took place on May 4, 1972: "Proceedings of the Symposium on Ethical Issues in Human Experimentation: The Case of Willowbrook State Hospital Research," sponsored by the Student Council of the New York University School of Medicine and published by its Urban Health Affairs Program.

267–71 On the press and Krugman, see *New York Times,* Mar. 24, 1971. On hepatitis B contagion and medical personnel see Alexander E. Denes, et al., "Hepatitis B Infection in Physicians," *JAMA* 239 (1978): 210–12; James W. Mosley et al., "Hepatitis B Virus Infection in Dentists," *NEJM* 293 (1975): 729–34; W. Thomas London et al., "An Epidemic of Hepatitis in a Chronic-Hemo-Dialysis Unit," *NEJM* 281 (1969): 571–78; James L. Rosenberg et al., "Viral Hepatitis: An Occupational Hazard to Surgeons," *JAMA* 22 (1973): 395–400. On transmission through other fluids see Victor M. Villarejos et al., "Role of Saliva, Urine, and Feces in the Transmission of Type B. Hepatitis," *NEJM* 291 (1974): 1375–78. A useful review is Wolf Szmuness et al., "Sociodemographic Aspects of the Epidemiology of Hepatitis B," reprinted in G. Vyas et al., *Viral Hepatitis* (Philadelphia, 1978), pp. 297–320; see also in that volume James E. Maynard, "Modes of Hepatitis B Virus Transmission," pp. 126–37. On guidelines see Center for Disease Control, "Morbidity and Mortality Weekly Report" 25 (1976); Supplement: "Perspectives on the Control of Viral Hepatitis, Type B." New York amended its guidelines in keeping with the 1976 policy: State of New York, DMH, "Guidelines on the Control of Hepatitis B," Memo No. 76-4, Mar. 24, 1976.

271–74 On the scare, Arthur Nareff to Irving Anker, "Hepatitis 'B' Carriers," Aug. 3, 1977 (N.Y. Board of Education Files). Interview with Francis X. Kelley, Oct. 3, 1979; Donald Lyman to Dr. Baker, Aug. 4, 1977, "Hepatitis B Among Mentally Retarded in the New York City Schools," Aug. 4,

pages

1977 (Department of Health Files). Curtis Bakal, "Hepatitis B Final Report, September 1, 1978" (DH Files), contains the questions that P.S. 69 parents posed to Department of Health officials, pp. 37–38. William Goldman and Edward Galaid to John S. Marr, "Hepatitis B Carriers at P.S. 69 Staten Island, September 27, 1977" (DH Files). Interview with John S. Marr, June 1, 1979; Marr to Olive Pitkin, "Hepatitis B Carriers at P.S. 69 Staten Island," Sept. 27, 1977 (DH Files). Interview with Lloyd Novick, July 31, 1979; interview with Joyce Coppin, Apr. 1979; interview with Helen Feulner, Mar. 14, 1979. *Staten Island Advance,* Sept. 29, 30, 1977, Oct. 8, 1977. Hannah Flegenheimer to Helen Feulner, "Segregation of ex-Willowbrook Children at P.S. 69 Staten Island," Feb. 16, 1978 (WRP Files). Olive Pitkin to Feulner, Oct. 11, 1977 (DH Files).

274–79 We had frequent meetings with Curt Bakal over this period and a summary interview on Apr. 4, 1979; Bakal to Lloyd Novick, "Individual Investigation of Hepatitis B Carriers in Schools, November 1977." New York City Department of Health, *Proceedings of the Advisory Committee on Hepatitis B,* Dec. 20, 1977 (DH Files). Interview with Robert McCollum, Dec. 20, 1979; interview with Wolf Szmuness, Oct. 25, 1979. Pascal J. Imperato to Irving Anker, Feb. 27, 1978. Imperato attached to the letter the New York City Department of Health "Guidelines for the School Management of Hepatitis B Carriers," February 1978 (DH Files). For Bakal's account see, Curtis Bakal et al., "Deinstitutionalized Mentally Retarded Hepatitis B Surface Antigen Carriers in Public School Classes," *American Journal of Public Health* 70 (1980): 709–11; their commentary on the events followed, pp. 712–15. For another account of the December meeting see Donald Lyman to Judith Retig and Fran Bernstein, "HBsAg Among Mentally Retarded NYC Schools," Dec. 22, 1977 (State Department of Health Files). Interview with Retig, Aug. 3, 1979.

279–81 Interview with Philip Ziring, Oct. 3, 1979; Curt Bakal to Lloyd Novick, "Meeting with Metropolitan Placement Unit," Feb. 23, 1978 (DH Files). We were present at Bakal's meeting with Brooklyn case managers, Apr. 21, 1978. Willowbrook Review Panel, "Minutes, March 18, 1978"; Curtis Bakal, "Hepatitis B Final Report," pp. 19–20. James Clements to Irving Anker and Pascal J. Imperato, "Review of the February 27th Department of Health Guidelines," Mar. 22, 1978 (WRP Files).

281–86 Curtis Bakal and Laura Jenks-Daley to Dear Parent or Guardian, Apr. 18, 1978; for a report of Bakal's encounter with the parents from Floral Park, Queens, see Curtis Bakal, "Hepatitis B Final Report," p. 23. See also Bakal to Cecelia O'Shea, May 29, 1978 (DH Files). Interview with Neal Rosenberg, Aug. 4, 1979; interview with George Shebitz, June 6, 1979; interview with Helen Feulner, Mar. 14, 1979; David Rogers, *110 Livingston Street* (New York, 1968). For Bakal's comments on the Board of Education see "Hepatitis B Final Report," pp. 11–12. Gordon Ambach to Irving Anker, Mar. 21, 1978; Anker to Ambach, Apr. 14, 1978; Reinaldo Ferrer to Anker, May 3, 1978 (DH Files).

286–87 See Bakal, "Hepatitis B Final Report," pp. 29–36. The figures, as we note, always kept changing so the numbers are not to be trusted. Reinaldo Ferrer to Frank Macchiarola, Aug. 2, 1978, "Guidelines for School Management of Mentally Retarded Hepatitis B Carriers, New York City,"

pages

Aug. 14, 1978 (DH Files); Ferrer to Macchiarola, Aug. 28, 1978 (DH Files).

287–95 *Hearing on the Board of Education,* Sept. 11, 12, 1978; *Hearing on the Board of Education,* Nov. 9, 14, 28, 1978. The first Bartels opinion was delivered Sept. 14, 1978 (466 F. Supp 79); the second was delivered on Feb. 28, 1979 (466 F. Supp 487). The Court of Appeals decision came down Dec. 10, 1979 (612 F.2nd, 644).

12. Politics, Politics, Politics

299–301 New York City Fire Department, "Inspection Report: Gouverneur Division of Willowbrook," Feb. 20, 1976, 5 (MPU Files). Alan Saperstein to Philip Toia, June 1976, and Mr. Wick to Mr. Dunn, "Gouverneur Division Manhattan Developmental Center," Aug. 10, 1976, discuss the cutoff of federal dollars (MPU Files); Jose Rivera and Willie Mae Goodman to Gouverneur Parents Association, Mar. 31, 1978 (WRP Files). New York State DMH, "Plan to Improve Services for Gouverneur Clients," Sept. 16, 1977; Barbara Blum to Thomas Coughlin, "Flower Fifth Avenue Hospital," July 1, 1977 (MPU Files). New York Medical College Mental Retardation Institute, "Budget for Proposed Rehabilitation Center and ICF/MR," Feb. 17, 1978 (WRP Files). OMRDD, "Summary Rationale: Delafield Hospital," Feb. 20, 1977; Thomas Coughlin to James Clements, Aug. 20, 1977 (WRP Files). The panel recommended removal of the Gouverneur clients on Aug. 8, 1977; Willowbrook Review Panel, *Report to the Court, June 1, 1977–December 31, 1977,* p. 6.

301–5 New York State Department of Audit and Control, "Review of the Financial Status of New York Medical College—Mental Retardation Institute, October 2, 1978"; Anonymous, "Background Information and Assumptions Relating to the New York Medical College/Flower Fifth Avenue Hospital Program, February 3, 1978" (MPU Files). *New York Times,* Jan. 19, 1978. M. Ford, W. Talley, and J. Cooledge, "Report for the Willowbrook Review Panel: Visit August 9–12, 1978," pp. 2, 7, 8, 14; John Cooledge and William Talley, "Report to the Willowbrook Review Panel: Consultant's Third Visit," Oct. 13, 1978, p. 9; James Clements to Thomas Coughlin, Dec. 14, 1978 (WRP Files). Jennifer Howse to Coughlin, Oct. 10, 1978 (MPU Files).

305–8 *Hearing on Flower Fifth Avenue Hospital,* Aug. 1, 1979, p. 167; Sept. 5, 1979, p. 218, Sept. 20, 1979, pp. 677, 700, 914, 1145, 1150.

308–10 OMRDD, "Criteria for Admissions to a Privately Operated Community ICF/MR," Sept. 13, 1979; Michael Mascari to Alan Saperstein, Mar. 13, 1978; Robert Norris, "Non-Publically Operated ICFMR's: A Discussion Paper," Aug. 2, 1976, p. 19 (MPU Files). The best single source for understanding the fiscal and programatic implications of the change is New York State Commission on Quality of Care for the Mentally Disabled, "Converting Community Residences into Intermediate Care Facilities for the Mentally Retarded: Some Cautionary Notes," October 1980. Interview with Clarence Sundram, Oct. 13, 1978. Interview with Michael Mascari, Jan. 11, 1980. New York State DMH, "Plans of Compliance for Meeting Requirements of Section 45 CFR 249.33, Intermediate Care for the Mentally Retarded," 1976 (MPU Files).

pages

310–14 On Introne's position, see OMRDD, "Operational Plan for Placements," Jan. 31, 1980 (MPU Files). On ICF/MR implementation see New York State Health Planning Commission, "ICF/MR Development in New York State: Issues and Recommendations," July 18, 1977 (MPU Files); U.S. Department of Health, Education and Welfare, Health Care Financing Administration, *Interim Interpretive Guidelines for the Application of the Regulations for Mental Retardation on Persons with Related Conditions,* 45 CFR 249, p. 13, Nov. 28, 1977; OMRDD, *Five Year Comprehensive Plan for Services to Mentally Retarded and Developmentally Disabled Persons in New York State* (Albany, 1978). Interview with James Introne, Nov. 7, 1979. See, too, Bruce Vladeck, *Unloving Care* (New York, 1980), especially chaps. 3, 6. In June 1984, HHS finally acted on this threat, attempting to deny New York State $58 million because of overcrowding at six of its mental retardation institutions. Willowbrook was not one of the six.

314–16 Jennifer Howse to John Bartels, December 1979; Murray Schneps to James Introne, January 1980 (WRP Files). The panel's formal recommendation was Dec. 13, 1979. New York State Senate, *Report of the Senate Finance Committee on the Executive Budget, Fiscal Year April 1, 1980 to March 31, 1981,* p. 72; Introne to James Clements, Mar. 31, 1980 (WRP Files). On the response of the voluntary agencies see Leslie Park, "Memorandum to Senior Staff: (UCP, City/April 28, 1980), My position with reference to termination of the Willowbrook Review Panel."

316–19 *Hearing on the Willowbrook Review Panel,* Apr. 7, 1980, pp. 9, 10, 6, 9, 11, 30; Apr. 9, 1980, pp. 42, 43, 47; *New York State Association for Retarded Children* v. *Carey,* 72 C 356, 357, *Order and Decision,* Apr. 10, 1980, pp. 14–15.

319–21 *New York State Association for Retarded Children* v. *Carey,* "Brief of Plaintiff Appellees," pp. 80, 72, 89, 95, 25, 26; *New York State Association for Retarded Children* v. *Carey,* U.S. Court of Appeals Second Circuit, No. 1215, p. 1235, Docket Nos. 80-7289, 80-7295, June 4, 1980, pp. 3332, 3331.

13. Willowbrook Revisited

322–26 David J. Rothman and Sheila M. Rothman, "The Conflict over Children's Rights," *Hastings Center Report* (1980), pp. 7–10. *Pennhurst State School and Hospital* v. *Halderman,* 445 U.S. 1 (1981). John R. Bartels to Willowbrook Review Panel, June 1, 1980. Chris Hansen and Rob Levy to John, Helen, et al., "En banc for Willowbrook," May 1, 1980 (NYCLU Files).

326–30 James Introne to Bruce Ennis, Aug. 11, 1980; Chris Hansen to Ennis, Aug. 15, 1980; Ennis to Introne, Aug. 19, 1980; Introne to Ennis, Sept. 8, 1980; "Plaintiffs' Draft of Revised Order of Consent," Oct. 14, 1980; Hansen to Ennis et al., "Introne—Willowbrook Settlement," Oct. 14, 1980; Paul Litwak, "Proposed Mission Statement for Willowbrook Review Panel," Oct. 24, 1980; Litwak to Hansen, Nov. 20, 1980; Jonathan Siegfried to Introne, May 12, 1981 (NYCLU Files).

330–35 The various drafts of the settlement are on file at the NYCLU. See especially, Chris Hansen to the Willowbrook Review Panel, Sept. 29, 1981, for

pages

the draft that was almost signed. We were present at the negotiating sessions and also at the plaintiffs' strategy sessions.

335–38 On Rivera's negotiations see Paul Krietzman to Paul Dolan, Nov. 5, 1981 (MPU Files). Interviews with Geraldo Rivera, Dec. 14, 18, 19, 1981. The program was aired Jan. 7, 1982.

338–42 On discovery see Chris Hansen to Judge John Bartels, June 25, 1981 (NYCLU Files) and John Bartels' *Order* of July 7, 1981, 72 c. 356/357. *New York Times,* Dec. 11, 1981. *Hearing to Modify the Consent Judgment,* December–January 1981. Testimony of Dec. 10, 1981, pp. 13–16, 132, 134, 137; Dec. 11, 1981, p. 674. Watts testimony, December 1981, 2097–98. On the Bronx facility see "Plaintiffs' Post Trial Memorandum," Feb. 23, 1982, 74.

342–48 OMRDD signed two contracts with LeBoeuf, Lamb to represent it in this case. They are Contract Nos. C 165924 with Amendments 1, 2, and 3, and Contract C-99420n with Amendments 1, 2, 3, 4, and 5 (copies with New York State Department of Law). Defendant's Post Trial Brief, February 1982, pp. 26–27, 28, 16, 22, 21, 32. Testimony of Ed Matthews, Jan. 9, 1982, pp. 3822, 3826; testimony of Frank Padavan, January 1982, pp. 3575, 3590; testimony of Barbara Blum, Jan. 10, 1982, pp. 4078, 4052, 4054, 4056, 4063, 4074, 4094, 4077, 4100, 4104.

348–52 John R. Bartels, *Order* of Apr. 28, 1982, 14, 16, 29, 31, 48, 49, 52, 57, 59, 66; U.S. Court of Appeal, Second Circuit Docket, Nos. 82-7, 82-7591, Mar. 31, 1983, pp. 11, 21, 20, 23, 27, 28.

Leaving the Field

353–65 The September 30, 1983, statistics on the Willowbrook class come from "Location and Status Report," of the New York County Service Group, the successor to MPU.

The two court decisions discussed here are *Youngberg* v. *Romeo,* decided by the Supreme Court, June 18, 1982 (102 S. Ct., 7–17); *Society for Good Will to Retarded Children* v. *Cuomo,* United States District Court, Eastern District of New York, Memorandum and Order, 78-Civ.-1847, Aug. 10, 1983. The Carolene Products case is discussed fully in Owen Fiss, "The Forms of Justice," *Harvard Law Review* 93 (1979): 1–58. For the case itself see 304 US, 144, 152, n.4 (1938).

On the link between Willowbrook and decision making on newborns, see Joseph Goldstein, Anna Freud, and Albert J. Solnit, *Before the Best Interests of the Child* (New York, 1980).

In June 1984 the Court of Appeals reversed Judge Weinstein, thereby demonstrating just how problematic and controversial judicial intervention had become.

Index